PUBLIC
INSIDE THE TERRORDOME
ENEMY

PUBLIC

INSIDE THE TERRORDOME

ENEMY

TIM GRIERSON

OVERLOOK OMNIBUS

This edition published by Omnibus Press and distributed in the United States and Canada by The Overlook Press, Peter Mayer Publishers Inc, 141 Wooster Street, New York, NY 10012.

For bulk and special sales requests, please contact sales@overlookny.com or write to us at the above address.

Copyright © 2015 Omnibus Press
(A Division of Music Sales Limited)
14/15 Berners Street,
London, W1T 3LJ, UK.

Cover designed by Fresh Lemon
Picture research by Sarah Datblygu

ISBN 978-1-4683-1138-9

Printed in the EU.

A catalogue record for this book is available from the British Library.

Cataloguing-in-Publication data is available from the Library of Congress.

Visit Omnibus Press on the web at www.omnibuspress.com

To My Beautiful, Wonderful Wife Susan.
We've Got It All.

INTRODUCTION

THE story of Public Enemy is actually two stories. The first one, you probably already know: an upstart crew from Long Island forms a band in the mid-eighties and changes the face of hip-hop, bringing political commentary and album-length focus to a budding art form that was, at that point, still widely considered a singles-only novelty. The PE albums from this period are seminal: *Yo! Bum Rush The Show*, *It Takes A Nation Of Millions To Hold Us Back*, *Fear Of A Black Planet* and *Apocalypse 91… The Enemy Strikes Black*. In only four years and four albums, Public Enemy built their legacy, cementing their position as one of the most important and influential hip-hop groups. It's this story that played a large part in them being inducted into the Rock and Roll Hall of Fame in 2013.

But that era ended in 1991. The other story is what happened next. That story is less discussed and when it is, it's done only in an abbreviated, bullet-point style. The critical and commercial disappointment of 1994's *Muse Sick-N-Hour Mess Age* will be brought up, perhaps 1998's *He Got Game* gets a mention, and then? A respectful silence, indicative of a cultural consensus that PE were never as great again. (Of course, there might also be the occasional disapproving comment about how far band member Flavor Flav fell in the 2000s, reduced to becoming a pathetic reality-television star.) Fans were content to let Public Enemy drift into a kind of hallowed irrelevance: the group still toured the world and were treated as icons, but their subsequent albums failed to spark audiences the way their early music had. Public Enemy were still around, but everyone had forgotten about them.

Public Enemy exists as an attempt to merge, reconcile and clarify those two stories. There has been plenty of official documentation of PE's early years, including two books written by frontman Chuck D (one a memoir, one a breakdown of his lyrics) and a band-approved biography written by journalist Russell Myrie in 2008 entitled *Don't Rhyme For The Sake Of*

Riddlin': The Authorized Story Of Public Enemy. But for anyone curious about Public Enemy's post-*Muse Sick* narrative, there simply hasn't been much to find online or in print. (Even Myrie's engaging book thins out after *He Got Game*. Only about 40 pages of the 252-page biography are devoted to anything after that soundtrack to the Spike Lee film of the same name.)

This imbalance isn't entirely surprising. Even the staunchest PE supporter has to acknowledge that the group lost hold of the zeitgeist shortly after *Apocalypse 91*, signalling the end of a golden era. Some of the fundamental architects of Public Enemy's dense, innovative sound had left by that point, and a new, less confident regime took their place. Most importantly, there isn't a single album that PE put out after *Apocalypse 91* that matched the fury, speed and brilliance of those four initial records: they never again released a must-own record.

But this isn't to suggest by any stretch of the imagination that Public Enemy have stopped being a fascinating, vital group. Quite the contrary, the growing list of obstacles that Chuck D, Flavor Flav and the rest of the band have had to face has made them a more compelling and rugged band. Some of those obstacles have been internal – tension between band members, a rotating crop of producers – while others have been external, including label woes and the difficulty of recording socially conscious hip-hop in a period when rap was becoming more commercial and less political.

Yet through it all, Public Enemy have survived to deliver music that's been angry, thoughtful and engaged. They haven't had a gold album in the United States in more than 20 years, but the records they've produced since are a fascinating document of a band in flux mirroring the uncertainties and growing pains of the nation around them. It is impossible to listen to Public Enemy's songs and not hear the pulse of what was going on in the country at the time they were made. The rise of crack and the callousness of the Reagan administration are buried in the enraged grooves of the group's eighties records. The economic upturn of the Clinton nineties – juxtaposed by the celebration of gangster culture in mainstream hip-hop – forms the background of *Muse Sick* and *He Got Game*. And, significantly, the advent of the world wide web's information overload, not to mention the crippling paranoia and anxiety of the post-9/11 era, informs PE's dark, sometimes corrosive 21st century albums. Just because the world stopped paying attention to them doesn't mean they stopped paying attention to the world.

I'm hardly immune from criticism in this regard: I, too, had started sleeping on them. Like many Public Enemy fans, I discovered their music in my impressionable youth, immediately responding to the hardness of their beats and the steeliness of their lyrics. In their late eighties heyday, Public Enemy rocked more mightily than any rock band and were certainly more dangerous than Metallica or Guns N' Roses. Where other groups made noise, Public Enemy raised a ruckus, one that was filled with the righteous indignation of the oppressed. Bands such as U2 and Midnight Oil touched on current events, but no one addressed issues of race and class as brilliantly as Chuck and Flav.

But as was the case with plenty of the band's acolytes, I lost interest along the way, disappointed that *Muse Sick* and later albums didn't sound like *Nation Of Millions*. But as Chuck has said on numerous occasions, he's not interested in making the same album again and again. To be fair, part of the reason why he's not is because he *can't*. Once lawyers started clamping down on the wizardly sampling that formed the bedrock of *Nation Of Millions* and *Fear Of A Black Planet*, Chuck's record-making strategy became too expensive to pursue. But in recent years, I started exploring PE's post-*He Got Game* catalogue and was stunned at how much great music had been there under our collective noses. None of the albums were a "must-own" in the same way as *Nation Of Millions*, but that's because they were pointedly different, incorporating new techniques to embody the rebelliousness and political consciousness that had been the band's hallmark practically since the beginning.

Consequently, *Public Enemy* is an investigation, an apology and a form of advocacy. While I cover the entirety of PE's career, I'm especially interested in connecting the dots between their past and present. If you once loved this band, this book is here to explain why you should still love them, and why their albums are still worth your time. And if you remained loyal, hopefully *Public Enemy* will validate why you did.

It's probably important now to note that this book was not authorised by the band or its management, which means that there aren't new interviews with Chuck, Flav or their current central producer Gary G-Wiz. But I'm quite pleased with the individuals who did speak with me: the engineers, mixers, producers, musicians, DJs, tour promoters, video directors and lawyers who share their stories of working with the band from *Yo! Bum Rush The Show* to their twin 2012 albums, *Most Of My Heroes Still Don't Appear On No Stamp* and *The Evil Empire Of Everything*. Their insights are invaluable to the story I wanted to tell of a group who are as important as any in the last 30 years — not just in hip-hop but in music as a whole.

Not to say that I think they're infallible, however. I walk away from the experience of chronicling Public Enemy with more respect and admiration for their music than when I started. But this book is also clear-eyed about where they've fallen short, both as a band and as individuals. Writing about that wasn't always easy considering that, as a white man from the Midwest now living in Los Angeles for over 20 years, I can't pretend to share the same racial, cultural or geographic perspective as the group I'm writing about.

So, for instance, the black nationalism advocated by Public Enemy, specifically by Chuck D and the notorious Professor Griff, is, to my mind, a laudable attempt to preach self-reliance and self-respect rather than succumbing to a culture of victimhood. Nonetheless, the movement's chauvinistic, occasionally bigoted slant is deeply troubling, and (as you'll see) the group didn't always navigate those waters commendably. But throughout the book, I temper such criticisms with an acknowledgement that I have not walked a mile in these artists' shoes. I have not experienced the racism they have, and I don't want to diminish the daily impact discrimination can have on one's soul and world view. As a result, I try to approach such issues with a spirit of fairness, staying open-minded and letting the band have their say.

Because Public Enemy did not participate in this book, I combed through decades of interviews, as well as drew from the band's authorised biographies and memoirs. (Flavor's autobiography, *The Icon The Memoir*, was easily the toughest slog of the bunch.) Constructing my book, I realised that I was doing what Public Enemy have done so expertly: stitching together snippets from different sources to create an intriguing new whole. And I did it out of love. This was a band that meant so much to so many people, and too many of us turned away, not bearing witness to the many exciting and intriguing chapters to come in their history. "In 1995, you'll twist to this / as you raise your fist to the music," Chuck D declared in 1990 on the volcanic *Fear Of A Black Planet* track 'Brothers Gonna Work It Out'. We're far past 1995 now. But with any luck, *Public Enemy* will serve as proof that the rapper's forward-looking declaration has lost none of its urgency, accuracy or power.

CHAPTER ONE

IF life had worked out differently, maybe the man behind hip-hop's finest voice would have gotten a job in a world far removed from music. "I always wanted to be in sports, a statistician or a broadcaster," Chuck D said in a 1990 interview. "I got my voice number one by heredity – from my pops – and number two, doing all my imitations of Marv Albert."

Carlton Ridenhour was born in Queens, New York on August 1, 1960, a couple of weeks before the Beatles (then with Pete Best on drums and Stu Sutcliffe on bass) started performing in Hamburg, Germany. The man who would become famous as Chuck D probably wouldn't be too pleased about having his birth connected to a moment in Fab Four history: he's always been more of a Stones guy. When an interviewer from *The Guardian* asked him in 2014 if Public Enemy were "the Beatles of rap", Chuck responded, "I would say Run–D.M.C. were more like the Beatles of rap. We might have been the Rolling Stones of the rap game." That wasn't a dig at Run-D.M.C., a forerunner of Public Enemy and a band he deeply admired and championed. But even as a child, Chuck felt closer to the Stones, probably because their music was louder and more dangerous than their peers'. "As an artist I don't make soft music," he wrote in his 1997 memoir, *Fight The Power: Rap, Race, And Reality*. "I make my music hard and aggressive, which is an extension of the mixture of music I listened to growing up."

Chuck came of age in a house where R&B, soul, rock and pop were played. He even dug the jazzy soft-rock of Chicago, "which wasn't aggressive but had a message". His parents seemingly always had records on. "My pops was into jazz; to this day, I don't have a sharp liking for it, though I guess it's in me," he told *Playboy* in 1990. "My moms played all the soul. She'd play Al Green over and over and *over* – the same record, over and over again – and then Stevie Wonder over and over, and then

Aretha, Aretha, Aretha." Elaborating in a 2014 *Billboard* interview, Chuck noted, "My mother was into Stax, Motown, Atlantic. My grandmother would have Etta James, Muddy Waters. I didn't feel a need to get my own records until I was 17, 18."

Marv Albert was the broadcaster for New York Knicks games when Chuck was growing up, and the young man's allegiance to New York sports was cemented around the same time. In an interview from Public Enemy's early years, Chuck declared, "I'm a sports motherfucker. I used to say, 'I don't give a fuck about music or the goddamn party, give me the Mets, the Knicks, the Jets, and I'm straight.'"

Chuck also loved comic books and collecting baseball cards. When he went to college at Adelphi University, he studied graphic design and communications. As he told Adelphi's graduating class in May 2013, when he was given an honorary doctorate from the university, his career strategy was, "I could work in an art department of a record company." And unlike other notable rap artists, he came from a relatively middle-class upbringing: stable if hardly rich. "People go on about this, about us having cars when we were kids, but, *I* know, a black suburban neighbourhood is still a black neighbourhood," he told *Melody Maker* in 1987.

In the early seventies, Chuck's family moved to Roosevelt, Long Island, thus beginning Public Enemy's proud association with what would later be dubbed "Strong Island" in hip-hop circles. Looked down on by residents of New York's five boroughs, who consider it a suburban wasteland, Long Island was a different world for those who moved there from other sections of New York City. Johnny "Juice" Rosado, a musician and DJ who worked with PE over the years, left the Bronx with his family to settle into Long Island when he was a kid. "When I moved to Long Island, I'm like, 'I'm in the fucking country,'" Juice says. "'Goddamn, man, I don't wanna be here.'"

"We were a black *community*," Chuck once wrote about Roosevelt. "Black fathers were not just fathers to their own children, but they responded and contributed in different ways to the entire community. . . . In 1969 the black population of Roosevelt was about 60 per cent, in 1970 the black population jumped to around 75 per cent, and by 1972 Roosevelt was damn near 90 per cent black."

It was also the incubator for the talent that would eventually become Public Enemy. Kerwin Young, a musician and producer who assisted on several PE records, grew up in the projects in Queens but moved to Roosevelt when he was nine. He ended up living a street away from Chuck, who also lived close to the man who would become PE's DJ, Terminator X. "Eddie Murphy lived by us," Young says. "It was something, being 10 or 11, going to the barbershop with my father and seeing Eddie Murphy in the barbershop when he was on *Saturday Night Live*." As compared to the projects, Roosevelt was, according to Young, "quieter and slower, 'cause it's houses. And it's a little backwards: they still wore bellbottoms when we moved out there from the city – it wasn't up-to-date with clothes. And they didn't even know about 'Rapper's Delight'," the 1979 Sugarhill Gang single that's generally considered ground zero for hip-hop's development.

But if Roosevelt was a little behind the curve culturally, it would catch up fast enough. In *The Men Behind Def Jam: The Radical Rise Of Russell Simmons And Rick Rubin*, Bill Stephney, who would soon become part of the Public Enemy story, told writer Alex Ogg, "[W]hen rap was developing in the mid-seventies in the projects of Harlem and the Bronx, basically those people were our cousins [in Long Island]. Every weekend we'd go visit them and we'd be an extended part of the hip-hop nation."

"Roosevelt was one square mile, predominantly black," Young says. "[White radio shock-jock] Howard Stern had gone to the high school, and the group Guy was there – I went to high school with Damion Hall, who was two years ahead of me." Asked what inspired such an explosion of talent in such a relatively small area, Young responds, "Everyone worked together. If someone knew you did music, they'd invite you to come by the studio. We all knew each other from the barbershop, or they knew Griff. Griff knew everyone, so we went out working with him in his studio in Roosevelt. I would say that there had to been at least six home-recording studios in Roosevelt."

The "Griff" he's referring to is Professor Griff, who was born Richard Griffin. Chuck and Griff were born on the same day in 1960. But within Public Enemy, Griff first became friends with Hank Shocklee, whose birth name was James Hank Boxley III. Neighbours, Shocklee and Griff threw a party in ninth grade. "All I remember is everybody had the crazy big afros and platform shoes," Shocklee told *Spin* in 1989 about the party, which took place around 1973 or '74.

Shortly after, Shocklee formed Spectrum, a mobile DJ unit, with his brother Keith, who would eventually be part of Public Enemy as well. Chuck loved Spectrum – and more importantly, it opened him up to the possibility of doing something musical in his future. "I was fascinated with deejaying, seeing someone stand with two turntables and make the records do all kinds of new and exciting things," he said in a *Los Angeles Times* interview from early 1988. "The great thing was the way the DJ would take a record you liked and concentrate on just the part you loved the best – going over it again and again in a way that made what he was doing better than the original record. Then, the guys would start talking over it. . . . That was for me."

When Chuck settled on his MC moniker, he went with "D" because of his middle name, Douglas. In a 1999 interview with *NME*, he explained, "Back in the seventies, if you happened to have anything like an 'E' or 'B', that's what you used. I didn't call myself Chuck R because that had no ring. First I was Chuckie D, but when I got older I just took the 'ie' off."

Speaking about the differences between Chuck D and Carlton Ridenhour, Johnny Juice offers, "[Ridenhour] is the geek. He's the nerd. He was the guy that got his ass kicked. He was the big, thick-glassed-nerd dude that got his ass kicked. That's why Chuck D is the antithesis of who Carlton Ridenhour is."

He tried his hand at rapping in front of an audience at a regular college party known as Thursday Night Throwdown. This was October 1979, a period in which Chuck had been booted from Adelphi for poor grades. "I was going to school every day," he once said, "I just didn't go to class." Too busy partying, shooting hoops and trying to pick up coeds, Chuck was directionless when he took the mic for Thursday Night Throwdown. A group of contestants would take turns rhyming over records, and Chuck was the final entrant.

"Back in the day it wasn't about your rhymes," he said at a Red Bull Music Academy seminar in 2008. "You had to sound good because most [sound] systems were inferior." He brandished that powerful, booming voice of his, catching the attention of Hank, who was at the party. "When I get on the mic I know no one's going to be louder and all I have to do is be clear, put some words together," Chuck explained about his technique that night. "Everyone else is sitting down because they're not loud and clear and rocking the music like that. Later on, when people talked about flows, you're talking about enhanced systems, studios which master it your way, but when it comes down to it, you've either got the pipes or you haven't. . . . [T]he whole thing about microphone kings, masters of ceremony, was they had to cut through because systems were wack."

Hank had gone to Thursday Night Throwdown specifically to fill a gap in Spectrum: they were the only DJ crew without an MC. "We went searching for one at a function at Adelphi University because they used to have Thursday night gigs," he recalled in *Ego Trip* in 2011. "But most of those motherfuckers was wack. We were bored out of our minds listening to these wack-ass MCs rapping. And then this one kid grabbed the mic and he made an announcement. And he did such a good job of making the announcement, it fucked me up. And that kid happened to be Chuck D. I liked the way his voice sounded, so I said, 'Yo, do you wanna get down with us?' I was throwin' parties, so Chuck came down and lit it up."

They had met before. In an iconic story of Public Enemy's early days, Chuck had gone up to Hank after an unsuccessful Spectrum event and told him that the party had flopped because their flyers were terrible, not least because the name Spectrum had been misspelled. Soon, Chuck was designing fliers and rhyming for the group. He also tweaked their name. As Keith recalled to *Ego Trip*, "[Chuck] said we might as well call ourselves 'Spectrum City' because we had our own little world."

"I left school after my freshman semester," Chuck confessed to *Spin* in 1992. "I had no direction. Rap actually gave me the direction to go through school. I wanted to apply my design and artistic skills to this new music. So the hip-hop scene and rap became my motive for living."

The Spectrum City world would soon include Griff, who had returned from a stint in the Army to form Unity Force, a security company that kept order at the group's events. They would eventually segue into the Security of the First World, or the S1Ws, the tightly choreographed unit of uniformed individuals on PE's tours and promotional photos.

Johnny Juice wasn't part of Spectrum City, but when he met Griff at the beginning of PE's run, he sensed the man's antagonism. "Griff automatically came at me," the DJ recalls. "Griff heard I was a martial artist – Griff's a martial artist, too. He asked me, 'What style?' I told him. He said, 'What belt level?' I told him. He tried testing me automatically: 'Do a black belt kata right now.' He tried to spar with me, and I was a lot quicker than he thought, and he was like, 'OK.' It was just a little game."

As Spectrum City began to build its reputation in the late seventies and early eighties, rap was honing its sound. At the time, it was a one-off format, as acts were mostly delivering individual tracks as opposed to full-length albums. "In the early eighties, the music was on par with a lot of the R&B records," says Young. "So, you had songs with dance beats. It was party music."

Spectrum City understood the importance of bringing the party, but their approach to deejaying also informed how they would eventually start making hip-hop music. As Hank Shocklee recalled to *Option* in 1991, "We were doing stuff in the nightclubs back in the early eighties that *no one* was doing: mixing sets, calculating the moods of our audiences. We'd go from reggae beats to soul to disco to slammin' punk rock; then we'd hit them with the sound effects and lights and everything, and then bring the mood back to the floor. And then, all of a sudden, out of all the buzz and dramatic stuff, you'd hear, like BLIP-BLIP-BLIP – WHOOOMMMP! . . . and we'd be" – he slammed his hand down on the table for effect – "*right smack* into our crazy hip-hop set. And all of this was long before *Yo! Bum Rush The Show* ever saw the light of day."

They were extending into other worlds as well. In the early eighties, Chuck became friendly with Bill Stephney, a fellow Adelphi student who was also studying communications. Stephney told *The Source* in 1990, "Bear in mind now that Adelphi is a 95 percent white institution, and you had all these courses that, of the thousand black students that attended there, not many took." But one class they both attended was "Black Music and Musicians". "We were the hoods . . . the b-boys, the malcontents, everything," Stephney recalled, noting that another future Public Enemy associate, journalist Harry Allen, was also in the class.

Stephney's interest in radio drew him to host a show on Adelphi's

WBAU, *The Mr. Bill Show*. A fan of Spectrum City – "They deejayed all the parties where hundreds if not thousands of kids would show up," he told Russell Myrie – Stephney, who eventually became WBAU's programme director, invited them on the air. Chuck's drive to get Spectrum City on WBAU was provoked in part because of the group's failed efforts to sell their mix-tapes. "I wanted to go from making tapes to getting free radio airplay and promotions for Spectrum, and simultaneously advertise the radio station," Chuck wrote in *Fight The Power*. "That way people could record a tape every week on their own. We wouldn't make any money off of it, but we would receive more notoriety."

While on WBAU, Spectrum would bring into the studio up-and-coming rap acts – such as Run-D.M.C. for their first interview – and play songs. That turned into the group landing their own weekly show on Saturday nights, *Super Spectrum Mix Hour*, but they struggled to fill time because of their devotion to hip-hop. "We wanted to play all rap records," Hank explained in an edited 2010 video interview. "And I would get, you know, 35 rap records within three months. You can't keep playing the same records all the time, so we had to come up with something. So I would just bring in local rappers and have them come in: 'Say whatever, do whatever, just put some raps on these beats.'"

Hank was essentially putting together early Public Enemy tracks. They weren't the first official PE songs, though. In 1984, the group had recorded 'Lies' and 'Check Out The Radio', minimalist records with stark horn samples and tough rhymes. Chuck D was still Chuckie D at that point – he gave a shout-out to himself and his crew on 'Check Out The Radio' – and while the songs weren't stunningly innovative, they made an impact on those around Spectrum City. "Run-D.M.C. loved 'Check Out The Radio'," Chuck claimed in *Fight The Power*. He also credits the song's "low-tempo vibe" for inspiring the Run-D.M.C. track 'Together Forever (Krush-Groove 4)' and the Beastie Boys' 'Slow And Low'.

Presumably discussing the process of making 'Lies' and 'Check Out The Radio', Shocklee recalled in the same 2010 video interview about the difficulty he faced in recording early Spectrum City material. "We went in and we had a producer produce the record," recalled Hank, commenting that the producer "didn't take any chances. He didn't do anything that I thought was different. . . . So I said, 'Well, let me go in and let me kinda, like, do something with the remaining time that we have.'" Hank's strategy was to slow down the beats per minute, or BPMs. "That was revolutionary at that time," said Shocklee, "because everything was 110, 115, 120 beats per minute. That was your norm on radio. I just said, 'I don't care about radio.' I wanted to do something that felt comfortable on the *street* level. Bringing the beat down to something that was, like, 90 made it easier for the rappers to put in more lyrics – more words – now. We could talk about more things that are more relevant [than] you could say with a normal pop record or a normal R&B record."

Lyrical content would be one of the ways that Public Enemy would eventually distinguish themselves from their hip-hop peers. Though Spectrum City knew how to entertain a crowd, Chuck had been influenced by parents who were socially conscious. "They came out of the sixties believing that young black people should be fed the right information on our culture and history to be active participants in America," he told the *Los Angeles Times* in 2004. "They set the tone for what we would rap about." In the same interview, he remembered the African-American classes he took during his summers in high school. "That was a rare programme," he said. "We formed our foundation of nationalism from that experience. It was wonderful. From that experience we learned that black was beautiful."

That need to speak out first asserted itself on the WBAU radio show. "I wasn't 'political'," Chuck told *Spin* in the fall of 1991, "but I would say things on the radio and in my raps about the community. You know, you play the rap jams, then you kick in with like, 'This goes out to the brothers there on the corner – man, you gotta stop all that crazy shit.' Stuff like that, looking out. As I saw it, I was just being a responsible adult."

Spectrum City's radio show featured underground rap songs from artists trying to get their music out to New York audiences. The group would have the acts come to their base of operations, which was located at 510 South Franklin in Hampstead, Long Island, to make their tapes. Before the crew was based at 510, they were headquartered at Hank's mom's house. But the show also included a track Spectrum City made in response to a local rapper who was talking shit about Chuckie D.

'Public Enemy No. 1' might not have happened if the group hadn't become familiar with a young man named William Drayton. Born in Roosevelt on March 16, 1959, he was obsessed with rap music, starting off as a DJ but wanting to segue into rhyming. "People had been deejaying for a while," Drayton wrote in his 2011 autobiography, *The Icon The Memoir*, about rap's late-seventies/early-eighties scene, "but the idea of talking over the record and hyping the crowd as the master of ceremonies, the 'MC,' was pretty new."

However, Drayton wasn't just a rapper and DJ: according to his memoir, he could play everything from piano to drums to bass to violin to xylophone. Chuck once said of the man, "He can play 15 instruments. I can't play lotto." Drayton also dabbled in angel dust, vandalism, joyriding and drug dealing. Plus, he claimed to have lost his virginity when he was six. "The girl was the same age as me," he told *PopEater* in 2011. "We kind of felt a little something funny. We knew it was kind of wrong yet we felt it was kind of natural. I mean, I call it a lost virginity when the penis penetrates the vagina, I do consider that a cherry pop."

He first came across Spectrum City when a good friend of his, T.A., who was a member of the early rap trio the Townhouse Three, met up with Chuck's crew to make a tape. Drayton tagged along.

Chuck wasn't overly impressed with Drayton. On *The Arsenio Hall Show* in early 2014, Chuck recalled on their first encounter, "I told him, 'You can't smoke up here. Go across the street where they selling them cheap chicken wings and smoke over there.'" Nonetheless, Drayton liked Spectrum City and contributed keyboards to T.A.'s song. From there, Drayton started hanging out with Spectrum City, working his way up from roadie to hype man. He, too, got a show on WBAU, named after his hip-hop moniker, MC/DJ Flavor. "What I was doing was walking around the neighbourhoods collecting tapes that people made," Flavor explained about his show's format. He'd play the tapes on his programme: "People tuned in 'cause having their jam on the radio made them feel like stars."

It was Hank who suggested that Drayton change his rap name from Flavor to Flavor Flav: after all, it had worked for Melvin "Melle Mel" Glover of Grandmaster Flash & the Furious Five, who had one of rap's first breakthrough singles with 1982's 'The Message'. Flavor returned the favour when he told Chuck about a conversation he'd had with a member of the Play Hard Crew, who was dissing Chuck's rhyming skills and challenging him to a rap battle.

"I wasn't into battling," Chuck wrote in *Lyrics Of A Rap Revolutionary*. "I was just into making tapes to put on the radio. I was trying to help MCs, not battle them." Rather than battle this naysayer, though, Chuck decided to make a song in response.

For years, Chuck had loved 'Blow Your Head', a song from 1974 by Fred Wesley and the J.B.'s off the James Brown-produced *Damn Right I Am Somebody*. The rapper had heard it plenty back in his roller-skating youth. He decided to bite the trippy instrumental intro for what would become 'Public Enemy No. 1'. To do this, he made a "pause tape", which meant putting a tape player's "record" function on pause and then un-pausing it when you wanted to record a snippet of something. Do this enough times in a row – pausing, then un-pausing, pausing, and then un-pausing – and you could create a loop (or repetition) of a particular sound, riff or drumbeat. Before samplers were invented, pause tapes were a way for DJs to create loops.

Chuck made his pause tape at 510 South Franklin and then asked Flavor to throw his voice onto the beginning, essentially repeating the story he'd told Chuck about the rap-battle challenge. Flavor's impromptu spoken-word opening gave the track an instantly gritty authenticity, as well as created a dramatic intensity that segued perfectly into Chuck's litany of brags and putdowns. Unknowingly, the two rappers were right then forming one of the great hip-hop vocal tag teams.

"The simple reason why we work together is just the contrast in our voices," Chuck told *The Source* in 1994. "People try to come up with intellectual reasons for 'the noise' and it ain't nothing intellectual. We was just making [WBAU] tapes and needed voices to cut through that shit. Flavor got a powerful trebly voice, with cut. I got some bass with treble and pitch, which also cuts. So you put me and Flavor together and it's basically like Bobby Byrd and James Brown."

A talented musician in his own right, Byrd would forever be remembered as the man who discovered Brown, eventually becoming his sideman and musical foil, both onstage and in the studio. When Byrd died in 2007, Keith Jenkins, guitarist in Brown's band the Soul Generals, told *The Augusta Chronicle*, "You listen to those records and those voices together, it was incredible. Whether they were singing in harmony on something like 'Licking Stick' or doing call and response on 'Sex Machine', it was always something special."

This was what Flavor would provide for Public Enemy. They never did much harmony, but the yin-yang of Chuck's and Flav's voices provided dynamic counterpoint, like two different arguing styles working in unison to win you over to their cause. 'Public Enemy No. 1' provided the blueprint – and it also became a mid-eighties New York sensation.

"That record was the number one smash hit on WBAU for . . . I dunno, *three* months or so," Hank Shocklee said in 1991. "Out of all the stuff we were playing – even the new records that were coming out – *that* was the number one song. By the time we put it on *Yo! Bum Rush The Show* it was old. We put it on that first album for the world to hear, because the record was already a hit in Long Island and Queens."

According to *Don't Rhyme For The Sake Of Riddlin'*, there are conflicting stories about how 'Public Enemy No. 1' got the band noticed by a nascent hip-hop label called Def Jam. Was it Run-D.M.C.'s DJ, Jam Master Jay, who brought it to the attention of a white New York University student named Rick Rubin? Or was it a radio DJ named Andre Brown, who went by the name Dr. Dre and was also a student at Adelphi when Chuck was attending, who played it for the Beastie Boys? (This Dr. Dre, by the way, is the one who became one of the hosts of *Yo! MTV Raps*, not the Dr. Dre of N.W.A. and *The Chronic*.)

No matter: Rubin and his partner, a budding African-American entrepreneur (and brother of Run-D.M.C.'s Joseph Simmons) named Russell Simmons, had founded Def Jam and were interested in signing Spectrum City. They'd already landed LL Cool J and Beastie Boys, and so by the mid-eighties the label had established itself as a hitmaker in the hip-hop realm. And Beastie Boys' debut, *Licensed To Ill*, was still to come. In a 2005 interview with *The A.V. Club*, Rubin reminisced about the charismatic young LL Cool J, noting, "There were no stars in rap music [at that time]. It was really just a work of passion. Everyone who was doing it was doing it because they loved it, not because anyone thought it was a career. We didn't even think about having a hit single. We just tried to do something we liked. There were no expectations whatsoever. The only hope was that we'd sell enough records to make enough money to make another record. If it didn't cost us money to have Def Jam, we'd be happy. If it supported itself, and we could keep doing it, we'd be doing it."

Chuck was initially resistant to Rubin's courting – and Simmons wasn't sold on Chuck. "It's not that he didn't want to put [their album] out," Rubin said about Simmons. "I just don't think that he cared about it as much as I did. He didn't understand why I was so excited by it. I remember him saying something like, 'You make records with the Bangles [who contributed a hit single, a cover of Simon & Garfunkel's 'Hazy Shade Of Winter', to Rubin's *Less Than Zero* soundtrack]. Why do you care about this?' I'm like, 'This is what I like.'"

In *Fight The Power*, Chuck addressed his mixed emotions about signing with Def Jam. True, he and Hank had been actively courting a label deal, fearful that they'd squandered the momentum of 'Public Enemy No. 1'. Still, "I felt I would be a better director than artist," he wrote, "but Rick Rubin was adamant about me being the vocalist in the group. I was in a situation where I received an offer that I couldn't refuse, and I had to do it." Chuck had enjoyed not being in the spotlight at Spectrum City, and he also wanted to focus on the group becoming a talent promoter. Signing up to be an MC wasn't exactly part of his grand ambitions.

"I contacted Chuck about signing them, and he said no, that he was too old, and hip-hop was a young man's game," Rubin told *The A.V. Club*. "LL was really popular at that time, and he was 16. Chuck was an old man, probably 21. He felt like his artist days were past him. I put his number up on a post-it note on my phone, and I would call it every day and just keep bugging him."

"Rick kept calling and calling and saying, 'Let's do a record, let's do a record,'" Shocklee said in 1991. "We were, like, 'Sheesh, we don't wanna do a record.' We was doing concerts and we was doing the radio show." In addition, the Spectrum City crew ran a nightclub and had a video show called WORD, which stood for "World of Rock and Dance". "We were, like, 'No way, we don't wanna do a record.'"

Finally, Chuck relented. As Rubin recalled, the rapper said, "'OK, I'm ready to do it. It's called Public Enemy. Here's the whole vision.' He had it all worked out. They weren't going to be like any other hip-hop group. They were going to be more like the Clash. They were going to have lyrics that meant something, and uniforms, and a militaristic feel, the whole thing."

Coordinated by Stephney, who was actually vice president of promotion at Def Jam, Chuck and Hank met with Rubin, playing him four songs that would end up on the band's debut album, *Yo! Bum Rush The Show*: 'Public Enemy No. 1', 'You're Gonna Get Yours', 'Sophisticated Bitch' and 'My Uzi Weighs A Ton' (which was called 'The Return Of Public Enemy' at that early stage). The new name, Public Enemy, had been suggested by Hank since a couple of tracks had that phrase in the title. And then Chuck, who loved graphic design and had even done a strip for the Adelphi school paper, focused on the band's logo.

PE's "b-boy in the crosshairs" symbol continued Chuck's belief from Spectrum City that great enterprises need great visuals and marketing. It was Chuck who had told Hank that his party stunk because the flyers were lame. And it was Chuck who had designed jackets for the Spectrum City crew to wear – the very jackets that helped Stephney realise they were responsible for the parties he enjoyed attending. The silhouette at the logo's centre was based on E Love, a friend of LL's. And then for the name "Public Enemy", Chuck "did the stencil letters, and put a crossbar in between them, and bam, it looked like they were made for each other," he wrote in *Fight The Power*. The crosshairs graphic is iconic enough that most don't need the stencilled letters next to it to identify the band. But putting them together, as they are on every PE album cover except one, is powerful, echoing the band's overall militaristic mindset.

Closet geek that he is, Chuck had a unique perspective on why he wanted Public Enemy to be a band rather than a solo project. "I'm a big *Star Trek* fan from back in the days, the original one," he wrote in *Lyrics Of A Rap Revolutionary*, "so I wanted to hook us up like we were on the USS Enterprise. Originally when I set up the Public Enemy characters . . . I looked at it like we were the Enterprise characters, their personalities is what carried that TV show. That's pretty much the same way it works for

Public Enemy." This meant that Professor Griff would be part of the crew, as would the S1Ws. So would Harry Allen, the group's so-called Media Assassin. So would Bill Stephney. But the group needed a DJ.

They turned their attention to Norman Rogers, another Roosevelt neighbour. "My family lived in the Bronx when I was born and we moved to Roosevelt when I was around three years old," Rogers says via email. "None of my family was directly involved with the music industry, but one of my father's jobs was security at Madison Square Garden and he would 'get me in' to concerts there when I was growing up. I saw acts like Earth, Wind & Fire, the Commodores, the Jacksons, the Whispers, Rick James, Prince, Parliament-Funkadelic, Hall & Oates, Shalamar . . . the list goes on and on. I remember seeing the guys at the soundboard and thinking I would like to do that job. I always loved music of all kinds. When I was very young I had a little blue AM radio that I would carry around listening to songs like Dionne Warwick 'Walk On By', Elton John 'Honky Cat' and others that were on the radio back then."

In love with all the hip-hop music he could get his hands on, Rogers would make his own pause tapes as a way to imitate the influential DJ Grandmaster Flash. "[I] would sound like Flash when he would repeat drum breaks and such while deejaying," Rogers recalls. "Then one day, a newer guy in the neighbourhood that was from Brooklyn had his turntables set up at another friend's house and was 'spinning' records, and I asked if I could try that, and he let me. I was hooked from that moment."

Originally, Rogers went by the name DJ Mellow D. "I had no clue what to call myself," he admits. "One of the local crews had an MC named Mellow Q or something similar, and I took the Mellow and, being my name was Norman, I didn't like Mellow N. I just picked D because it sounded good to me and it was sort of a play on 'melody'."

In some ways, Mellow D was the perfect moniker for Rogers. "Talk about somebody that's not confrontational," Johnny Juice says of Rogers. "He's *Mellow* D. That's what he really is." In *Don't Rhyme For The Sake Of Riddlin'*, Eric Sadler, a musician and fellow tenant of 510 South Franklin who would become a producer on PE's early records, described Rogers as "a big teddy bear, he's really like Yogi Bear, the most lovable, naïve, goofy kid that you could ever have". ("I would say Eric Sadler is mostly correct,"

Rogers says when asked how he feels about Sadler's characterisation of him.)

Chuck, who had gone to school with Rogers' brother, referred to Rogers as DJ Mellow D in 'Public Enemy No. 1', but the decision was made that he would now be known as Terminator X. ("[H]e was terminating all the nonsense," Chuck explained in *Fight The Power*, "and the X symbolised the unknown, a mystery. He's terminating all the things that we think we believe, that we really don't know about.") In the past, it's been said that Rogers initially didn't like this new name, but by email, he responds, "I don't remember not liking it per se, but it did seem a bit odd at first. Probably a bit gimmicky, but it grew on me fast." Plus, it was an exciting development for a guy who preferred his anonymity and hadn't given a lot of thought to becoming part of a professional recording band. "I never had any 'dream' of being part of a rap group," he writes. "I just loved music, deejaying and sound systems."

But the sticking point with Def Jam was Flavor Flav. "They said my voice was high, peaky and annoying," Flavor wrote in his memoir about the Def Jam brass. "They said the style for rap was a low, bass-sounding voice. I didn't sound like that, and since I didn't, they didn't think I added anything to the group."

In the book *Check The Technique: Liner Notes For Hip-Hop Junkies*, Chuck told writer Brian Coleman how he sold Def Jam on Flav. "Initially we wanted to bring Flavor through into the recording contract, and Rick and Russell pretty much detested the idea," the rapper said. "They were like, 'You gotta sign a vocalist, and what the fuck does he do?' And me and Hank said, 'Well, we can't really explain what he does, but he brings Flavor to the situation. You'll see.' I said I wouldn't sign with Def Jam unless they signed Flavor. We knew he was an integral part."

The group signed with Def Jam in the summer of 1986. The attorney who handled the deal was Ron Skoler, whom the band had met when they were putting out 'Lies'/'Check Out The Radio' through Vanguard. "I was a young lawyer at that time, out of law school just a couple of years," Skoler recalls. "I was in love with music and I wanted to be in that area and I was doing entertainment law. I always liked to keep my ears open. I had been into punk when that started – I loved bands like the Sex Pistols, the Clash, Buzzcocks, the Ramones. I was very open to hip-hop when that started happening. I remember listening to the early records of Grandmaster Flash & the Furious Five, the Sugarhill Gang, Kurtis Blow and all of that. I felt it was something unique, something exciting, something original. The lyrics at that time were basically just party lyrics or nonsense lyrics – but, you know, it was fun."

Skoler is about the same age as Chuck and Hank, and had also attended Adelphi, although he didn't know them back then. They had established a rapport, and so the two men approached Skoler about the Def Jam contract. "At that time, Def Jam was really an embryonic situation that was coming out of a college dormitory in Rick's room," says Skoler. "I think they had a distribution deal with Columbia that either was closed or they were closing it at that time. LL Cool J had already put a record out and the Beastie Boys were starting to come out. [Chuck and Hank] came to me and said, 'This is a way in the door.'"

The lawyer recalls that Chuck and Hank seemed more interested in forming a production company than in focusing on Public Enemy. "They were talking about various emerging artists that they knew from the Long Island music scene that they wanted to bring under their roof," he says. "And at that time, I was emerging as a lawyer in the music industry: I was representing Next Plateau Records that had Salt-N-Pepa, and [producer] Hurby Azor was my client as well. I was also representing DJ Red Alert and the Jungle Brothers, so I brought a lot to the table, too. They came and said, 'Listen, why don't we form a production company together?' They would attract artists, and I would attract artists, and we could put them under one umbrella. I said, 'Well, that sounds great.'"

One other person had to be added to the mix, though. "In my normal job, if you will, I was working in-house for a production company called PPX Enterprises," says Skoler, "which was owned by Ed Chalpin."

As writer Dan Charnas notes in *The Big Payback: The History Of The Business Of Hip-Hop*, Chalpin had an inventive way for making money in the music business in the sixties: he would record "'cover records', quick knockoffs of current hits, selling the sound-alikes in foreign markets where the imitations were less likely to be noticed". Older than Skoler, Hank and Chuck, Chalpin was also famous for signing Jimi Hendrix in the mid-sixties, prior to the guitarist's explosive solo career. The recording contract (which was for Hendrix's services as a sideman) soon became a nightmare for Hendrix: when the artist put out his own albums, Chalpin sued to ensure his rights. A 1968 *Rolling Stone* article mentions that Chalpin, through Capitol Records, was releasing archival material from Hendrix's early days in the band Curtis Knight & the Squires, even titling an album *Get That Feeling: Jimi Hendrix Plays, Curtis Knight Sings* to capitalise on the guitarist's solo fame. Warner Bros., which was going to be releasing the next album from the Jimi Hendrix Experience, wanted to stop Chalpin and Capitol. *Rolling Stone* writer Michael Lydon noted that Warner Bros. was "threatening court action to stop sales" of *Get That Feeling* and arguing that the album would "hurt the sales of their own record and Hendrix's growing reputation". As for Capitol, Lydon reported, the label insisted "that Hendrix's contract with PPX is still good and that they are on solid legal ground". As noted by Charnas, Chalpin successfully sued to get a percentage of Hendrix's Warner Bros. recordings. "Chalpin was often amenable to negotiation," Charnas wrote, "but he zealously guarded what he felt were his rights and was unafraid of a legal battle to protect them."

When Skoler began working for Chalpin, who isn't a lawyer, Skoler made him a deal: "I told him, 'The way I would work with you is, you give me a set retainer, give me an office, a secretary, and I'll handle your legal work. But I have to have the freedom to handle my own clients.' So, when Hank and Chuck came to me, I said, 'Look, I'll do this with you, but I have to bring Ed in also because I'm working for him. It's going to be done under his roof. We'll be using his office – we'll be using his secretary, his staff, all of that. Otherwise, it's going to be cutting into the time that I give him.'"

In *Fight The Power*, Chuck recalls, "Ed Chalpin was supposedly a big deal maker who was 'guaranteed' to propel our situation forward. We put our full trust in our lawyer, and together started a management company with both of them." As for his decision to start a management company, Chuck writes, "We didn't want to be signed to the Def Jam label, and be managed by Rush Artist Management [which was run by Simmons], and have to answer to both situations without having some kind of autonomy for ourselves."

Johnny Juice, who would help out on *Yo! Bum Rush The Show*, reiterates Skoler's claim that, early on, the group's heart wasn't entirely into Public Enemy. "For Chuck and them, it was meant as a way for them to actually become producers and managers," he says. "They wanted to create a management team. They were really trying to blow up their radio show – they wanted to run radio. Public Enemy was just a means to an end."

Whatever the case may be, Hank and Chuck joined forces with Skoler and Chalpin in a company they named Rhythm Method. "We met with Ed, and they liked him," Skoler says. "They were very happy to have him because he's a seasoned guy who's a great negotiator and was very adept at making deals and had brokered some very big deals before. I brought Ed in kind of kicking and screaming, because he didn't like rap music – he thought it was a trend." Perhaps not surprisingly then, Skoler never felt that Chalpin was as on board as he was about Rhythm Method. "Ed, I think, just went along for the ride," says Skoler. "He was helpful, but he was one of those guys that just wanted to cash in from Day One rather than really build something. I wanted to build the next Def Jam or the next Rush Management – that's where I was coming from."

The contract with Def Jam wasn't very advantageous to the band. "We got a low royalty rate," Skoler says. "They took all of our publishing. It was just a terrible deal, which we later renegotiated. But that's how we got started." As for Rhythm Method, which would manage Public Enemy, the company was owned equally by the four men. But an interesting predicament presented itself when they had to decide how to draw up the contract between Rhythm Method and Public Enemy, which was Chuck and Flavor Flav. Skoler asked Chuck and Hank how they wanted to proceed. According to Skoler, "I remember Hank said – and Chuck was going along with him – 'Well, we want to take a big piece because we're really looking to build Rhythm Method.' They felt that Public Enemy may not catch on because they didn't have a following. But they felt that we could parlay [Public Enemy] into signing nine or 10 other emerging acts that were interested in signing to an alternative company rather than Rush."

Skoler suggested that Rhythm not take more than 50 percent of Public

Enemy, but Hank and Chuck proposed 75 percent. "Bear in mind that if we took 75 percent, Rhythm Method was still owned by the four of us," Skoler says. "So, it would still go an equal amount to Hank and Chuck anyway. But I said, 'Hank, that's unconscionable to take 75 percent of any group.' And Chuck was like, 'Well, I'm the group.' I said, 'I understand that, but it's just weird – it doesn't look right.'" None of Skoler's other three partners saw a problem, so he gave up his protests: "I said, 'Yeah, OK, fine, what the fuck. If that's what you want to do, fine.' So, we signed that deal where Rhythm got 75 percent of Public Enemy."

"Hank and I didn't really know too much about the management aspect of the business," Chuck would later admit in *Fight The Power*, "but we knew we could handle the creative end and left it to the attorneys to handle the legal and business end." The legal and business end would get complicated later on. Right now, though, it was time to focus on the creative.

CHAPTER TWO

STEVE Linsley owns a valuable piece of *Yo! Bum Rush The Show* history.

"I actually have the original cassette that I need to get back to Chuck," says the musician, producer and photographer as he sits in an East Los Angeles restaurant. "Somehow it ended up in my pocket."

The cassette, Linsley says, is a mix-tape that was part of the blueprint of the beats and samples that would form much of Public Enemy's first album. "It's really, really raw," he says. "I think I listened to it once in the last 20 years. Technologically, the samplers back then were a fucking joke. You couldn't even record a snare drum that had the full dynamics of a snare drum. It was really limited."

When Public Enemy focused on recording *Yo! Bum Rush The Show* in 1986, they visited two studios. One was Chung King, which had developed a reputation not just in hip-hop but pop music. "Russell Simmons did all his first records there," recalled Hank Shocklee in 2005. "He did the Whodini record, he did the Kurtis Blow record, he did the Run–D.M.C. record, he did the Beastie Boys album and LL Cool J . . . Chung King was the studio to be at and Steve Ett was the number one engineer because he engineered all those records. So being in the studio with him was truly an honour and it was a very good experience, because in the studio they had, since 1973, a Neve board. They said that Carly Simon made records on this."

Although it was one of Shocklee's first visits to a studio, he quickly appreciated what Chung King's board could do. "The Neve board gave the sound a nice, warm, rich sound," he said. "That's why, when you listen to those old Def Jam records, you'll listen to the beat and that's basically a drum machine. You are talking about the early LL Cool J records, which were basically a DX or a DMX, one of the two, and that drum machine is very harsh. But going through the Neve, you know, the

Neve EQs and using the inputs from the Neve board, gave it a nice, warm tone. That's why those beats sound so big and so large and so fat, but yet so warm and inviting to listen to."

"Chung King was – not to say 'ghetto' – but it was another downtown studio that was accessible pricewise," says Linsley, who served as an engineer at the other downtown studio where *Yo! Bum Rush The Show* was birthed, INS Studios. "In those days, the uptown and midtown studios were, probably, hundreds of dollars an hour. Chung King was in Chinatown – it was pretty funky. INS was down in Tribeca, which is below SoHo, right before Wall Street, right near City Hall. [INS] was like all the other artist lofts – you know, this was before the rich folks got a hold of SoHo and Tribeca. You walked up two flights of stairs, and it was funky. I mean, like, carpet on the fucking walls. There was a wood door covering the window. I used to get yelled at all the time 'cause we'd open the window and, of course, the neighbours were like, 'Shut that noise off!'"

Linsley had ended up working at INS after his group, the Jim Carroll Band – he played bass – called it quits in the early eighties. A stint in England and then a move to New York finally cured him of wanting to be part of another band. "I did play in a band for a little while in New York," he recalls, "and it was just weird. Every time we'd do a show I'd say, 'What am I doing here?'"

Hooking up with INS was a way for Linsley to remain in music without having to perform. "I started engineering right at the [start] of rap," he says. "There had been some early recordings – the real pioneering stuff – and that's what was happening in New York. I ended up in this small studio downtown. A low-budget studio was actually a phenomenon – you still went into a recording studio, it's not like today where you can do everything at home. So a cheap studio was actually something, and a lot of the local rap and dance artists were attracted to that 'cause they didn't have big budgets."

If other white rock musicians were dubious about hip-hop's potential, Linsley felt an immediate kinship with Public Enemy's sound and politics. "Rap was like punk rock," he says. "I've always thought rap was the same kind of divisive, 'fuck it, we're just gonna make shit happen on our own' [thing]. I was in the late-seventies punk scene with Jim Carroll – it was a similar environment, where there were all these bands and they all had personality. Even the bands that didn't make it, the people really had a lot more individual personality." Such feelings were echoed by Rick Rubin when asked in 2005 by *The A.V. Club* why hip-hop appealed to him. "At the time, I was listening to a lot of punk-rock music, and it felt like an alternative to punk rock," Rubin recalled. "It felt like black punk rock. . . . [P]unk rock took the music out of Madison Square Garden and brought it back to this kind of naïve street level where anyone could do it, even those who are not really musicians. Hip-hop did the same thing, where you didn't have to be Luther Vandross or Herbie Hancock. You could just be a guy with an idea. That was enough for you to make a record."

For Linsley, there was an additional attraction. He had grown up in Berkeley, California, enjoying access to San Francisco's progressive radio programmes. When Public Enemy referenced Gil Scott-Heron & the Last Poets, Linsley was already familiar. "My parents were hippies, sort of," he explains. "I'm really glad my parents had that stuff around. There were little things that I [experienced] early that sort of got into my brain that made me connect with Public Enemy."

The demo that Public Enemy brought in to INS was the foundation for the album, and Linsley was struck by how focused the band members were. "They really had it mapped out," he says. "They had their loops, and once we figured out how to physically do them, it really rolled. Hank Shocklee seemed to be the driving force. He was, in a literal sense, the producer who's really taking control and shaping the sound. He was the boss in terms of what we were gonna sample and what we were gonna put together in the sounds."

Considering how ambitious they'd eventually become and how complex their music would get, the Public Enemy heard on *Yo! Bum Rush The Show* were almost charmingly freewheeling. Chuck D rhymed ferociously, but he also showed off his almost nerdy love of sports (lots of references to basketball and baseball) and even threw in shout-outs to Thor and the Green Hornet, betraying his interest in comics, pop culture and graphic design. ("Those early Saturday morning cartoons got me," Chuck told

Comic Book Resources in 2006. "CBS' Superman, Batman, Justice League. Then Space Ghost, then ABC's Spider-Man and Fantastic Four led me straight into [comics]. . . . You can show all emotions in comics.")

Working on their first album, Public Enemy, and especially Chuck, were ready to go from the first day. "[Chuck's lyrics] were all done," says Linsley. "They weren't making up anything at the studio. They came in like an army – they really were a fucking crack team. They were Marines landing on the beach. There was no bullshit. Not that it wasn't fun – I mean, with Flavor Flav around, you're going to have some fun."

Shocklee had been one of the early advocates for the mingling of Chuck and Flav's vocals on PE tracks. "Flav is dark but he lightened Chuck up," Shocklee once said. "Chuck's voice was baritone, Flav's voice is close to being a tenor, he is in that high-frequency zone and I never thought that the two vocals would work together, but those vocals really complement each other. Whereas you knew Flav and you knew Chuck and they were distinct and they were different parts. So that also added another element because when we produce records, I see a lot of producers spend a billion years on instrumentation and I think that instrumentation is part of it, but to me the most important part of any song is the vocal. I want to produce vocals like you produce music because that's the other side of it. So I make sure that all my instrumentation is outside of the frequency of the vocals and I want to make sure that the vocal frequency adds something to the body of the song."

Flav would later solidify his court-jester routine on the mic, but on *Yo! Bum Rush The Show* he's a much more aggressive presence, providing a live-wire danger as the foil on tracks like 'Public Enemy No. 1' and 'Yo! Bum Rush The Show'. He's not trying to make you laugh – he's trying to seriously unnerve you. When Flavor took centre stage on 'Too Much Posse', his rhymes had a lethal, don't-push-me edge. And on the steely grind of 'M.P.E.', he swings between threatening murder and boasting about his skill with the ladies ("I got to the beach / The ground was so sandy / Girls on my jock like ants on candy") – completely convincingly in both guises.

"On the first album, Flav [played] a really antagonistic asshole," says Johnny Juice, who scratched on the band's early records. "You listen to that album, it's 'I ain't gonna stop the bum rush, homes.' He was just a real belligerent asshole. He wasn't really the comic relief. In real life, there's that one dude that starts all the shit: that was Flav. It wasn't 'til the second album where it became comedy."

In his autobiography, Flav pinpointed his value in the band. "I brought something to the table that they needed," he wrote. "Not only was I part of a rap group that was bringing black power and social consciousness into the game, but I was also straight from the street, straight from the hood . . . I *was* the life they were rapping about. I wasn't a college boy like Hank and Chuck . . . I was a straight up nigga from the 'hood. I'd done drugs, run numbers, and been to jail. I wasn't perpetrating a street style. I *was* the street."

"Flavor was a gas, in those days particularly," says Linsley. "When he was young, you never met anybody like him. He's completely fucking unique in a great way. The roots of who he is today were there then – he was comedic, hyperactive. We had this really crappy, out-of-tune piano in the recording room for the vocals. In between breaks, he was on that piano all the time doing Frank Sinatra impressions. I remember him playing songs on the piano, just sort of mimicking people and being funny. In other rap acts, you got a posse backing up the lead guy, but that's not how it seemed with Flavor Flav. Even if he was being funny or just counterpointing Chuck, there was seriousness in his thing, too. It was like the music – everything had a purpose."

That shouldn't be a surprise considering that Chuck had a laser-like focus on his future. Hip-hop mattered to him, but he wasn't some wide-eyed kid who wasn't going to think through the ramifications of a life in music. As he explained in 2008, "April 1, 1987, our first tour with the Beastie Boys, I worked at a job until that Friday. I wasn't leaving my fucking job until I'd seen a clear answer, that I could make a living and support my family doing rap. And I'd already made a record. I wrote *Yo! Bum Rush The Show* while I was driving and working. I wasn't waiting for music to pay me, I better see it work. When I could see a little bit I put in my resignation, worked until the Friday and was on tour Monday. I had two days from going to a job to my own business."

Chuck's calm, pragmatic confidence extended to his rhyming on the debut. He'd already proved himself on 'Public Enemy No. 1', but throughout *Yo! Bum Rush The Show* he exudes the same sort of hard, booming authority that was popular in New York's hip-hop scene.

Looking back at *Yo! Bum Rush The Show* from the perspective of more than 20 years, Chuck told *The Quietus*, "We made it from a New York standpoint, because that's where we were at." That was reflected in the gritty urban desperation of the album's sound – you can practically see the dimly lit city streets and nasty subway cars – but it was also a by-product of growing up in the same general environment as other local acts.

In 2013, Chuck reminisced to *Vibe*, "*Yo! Bum Rush The Show* was recorded for 1986 during a time when we were being influenced by great people like Schoolly D, Run-D.M.C. and Whodini." Chuck had singled out Schoolly D previously in his memoir *Fight The Power*, declaring, "Schoolly D was a big influence on my vocal application, rhyming style and delivery." On tracks like 'I Don't Like Rock & Roll', 'Gucci Time' (which inspired the musical framework for *Yo! Bum Rush The Show*'s 'Too Much Posse') and 'P.S.K. What Does It Mean?', Schoolly D flaunted a smooth-yet-rough flow that oozed swagger with no-fuss execution. Chuck's all-business approach was similar: on the album-opening 'You're Gonna Get Yours', he lays out his case as an underdog not to mess with: "Object of hate / Who's the one some think is great? / I'm that one."

With hindsight, it seems like such a strange way to kick off the first PE album: 'You're Gonna Get Yours' is, essentially, a car song. On the track, Chuck pays homage to "the 98", a reference to the Oldsmobile 98 but also to the 98 Posse, a group Griff described to Russell Myrie as "a bunch of cats . . . who just possed up . . . They were just brutal with how they went about handling different things." The 98 Posse all owned that particular Olds model, and they initially clashed with Public Enemy's Security of the First World before reaching a truce. But for Chuck, the song was also a statement about PE's roots. "Long Island was different than New York City," he wrote in *Lyrics Of A Rap Revolutionary*. "In the city people catch trains, or they might catch a bus here or there . . . Nobody in the Bronx was rapping about cars back then, because young people didn't have cars in the Bronx. On the contrary, I rapped about cars, 7-Elevens and things that we did have out on Long Island."

But there was also a political edge to the track. In a *Spin* interview published in January 1988, Chuck explained, "'You're Gonna Get Yours' is about police arrest in black neighbourhoods. If you have a fly car and you drive around, the police will tend to stop you more often than not. And I've been stopped plenty of times. . . . Oldsmobile 98 is the ultimate homeboy car, you know? And just because you're drivin' it, a lot of times police will stop you because they think you're a drug dealer and they tend to stereotype. So basically, I'm attacking the stereotype. Drug dealers don't drive 98s."

'You're Gonna Get Yours' could have drawn more attention if the band had stuck with their first choice for the title: 'You're Gonna Goetz Yours', a reference to the 1984 shooting of four black men in the New York subway by a white man, Bernhard Goetz, who claimed that they tried to mug him. He was later found not guilty of attempted murder charges. Chuck eventually decided the inflammatory move wasn't worth it, convinced "that our use of the more controversial title might cause some unwanted legal ramifications down the line". This wasn't the only song off the album that necessitated a title change. 'M.P.E.' was going to be called 'Magnum PE' but, according to Chuck, "the people from *Magnum P.I.* said we couldn't".

From the start, Public Enemy knew they wanted to address current events head-on. Bill Stephney famously encouraged the group, "Let's make every track political. Statements, manifestos, the whole nine." This wasn't the predominant mode of eighties hip-hop, but Chuck had been exposed to the black-owned New York radio station WLIB while driving around in his dad's company's U-Haul coming up with songs for *Yo! Bum Rush The Show*. "They featured Gary Byrd in the mornings and Mark Riley in the afternoon," he wrote in *Lyrics Of A Rap Revolutionary*, "and both of them had powerful programmes. WLIB was a gigantic influence on opening up my mind on who we are as people and where we should go."

Not that he was yet fully confident in that mode. Although on 'Rightstarter (Message To A Black Man)', he chastises those "Just growin' not knowin' about your past / Now you're lookin' pretty stupid while you're shakin' your ass," the album finds Chuck hesitantly dipping his toe into political commentary. Take, for example, the minimalist 'Megablast', which lashes out at drug dealers with real potency. Unfortunately, Public Enemy hadn't yet figured out how to sharpen their storytelling skill and musical acumen to make the crack-epidemic narrative deeply resonate: it was a protest song without significant bite.

"That first album wasn't very political," Johnny Juice says. "It was very similar to [Boogie Down Productions'] first album, *Criminal Minded*. After the first album, KRS-One became peaceful, a man that wants to save his race – but on the first album, it was totally gangster about killing and sex and all that stuff. The same thing with PE: if you listen to their whole first album, it was very violent."

Still, *Yo! Bum Rush The Show* shone a light on a drug that was devastating poor and African-American communities, as crack reared its head on tracks like 'M.P.E.' and even 'Raise The Roof', an otherwise nostalgic look back at the band's DJ-party past. "When Reagan and Bush were around in the eighties," Chuck once recalled, "they knocked out plenty of opportunities, so people were responding to having a lot of guns in the community from nowhere, drugs in the community from nowhere. All of a sudden it goes from weed to cocaine in three years. So you talk to people, but you also have people in your family who were wiped out from these things."

Yo! Bum Rush The Show's political targets weren't always that gracefully attacked, unfortunately. 'Sophisticated Bitch', according to Chuck, "tells a fictitious story about a woman who plays black men. She's a sister, but she goes outside of that realm and chooses to use this brother to support her drug habit." It's a gold-digging tale so vindictive – it's supposedly written from the perspective of a bystander from the neighbourhood – that its depiction of her as a "ho" and a "bitch" feels misogynistic. (What also doesn't help is that the album's only appearances by women are in 'Sophisticated Bitch' and when Flav brags about the ladies clocking his jock.) The titular bitch's comeuppance at the song's finale – she gets beaten by her latest mark – only made the track's attitude more nauseating.

Chuck has said that he was trying to write about a specific instance, not condemning women as a whole. But 'Sophisticated Bitch' would start a trend of PE treating women in a dismissive or condescending manner on record. The song's best quality, though, remains its rock'n'roll arrangement, featuring Linsley on bass and virtuoso Living Colour guitarist Vernon Reid on the axe. Chuck and Flavor would pay Reid back by guesting on the anti-racism cut 'Funny Vibe' from Living Colour's 1988 debut, *Vivid*. Hooking up with one of the preeminent African-American guitarists, the creative force behind a major black rock band of the late eighties and early nineties, Chuck was making a stronger statement sonically than he was lyrically on 'Sophisticated Bitch'.

"We've always been pretty much rock'n'roll kind of guys," Hank Shocklee once said about the band's musical preferences. "We always liked the way rock'n'roll built up its heroes. . . . Like Iron Maiden – they're cult heroes. The way the whole concept is built around that huge mummified figure . . . that's incredible."

The work that took place on *Yo! Bum Rush The Show* was rough and experimental out of necessity. In an era where rap singles were more prominent in the culture than rap albums, Public Enemy were figuring things out as they went along. In an interview with Guitar Center, Johnny Juice (who's credited with "rhythm scratch" on *Yo! Bum Rush The Show*) remembered his first drum machine, the Korg DDD-1. "It had a small sampling bank in the back so you couldn't sample much, but I'd sample an 808 kick or a funky snare drum," he said. Making the album also required people with different backgrounds – some DJs, some musicians – to develop a shared language. "There was a lot of frenetic tension," Juice recalled. "'That chord does not transition to this chord well.' Who cares if it doesn't transition? Make it work! 'That noise totally destroys everything.' That was part of breaking new ground and trying something different."

"There was a lot of stuff that nobody had ever asked me to do on a record," says Linsley. "I remember the first day, we had to figure out how to manufacture this solo on a break, where the whole track breaks down to vinyl. I just remember being kind of freaked out by that – like, 'Wow, I never, never thought that you [could do that].' Somehow, they knew. They had that in their heads already: *the whole track is going to break down to just the DJ*."

But Linsley also contributed ideas, such as how to make Chuck's voice sound as powerful as it could. A fan of adding delays, he liberally applied them to the frontman's vocals. "When I put it on Chuck's voice, it just made it sound to me like he was yelling on the street," he says. "Steve [Ett]'s mixing – I'm not criticising it, I'm just saying it's different – the vocal processing on Steve's mixes was a lot less extreme of an effect. But I really kind of hammered it. When I heard Chuck D's voice through that thing, I was kind of smitten. It sounds like this urban environment: you imagine the guy rapping with the veracity that Chuck raps with, and it's literally echoing off the buildings in some ways. I like the sound of it, but I like weird stuff."

Linsley was in good company. Chuck loves odd, and Shocklee was a fellow devotee of intuition over stereotypically "good" music. "I don't listen to music! I feel it," the producer said in a 2013 interview with *Beats*. "I don't hear keys! I see frequencies." In a 1991 chat with *Option*'s Mark Kemp, he fleshed out his philosophy for PE's early sound. "When we started Public Enemy, I had a vision of what I thought music should sound like in the future," he said. "We started Public Enemy because we wanted to project this vision and the messages we had in as strong a way as possible. We worked hard on our sound . . . because we felt there was a critical need for that kind of power in rap."

But they didn't have a lot of time to execute that vision. Somewhat forgotten now because of the band's staying power is that Public Enemy had given themselves a tight deadline when they began. "The initial plan was to build each individual [band] member over time," Chuck D wrote in *Lyrics Of A Rap Revolutionary*, "but because of our crazy, anti-government ideas we strongly believed that we would only have about two years to do our thing before they caught on to what we were doing, and then we'd segue into something else, but our chief purpose would have been fulfilled. We knew that somebody would try to stop us with the type of messages we were going to be pumping out."

Such an attitude might have been mere incendiary bluster, but it was also understandable when entering into a new musical art form that had yet to prove if it was more than an explosive novelty. Although Run-D.M.C. had slowly built an audience, releasing their third album, *Raising Hell*, just as Public Enemy were preparing to record their debut, hip-hop still was in its infancy, with some dismissing it as a fad like disco.

Ironically, Linsley recalls that some of the primitive techniques PE used to make loops on *Yo! Bum Rush The Show* were similar to those on disco records. "Those perfectly timed disco records," he says, "they would have a drummer and he would play a really tight-ass eight bars. They'd cut that loop of tape and then played it through the tape machine, and then you'd re-record that."

But there was reason to be optimistic about rap's promise. In the summer of '86, Run-D.M.C. put out 'Walk This Way', their rap-rock remake of Aerosmith's mid-seventies hit. Reaching almost the top of the charts, 'Walk This Way' revitalised the Boston rockers' stagnant career, but it also made hip-hop seem accessible to those who may have initially resisted it, proving to naysayers that rap wasn't that different than the rock'n'roll they'd known and loved. And while Public Enemy were focusing on *Yo! Bum Rush The Show*, a white trio named Beastie Boys unveiled *Licensed To Ill*, a bratty collection of insanely catchy, juvenile rap songs bolstered by Led Zeppelin samples. By meeting the larger white audience halfway, hip-hop was beginning to plot its cultural domination.

As part of *Yo! Bum Rush The Show*'s trial-and-error process, two DJs chiefly contributed to the album's scratching, although others (like Keith Shocklee) were involved as well. Emblematic of its era, the scratching on the album is pronounced, serving almost as guitar solos (without the insufferable self-indulgence) on tracks like 'Miuzi Weighs A Ton', 'Yo! Bum Rush The Show' and 'Rightstarter'. "The DJ was first, the MC came after," Terminator X says by email when asked about hip-hop's roots. "Hip-hop in the beginning was centred around the DJ. Now, in the new rap music the DJ is irrelevant. Rappers don't include DJs other than at the show. The hip-hop DJ has gone the way of the band in R&B."

Asked how he would approach scratching on PE albums, Terminator responds, "I look at scratching on a song as adding an instrument solo. Like a sax player or a guitarist laying down a solo part. I'm not just making noise . . . I'm doing a wicked scratch solo. Sometimes a freestyle and sometimes a 'steady melody'. I try to make it fit into the music. I hear a lot of scratching that sounds like it's just 'on top' of the music and doesn't belong. I don't care for that."

Integration of the DJ was a key component of *Yo! Bum Rush The Show*, building on the tradition of groups like Run-D.M.C. but also working to make the turntable action sound like a proper instrument in a rock'n'roll band. Hip-hop did start with the DJ, but Public Enemy sought to prove that the burgeoning notion of a guy doing fancy tricks on the stylus wasn't the DJ's final destination.

"We wanted to make the statement, and this is something because I'm a DJ, I want to make the DJ a part of the instrumentation," Hank Shocklee said at a 2005 Red Bull Music Academy lecture. "So, if you listen to all the records, a lot of the stuff that you are hearing is cut in with turntables. So you might hear a bass line just being cut in instead of sampling that bass line, because we didn't want that feel. There is a feel when something is cut in as opposed to when something is played through the sample and it's another feeling when something is played out live. So it depends upon which particular record it was that we want to get that effect across, but I always wanted to make everybody feel the element of a DJ always being involved."

Because of the establishment of Terminator X's persona as the group's main DJ, it's been generally assumed that he was the main instigator of scratches on PE albums. On *Yo! Bum Rush The Show*, he's credited with "lead scratch", as opposed to Johnny Juice's "rhythm scratch". But when Russell Myrie published his band-authorised PE biography in 2008, there became a greater debate about how instrumental Terminator was to the group's turntables.

Writing about *Yo! Bum Rush The Show*, Myrie indicates that the principal DJ was Johnny Juice. Eric Sadler is quoted as saying, "Johnny Juice would come in and just tear it up . . . he's a technician, he would do the majority, but then we'd bring in Terminator who would do the kind of rubbing, kind of scratching slow style. And that would add a whole 'nother dimension to the fast stuff 'cause it was a different style." And, supposedly because of the album's low budget, Juice was favoured over Terminator X because he could knock out quality scratches faster. "A lot of times me and Terminator would be there at the same time," Juice said in *Don't Rhyme For The Sake Of Riddlin'*. "We didn't have a lot of opportunities to keep going over and going over to get it right. They'd give Norman two tries, and if Norman couldn't do it on the third try, they'd be like, 'Juice, see what you can do,' and I'd normally knock that out on the first take."

Asked about this today, Juice responds, "[Terminator] wasn't really a scratch DJ, so they wanted somebody that could scratch. That's why Chuck asked me [to be on the album]. Norman did a lot of scratches already, but a lot of them were simple rubs – if anything, he did the rhythm scratching, I did the lead. I just came in and I knocked out the whole album scratching in a day."

Terminator has his own opinions about the album sessions and *Don't Rhyme*'s impression of them. "Johnny Juice and I both did scratching on the PE albums," he says via email. "For me it was not a competition. I can't speak for Juice. There were a few early PE sessions where me and Juice were there at the same time. The rest is a matter of opinion."

Regardless of which version of the story you believe, Public Enemy were clearly invested in building up Terminator X in the band. The final track on *Yo! Bum Rush The Show* was 'Terminator X Speaks With His Hands', an instrumental that begins by reprising the beat from the album's slinky, funky 'Timebomb' before seguing into a loop of a skeletal drum machine and an annoying siren noise. That combination of beat and shrill whine would eventually become the prominent sonic assault of Public Enemy, but for now it was merely a minute of diverting filler. And the song's title established Terminator's silent-enforcer persona, a perfectly menacing counterpoint to Chuck's barked vocals and Flavor Flav's unhinged flow.

"I am not into the 'limelight' thing," Terminator says. "I love deejaying for the crowd but it is about the music, not the fame or attention for me. That comes with it, obviously, but for me it's all about [the] music." Terminator's entire persona hadn't been nailed down by *Yo! Bum Rush The Show*, though: on the album cover, he stands next to Chuck D, but without his signature shades. Still, he looks strong and defiant. "I am probably nothing like the 'Terminator X' stage persona," he says. "One of my friends told me it would blow him away how he would be hanging out with me, and then when it was time [for me to] go on stage I would put my shades on and turn into 'Terminator X'. The shades was my idea, by the way."

Like his bandmates, Chuck D was also trying to find his musical personality. Throughout Public Enemy's career, the rapper has rarely focused on himself in his lyrics. That was certainly true with *Yo! Bum Rush The Show*, helping Public Enemy separate themselves from other rap acts that featured storytelling and personal tales. But for Chuck, his lyrical themes weren't so much a conscious attempt to be different – he was just rapping about his experience.

"When I was born I had 'negro' on my birth certificate," he once said. "Malcolm X was killed in 1965, I remember that Martin Luther King was killed in 1968, I was eight. The Vietnam War was in 1963, all the way until 1971, I remember that. . . . These are the things that are inside me, as well as the music, like 'Say It Loud, I'm Black And I'm Proud' by James Brown, that said, 'We're black, we're not coloured or negro. We're black, we speak to the world because this is how we look.' Curtis Mayfield always spoke inspirationally. These are things inside me because music was always in the house. You speak a lot of words, you speak where you come from and what you know. People say I'm political, but this is where I come from and this is what's inside me. I think a lot of the time rappers try to copy a political stance that wasn't inside them in the same way. They may have been born in 1975 or 1982, different things going on. You can read back, but you can't actually talk from your personal experiences."

Chuck's sense of history extended to his love for the music of the past. "Chuck D was a disc jockey," says Linsley, "which gives one this great musical vocabulary. I grew up in the seventies listening to real disc jockeys. The disc jockey was somebody who knew fucking music and knew how to combine music, whether you're sampling songs or whether you're stealing loops. DJs understand music. They're librarians – and I say that in the highest possible meaning. You've gotta have respect for that."

Much has been made about the fact that Chuck D was older than his MC contemporaries, affording him an elder-statesman/big-brother status from the beginning. Even so, *Yo! Bum Rush The Show* occasionally reminds us that he was still a young guy, bragging about his car ('You're Gonna Get Yours', 'Timebomb'), throwing in some sexy come-ons ("I'm number one / You know it weighs a ton / And I'll be the burger / You can be the bun, girl / Surroundin', my steady poundin' / Get on down to my funky sound") and reminiscing about when Spectrum City used to rock frat parties ('Raise The Roof'). "This album was something where I just let my juices ride," Chuck wrote in *Lyrics Of A Rap Revolutionary*, and that exact quality would never be duplicated throughout the rest of PE's discography. Although an undeniably serious record that condemns apartheid in South Africa and praises black self-knowledge, *Yo! Bum Rush The Show* rose from an environment in which Chuck and his band members had learned how to entertain crowds on the radio and at parties. For all the many accolades heaped on Public Enemy, "fun" has rarely been an adjective associated with the group: the tone of their content and the dark density of their music chases away such a frivolous compliment. Still, *Yo! Bum Rush The Show* is the most "fun" album they ever made, reflecting the giddy freedom of a new art form revelling in its possibilities while still trying to figure itself out.

Even at this early stage, though, Public Enemy were led by Chuck's commanding, powerful voice. He sounded like a born leader rallying the troops, as opposed to an angry crank hectoring and ranting. Linsley, who's also an opera aficionado, praises Chuck's voice for its "sonority and authority", drawing a comparison between the frontman's rapping and an opera singer's delivery. "I like opera so much because, aside from the music, it's totally voice, which means it's totally body," Linsley says. "Some person manages to take this air from their body and, when it's good and intense, it has the same punch in the face as what Chuck does. Chuck's voice and delivery – everything about it – it's really like someone's punching you in the chest going, 'Pay the fuck attention.'"

According to Linsley, Def Jam didn't poke its nose around too much during the INS sessions. "Rick showed up a few times. Bill Stephney was the day-to-day guy," he recalls. "But from a musical point of view, it was Hank Shocklee who was really the orchestrator. But everybody really pitched in: it was really a cool little collective. It wasn't like Chuck was the star – everybody had a job to do. Hank had a job to do, Eric Sadler had a job to do, Flavor had a job to do, Chuck had a job . . . I really think that's partly why it's such a cohesive record. It was amazingly democratic and a lot like a rock band. Not a rock band with a big star – a real working rock band."

When it came time to put out *Yo! Bum Rush The Show*, PE's label decided to hold off on releasing it until the first quarter of 1987, despite initial talk it would be out by the end of '86. In *Don't Rhyme For The Sake Of Riddlin'*, Myrie puts the blame for the delay on the release of *Live/1975–85*, a massive three-disc live overview from Bruce Springsteen & the E Street Band. Unveiled in November 1986, the live set was CBS Records' attempt to continue cashing in on the blockbuster success of Springsteen's 1984 album, *Born In The USA*. If Chuck felt slighted – or, as he's mentioned in the press, concerned that *Yo! Bum Rush The Show*'s sound would become dated – Def Jam still benefited, as did Public Enemy. The same month as *Live/1975–85* came out, the hip-hop label put out *Licensed To Ill*, which went platinum in about four months. "Seriously, if it wasn't for the Beastie Boys Def Jam really would have been on a little bit more of an edgier ground and might not have pushed us through," Chuck later said to Myrie.

When *Yo! Bum Rush The Show* finally hit shelves, it wasn't greeted as the next sensation in hip-hop. "I *loved* their first album," Rubin told *XXL* in 2013. "But there's a reference on [*Nation Of Millions*] where Chuck says, ['They praised the music / This time they play the lyrics']. What he's talking about is that when the first Public Enemy album came out, on the mix shows – which was the only place that played hip-hop in those days – they would only play the instrumental versions of the songs. They wouldn't play Chuck, because it was too different." Further frustrating to the band was the fact that, according to Rubin, "At the time Public Enemy came out, they were the least successful group on Def Jam."

Ron Skoler, the group's attorney, loved *Yo! Bum Rush The Show* but recognised that it wasn't getting PE a ton of attention. "I'll never forget this," he says. "Right around the time the album came out, Public Enemy had a performance at the Capitol Theatre in New Jersey – it was two nights. They were the opening act. The show was the Beastie Boys, a group called Murphy's Law and Public Enemy. It was, like, a 99 percent white audience. Public Enemy got onstage and the audience didn't know what to make of them. I thought that they were great – they were brilliant. There were boos – they were not well-received on the two nights. It was basically a young, white rock audience – they didn't understand what this was. They looked at Public Enemy like they were from another planet or something. I remember driving back to New York City with them in the van after the first show. They were depressed, and I was able to cheer them up by saying, 'Hey, look, I got a copy of *Melody Maker* here. They just reviewed *Yo! Bum Rush The Show*, and they loved it.' I remember Chuck was reading that, and that raised his spirits."

History has created a perception that critics, especially in America, didn't take kindly to *Yo! Bum Rush The Show*. That's not inaccurate, with *The Village Voice*'s John Leland dismissing the album's content by sarcastically writing, "[W]hen Flavor Flav says he's got girls on his jock like ants on candy, or threatens to scatter suckers' brains from here to White Plains . . . yo that's when I'm hooked."

"You have to remember, this was a time when people like John Leland and some others were saying rap was supposed to be just dance music," Hank Shocklee observed in 1991. "And you still get that mentality out there; just look at what they've done with MC Hammer. He is getting pushed to the heights by the media. And I'm not dissing MC Hammer, because I think he's a very conscientious brother, and I admire his business acumen and his hard work. But the media wants to take Hammer and say that this type of rapping is the way it is. Now you know that's not true."

But, at the same time, other New York critics were able to see both the strengths and weaknesses in Public Enemy's debut. Writing in *The New York Times*, Jon Pareles was perceptive and mostly complimentary. "There are no tunes on the album, just raps and rhythms and noise – and a spirit of defiance that shades toward rage," he observed. "Like other recent rap albums, *Yo! Bum Rush The Show* is audio theatre with a dance beat." And while he faulted the young group for bravado, materialism and misogyny, he also noted, "[W]here the Beastie Boys dispense bratty adolescent fantasies and Run-D.M.C. generally sticks to self-praise, Public Enemy sometimes draws sociopolitical lessons." If hip-hop itself was discovering its album-length identity, then music critics as well were trying to wrestle with this music's potential. With that in mind, the final paragraph of Pareles's review was shockingly dead-on. "Public Enemy is weakest when it follows rap's macho conventions," he concluded. "Its songs are far more convincing – and unsettling – when Mr. D takes on money and power. At a time when most rappers typecast themselves as comedy acts or party bands, Public Enemy's best moments promise something far more dangerous and subversive: realism."

In March 1988, *Yo! Bum Rush The Show* landed at number 14 on *The Village Voice*'s influential annual Pazz & Jop music poll, which certainly suggested that the album had its share of fans. That didn't stop the band from bad-mouthing the poll's overseer, Robert Christgau, who gave *Yo! Bum Rush The Show* a favourable B rating but opined, "[T]hey make something personal of rap's ranking minimalist groove. But there's no fun in these guys, which given the intrinsic austerity of the groove means not much generosity either."

"John Leland from *The Village Voice* and *Spin*, Annette [Stark] from *Spin*, Christgau – man, they are my public enemies," Chuck said in an *NME* interview in October 1987. "[Stark] wrote a thing 'bout LL and took a lotta pot shots at us. I get pissed, man. I wanna be the critic's worst enemy. Leland disses me every chance he gets, he don't know me, never met me but he thinks I ain't for real. Man, I went lookin' for that dude at the *Spin* party. I wanted to fuck him up bad!"

Chuck's annoyance with Stark's *Spin* article stemmed from an observation she made in the midst of her profile of LL Cool J. The rapper was performing at the University of New Orleans Lakefront Arena, and PE were one of the opening acts. She wrote that the group members "march onstage in army active sportswear. The guy in the middle, the one who isn't dressed like he just finished filming *Platoon*, speaks to the crowd. 'There are people out there who don't want this show to go on. I'm talking about the fuckin' Klan, man.' The message falls on deaf ears. The logistics and the timing are off. 'Why don't you shut up,' the guy next to me calls out. 'We came here to party.'"

"Excuse my language," Chuck complained in *Spin* in 1988, "but that fuckin' bitch . . . [she] just tried to make a joke of what we stood for, sayin', 'These guys look like they came out of *Platoon*.' . . . [T]he whole article was sarcastic as far as rap was approached anyways. So I'm saying, that fuckin' bitch is trouble. Who the fuck is she? Fuck her, Christgau,

Leland, and the goddamn fuckin' bullshit-assed newspapers they write for."

Chuck's right that Stark's LL Cool J article has a strong scent of condescension on it. (At one point, she asks LL, "Why do rappers rub their balls?") But it's also a perfect time capsule of the mainstream (and largely white) media's confusion about rap music in the late eighties. Especially when acts like LL Cool J and Beastie Boys were mostly peddling entertainment, Public Enemy's political stance represented a strange, possibly scary, new message – one that Stark, and that guy next to her at the New Orleans show, refused to take seriously.

The problem was, Public Enemy didn't help their cause by opening their mouths. Calling Stark a "fuckin' bitch" twice in an interview was bad enough: when they did an interview with *Melody Maker* in the fall of '87, Chuck made some derogatory comments about homosexuals. But, first, he made some derogatory comments about women. Asked by Simon Reynolds if women fit into Public Enemy's world view, the rapper responded, "Of *course*, they have a place. Man is husband and woman is wife. You can only go to that point, with me. You can even have black women leaders to a degree. But I think that, where America has elevated a few women in a process of tokenism, in order to keep the black man down, as we said in 'Sophisticated Bitch', then I think it's maybe time to go back to some kind of *original* structure."

Reynolds noted that Chuck seemed more comfortable having fixed boundaries between the genders, races and even different sexualities. Chuck replied, "Borderlines have to be set because borderlines are *there*. If 10 whites and 10 blacks go to an interview, and 10 jobs are available, you can bet your life it ain't gonna be five/five, it'll be nine white jobs and one black. So, for us, there has to be cohesion. And men should be men and women should be women. And there's no room in the black race for gays, a black gay can't raise a kid, the kid's gonna be confused enough as it is being black. Lines have to be set. There has to be guidance. The shit has to be stable."

If all that wasn't wince-inducing enough, Chuck also commented that he's not much of a fan of house music, partly because it doesn't have enough soul and partly because its scene represents "'sophisticated', anti-black, anti-culture, anti-feel, the most *artificial* shit I ever heard. It represents the gay scene, it's separating blacks from their past and their culture, it's upwardly mobile."

The armed S1Ws also caused consternation. In her January 1988 article for *Spin*, writer Jessica Bendinger felt the need to point out that "the guns are unloaded". Explaining the S1Ws' wardrobe, Griff told *Melody Maker*, "We wear paramilitary uniform, because everybody wears uniform today – Khadaffi, Khomeini. What else do we do? We mingle with the crowd, we talk, we enlist."

Even Chuck's salute to his verbal dexterity, 'Miuzi Weighs A Ton', drew questions. No, he insisted, he wasn't talking about an actual gun. "My Uzi is my mind," he told *Spin*, "the bullets are the words I speak. . . . You know the mind is heavy. And words are heavy. The words are comin' at you rapid-fire. Like a machine gun – da-d-da-d-da-da-da-da-da. But it's not promotin' guns. It's not promotin' violence." A close inspection of the song's lyrics would have made that point for him: "I don't shoot bullets and I don't shoot blanks," he sings, a nod to his fully armed rhetoric.

But it was Public Enemy's brand of black militancy, powered by self-empowerment, that especially rankled with the press. Chuck openly supported and defended Minister Louis Farrakhan, the outspoken leader of the Nation of Islam. Farrakhan's profile rose after aligning himself in the mid-eighties with Jesse Jackson, a civil rights leader who unsuccessfully campaigned to become the first African-American presidential candidate. Farrakhan's preaching of black advancement struck some as bigoted, as he vilified Jews and other groups he perceived as trying to suppress blacks. He was also unkind to gays, saying in a 1996 speech, "God don't like men coming to men with lust in their hearts like you should go to a female. If you think that the kingdom of God is going to be filled up with that kind of degenerate crap, you're out of your damn mind."

"Basically I support the black leaders that want to take a stand," Chuck D explained to *Spin* when he was questioned about Farrakhan. "My whole issue is the us-against-us campaign and trying to convince black people to respect each other and love each other. And, politically, Farrakhan speaks for the same thing. But media blows it out of proportion.

When I say I support Farrakhan, a lot of people in the media just think I'm a racist and that I agree with hate-mongers. The media has always taken Louis Farrakhan out of context. You have to understand the man in order to judge the man."

Speaking with *Melody Maker*'s Simon Reynolds, Chuck argued for Farrakhan's importance by saying, "Right now, we need leaders. We're the only people who can raise ourselves. I don't think anything will be achieved in my lifetime, but a start can be made and maybe in the next century, we will be so strong and independent that only overt aggression will threaten us, a wave of lynching. Right now they don't need to destroy us, 'cause we're doing it to ourselves."

This would become one of the central challenges in Public Enemy's career: how do you make music about the plight of African-Americans that preaches self-respect without demonising others? Can you advocate self-knowledge and self-sufficiency when there are factions within the community that aren't interested in that message? Are flawed messages (and flawed leaders) better than giving up and doing nothing?

These questions would threaten to obscure the band's purpose at different occasions in the future, but especially with *Yo! Bum Rush The Show* there was a worry that the music would be overshadowed by controversies – partly because the songs weren't powerful and compelling enough to silence such concerns. That didn't stop the album from having its proponents. Beside Rubin, Linsley is also a staunch *Bum Rush* supporter. The musician/engineer, who went on to work with the Fat Boys, has remained a Public Enemy fan throughout their subsequent albums, but confesses, "For me, this record sets itself [apart] from their other records, sonically, because it's a little – I hate to say 'weird', but they get a little bit smoother [afterward]. I know most people would be like, 'Public Enemy? Smooth?' But [with *Bum Rush*], I think they got some expertise – they're right at the beginning of all this new technology. After this, things really took off."

The group couldn't know that at that time, of course. But they were already putting plans into motion for their next record. And they were sowing the seeds for future musicians to cultivate. In an interview with *Spin* in 1999, Tom Rowlands (one-half of the pioneering dance-rock collective the Chemical Brothers) enthused, "Hearing Public Enemy's *Yo! Bum Rush The Show* spun my world around totally." That first taste came while Rowlands was in his car. "I remember hearing 'Miuzi Weighs A Ton'," he said, "and I'd never heard music so powerful. It was just power, funky power, so powerful and tight and controlled."

You have to wonder how young Tom handled what Public Enemy did for a follow-up.

CHAPTER THREE

"WE wanted to . . . put together a concept album in the same realm as the classic albums," Chuck D said in May 2008. "The Beatles, Earth, Wind & Fire's *Gratitude*. We wanted to put together something that signified a live album, but also some great studio work. We had knowledge of James Brown *Live At The Apollo*, we had knowledge of *Sgt. Pepper* and *Revolver* by the Beatles, we were record collectors. So we wanted to make a *What's Going On* of rap."

The Public Enemy frontman was speaking with *The Quietus* while the band were in the midst of celebrating the 20th anniversary of their most acclaimed album. They were performing it in its entirety at select concerts. They were doing interviews where they were asked if the album still felt as radical as it did in its time. "I think the thing about *It Takes A Nation Of Millions* is, it's a global experience," Chuck would say.

Black pop has featured its share of provocative album titles: *Free Your Mind And Your Ass Will Follow*; *There's A Riot Goin' On*; *America Eats Its Young*. But nothing compared to Public Enemy's sophomore record. *It Takes A Nation Of Millions To Hold Us Back* was a gauntlet thrown down even before anyone had a chance to hear a second of the album. It was a line from *Yo! Bum Rush The Show*'s 'Raise The Roof' that, when it subsequently appeared in a story about the band in Toronto, inspired Hank Shocklee to suggest to Chuck it would make a fine album title. "[The meaning] was twofold," Chuck explained on *Tavis Smiley* in 2007. "It could take a nation of millions to hold us back as adversaries, or it takes a nation of millions *of us* to hold ourselves back." And with that double-edged meaning, Public Enemy would begin one of their grand, career-long crusades: looking at the instruments within mainstream society that were suppressing black Americans, while simultaneously criticising those within the community that were doing comparable damage.

Chuck took that crusade deadly seriously, wanting to be a hip-hop role model. "I look at myself as an interpreter and dispatcher," he told *Spin* in September 1988, later adding, "Two years ago black kids used to think that saying nothing was all right; getting a gold rope, a fat dukey gold rope, was dope, was the dope shit; it's all right to sniff a little coke, get nice for the moment . . . 1988, it's a different thought. Because consciousness has been raised to the point where people are saying, 'That gold rope don't mean shit now.'"

For all its intellectual heft, political rhetoric and no-bullshit aesthetic, *Nation Of Millions* is also an album inspired by Chuck's reaction to the band's critics, his personal accounting of the terror of drug abuse, and a good amount of love for sports, sci-fi and pop culture. It's a deadly serious album leavened by some well-placed humour and the infectious spirit of some talented young guys hell-bent on changing the world.

"When we made it there weren't that many rap albums out, maybe 20," Chuck told hip-hop writer Jeff "Chairman" Mao in 2008. "To me the greatest rap album that signified rap as an album format in the marketplace was Run-D.M.C.'s *Raising Hell*. That was power, and Run-D.M.C. being able to handle a stadium. When we made *Takes A Nation*, we knew what we were not going to make. . . . It has a lot of things going on: it had the sonic changes, it was the first album that said we're not going from track-to-track – before De La Soul put skits in there, it was the first album that broke the monotony of going track-to-track – it had the meaning of voices, the arrangement of samples. It was the first album unto itself, the juxtaposition so it plays like a radio show. We wanted to make it exactly 60 minutes, so it's an hour of introduction into the world of 1988."

The songs on *Nation Of Millions* began forming almost immediately after *Yo! Bum Rush The Show*. Peeved about *Bum Rush*'s delay getting into stores, and concerned that acts like Eric B. & Rakim were outclassing them with their more innovative tracks, Chuck and his production cohorts were desperate to prove their credentials as cutting-edge artists. Referring to Eric B. & Rakim as well as Boogie Down Productions, Chuck said in a 2013 *Vibe* interview, "They fucking changed the world, man. Hip-hop became much more aggressive and much faster. And Public Enemy had to get with that, so myself and Hank had to develop something in 1988 that was a lot faster, funkier, and also saying something serious that the people could feel."

One particular Eric B. & Rakim track, 'I Know You Got Soul', spooked Hank Shocklee and Chuck. "The minute we heard that shit," Shocklee said in 1990, "we knew the motherfucker was the greatest record ever made. . . . But we also knew the limitations of the record – that record was, to us, a pop record. We wanted to make something where, you know, the b-boys, the underworld, the gangster motherfuckers . . . we wanted to make a record that would reach *those* motherfuckers."

The first salvo was 'Rebel Without A Pause', a track highlighted by sampled horns from 'The Grunt', a 1970 instrumental from James Brown's band the J.B.'s. The screech of a saxophone became the song's jittery, ear-piercing centre, signalling either a distress call or a wilfully obnoxious bit of repetitious noise. But underneath that was endless complexity. "That record has four different beats," Hank Shocklee said in 2005. "One is the change beat, one is the original verse beat. The other is the short verse beat, and the fourth being with the ride on the beat. And it has 10 different turnarounds, all those little kicks, all that stuff is programmed. Each one does not repeat itself, so it gives you the illusion of the record . . . constantly getting better as opposed to it just staying linear."

Chuck had a similar approach to the lyrics. Writing in *Lyrics Of A Rap Revolutionary*, he mentions that the original germs of an idea came to him while Public Enemy toured with Beastie Boys in 1987. "It's a song where I wanted to say a whole bunch of phrases . . . and do a whole bunch of name identification that people could relate to or associate with the black militant and black nationalist movements," he wrote. Prodded by a belief that listeners' short attention spans would discourage concentrated lyrical attacks, Chuck "didn't give four minutes to the same thought".

Consequently, 'Rebel Without A Pause' moved from boasts of Chuck's lyrical acumen to praise for the Black Panthers to disses of black radio to a salute to the band's Long Island roots. In between, there's also a dedication to JoAnne Chesimard, who is alleged to have killed a state trooper in 1973 and fled to Cuba, and a beautiful dig at US President Ronald Reagan: "Impeach the president / pullin' out my ray-gun." Chuck wanted to flatten his critics while also dropping political rhymes. Perhaps most importantly, he also wanted to prove how hard he and his crew were.

"Our whole thing was anti-R&B because of the favouritism it had over the radio dial back then," Chuck wrote. Furious that some considered hip-hop not to be "real music", Public Enemy "musically rebelled against the melodies and strings". The band's philosophy, he explained, was, "We don't make records that girls like and want to hear, end of story. Once you make a record that your girl likes, what are you doing? Who are you, Babyface?" Alas, the hyper-macho tendencies of *Yo! Bum Rush The Show* weren't going to dissipate on PE's new material.

Chuck sweated over his lyrics and his vocal approach, determined to get them right. And when that was finished, the band handed the song over to Terminator X. In *Don't Rhyme For The Sake Of Riddlin'*, Eric Sadler, assistant producer on *Nation Of Millions* and part of the band's musical brain trust, is quoted as saying that PE were considering letting Johnny Juice scratch on the track but that Terminator said, "Nah, fuck that man, what are you talking about? I got some parts for this, I got some ideas for this." Reached by email, Terminator X recalls what inspired his indelible "rock'n'roll" sampled scratch that highlights 'Rebel Without A Pause'. "I had set up my turntables in my father's garage and I was looking for something good to scratch on the track," he writes. "One of the records I decided to play around with happened to be Chubb Rock's 'Rock -N- Roll Dude'. I was messing around with it and when I did that particular scratch, I immediately knew . . . [I]t sounded kinda like I was playing guitar. I didn't take time to come up with any alternatives. I said, 'This is it!'"

"I was disappointed when I first heard it," Shocklee would admit. Listening to the track at home, he thought, "There is something in here that I like but there is something that I don't like about it." Then, he hit on an idea: what if they took the bass out? "Once Steve [Ett] pulled the bottom off, the whole shit popped out like crazy," he said, "and it was my favourite piece in life. . . . I thought that that was probably the most brilliant piece of scratch work on a record to me ever."

In an epochal story, Chuck tried to convince the Def Jam brass that 'Rebel Without A Pause' needed to be Public Enemy's next single, even though the label was in the midst of putting out the next *Bum Rush* track, 'You're Gonna Get Yours', to radio. Despite Russell Simmons' resistance – "I don't want y'all to put out B sides, because it would ruin the album sales," Simmons said, according to Chuck in *Fight The Power* – the group went ahead and made it the flip side of the 'You're Gonna Get Yours' single, a decision that infuriated their label boss a little less when it became an instant radio smash.

As Chuck wrote in his memoir, "That was one of the few records where after we cut [it] I said, 'I know it's a hit. It's going to come out and smack everybody.'" The song's impact could be felt even on those who weren't yet part of the PE fold. "I used to work at Tower Records," says Chris Shaw, an engineer who would contribute to *Nation Of Millions*. "I used to work the late shift, and I remember walking to the subway at, like, one o'clock in the morning, and there was this crew of kids walking toward me on the sidewalk from a block away. One kid with his boom box, he was blasting 'Rebel Without A Pause' at full tilt. And I just remember being frightened. It wasn't the guys that scared me – it was the combination of the guys and this squealing saxophone. I just thought, 'I'm going to die. They're out for blood.' I had no idea what was going on, and then, like, eight months later, I was in the studio making a record just as obnoxious with Public Enemy."

"That was like a saving grace," Bill Stephney told *The Source* in 1990, speaking about the impact 'Rebel' had for the band. Before that song, he said, "We were getting lots of press, lots of notice overseas, but we weren't getting the street buzz that we thought that we should have gotten. Once 'Rebel' came out, forget it, that really established Public Enemy." Asked what made the difference, Stephney responded that the track "had within it the urban terror that everybody felt Public Enemy should speak about."

For a 2004 *Rolling Stone* issue celebrating the greatest rock artists of all time, Beastie Boys' Adam Yauch wrote about the song's importance. "I remember the first time I heard 'Rebel Without A Pause'," he wrote. "We were on tour with Run-D.M.C., and one day Chuck D put on a tape they had just finished. It was the first time they used those screeching horns along with this incredibly heavy beat – it was just unlike anything I had ever heard before. It blew my wig back."

The seeds of *Nation Of Millions*' success were sowed by 'Rebel Without A Pause', but also by that oldest of musical traditions: tireless roadwork. It didn't come easy at first, though. Hank Shocklee said at the 2005 Red Bull Music Academy seminar that when PE started touring, "Chuck was very, very introverted, he was not a person that wanted to be in front of large crowds, he did not want to be around a lot of people. I tell you a story. At his first tour when he was with the Beastie Boys, Chuck used to perform with his back to the audience . . . [I used] to get all kinds of calls like: 'Oh, why doesn't Chuck turn around?' Because he couldn't face the crowd."

As Chuck himself admitted, being a frontman wasn't his natural inclination: "It handicapped me in one way, because I had to be this guy that I really didn't want to be at that time." But Chuck worked through those issues to focus on his plan of touring internationally, bringing US hip-hop to European audiences. "Not only did our records strike people as being different, but we had set up a strong European base through massive press interviews," Chuck wrote. "I was saying things in interviews that they had never heard from a rapper before."

Unfortunately, some of those comments were similar to those he made to *Melody Maker* about there being no room in the black race for gays. Nonetheless, Public Enemy's gung-ho attitude won over crowds in London. Where American crowds had booed Public Enemy while worshipping Beastie Boys, London audiences embraced the military precision of the group's sets. As Chuck recalled, Public Enemy revelled in their underdog status, the opening act on a Def Jam tour that featured heavier hitters LL Cool J and Eric B & Rakim. "It was freezing cold over there, and we were sleeping on the bus," Chuck wrote. "It was like being in the service. We weren't getting much food, so all we had to look forward to was the next show. It didn't matter to us, because we had the eye of the tiger."

"At the beginning, Public Enemy had one of the worst stage shows ever," Johnny Juice recalls. "It was bad, and every time PE got off the stage everybody [was like], 'You old dudes are wack. You guys gotta step your game up.' Griff took that shit personally: 'Fuck that.' Griff is one of those chip-on-the-shoulder dudes. Griff's about a half-inch taller than me, and I'm only five-two. Talk about Napoleon complex, that's Griff. So he started introducing martial arts [moves] into it – and little by little, Public Enemy just started whipping everybody's ass on the stage. By the time it got to London, it was like, *bam.*" Air-raid sirens had been introduced as part of the sound design, and the band's demeanour was more confident. "By the time that [tour] was over, motherfuckers was like, 'What the fuck happened to these guys?' Public Enemy learned from everyone – even though they were the oldest motherfuckers there, they really learned about showmanship and working the stage and the crowd."

After hearing tapes of their London shows, Chuck wanted to include snippets of their sets in the group's forthcoming album. It would serve as a conceptual framing device for the record, and it would prove to doubters just how big Public Enemy were getting. "Our point was to say that hip-hop could be a live genre and it could be international," he later told *Vibe.* "We were coming at you with a higher speed that was going neck-and-neck with anything that you call rock'n'roll."

Rock was clearly in PE's crosshairs. A genre the band admired but also resented – rock diehards remained resistant to rap since it didn't feature "real instruments" – rock'n'roll didn't provide much of the musical foundation for *Nation Of Millions*, but its attitude powered every second of the album.

"In some ways, I see rap as closer to rock these days than to soul," Chuck D said in a *Los Angeles Times* interview from February 1988. "Rap and rock both grew out of black music and they have the same aggressive, questioning attitude. We found in doing shows with the Beastie Boys and shows before almost all white audiences in Europe that white audiences pick up on lyrics faster than black audiences. With a black crowd, they will only pay attention to the words if you prove to them that you are what is happening. When I first started out, I was happening kinda slow, but now I am at a level where I am in the top block and what I say is now import-ant. That's why the message on [*Nation Of Millions*] is going to be even stronger, deeper issues."

The connection between rap and rock was made explicit in 'Bring The Noise', one of the other early tracks composed for the record. A hip-hop statement of purpose, 'Bring The Noise' opens with a disembodied voice dismissively taunting "too black . . . too strong . . ." The rest of the track answers that charge, asserting the group's (and, by extension, hip-hop's) right to be as loud and militant as they want.

"It was mad, mad fast," Chuck recalled in *Lyrics Of A Rap Revolutionary* about first hearing the song's beat, which had been dreamed up by Hank Shocklee and Eric Sadler. "'Rebel Without a Pause' was already faster than a lot of other songs, it was 104 beats per minute. This track was 109 beats per minute." Struggling to find a lyrical angle, Chuck hit upon the criticism that hip-hop was just noise – and that Public Enemy's music was too provocative.

"People are saying that records I made on my last album and 'Rebel Without A Pause' were the most offensive records ever," he groused to *Spin* in early 1988, "just on the basis of how I sounded. . . . [Black radio stations] figure our message is too black and too strong and not realising that black radio is before the downfall of the black American mind."

Bill Adler, the band's publicist at Def Jam, acknowledged the struggles the label had getting hip-hop acts on radio. In a 2014 interview with journalist Chairman Mao, he recalled, "[P]romoting rap to the press was very, very easy compared to Bill Stephney's job. Bill had to promote to radio. That was a tough job. Radio – not just rock radio but black radio – both of those formats were very resistant and hostile to rap music. So getting our records on even black radio at the time . . . was very difficult. My job was just to get us in newspapers and magazines. And those media were much more open to rap. . . . [A] lot of the black mainstream media were less inclined to cover us than rock media or white media. *Rolling Stone* covered us before *Ebony* did. *People* covered us before *Jet* did. Along the same lines, we were booked onto *American Bandstand* before we were booked onto *Soul Train*. And it was very disappointing to Russell [Simmons]. Russell's a guy with a ton of race pride. He would have expected or at least he would have loved to have had black media embrace this new community of black artists right from the beginning. But like I said, they seemed kind of reluctant."

Musicians bitching about not getting radio play is nothing new, but 'Bring The Noise' laid waste to the group's detractors while seeking common ground with artists with whom Chuck felt an affinity, whether they be Yoko Ono or Anthrax. Chuck also saluted Run-D.M.C. and reminded white listeners, "Beat is the father of your rock'n'roll." This was a declaration with genuine sting. When Kiss announced they wanted to 'Rock And Roll All Nite' in the mid-seventies, it was a brash assertion undercut by a lack of true urgency. Maybe some rock purists scoffed at Kiss because of their make-up and theatricality, but the quartet were still part of a sonic tradition less removed from the Beatles and Stones than Public Enemy were almost 15 years later. PE's skin colour, their politics and their sound were largely foreign quantities in the white rock'n'roll world – and so 'Bring The Noise' was more than just some cozy suburban rebellion. Proclaiming that they ride in limos like rock stars – more of a fantasy at that stage in PE's career than a reality – and that they're fighting to be accepted, Chuck was forcefully reshaping the definition of rock'n'roll.

In the process, the band also wanted to change the perception of noise. "Most people were saying that rap music was noise," Hank Shocklee told *Rolling Stone* in 1989, "and we decided, 'If they think it's noise, then let's show them *noise*! But we're also gonna give them something to think about.'"

Toward that end, Public Enemy went to Greene Street Recording to work on *Nation Of Millions*. In a short time, the SoHo space had built a reputation for being one of the go-to rap studios in New York. "Greene Street had some really huge records," says Shaw. "They did Kurtis Blow's 'The Breaks', Run-D.M.C., a lot of big dance records like Shannon's 'Let The Music Play'. It was a pretty well-known spot – people were coming down to Greene Street because they liked the sound of the records that came out of there."

Specifically, artists were coming because of the studio's chief engineer, Rod Hui, who had been responsible for Greene Street's most iconic tracks, including Run-D.M.C.'s 'It's Like That' and 'Sucker M.C.'s'. "Hank Shocklee really loved the sound," Shaw says, "and Chuck loved those first two Run-D.M.C. records. They wanted to work with Roddy. Russell Simmons pointed them toward Greene Street."

"Rod was like our godfather," recalls Nick Sansano, who, like Shaw, worked as an engineer at Greene Street when Public Enemy came around to make *Nation Of Millions*. "He was our mentor." About 11 years older than Sansano, Hui "took me under his wing when I started to work there.

He was showing me the ropes. He was one of the first specialists of hip-hop recording and mixing. I learned through him, and [because of] him and my association with Greene Street, I started to work with Hank, Eric and Chuck."

At that time, Greene Street (like other studios) had a staff of employees. (Now, it's more common for studios to simply go freelance.) "People were on staff as engineers, even producers, mixers, assistant engineers," Sansano says. And individual employees would start to develop an identity as being specialists in certain genres. Sansano and Shaw became known as the studio's hip-hop people, although Shaw was initially one of those who wrote rap off.

"I went to NYU for recording," Shaw says. In 1986, he was a year from graduating, and the school informed him that he was required to do an internship. After being turned down by "all the big studios in Manhattan", he finally landed an internship at Greene Street, which was two blocks from New York University's campus. "While I was sitting there waiting for the interview with the studio manager, I'm looking at the walls and I'm seeing all these hip-hop records," Shaw remembers. "To be honest with you, I really wasn't a huge fan of hip-hop. I thought it was really a novelty. I liked Run-D.M.C.'s 'Rock Box', 'cause it had more of a rock edge to it. But to me, hip-hop was this fad that I thought, within two or three years' time, would fade into the distance. I was a progressive rock snob: I listened to punk rock and Kraftwerk and Brian Eno and King Crimson. I just thought hip-hop was . . . I never really regarded it as music. I regarded it more as an extension of dance music, another progression of R&B. I never thought it would stick around, and I wasn't really too thrilled about the idea of working in a hip-hop studio."

But that hesitation quickly melted away when Shaw started working with rap acts. "The way I saw hip-hop records put together with samples, it was almost like a form of *musique concrète*," he says. "It became infinitely interesting to me: 'Holy cow, you're making records where the record is all about processing the samples.' At the time of Public Enemy, most people were just looping a drumbeat and that was it – there was nothing really creative beyond that. Then when these guys came in, especially Eric Sadler, I watched them mangle things by filtering them, distorting them, turning them backwards and just doing all kinds of things to manipulate the sound. It was an eye-opening experience for me."

Sansano had worked on other hip-hop records before *Nation Of Millions* but says that the Public Enemy experience created a huge learning curve – especially because the band played the samples by hand, eschewing the smoothness of a sampler. "They was doing all the micro-sampling and the snippets and lots of different sounds and lots of changes – lots of small little details whose sum effect was greater than any of the individual parts," he says. "You had to rethink the logistics of how you would capture all of it. Now with Pro Tools and Logic and digital audio workstations, there are unlimited tracks and flexibility. At that time, we had essentially 22 tracks [available] – 'cause one track handled the time code, so you could lock all your sequences and drum machines to the tape, and one track handled your click track, so you can establish a tight synchronisation with your machines. So, over 22 tracks, you have bits of everything: all the samples, all the bits and pieces, all the changes, all the vocals. It really made you think in a completely different way. It was easier when hip-hop production was more akin to R&B production – early hip-hop was a drumbeat, a bass line, and the vocals, maybe a guitar or something. It wasn't all that much different from, I don't know, a programmed R&B track or a pop track. But with Public Enemy, you had to be willing to reinvent what you did, throw the rules out the window, and say, 'All right, we'll make this work.'"

As on *Yo! Bum Rush The Show*, the group came into the studio very prepared for *Nation Of Millions*, with song structures and lyrics already in place. "We'd be a little bit more improvisational where they would go to records and find samples that they wanted," Sansano says, "and one of the DJs would scratch something in, but it wasn't a haphazard thing by any stretch of the imagination." If the PE brain trust felt that a particular sample wasn't giving a song the oomph it needed, they would switch it out, trying different combinations. And they encouraged the engineers to push the volume and distortion.

In a 2006 interview with *Scratch*, Hank Shocklee recalled that record companies were always wary of putting out albums that "hit the red" – in other words, featured distortion because their volume levels went into the red/unsafe levels. "Sony didn't even let it hit the red at all," Shocklee said. "Sony would bring it back maybe two or three DB below before it reaches zero. So Sony would basically have all this hiss on the tape. You'd get music but you'd get a lot of tape hiss. So one thing I wanted to do is I wanted to saturate it. I wanted to hit it hard . . . I learned that from being with Steve Ett in the studios at Chung King. When I recorded with Steve, he was recording in the red. If you're in a recording studio, all engineers always want to make sure that they're never distorting. Tape distortion is like the biggest no-no in the business when you're an engineer. So they always would be very cautious to make sure they were not. And Steve Ett was pushing it into the red."

Shaw was more than happy to follow Ett's example. "When Hank and Eric would work with standard R&B hip-hop engineers, those guys were really all about smoothing things out," says Shaw. "With me, they'd be like, 'Hey, can you make that noise louder?' I was like, 'Yeah, sure, absolutely,' and I'd make it the loudest in the track and blow it up even more. They would say, 'We can't get black engineers to do that – we'll get the white guys to do that for us. They're into the noise.' They approached making hip-hop records more like making rock records."

The Greene Street sessions were an intimate affair. "When I started at Greene Street, it was a one-room facility," remembers Shaw. "There was one control room, one live room and that was it. When I started there as an intern, they decided they were going to build a second room for mixing and overdubbing. So once that room came online, Roddy couldn't be the only engineer at the studio, because there were two rooms to be run, so all the assistants basically stepped up and became engineers. People were constantly running back and forth between the rooms. It was that kind of little community – everybody who worked there at Greene Street, it was sort of like a clubhouse."

Shaw recalls that the band would show up around eight in the evening, with sessions running sometimes past dawn. With each new track, Sansano says, one of the first steps was "recording basics, which means literally establishing synchronisation between [Public Enemy's] machines and our tape machine, starting to lay out exactly the grid of how the tracks could work so we can continue to build and swap out sounds. Very often with

that style of music, even to this day, you may start out with this one particular kick drum sound or snare, and then once you add some of the core
samples and even after you add vocals, you might have missed your mark
on how the kick or snare speaks through the production. So, you gotta be
really careful. Now, it's so easy because you can just go into your digital
audio workstation – it's literally a two-second operation – but back then,
you had to be really careful that what you're doing was changeable. So,
when you start those sessions, what you're doing as the engineer is making
sure that you've established what we call 'synch' or 'lock' between what
they've got going on their sequencers and then what you can provide."

Once that step was nailed down, the engineers had to turn their attention to what Sansano calls "recording things the way they would appear at
the end of the day". Sansano had come to Greene Street after graduating
from the Berklee College of Music, getting a degree in music production
and audio engineering. He now teaches at the Clive Davis Institute of
Recorded Music, and a lesson he imparts to his undergraduates is the same
he and the other Greene Street engineers used to preach.

"When you get to the end of the record, you shouldn't be at the beginning of the record," he says. "You shouldn't just put all your ideas down
in a really generic way. You've got all your elements down – your music,
your vocals, your everything – and then you begin the mix process of
compiling everything, giving it the balance it needs to work. Very often,
people just lay [elements] down, not randomly, but without consideration
for the musical arrangement and everything else. And then when they get
to the mix, they're really not mixing – [only then do] they start to make
decisions about the colour of the record, what should be there, what
should not be there, and it's like, 'Well, what the hell have you been doing
for two weeks up to this point?' That's something that we took care to do
from the beginning, because their vision was so clear – and they had so
many elements – that when we committed some of these ideas to tape, it
would be as if, 'OK, this won't need much change after we process it.'"

Unlike Shaw, a fan of noise and Brian Eno, Sansano describes himself
thus: "I'm a much better musician than I am a technician." At first, he was
thrown by PE's sonic density until Hui gave him an insight. As Sansano
recalls, "He said, 'Yeah, this is crazy, crazy complicated music, but what

we have to do is fight to make all these elements heard individually so it doesn't come off as a completely meaningless cacophony, yet still have the impact.' I thought, 'Oh, you mean like writing a really good chart?' Because that's exactly what happens when you write a good chart: it mixes itself in a way, 'cause all the considerations that a mixer would take into balancing frequency domains, balancing dynamic range, building in dynamic range – that's all the stuff we were taught in music school that a composer or arranger should do on the paper. That explanation opened the door for me to say, 'Oh, I get it.' No matter how complex it is, you try to find a way to have individual elements heard without sacrificing the global effect of the music. I think that you had to be somewhat musical as a mixer and an engineer in order to do that."

Or, as Chuck D once said, "I like noisy shit, but you can't just like it. You have to have the ability to be heard over it."

If it was the Greene Street personnel's job to execute the mechanics, it was still Public Enemy's responsibility to provide that blueprint. "Chuck and Hank had the vision for how the record should go," Shaw says. "They were looking at the forest, whereas guys like Keith and Eric were looking at the trees. They were all individuals, so there would be times where they'd be butting heads about a specific sample or a specific part, but it was always Hank and Chuck saying, 'We understand that you want that to work that way, but in the scope of the record, it can't be that way because . . .' Chuck and Hank were always very aware of all that stuff going on."

Hank especially took pride in letting noise carry the day. "I'd actually get into arguments with Hank," Shaw says. "He would try to work a sample into a song, and harmonically it just was not working. There would be this massive discordant clash between a bass loop and a music loop. I'd say, 'Hank, maybe we should do this so it works musically with the other thing.' Hank would just look at me and say, 'Fuck music! I don't care if it works musically. I want it to be discordant. I want people to feel irritated when they hear the song.'"

In a 2010 interview with Propellerhead Software, Hank said, "There was no way I could use the same rules that, for example, Marley Marl was using for his groups or Hurby Azor was using for Salt-N-Pepa and

Kid 'n Play. When you listen to a lot of those records, those records sounded 'correct'. The chords were 'nice' . . . but those records were well-constructed in a way that, to me, was more pleasing and more comfortable to you. I didn't want to do that."

But this didn't mean that Shocklee didn't take a lot of pride in the building blocks of songwriting: craftsmanship, tone, pacing. "When Public Enemy decided to make records," he said in 1991, "it was important to us to have real songs; pure rap songs, mind you, on our own terms. And every song that we develop has a structure. It's not *all* chaos. As a matter of fact, our song structures don't get boring or tiring after X amount of time, because each structure and pattern changes and evolves. We took deejaying and songwriting to a level that nobody had gone to before. Not just to the point of counting beats per minute, but actually calculating mood."

Shaw witnessed Shocklee's dedication for both clarity and chaos firsthand. "Hank's thing was, he'd redo a mix for Chuck, and Chuck would put it in his crazy little red Sony boom box that he had," says Shaw. "He'd crank the volume up to 10, and he'd push the bass boost button and he'd listen to the mix. It would be nothing but distortion coming out of the box, 'cause he'd push it so hard. And then after Hank finished listening to it, he'd turn it off and look at me and say, 'Yeah, we need to bring the hi-hat up.'" Shaw laughs. "I was like, 'How could you tell? The boom box is distorting, you have it turned up so loud – how can you tell that the hi-hat isn't loud?' He goes, 'Believe me, the hi-hat needs to come up.' And sure enough, he'd be right."

The musical aggression was a sonic chip on the band's shoulder, a way to double-down on the criticism they received from not just the press but also their peers. And sometimes their rebuttals were made explicit on *Nation Of Millions*. The Flavor Flav solo track 'Cold Lampin With Flavor' kicks off with a voice saying, "I guarantee you: no more music by these suckers." It belonged to Mr. Magic, a New York DJ who said it during his radio show after playing (and then dissing) 'Public Enemy No. 1' in early 1987.

As Flavor explained in *Don't Rhyme For The Sake Of Riddlin'*, "He was like, 'Yo, we don't know who these guys are, we don't know who the hell they think they is, but we will have no more music by these suckers, they

sound like suckers, so there will be no more music by these suckers.'"
Flavor had been listening to the radio in the hopes of hearing PE's new
single, and when 'Public Enemy No. 1' came on, he recorded it, only to
be surprised by Mr. Magic's dismissal of the group afterward. The
comment, which Flav captured on his tape, became another element on
Nation Of Millions to demonstrate the obstacles Public Enemy were
combatting.

But it was through those obstacles that the band began establishing its
voice. The Public Enemy of *Yo! Bum Rush The Show* was hard, militaristic
but also, oddly, somewhat slight. (Chuck D's politically volatile bluster in
interviews wasn't matched by the album's austere, one-dimensional bat-
tering.) With *Nation Of Millions*, PE responded to being kicked around.
They remembered being heckled by revered MC Melle Mel when the
group performed for the first time at the Latin Quarter in 1987. Among
other things, he objected to the fake Uzis toted by the S1Ws. Chuck D, a
long-time fan of the legendary MC, was crushed, although Melle Mel
came around after the release of 'Rebel Without A Pause'. They were
angry that label politics had delayed *Yo! Bum Rush the Show*, making the
album sound passé. And Chuck specifically had become more politically
aware, convinced that he needed to educate his community.

"Sonically, [*Nation Of Millions*] said all the things we grew up with in
the sixties and seventies, all the voices from that time that were forgotten
in the eighties," Chuck explained at a 2008 Red Bull Music Academy
seminar. "In the eighties, Hank and I were hanging a flyer on a pole of
Malcolm X looking out the window with a rifle, defending his house,
which is a famous shot later used by KRS-One [for the album cover of
Boogie Down Productions' 1988 record, *By All Means Necessary*]. Some
guy came by and said, 'Who's this Malcolm the Tenth?' Me and Hank
said, 'Shit, we need to let these people know in the middle of Reagan and
Bush where we come from.' That had been forgotten and it was only
10–15 years prior, 20 years prior to him being killed. That's what gave the
meaning to Public Enemy."

That meaning was also, in part, supplied by the political speeches that
Professor Griff would play while the group was travelling from gig to gig.
"Griff never got a lot of the credit he deserves," Johnny Juice says. "The

whole militarism that happens on stage – the whole speeches by [Nation of Islam leader] Khalid Muhammad or Malcolm X – that was also Griff's idea. Griff made Public Enemy into what you *see* now, the imagery. Chuck was on the first album, but without the militarism and without all the Malcolm X stuff, it didn't have the same feel. But when that stuff came on the second album, all of a sudden it was a different animal. Chuck was still Chuck, but Chuck accentuated all that stuff. That stuff brought the Chuck out of Chuck."

Sound bites from Khalid Muhammad, Malcolm X and Jesse Jackson became part of *Nation Of Millions'* aural tapestry, connecting Public Enemy's present-day mission with past African-Americans struggles. In the same manner, the band scoured their records for sonic reference points, drawing from James Brown and Isaac Hayes to place PE in a proud tradition of black music. "You talk to Chuck or Keith or me and we know our records backwards and forward," Hank said in 1991. "We're record librarians. And Chuck and I are arrangement fanatics, too; we know arrangements, concepts, songs, ideas, beats. So we put that together and say, 'This is what we wanna do.' Then there's Sadler. Eric Sadler knows the machinery. He was in a band, so he has a musician's head. He'd say, 'Yeah, we can go do this, but we can't go *that* far out. Give it at least some kind of musical structure.' Then once we knew what we wanted, we put together songs, which is ultimately what you want to do, right?"

In a 2011 interview with *Vibe*, Chuck recalled, "You had four people in the room beat-digging, evaluating and seeing what sounds worked and didn't work. But at the end of the day, the music had to make some kind of sense."

Different estimates put the total number of samples on *Nation Of Millions* at between 100 and 150. Previous hip-hop records had used samples, but none had incorporated them as densely as what Public Enemy were attempting. "I have a lot of memories about them doing like 'Night Of The Living Baseheads'," Shaw says. "That pretty much is the most intensive sample track on the record – it's only in short bursts, lyrically, throughout the entire track. You know there were so many samples on that one particular song that if you looked at the track sheet, there would be pieces of legal-pad paper stapled to the back – it would be a list, in chronological order, of what happened in the song and what sample would appear on that track at what point during the song."

'Night Of The Living Baseheads' saw Chuck evolving far beyond the anti-crack attacks on *Yo! Bum Rush The Show* to deliver a stirring, grim report on drug addiction. It was inspired by what the rapper saw around him. In *Lyrics Of A Rap Revolutionary*, Chuck wrote, "I used to notice in the area where the Rush and Def Jam offices were located in lower Manhattan that baseheads would break into cars. I'd see crack vials all over the place, and a lot of times people would come right up to the car, looking like zombies, like a scene from the movie *Night Of The Living Dead*." A repeated screeching horn, occasional frenzied scratching and rampant micro-sampling created a horror-film mood for Chuck's vision of a post-apocalyptic New York terrorised by crack. But the song was also personal for him: the final verse, which describes a former rapper who has become a lawless basehead, was prompted by "a rapper that I looked up to who was on the pipe at the time . . . [t]elling the story of how anybody can get caught up in this".

Grabbing everything from Run-D.M.C.'s 'Sucker M.C.'s' to David Bowie's 'Fame', 'Night Of The Living Baseheads' demonstrated Sansano's philosophy that a seeming cacophony can feel like a coherent piece of music. Not bad for a song that required such painstaking stitching to construct. Shaw recalls hanging out with Hank for a full day simply filling in all the samples, including playing with Chuck's vocals. "Chuck put the vocal down," says Shaw, "and we'd try to find samples of the exact same lyric in other records. So all this research had to be done: Hank and Keith would just scour through records to see if they'd find a sample of somebody saying the word 'one' or 'trouble' or 'dance.' Scouring and scouring – there were many, many nights like that." The effect made Chuck's vocals sound more forceful – not just the words of one man but a whole community. And yet at the same time, it added another layer of dehumanisation and unease to the song, as if Chuck's very words were being scraped away and replaced with disembodied ghosts from the past.

The dexterity of sampling mixed with a personal lyrical perspective continued on the next track. 'Black Steel In The Hour Of Chaos' was its own horror story: an imaginary account of Chuck violently leading a prison jailbreak after being incarcerated for draft-dodging. The scenario seemed anachronistic – in the late eighties the US wasn't at war, and the draft had been ended in the seventies – but Chuck was recalling a potent childhood memory. "Back when I was seven years old I saw my uncle come to my grandmother's house to get his draft papers for Vietnam," he told writer Brian Coleman for his book *Check The Technique: Liner Notes For Hip-Hop Junkies*. "Of course as a kid you're trying to see what's going on. I saw their faces drop. I thought about the whole draft policy – it just stuck with me. I was like, 'If I have to go to jail for not fighting in a war, then breaking out is righteous.'" He also held onto the words of his mother from when he was a boy: "Whatever you do, don't go to war for this country. Be a conscientious objector."

One of the group's longest tracks, clocking in at just under six-and-a-half minutes, 'Black Steel In The Hour Of Chaos' builds powerfully from its sample of a few piano notes from Isaac Hayes' 'Hyperbolicsyllabic-sesquedalymistic'. Evoking John Carpenter's chilling *Halloween* theme, the sample suggests terror and urgency as Chuck relates first-person how he ended up in jail and how he meticulously led the escape. Shaw heard the song at an early stage before vocals had been added. "I opened the door to the A room," Shaw recalls, "and they had just finished laying down the basic track. No vocals, no extraneous samples. It was playing on the big speakers at full volume, and I just walked into this room and was assaulted by this massive song. I remember standing there completely shell-shocked for five minutes. Like, 'What the fuck is this?' It was insane. I was completely blown away by it. I thought, 'I've got to get in on as many of these sessions as I possibly can, 'cause this is some of the weirdest shit I've ever heard in my life.'"

Though 'Black Steel' could be seen as an antecedent to the gangster fantasies of N.W.A. and others, the track had a political perspective and a gripping narrative with impressive cinematic complexity. "The true message of the jam is don't let anybody try to hold you back from what you believe in," Chuck wrote in *Fight The Power*. "It was a jam that was far ahead of its time. [The song] was dedicated to my brothers and sisters in the lockdown, because there's way too many black people in the prison system." The song doesn't just feature Chuck's deft as-it's-happening storytelling, however – there's also a running subplot with Flavor Flav calling Chuck to let him know that the rest of the band will be there to spring him. This created a cunning suspense within the song: would Chuck's antiwar antihero be able to free himself? And would the S1Ws get there in time?

"That phone call [conceit] . . . sometimes that stuff seems like it's really easy," Sansano says, "but to make it not seem cheesy and have a flow and a conversational quality, it takes a little bit." Apparently, it required the engineers trying different phones until it sounded convincing. Finally, according to Shaw, "Flavor Flav did his vocal from a lounge on the intercom. We took the phone from the control room, stuck it out in the vocal booth with a microphone on it, and we had a headphone cable out into the lounge. Flavor was doing the ad-libs on the phone – we had the speakerphone mic'd up – and Hank kept on interrupting: 'No, don't say that, say this, don't say this, don't say that, say this.' At one point, Flavor is like, 'Yo, don't stop me, Hank!' And that's in the [final] track."

And just as Chuck and his production cohorts were sharpening their musical landscapes, Flavor was finding his role. 'Cold Lampin With Flavor' caught him in a still-dangerous mood, but it also showed him flashing some of the maniac-psycho humour that would become part of his trademark. No more proof of that was necessary than this hilarious, brilliant, bizarre verse . . .

> *We got Magnum Brown, Shoothki – Valoothki*
> *Super-calafraga-hestik-alagoothki*
> *You could put dat in ya don't know what I said book*
> *Took-look-yuk-duk-wuk*

Mocking his own indecipherable strangeness while asserting his lyrical potency, Flavor was a weapon: the unpredictable jagged edge of an angry, thoughtful group. Sansano recalls that, as opposed to Chuck's planned-out lyrics, Flav was more off-the-cuff. "You never know exactly what he was gonna bring, or even if he was gonna show up," says Sansano. "But he's the wild card, so he had a little bit of latitude. On a good day, he would be hilarious – and on a bad day, he would need Chuck to tell him exactly what to do."

Ron Skoler recalls the day Flavor came into his office to play 'Cold Lampin', performing the lyrics with a backing track he brought with him. "This guy was always kidding around, always joking, always happy," Skoler recalls. "I remember one time, he showed up in the office, and I said, 'How is everything?' And he goes something like, 'I'm potted like a plant.' He would just say these things."

It was one particular visit to Skoler's office that inspired his coinage of the term "cold medina", which shows up in the *Nation Of Millions* lyrics. "I had some law books in the office on a shelf," Skoler explains, "and one of the law books, it's like a series of research books called *Medina's Bostwick*. I said to Flavor, 'What's going on?' He goes, 'Everything is cold medina.' I said, 'What does that mean?' He got it from looking at *Medina's Bostwick*."

Soon, "cold medina" would be adopted by Beastie Boys in their '89 song 'Looking Down The Barrel Of A Gun' and, most memorably, by Tone Loc for his huge hit from the same year, 'Funky Cold Medina'. As Flavor recalled in a 2011 interview at the Grammy Museum in Los Angeles, "Tone Loc, one day, said, 'Yo Flav, what's "cold medina" man?' I said, 'It means cold pumpin', no slumpin', it's the bag you wanna be jumpin'.' I said, 'Yo, you should use that in one of your records, man, I'm tellin' you.'"

Nation Of Millions also gave birth to Flavor's "Yeeeah, boyee" catchphrase, wielded memorably at the start of 'Bring The Noise'. In *The Icon The Memoir*, Flav explained that it came about from LL Cool J. "You'd say something like, 'That's a slamming beat, yo!,' and LL would say, 'Yeah, boy!' like that," Flav wrote. "He said it so much, I kinda picked it up." To make the phrase his own, he extended both words "and let my voice go up a bit at the end." From such humble origins came a persona – and immortality. Flav claims in his memoir, "I became one of the most sampled voices in the history of music. Nobody's voice has ever been sampled more than Flavor Flav's, to this day."

The album also popularised Flav's signature accessory – the large clock worn around the neck – that can be seen on *Nation Of Millions*' inner-sleeve photography and cover. "We started off wearing stopwatches as a fad," Flavor told *The Daily Beast* in 2011, "and one day, this lady came through our project selling shower clocks. My boy took the stopwatch off my neck, put this big clock around my neck, and everybody was laughing in the hallway saying that it looked funny. Then, they dared me to wear it onstage during the show. So, when we went to open up for the Beastie Boys in Passaic, New Jersey, I wore the clock. When we got these photos back from *Newsday*, the *New York Post*, and the clocks looked dope. . . . Chuck D wore a clock for maybe [the first] three or four years. After that, Chuck D took his clock off, but I kept mine on."

Another Public Enemy personality, Terminator X, was also built up on the album. Beyond being shouted-out in 'Rebel Without A Pause' and 'Bring The Noise', he was front and centre on 'Terminator X To The Edge Of Panic'. Starting with a snippet of the band's '87 London shows, the song pays homage to PE's DJ, admiring his skill to "be bad by his damn self". It also features one of the group's most indelible lyrics: "Who gives a fuck about a goddamn Grammy," an award Public Enemy have still never won.

"I came up with the track and presented it to Chuck," Terminator X says by email when discussing the song's origin. "Chuck came up with the name and did the verses. Either Chuck or Hank added the Spoonie Gee 'Love Rap' drum loop sample to the track as well." And, in another sign of the group's pop-culture love, Terminator acknowledges, "I am a fan of Queen's music and also a sci-fi fan and decided to play around with Queen's *Flash Gordon* theme," which lent 'Terminator X To The Edge Of Panic' its playful/boastful declaration the DJ was the "saviour of the universe".

'Terminator X To The Edge Of Panic', along with 'Cold Lampin With Flavor', was a moment of relative lightness on an album of otherwise focused assault. If you didn't know better, you'd swear 'Edge Of Panic' was *Nation Of Millions*' block-party cut. "The music to that is 'Rebel Without A Pause' backwards," Chuck said in *Check The Technique* with a laugh. "We was rockin' that freestyle out, around '87. We had the track backwards, and we wanted Terminator's name to shine more. We put some Farrakhan speeches on it and we had something out of nothing. It was one of those things that was put together at the last minute."

It wasn't the only such song, though. One of the album's closing tracks was also one they put together near the end of the sessions. Chuck was reading *Life* when he noticed a caption to a picture of Malcolm X that read, "What ever happened to the prophets of rage?" From that, the frontman conceived 'Prophets Of Rage', built around a beat that Hank and Eric had written but abandoned. In *Lyrics Of A Rap Revolutionary*, he admitted that he'd been reading the article while sitting on the toilet, scribbling the title down on some toilet paper.

"I like to make the title to a song first because it helps me write the rest of the song," he revealed in *Check The Technique*, and it's a process he still follows today. As for his vocals on 'Prophets Of Rage', he said, "I stretched the limits on that one. I was just never satisfied with my takes." Laughing, he added, "I was known as the Hundred-Take Man."

"Vocals are always the hardest thing," Sansano says about the recording process. "You have the most sensitivity to vocals because we're just so predisposed to reacting to such minute changes in inflection in the human voice and sound of the human voice. When people say there are the intangibles of a great performance that no one can describe, it's not all that intangible. You as a person detect the sincerity and believability of the performance. Can somebody listen to a vocal performance and have this seamless experience that is purely emotional? Chuck really knows how to control his voice and how to execute what he wanted. But he struggled to make sure the vocals were exactly what they should or could be."

Chuck had good reason to be exacting. As elsewhere on *Nation Of Millions*, 'Prophets Of Rage' was a precise examination of why blacks had a right to be hostile, condemning those who would question his authority ("If you don't think I'm a brother / Then check my chromosomes"), saluting jailed South African activist Nelson Mandela and dissing UK Prime Minister Margaret Thatcher. "It was a time of heightened right-wing politics, so the climate dictated the direction of the group," Chuck explained in a 2005 interview in *The Progressive*. "The Berlin Wall was up. Nelson Mandela was in prison. Margaret Thatcher was running the UK. Reagan was out of control in the White House. And [George] Bush Senior was vice president soon to be president. You can say we were up against it." But 'Prophets Of Rage' was also critical of African-Americans who sowed self-destruction by selling drugs or being ignorant of their history.

When Chuck D finally sat down with John Leland, who had been dismissive of *Yo! Bum Rush The Show* in his *Village Voice* review, for an interview in *Spin*, they discussed whether Chuck considered himself a prophet. "I guess so," the rapper replied, later saying, "What is a prophet? One that comes with a message from God to try to free people. My people are enslaved within their own minds."

To further illustrate that point, *Nation Of Millions* also contained the song 'She Watch Channel Zero?!' Swiping the metal band Slayer's demonic guitar riff from 'Angel Of Death', the track lamented a woman addicted to daytime television. Although Chuck hails her as a beauty, the main character behaves in such a way that "There's a five-letter word to describe her character." That five-letter word would presumably be "bitch", an unfortunate continuation of the previous album's 'Sophisticated Bitch': when women showed up on PE albums, they were usually criticised for their attitudes. Chuck swore he wasn't being misogynistic – when the band started, "I didn't even know what the word 'misogynist' meant," Chuck said in 2006 – but rather, as he wrote in *Fight The Power*, that he wanted to focus on "how we as a people, especially some sisters, believe what we see on TV and soap operas, when there's really nothing there for *us*."

The use of Slayer was exciting, but also radical. "There was a definite respect between hip-hop and the alternative metal and alternative rock of the day," says Sansano, but it wasn't felt in all corners. 'Angel Of Death' was the opening cut off Slayer's 1986 album, *Reign In Blood*, which had been produced by Rick Rubin. In author D.X. Ferris's 33⅓ book about *Reign In Blood*, he quotes Hank Shocklee, who says, "At that time, hip-hop and rock, especially heavy metal, were so far away from each other. Rick's genius was taking rock and hip-hop and marrying them together." Rubin had convinced the group to join Def Jam, which was known for its rap acts. "Slayer, that was like *the dark side*," Shocklee told Ferris. "They were enigmas. But they were always cool. In a strange way, they did fit in. They were the extreme of the Beastie Boys. As far as I'm concerned, the whole Def Jam family was a very, very weird family anyway. It was more like the Addams Family than anything else." In a sense, Public Enemy's sampling of their Def Jam head-banging brothers suggested that the two bands had more in common than outsiders might have presumed.

Speaking with *XXL* in 2013, Rubin confessed, "I played more of an advisory role with Public Enemy. I really trusted them to make the music that they wanted to make . . . they created their whole own world of music. They would always ask me to come to the studio and I would check in on things and I'd make suggestions and stuff, but for the most part, the closer it was to Chuck's vision, the better."

Rubin did play a very small part, however, in 'Don't Believe The Hype'. The track was written in response to Rubin putting together the soundtrack for the 1987 drama *Less Than Zero* and asking the band to contribute a tune. After completing 'Don't Believe The Hype' for Rubin, Public Enemy had misgivings: this was the first song they executed after 'Rebel Without A Pause', making great use of an understated guitar lick from James Brown's early-seventies cut 'I Got Ants In My Pants (And I Want To Dance)', but decided it was inferior because it wasn't as intense as 'Rebel'. Consequently, Public Enemy instead submitted 'Bring The Noise', leaving 'Don't Believe The Hype' to gather dust until they could decide what to do with it. In her history of Def Jam, *Def Jam, Inc.: Russell Simmons, Rick Rubin, And The Extraordinary Story Of The World's Most Influential Hip-Hop Label*, journalist Stacy Gueraseva reveals that Rubin wasn't too enthused about 'Don't Believe The Hype' either, and that he was much happier to have 'Bring The Noise' on the soundtrack.

Thankfully for the band, an outside influence helped them realise what they had on their hands. In *Check The Technique*, Chuck commented, "Hank went to this spot on the Lower East Side and heard [Run-D.M.C.'s] D.M.C. play ['Don't Believe The Hype'] in his car, and it renewed his interest." Darryl McDaniels had somehow gotten access to 'Don't Believe The Hype', his fortuitous run-in with Shocklee provoking the band to include the track on *Nation Of Millions*.

When Chuck spoke with Leland for *Spin*, they talked about the track, which had been partly inspired by naysayers like Leland. (In the same interview, Chuck tells Leland about 'Bring The Noise', "Oh yeah, that was about you. I was talking right about you.") "'Don't Believe the Hype' is about telling people, 'Listen, just don't believe the things that are told to you,'" Chuck explained. Over the song's lean, funky groove, the rapper sticks up for Farrakhan, gets in the face of "suckers [and] liars", takes journalists' "pens and pads" away from them, denies that he's a racist, and compares himself to John Coltrane, whose adoption of free jazz mid-century drew criticism from some former fans. "[A] lot of writers came crashing down on him because of his radical stance," Chuck told Leland. "He started becoming more and more radical until the day he died, started speaking his mind. A lot of people thought he was losing it. Today they recognise the man as a genius."

In that same interview, Chuck D vocalises one of his most iconic phrases, which would be mangled and reshaped over time. Complaining about the media's distorting effect on individuals, he mused, "Rap serves as the communication that they don't get for themselves to make them feel good about themselves. Rap is black America's TV station. It gives a whole perspective of what exists and what black life is about. And black life doesn't get the total spectrum of information through anything else."

Rap is black America's TV station. In subsequent years, those six words would be turned into many variations on "rap is CNN for black people", attributed to Chuck and perhaps one of the most potent descriptions of hip-hop's cultural value ever uttered. When Chuck's memoir *Fight The Power* came out in the late nineties, even he got into the act, writing, "That's why I call rap the black CNN." In the process, "Rap is black America's TV station" – Chuck's original evocative turn of phrase – got lost to history, although its essential point remains.

By this time, Chuck D was already well on his way to making a name for being "outspoken". In the band's early concerts, one of his bits of onstage patter was to tell the crowd that the Ku Klux Klan were outside trying to keep the show from happening. "Until we had more jams, five-minute speeches were part of our show," Chuck wrote in *Fight The Power* about the band's early touring days. "We knew how to keep an audience on our side but at the same time say enough to make them feel guilty, then at the end make them feel like they're with us even though they fucked up." In his *Spin* interview with Leland, he acknowledged that Klan business was totally invented. "But at the same time," the rapper said, "I was letting people be aware that these forces exist." When Leland accused him of manipulating the truth, Chuck responded, "You tell me another way to tell the truth to black people if they don't want to hear the truth straight out. I'm open to answers."

As a result, it's always been hard to accept Chuck's claim that *Nations Of Millions'* 'Louder Than A Bomb' was inspired, as he explained in *Lyrics Of A Rap Revolutionary*, by the fact that his home phone "mysteriously would go dead between 11pm and 1am every night. I would complain to the phone company and they would repeatedly answer that there was nothing wrong with the line." Chuck admitted, "I never knew if [the FBI] were actually tapping my phones, but [I was] not being naïve about it and knowing that they have tapped peoples [*sic*] phones for less," comparing himself to black activists like Martin Luther King, Jr. and Malcolm X.

But whether delusional fantasy or legitimate concern, Chuck's paranoia fuelled a great track, which bit Kool and the Gang's 'Who's Gonna Take The Weight' for its intro. At this early stage of their career, Public Enemy seemingly could take any idea and spin it into gold. Even the album-closing 'Party For Your Right To Fight', a full-throttled accusation that the US government has targeted black leaders and conspired to hold down African-Americans, managed to twist the title of Def Jam labelmate Beastie Boys' hedonistic mega-hit '(You Gotta) Fight For Your Right (To Party!)' so that it became a black-power anthem. After all, the party that Public Enemy's song was referencing was the Black Panthers.

Part uptempo rocker, part political rant, 'Party For Your Right to Fight' sampled the Beasties and tipped its cap to deceased Nation of Islam leader Elijah Muhammad, calling the power elite "grafted devils" and quoting the album's title as its final lyric. Inflammatory and inspiring, it was the final detonation on a disc full of them. Public Enemy initially planned on calling the album *Countdown To Armageddon* – which instead was used as the title for the opening cut, a snippet from the band's galvanic arrival on the London stage – before settling on *It Takes A Nation Of Millions To Hold Us Back*.

"I fought long and hard with Def Jam over that title," Hank Shocklee said in a 2013 interview with *Electronic Beats*. "I thought at that time we needed to make a statement that would signify the rising of a nation's consciousness, the underclass movement. Also, the sequel to the critically acclaimed first album, *Yo! Bum Rush The Show*, needed to show all those that didn't believe in our mission that it was going to take more than non-belief to stop us."

"Our deal with Rick and Russell was, 'We deliver the music and everybody just leave us the fuck alone,'" Chuck told *Vibe* in 2011. "Bill Stephney should get more credit. He was an important figure during our '87–'89 years. He kept a lot of shit at bay. There were things jumping off at the label, but we were not affected by a lot of those different things."

Critics weren't going to stop them, either. Where *Bum Rush* had its share of mixed reviews, *Nation Of Millions* was a sensation, winning that year's Pazz & Jop poll. Interestingly, its closest competition was the hugely influential noise-rock band Sonic Youth's *Daydream Nation*, which was co-produced by Sansano and recorded at Greene Street, in part because of that group's admiration for Public Enemy. "When I met Sonic Youth to audition for the gig," Sansano recalls, "I played them a piece that I'd been working on [with Public Enemy]. They were like, 'Well, that's what we want.' It wasn't two parallel worlds – it was the same exact world."

When *Rolling Stone* selected the 100 greatest albums of the eighties in the fall of 1989, *Nation Of Millions* landed at number 12, the highest-ranking hip-hop record on the list. Since then, its reputation has only grown. *Nation Of Millions* is generally picked as the best rap album ever made – or, at the very least, one of the most important and groundbreaking, the first to demonstrate the viability of hip-hop as an album art form. It's inspired plenty of scholarly appreciations, including music critic Christopher R. Weingarten's superb 33⅓ tribute to the album, in which he places *Nation Of Millions* in its historical context alongside James Brown, *Wattstax* and other black cultural totems that informed its making – whether because Public Enemy sampled them or subsumed their influences. If that wasn't enough, in the first line of his book Weingarten declares *Nation Of Millions* "the greatest anti-government record ever made".

Little wonder that the album's creators enjoyed gloating a little in hindsight. "When I first delivered those records," Hank Shocklee said in 2010 about PE's early albums, "they were 'the worst records ever' – to the record companies and everything. You're talking about what was 'acceptable standard' then, and the acceptable standard was musicality . . . and ours was the total opposite of that. It didn't have any musicality, but at the same time, it had a lot of musicality to it. But the musicality was in listening to the records, the little samples and snippets and everything else that was inside it. The people that we was bringing it to, they didn't understand. . . . The major labels, they thought it was just sheer garbage. There was so many situations when people said, 'This stuff will never sell.' "

Nation Of Millions went gold within a few months, platinum a little more than a year after its release. If *Bum Rush* had suffered because of label delays, Public Enemy's new album caught the zeitgeist. In 2013, electronic musician (and fellow New Yorker) Moby explained what PE's early records meant to him and the city. "You can refer to musical culture in New York as before and after Public Enemy," he said, "it changed the city. New York was so dangerous then, it had the highest murder count, people were getting stabbed and shot and the crack epidemic was decimating communities and people were dying of AIDS. You'd go out to nightclubs in the late eighties and you'd hear these apocalyptic Public Enemy songs that perfectly described the city that you lived in, but they were oddly celebratory and you could dance to them."

But the album's impact could be measured in other, smaller ways. When Shaw had first interned at Greene Street, he was surprised how few applicants there were. *Nation Of Millions* raised the studio's profile, but it also changed its complexion. "Greene Street, it's owned by a Jew, the chief engineer is Chinese and everybody who works there is either Irish or Italian," Shaw recalls. "There wasn't a black person on staff – and not because the owner or the studio manager didn't want to hire any black people. Nobody applied. When *Nations* came out, all of a sudden all these black kids started showing up at the studio: 'Hey, we want internships.' 'I want to work here.' "

In 1994, Chuck looked back at *Nation Of Millions* and considered how its era helped provoke its making. "You're talking about a classical period of rap . . . when rap *albums* were rare," he said. "What we did in 1988 is that we introduced a different tempo and a much-needed pace to the music as well as a different thought. . . . *It Takes A Nation* was something where the blueprint was set out for us to lead right in that path, because we saw what was needed. [There] was not a lot of product out there, as far as albums or album concepts."

And perhaps that's what makes *Nation Of Millions* still so epochal. It's a stellar collection of songs, but it's the conceptual glue between those songs that makes it even stronger. If the London concert snippets provided a heft and thematic unity, then the rush of one track into another created a whirlwind forward momentum, a sense that the album as a whole was a journey. And just as Shocklee had insisted on a track-by-track basis, *Nation Of Millions* as a whole never felt linear – instead, it seemed like it was getting better, stronger and faster as it went along.

And it wasn't just hip-hop that took notice. Soon, rock began to accept rap – and not just Anthrax's Scott Ian wearing a Public Enemy T-shirt in concert, a gesture that inspired Chuck to give the band some love in 'Bring The Noise'. In Bob Dylan's 2004 memoir *Chronicles: Volume One*, the singer-songwriter recalls that he had become friends in the eighties with Kurtis Blow, who turned him on to rap acts like Ice-T and Public Enemy. "These guys definitely weren't standing around bullshitting," Dylan wrote about this first wave of rap stars. "They were beating drums, tearing it up, hurling horses over cliffs. They were all poets and knew what was going on. . . . With Ice-T and Public Enemy, who were laying the tracks, a new performer was bound to appear, and one unlike Presley. He wouldn't be swinging his hips and staring at the lassies. He'd be doing it with hard words and he'd be working 18 hours a day."

Dylan backed up those convictions when he hired Shaw to be his engineer in 2000. "I got that gig because I worked with Public Enemy," says Shaw. "Bob's manager talked to my manager about what bands I had worked with, and he started rattling off all these singer-songwriter guys I'd worked with – and they just weren't interested at all. They were like, 'Well, Bob has worked with a billion of these guys – what makes Chris different?' And my manager says, 'He used to work with Public Enemy.' And that was the thing that got me the gig. Bob really loved Chuck D."

CHAPTER FOUR

BEFORE 1989, casual Public Enemy fans probably didn't know who Professor Griff was. They could name Chuck D, Flavor Flav and even Terminator X, but the rest of the supporting cast faded into the background. Griff would show up on occasion in *Nation Of Millions* to throw out a line: "I ain't no toast" on 'Louder Than A Bomb' and the bit about succotash for 'Night Of The Living Baseheads'. And his is the first voice we hear from the band on the live opening track, 'Countdown To Armageddon'. But even though he got his own photo alongside the other band members in the liner notes, and was identified as "Minister of Information", Griff didn't seem particularly integral to what made Public Enemy run.

But that public perception overlooks Griff's involvement with the band from the very beginning, organising the S1Ws, serving as road manager and cultivating the political consciousness that became a cornerstone (musically and thematically) on *Nation Of Millions*. "The first time I ever really had an in-depth conversation with him and got to really know him was when he picked me up at my office to take me to the album shoot for *It Takes A Nations Of Millions To Hold Us Back*," Ron Skoler recalls. "It was at a police station on, like, 32nd Street or 33rd Street in New York – it was a jail cell in an actual police precinct, where they filmed the Pogues' video for 'Fairytale Of New York' in the drunk tank. Griff drove me over and we were talking, and I got to know him a little bit. He was a very nice, soft-spoken, polite, intelligent person, and we've become friendly since then – we always kid around with each other. He was just a very nice guy. I think people got a very different image of him."

The world would come to know Professor Griff by the summer of 1989, but the problems had been there for a while. Even as *Nation Of Millions* was about to be released, there were complaints about Griff's comments to the press. At the New Music Seminar in New York in July

'88, an anonymous pamphlet had been placed on the chairs of attendees for a panel about racism. With the heading "Don't Believe The Hate", the pamphlet contained quotes from Public Enemy – actually from Griff – in which different groups were denigrated: whites ("White people's hearts are so cold they can't wait to lie, cheat, and murder. . . . Whites are the biggest murderers on earth"), homosexuals ("There's no place for gays. When God destroyed Sodom and Gomorrah, it was for that sort of behaviour") and Jews ("If the Palestinians took up arms, went into Israel and killed all the Jews, it'd be all right").

Spin's John Leland spotted the pamphlet and later asked Chuck D whether he agreed with Griff's statements. "I back Griff," the rapper replied. "Whatever he says, he can prove." Chuck argued that some of the comments were taken out of context: Griff's observation about Palestinians killing Jews, he said, was part of a larger discussion about humanity's penchant for conquering and killing others.

But those Griff quotes, excerpted from UK interviews, weren't isolated incidents. In August 1988, *Rolling Stone*'s Michael Azerrad was one of approximately 100 journalists invited to cover a PE concert at Rikers Island in which the band played for the inmates. During the show, Griff reportedly told the white attendees, "When y'all lived in the caves of Europe in the Caucasus Mountains, and you did, you made it with animals. And you still do it today! That is the truth, brothers!" This was a refrain of something Griff had said to *Melody Maker* a few months earlier: "White people are actually monkeys' uncles because that's who they made it with in the Caucasian hills."

By comparison, Flav, who spoke before Griff, used the Rikers show to tell the incarcerated crowd that he, too, had once been imprisoned when he was busted with two keys of cocaine. "Those were the keys to my jail cell, man," Flavor said. "Don't be like me."

"He speaks for himself," Chuck said about Griff when Leland asked him if the Minister of Information spoke for the band. "At the same time, Griff's my brother in Public Enemy. People are gonna see that Griff said this, and in the same interview, I said something else. It's up to them."

Johnny Juice had already left Public Enemy and joined the military by 1989 – an unhappiness over lack of money and credit prompted his exit –

but he sensed that Griff could be a major liability for the band when it came to the press, who would naturally associate his actions with those of the group.

"I knew it was gonna happen," Juice says. To illustrate his point, he tells a story. "I remember doing a show in L'Amour East, which is a club on Queens Boulevard – real dope show. Griff was starting to produce these girls called the She Rockers, and they opened up the show. Griff was like the host. Griff barely spoke onstage when he did PE stuff, except for doing the [S1W] cadences, but that night this dude showed the other side of him that nobody knows. Griff's a funny dude, the funniest dude in Public Enemy. Chuck and Griff, they easily are funnier than Flav – it's not even close. Flav is the clown that you laugh *at* – these guys, you laugh at what they say. Griff's a funny dude, Griff's smart as fuck – he loves to snap on them. I was DJ for the She Rockers, and Griff starts snapping on me, making jokes – he starts doing beatboxing."

Juice remembers it being a fun night, but later after the Public Enemy portion of the programme was over, people were hanging backstage, and Russell Simmons approached the group. "He looks at Griff and he goes, 'Can you excuse us?,'" says Juice, who adds that once Griff left the room, Simmons asked Chuck, "'Why the fuck is Professor Griff doing the beatboxing on stage?' Chuck was like, 'What? It was a great show.' Russell said, 'Yeah, but that's not the imagery of the S1Ws.' Chuck was like, 'At the Public Enemy show, he did what he does.' Russell goes, 'Yeah, but before that, he did this whole hosting thing – and people are not gonna be able to separate it.' Russell's whole point was he thought Griff was trying to steal too much of the spotlight. And he might've had a point."

But if Griff had the potential to be a powder keg, the rest of the band did their best to make sure it didn't explode, limiting his exposure to the media in the wake of his comments to the UK press. Besides, Public Enemy had plenty else on their plate. Before the group went to tour Europe in the fall of '88 with Run-D.M.C., they met with filmmaker Spike Lee.

A blunt, monstrously talented writer-director, Lee had been born in Atlanta but moved to Brooklyn as a boy, eventually earning a graduate degree from New York University's film school. Inspired by the American independent film movement of the eighties, which was spearheaded by directors like Jim Jarmusch and John Sayles, Lee made pointed, politically conscious indies. After enjoying success with his college comedy-drama *School Daze*, Lee set his sights high for his next film, which he started writing on Christmas morning, 1987. "I want the film to take place over the course of one day," he wrote in his journal, "the hottest day of the year, in Brooklyn, New York." By July of the following year, he was shooting *Do The Right Thing*, an ambitious slice-of-life film that would confront issues of race and class in America, all through the perspective of a group of characters living on one block in Bedford-Stuyvesant, better known as Bed-Stuy.

In his journal, Lee laid out his hopes for the film, quickly latching onto its cathartic finale of a riot provoked by racial tension and the rising temperatures. But he also began thinking about the characters, including Radio Raheem, a quiet, intimidating-but-sweet African-American youth who would walk the streets blasting his oversized boom box. "Radio Raheem is the misunderstood black youth," Lee wrote. "White people cross the street when they see him coming. The Bernie Goetzes of the world want to kill him. . . . The song Radio Raheem plays on his box has to be by Public Enemy, my favourite politically conscious rappers. Their new jam, 'Bring The Noise', is viscious. I gotta get them to do this like Brutus."

When Lee eventually sat down with the group to discuss writing a song for the film, Chuck recalled the filmmaker's direction was simple: "Hey look, I've got this movie based on all this tension going on in the New York area, the clashing neighbourhoods, and I'm looking for an anthem." The last bit especially stuck in Chuck's head: "I'm looking for an anthem."

"We knew the song was coming out in the summer of 1989," Lee said in 2013, "and in the summertime, there's always one song in New York that, if it's a hit, you can hear it everywhere: on the subway, cars, coming out of people's houses. I wanted this song to be an anthem that could express what young black America was feeling at this time. At this time, New York City under Mayor Ed Koch was racially polarised, and I wanted this song to be in the film."

Lee has said that Public Enemy's first stab at an anthem didn't meet with his approval, forcing Chuck and the group to give it another try. But when *Rolling Stone* spoke with PE in the summer of 2014, Hank Shocklee offered a slightly different take on the events. "He got the preproduction version," Shocklee said. "It was a sparse outline of the idea of the song. Spike, with all due respect, is not a rap guy, so he's not gonna understand where it could go until it's a finished production." Shocklee also provided his version of how he convinced Lee of what direction the song should take. "Spike's original idea was to have Public Enemy do a hip-hop version of 'Lift Every Voice And Sing', which is kind of like a Negro anthem or spiritual," the producer said. "But I was like, 'No.' I opened the window and asked him to stick his head outside. 'Man, what sounds do you hear? You're not going to hear 'Lift Every Voice And Sing' in every car that drives by.' We needed to make something that's going to resonate on the street level. After going back and forth, he said, 'All right, I'll let you guys go in there and see what you guys come back with.'"

As with a lot of PE songs, 'Fight The Power' started as a title. It took its name from an Isley Brothers single that Chuck heard as a kid. "The record was startlingly powerful to me because it was the first record that I ever heard use a curse word," Chuck wrote in *Lyrics Of A Rap Revolutionary*. But he and Hank didn't want to do a cover of the song – they wanted to make something new. While on a flight over Italy, Chuck wrote the bulk of the lyrics. In his memoir, *Fight The Power*, Chuck explained, "When I'm on a plane or on a bus writing with my headphones up loud, I'm in my own world and people can hear me talking out loud."

The words he came up with were like a stack of slogans and provocations put to rhyme. He dissed Bobby McFerrin's feel-good number one hit 'Don't Worry, Be Happy', as well as white icons John Wayne and Elvis Presley, while preaching black unity. He also drew from Lee's description of a central location in *Do The Right Thing*, an Italian pizzeria, which only hangs pictures of famous Italian-Americans on the wall, even though the clientele is largely black. From that, Chuck came up with the line, "Most of my heroes don't appear on no stamps," a protest of the US Postal Service's commemoration of famous white individuals at the expense of comparable African-American figures.*

---

* The first stamp featuring a black man, Booker T. Washington, appeared in 1940.

While defending his own heroes, Chuck shot down other people's. He labelled Elvis a racist. Flav joins in, yelling, "Motherfuck him and John Wayne." "Elvis' attitude toward blacks was that of people in the South at that particular time," the rapper said in *Playboy* in 1990. In later years, Chuck would back away from his contention that Presley was a racist. (And music historian Peter Guralnick has written persuasively on the fact that Presley was actually quite inclusive of blacks and supportive of the African-American artists who inspired him.) But nonetheless, the rest of Chuck's comment to *Playboy* remained a fair argument: "The point of the song is not about Elvis so much, and it's not about the people who idolise that motherfucker, like he made no errors and was never wrong. Elvis doesn't mean shit. White America's heroes are different from black America's heroes. John Wayne could go around in these movies and kill Indians and he was all right. But a black man like Louis Farrakhan comes out for the uplifting of black people and whites pick at things and throw shit at him."

Looking ahead to the following summer, when the movie would come out, Chuck opened the track with a staccato "1989 / the number / another summer," which set the stage for *Do The Right Thing*'s timeframe and tone. The band hadn't seen the film when they wrote the track but, according to Chuck, he wanted to make a song that "tried to hinge upon the feelings of defiance, pride, attitude, nationalism, a little bit of rhetoric, who we have as our heroes, and who we are as a people, and giving them a top notch place in our history."

'Fight The Power' sampled from everywhere, swiping Bobby Byrd's "You got it!" from 'I Know You Got Soul', the background wails at the end of Sly & the Family Stone's 'Sing A Simple Song', and the furious groove of 'Hot Pants Road' from the J.B.'s. "'Fight The Power' was basically my version of what I consider to be an inspirational record," Shocklee once said. "I wanted to take PE at that point and move them into inspiration. Instead of identifying the problem, I wanted now to start to identify solutions."

The song, which also featured live saxophone from Branford Marsalis, appeared throughout *Do The Right Thing*, first in the opening credits. There, it blared atop images of young actress Rosie Perez as she vigorously danced and shadowboxed on a stage. The shoot was eight hours for what ended up constituting less than four minutes of film. "I developed tennis elbow from throwing those punches," Perez said in 2013.

Announcing itself as the film's musical (and spiritual) theme, 'Fight The Power' would then pop up in *Do The Right Thing* whenever Radio Raheem (played by Bill Nunn) appeared onscreen, his boom box's loud volume sometimes making its presence felt before the character did. The band had no idea how much the song was going to be used in the film. In a 2005 interview, Shocklee said, "You know, to me I'm like, 'Yo, if it works for you, then that's cool.' . . . But I personally thought I got kind of used, because when you do it for a movie, you license that for a particular scene, that happens one time. What [Lee] did was kind of like sample me in a movie. So what he did was pay me for one spot in the movie and then random spots a billion times throughout the whole movie that I didn't get paid for. And I didn't even know that you are supposed to get paid for it, you know, every time that he plays it in the movie. So we got our one little cheque for that and that's . . . whatever."

The song's antagonistic back-and-forth vocals between Chuck and Flavor hinted at the racial unease simmering underneath the movie's seriocomic look at Italians, Koreans, blacks, Puerto Ricans, drunks, cops, the young and the old who were all trying to live together peacefully. *Do The Right Thing* implicitly referenced recent real-life New York racial incidents, such as the 1986 beating death of a black man, Michael Griffith, by a group of whites in the Howard Beach section of Queens. The movie was melancholy and angry, but the song was stirring, as if Public Enemy were giving voice to the pragmatic reality of New York's stewing melting pot.

"'Fight The Power', when that came out in New York, that's all you heard on the streets," Steve Linsley remembers. "I'm telling you, you heard that sound every time you went outside, that horn. That was a big jump up for them."

In '94, Chuck admitted that, while he likes 'Fight The Power', he also was wary of it in one regard. "I think 'Fight The Power' was a record that, when I did it, I wasn't happy with it," he claimed. "It was a record that PE was *supposed* to do. 1989 was a year after '88, where we had *Takes A Nation* and we got known to the world as a group that was heavily pro-black . . . a nationalist-pride, 'keep yourself black and proud'-type group. 'Fight The Power' was something that was just, like, a *layup* at the time." Being associated with *Do The Right Thing*, although enormously helpful to the band, also added to Chuck's sense that the song was a little too obvious. "All those pieces *fit*," he said. "They were supposed to be like that. As an artist, you want to do some things like that, but you don't want to be *defined* by moves that you were supposed to make, as opposed to moves that you took a chance on."

Even at that moment of great success, Chuck was hungry to explore the unexpected, to throw his audience for a loop. This would become a defining element of his artistry: an almost stubborn refusal to repeat himself.

Still, Public Enemy had every right to enjoy their moment. A breakthrough album followed by a smash single connected to a much-debated, must-see movie: it was everything a rising band could have asked for. But in the midst of all that momentum, the powder keg went off.

★   ★   ★

When David Mills died of a brain aneurysm on March 30, 2010, he was only 48 years old. Obituaries mentioned his television career, writing episodes for acclaimed dramas such as *NYPD Blue*, *Homicide: Life On The Street* and *ER*. He won two Emmys for the miniseries *The Corner*. A passionate music fan who fell in love with New Orleans jazz while working on the HBO series *Treme*, the show he was co-executive producing before his death, Mills received plenty of heartfelt eulogies from friends and colleagues in the business. Only the longer pieces delved into his life before transitioning into television. Previously, he had worked as a journalist, and it's in that capacity that his path and Public Enemy's intersected.

The meeting between Professor Griff and David Mills on May 9, 1989 is probably the most infamous single encounter in the band's history. Not surprisingly, then, it's one fraught with contradictory stories. There are only two people who know what happened – one is dead, and the other hasn't always told the same story.

In *Fight The Power*, Chuck provides background on the tensions that were eating up the band leading up to the Mills interview. Touring relentlessly had caused plenty of strain. "By 1989 everybody had started families, continued families, and added on to families, so we were all dealing with family life," he wrote. "It takes a lot of mental preparation to be on the road." Add to this that, according to Leland in a September 1989 *Spin* exposé, Chuck was so hard-up for money, even after *Nation Of Millions*, that he had to grab a day job for a while that brought in $300 a week.

But Chuck also had to learn how to be a manager of people, a skill that was tested when members of the S1Ws became unhappy with Griff. "Some of the S1Ws resented that he was in a power position and thought he was mismanaging and misusing that power," the frontman wrote.

Not used to being in charge, Chuck didn't take to being an authority figure naturally. Johnny Juice, who knew Chuck when Public Enemy were working on *Yo! Bum Rush The Show*, says, "He's scared of confrontation." Juice realises how strange that sounds considering the stentorian voice Chuck brings to PE records, but the DJ argues, "He was a very quiet dude – that's the kinda person he was. He was a non-confrontational, peaceful guy, but he really wanted to be this [tough guy], so he became the guy."

Chuck has claimed that part of his plan for PE albums would be to build up individual members, introducing Terminator X on *Bum Rush* and then bringing Professor Griff out of the shadows on *Nation Of Millions*. But because Griff and Flav didn't get along – the strict, serious Minister of Information was angry about the hype man's tardiness and being forced to babysit him – it wasn't so easy for Chuck to execute his plan of a united front when it came to the media. (In *The Icon The Memoir*, Flavor tells a story from the *Yo! Bum Rush The Show* days in which he showed up at the studio high on crack cocaine and weed. Griff confronted him, broke his boom box and fractured Flav's ribs and shin. "I would come to the studio with a gun on me," Flavor writes. "If Griff had even made a move in my direction, I would have shot him at close range, no errors.")

When Public Enemy arrived in Washington, D.C. for a show in early May of 1989, Chuck was supposed to speak with Mills, a reporter for the conservative paper *The Washington Times* who asked to discuss some of the band's more incendiary quotes. But when the appointed time for the interview arrived, Chuck had a conflict: he wanted to talk to a tour promoter about getting some dates with LL Cool J. In *Fight The Power*, Chuck claims that at the time, "We were the most interviewed music artists around. People wanted to know what we were about." Chuck took care of around 75 to 80 percent of the interviews, and left the rest to Griff. With Mills waiting for him, Chuck asked Griff to field this one.

If Chuck was feeling intense pressure from all sides, Professor Griff wasn't far behind. Chuck mentions in his memoir that while they were in DC, Griff confided in him "about a personal problem he was having in his family that was building up". According to Leland's reporting, Griff separated from his wife during this period, later moving in to his mom's house.

When Griff spoke to the *Miami New Times* in the summer of 1990 about what happened during the Mills encounter, here's how he put it: "It was supposed to be a musical interview. It led into a discussion of Jewish control of the music industry, the media, TV, and movies. It was music, music, music, and then he slips in a question about who controls the music industry. I was caught off guard, and it was at a time when there was a lot of tension [within Public Enemy]. He made it sound like I was lashing out. I was under a lot of stress."

Be that as it may, the quotes that ended up in *The Washington Times* were alarming. Griff said that Jews were the cause of "the majority of the wickedness that goes on across the globe". He suggested that Jews were behind a conspiracy to "finance these experiments on AIDS with black people in South Africa". He referred to "faggot little hit men" within the Jewish community that would try to silence him. It was ugly.

At first, the story didn't get much traction. Remember that this was before the internet, back when the smallest piece of controversy couldn't bounce around the globe within minutes of it being published. But about three weeks later when *The Village Voice* ran a piece about Mills' interview, Public Enemy were suddenly embroiled in a major scandal.

Skoler, who is Jewish, talked to Griff after the Mills interview sometime later. "The way he explained it to me was, he was relaxing in the hotel, hanging out, and a reporter came over to him," the lawyer says. Skoler's impression was that Griff and Mills were having a good time and joking around. "Like, 'Let me ask you some questions about the Jews,' and Griff was like, 'Oh yeah, come on, man, why do you think they call it jew-ellery.' Things like that, which was in Griff's mind a joke."

If Skoler's memory is correct, then Griff's joke was a callback to a previous TV interview in which Griff said, "I think that's why they call it 'jewellery', because the Jews in South Africa, they run that thing."

"Believe me, I took no offence," Skoler says, "and I take him at his word. These were just comments that were silly to make, especially when he didn't know the guy, and I think that they were taken out of context and absolutely blown out of proportion and misquoted."

Robert Christgau, a vocal champion of *Nation Of Millions* and the senior music critic on the *Voice*, wrote a piece that summer noting that Griff's comments occurred about 40 minutes into his talk with Mills, which would theoretically back up Griff's contention that the interview segued from music into other matters. And as far as the Minister of Information's claim that he was manipulated by Mills, the reporter responded to the *Miami New Times*, "Griff's entitled to his opinion," adding, "Why, in all this time, has nobody heard Griff speak on the substance of the question – whether he believed the things he said?"

In a 2014 interview with hip-hop writer Chairman Mao, Bill Adler, Public Enemy's publicist at the time, said, "It was tough for me – *I'm Jewish*! And I don't believe, by the way, that you have to be Jewish to abhor anti-Semitism. You don't have to be black to hate anti-black racism. But having said that, I probably did find it particularly painful when Griff started saying this ridiculous anti-Semitic stuff. The story broke in America in May/June of 1989, but Griff had started to give these terribly anti-Semitic interviews to the English music press in 1988. And I don't think I focused on it somehow. Not least because it wasn't bouncing back to me in America. But by the spring of '89 when this stuff starts to blow up, I sat down with Griff."

Adler had always thought that he and Griff had a good rapport, so he hoped he could get some clarity in a one-on-one chat. Instead, he walked away from their talk even more discouraged. "Griff kind of repeated a lot of the things he'd said to the press," Adler told Mao. "It was almost funny.

Because the thing about Griff is his style is basically Nation of Islam, Fruit of Islam – which is sober, dignified, soft-spoken. Not to say that he doesn't have gravitas. But he's not a frother. He's not screaming. And even so, a lot of things he had to say they were just . . . in effect, they were wild-eyed."

What was especially disheartening for Adler was that Griff would cite *The International Jew* as a source for his beliefs. The book's contents, written by Henry Ford in the twenties, had been subtitled "The World's Problem" when they first appeared in print. Denigrating everything from the movie business to "Jewish jazz", Ford's missives were anti-Semitic and moronic. "I understood that there was gonna be no reasoning with Griff," said Adler, who stopped working for the band as a result. He talked to Chuck about his concerns but, according to Adler, "I think what it came down to for Chuck is that he felt put on the spot. He didn't endorse what Griff had to say. He didn't share the politics. But he did not like anybody telling him how to run his group. That's really what it came down to for Chuck. And so you see what happened is, in effect, he chose Griff. . . . And for me, after I spoke to Chuck I thought, 'Well, this is basically a mess and I'm not gonna help them manage this crisis.'"

Johnny Juice has also observed Chuck's occasional circle-the-wagons tendency. "Chuck is very gracious, but he does have this 'Fuck you, I'm Chuck D' [thing]," the DJ says. "When you tell him certain things, he's like, 'Come on, man, I know what I'm doing.' I'm like, 'Chuck, when we first started, none of us knew what we were doing. We learned at the same pace. You have a lot of experience, but we all bring different experiences to the table.' But he would tell you, 'No, trust me, you don't under-stand.'"

Amid the Griff controversy, Public Enemy were touring, where the scandal soon ensnared them. Darryll Brooks, along with partner Carol Kirkendall, was handling tour promotion. "Our insurance went from, like, 35 cents a head to $1.50 a head," Brooks says. "That impacted on our tour."

Kirkendall adds, "It got ugly for a while, but it really didn't last long. I mean, as soon as things calmed down, things calmed down. Money was the key. It's terrible to say, but if groups sold tickets and people made money, they eventually found a way to get past those hurdles."

Asked if the controversy affected ticket sales, Brooks replies, "It didn't hurt. It only hurt from the economic standpoint, because we were spending an additional $10,000 or $15,000 that we didn't normally have to spend. . . . We knew the fight we would have to fight because we were the ones that were getting hit by insurance companies and by the buildings saying, 'Hey, the insurance company said they're not going to let you have that rate. You have to do this in order to get a contract from the building.' And we had to pass that cost back into the group."

But this wasn't necessarily anything new to old pros like Brooks and Kirkendall, who had been some of the earliest promoters of hip-hop tours. Brooks recalls a sold-out show Public Enemy was going to hold at the Spectrum in Philadelphia around the time of *Do The Right Thing*. "The building manager, because of all the gang stuff that's been happening in different spots around the country, is very concerned about gangs coming to the building, because he's heard so much about this 'rap music'," recalls Brooks. "So, we're trying to comfort him, especially me. Out of his office, he sees kids walking down the hallway with chains around their necks, and he calls security. I said, 'No, no, they're not trying to have any problem. That's just how they dress.' We go past the soundboard and [Public Enemy] are singing 'Fight The Power'. He panicked – he thought there was going to be a riot [during the show]. I had to tell him, 'It's all right, this is a soundcheck. It's on a Spike Lee movie.' It was that kind of crazy. It was culture shock [for the building manager] to see that kind of energy, and he didn't understand it."

In *Fight The Power*, Chuck acknowledges mistakes he made leading up to and after the Mills interview. But even in 1997, when the memoir was published, the rapper remained defiant. "Some of the comments made during the interview obviously bothered David Mills," Chuck wrote. "It could also be added that David's girlfriend at the time was white and Jewish and was at the interview, and she may have been offended by what Griff said, which I suspect sent David into another zone." Even if that was the case, Chuck's deflection suggested that, years later, he was still more willing to blame others than to look at the fault within his own house. Or, at the very least, he wanted to stand behind his friend, no matter what.

Public Enemy walk the streets of New York. This photo was taken during the band's early days, when Chuck D still wore a clock around his neck like his cohort Flavor Flav. © GLEN E. FRIEDMAN, FROM THE BOOK MY RULES

Concert promoter Darryll Brooks is flanked by Ice Cube and Chuck D. As one of the first promoters of hip-hop shows, Brooks knew well how venues would freak out about rappers and their entourage. "No, no, they're not trying to have any problem," he remembers telling nervous building managers. "That's just how they dress." DARRYLL BROOKS

Public Enemy enjoy a relaxed moment backstage. Second from the left is Darryll Brooks, a concert promoter who worked with the band in the late 1980s at the height of the controversy surrounding Professor Griff's comments. DARRYLL BROOKS

Professor Griff and Public Enemy collaborator Kerwin Young in the summer of 1989. After Griff left the band, he recorded a solo album, *Pawns In The Game*, which was co-produced by Young. COURTESY OF KERWIN YOUNG MUSIC PUBLISHING INC.

Chuck D performs at the Hammersmith Odeon in 1986. "At the beginning, Public Enemy had one of the worst stage shows ever," DJ Johnny Juice says. But the band quickly improved. "By the time that [tour] was over, motherfuckers was like, 'What the fuck happened to these guys?'" MICHELE POORMAN/PYMCA/REX

Public Enemy strike a pose during a 1988 photo shoot. JACK BARRON/REX

Chuck D, Flavor Flav and Terminator X are well protected by the Security of the First World. KEVIN CUMMINS/GETTY IMAGES

Flavor Flav lets us know what time it is while hanging out in Chicago, Illinois, on December 11, 1988. "I'd done drugs, run numbers, and been to jail," Flav wrote in his memoir. "I wasn't perpetrating a street style. I *was* the street."
RAYMOND BOYD/MICHAEL OCHS ARCHIVES/GETTY IMAGES

Professor Griff on the streets of Shepherd's Bush, London, 1988.
NORMSKI/PYMCA/REX

In fighting form, Professor Griff performs with Public Enemy in New York City in August 1988.
MICHAEL OCHS ARCHIVES/GETTY IMAGES

Flavor Flav, Terminator X and Professor Griff share a euphoric moment onstage at Montreux in May 1988. ANDRE CSILLAG/REX

Chuck D, director Spike Lee and Flavor Flav confer during the making of Public Enemy's 'Fight The Power' video in 1989.
MICHAEL OCHS ARCHIVES/GETTY IMAGES

Chuck and Flav get down to business while the cameras roll on the set of the 'Fight The Power' video.
MICHAEL OCHS ARCHIVES/GETTY IMAGES

In January 1991 in Chicago, Illinois, Flavor Flav and Chuck D hang out with Anthrax on the set of the 'Bring Tha Noize' video. The song, from *Apocalypse 91 … The Enemy Strikes Black*, was a rap-rock collaboration between the two groups.
RAYMOND BOYD/MICHAEL OCHS ARCHIVES/GETTY IMAGES

Public Enemy perform on *Saturday Night Live* on September 28, 1991. The band requested a moment of silence during the broadcast in honour of Miles Davis, who died earlier that day. RAYMOND BONAR/NBCU PHOTO BANK

Chuck D heads over to Rockefeller Center to take part in Public Enemy's *Saturday Night Live* performance. The group performed 'Can't Truss It' and 'Bring The Noise.'
RON GALELLA, LTD./WIREIMAGE/GETTY IMAGES

Flavor Flav with his family. The prankster rapper would revitalize his career in the 21st century by becoming a reality-television star.
JEFF KRAVITZ/FILMMAGIC/GETTY IMAGES

Flavor and Chuck D kick back at the 11th Annual MTV Video Music Awards on September 8, 1994, at Radio City Music Hall in New York City. RON GALELLA, LTD./WIREIMAGE/GETTY IMAGES

In the midst of a PR crisis, it can be difficult to know what to do. Is it better to say nothing in the hopes the controversy dies down on its own? Do you tackle it head-on? And if so, is it better to be apologetic or mount a counter-defence? There's no perfect answer, with each situation unique. But in retrospect, Public Enemy did other groups a favour by showing precisely how *not* to conduct oneself in the midst of a media firestorm.

Among his many errors in judgment, Chuck in a huff called RJ Smith, the *Village Voice* journalist who had written about the *Washington Times* interview, and was quoted as saying, "Listen to me, RJ, any shit that comes down on me, it's coming down on you. And that's a goddamn threat! Write this down! I ain't gonna write no goddamn white-boy liberal letter to the editor, no article either."

Then there was the series of public flip-flops about what the band would do. At first, it appeared that Griff would merely have a diminished role in Public Enemy. Mid-June, the band sent out a press release announcing that he was no longer their Minister of Information. "Black power is only a self-defence movement that counterattacks the system of white world supremacy," Chuck wrote, "not white people or the religious sects they choose. It does not mean anti-white, it means anti-a-system that has been designed by the European elite." But then the statement was withdrawn, adding drama to a press conference the group held soon after on June 21 in New York. It was there that Chuck let it be known that Griff was fired. "You can't talk about attacking racism and be racist," he said, while also being specific about his feelings on the Nation of Islam by declaring, "I follow the Nation because Minister Farrakhan and the Nation show us economic self-sufficiency in America, and that's my sole use for this information." In other words, Chuck was distancing himself from the anti-Semitic rhetoric that had slipped into Farrakhan's philosophy. "Our job is not to offend anybody," Chuck said. "We're not anti-anybody. We're pro-black."

But events kept piling up. A few days afterward, Chuck spoke with MTV's Kurt Loder. "The group is over," Chuck D revealed on *Week In Rock*. "It's our way of boycotting the music industry . . . We got sand-bagged. There was a conflict between the group's idea of how to discipline Griff and the industry's idea of how to discipline Griff." In the same interview, he accused his label of suppressing his follow-up to *Nation Of Millions*, which was news to executives at his label since they hadn't even heard the album yet.

(In *Fight The Power*, Chuck came clean: "I hadn't stepped in the studio for one day and had not written a song, but everybody was like, 'Yo, they stopped the album.' . . . When in doubt confuse them.")

Then on August 9, Public Enemy had a new statement to make. Even though their label had announced that the group had, indeed, broken up, Public Enemy revealed they were getting back together. In an interview with *The New York Times* shortly following the announcement, Chuck denied that his band had called it quits. "I said Griff had to lose his position," the rapper told writer and critic Jon Pareles. But that didn't mean Griff was being excised from the band: According to a new statement, he would no longer be Minister of Information but, rather, "supreme allied chief of community relations", which meant that "his duties will include service to the black community with special attention to local youth programmes".

"Griff's statements were wrong and I apologised," Chuck said in the *New York Times* interview. "He also apologised to me. Griff wasn't clear in his thinking and he wasn't 100 percent right. He's not going to make those statements any more, and he won't do interviews. He's definitely going to talk – you can't tell any man to be quiet, this is America – but he won't be dealing with any kind of major media. He's going to tell black kids to be the best they can be."

Commenting on that period for *Fight The Power*, Chuck, perhaps disingenuously, claims, "I was making erratic moves to keep outsiders guessing. I shut down the group, then I started the group again without Griff. I only did that to be confusing. My whole thing is if you're vulnerable, be confusing."

As Griff himself described it in the summer of 1990, "I was suspended by Public Enemy. Then I was fired. Hired. Fired again." In fact, Chuck's conversation with Pareles wasn't the end of Griff's ordeal. By the end of '89, Griff had supposedly been completely booted from the group, although a March 1990 article in *NME* claimed that he was still a part of Public Enemy. But when Griff talked to the *Miami New Times* for a long profile that ran in June of 1990, it was clear he was out – and bitter about it.

"There was no investigation," Griff said, "they had no right to speak. The majority of people [at the record labels] never heard what I said, nor did they just talk to me the way you're talking to me right now. They would rather fire me. That dollar, chump change . . . was being threatened. I feel sorry for Chuck. We grew up together and put Public Enemy together. And then I was fired over the phone, on TV and the newspapers. They just kicked me to the curb. And that's when my family was threatened," alluding to anonymous threats he'd received in the wake of the *Washington Times* interview. (Weirdly, when PE released their next album, *Fear Of A Black Planet*, Griff's photo was included alongside the other band members' in the inner sleeve. His title was "The Last Asiatic Disciple".)

Griff would say that his Mills comments were taken out of context. But he also reached out, meeting up with Sam Rogatinsky, the president of the National Holocaust Awareness Student Organisation, to discuss his views. The *Miami New Times* was there to document the interaction, which left Griff saying, "My views change with time, and my views about [Jews] have changed. This could be a process of me maturing."

But he also wanted to prove his musical worth. Kerwin Young, a musician and DJ who had worked with Public Enemy, assisted Griff on the making of his first solo album. "We rushed to get *Pawns In The Game* done," Young says. "We didn't take our time doing it. We started the demos in September '89 and we wrapped up in October, and then late November we headed to Miami and we did the album. We recorded the album in a week. We finished it in, like, December or January."

While no doubt Griff's rush to finish *Pawns* was partly driven by his desire to capitalise on the controversy, Young says that Griff knew Public Enemy would have their own album out in early 1990. "He wanted it to come out and kind of put a choke on Public Enemy's release," says Young. "He wanted to compete."

The trip to Miami was due to Griff signing a deal with the label fronted by 2 Live Crew's Luther Campbell (a.k.a. Luke Skyywalker), one of the city's most successful rap artists. (Skoler helped advise Griff on the deal.)

But if Griff had hoped that getting out of New York would help distance him from the media spotlight, he was going to be disappointed.

"It followed us there," says Young about the controversy. "The engineer that worked with Luke had made a phone call to a journalist. Griff found out, and I would say there was a slight argument there in the studio, some tension. But for the most part, Griff tried to disassociate himself from the controversy that surrounded him and was totally focused on doing this album. He kept his spirits up. I shared a room with him in the hotel, so we were pretty close. We had a cool group of guys [on the album] and Luke was great to work with, and Miami was good. But the element that surrounded Griff – that air of 'You're blacklisted, we don't want you here' – you felt that. When I went back to 510 [South Franklin], I could feel some tension from some of the guys that had worked with Griff."

Pawns In The Game got as high as number 127 on the *Billboard* charts. But because Griff had been known as more of a peripheral figure in Public Enemy – Simmons memorably referred to him as the band's "racist stage prop" – there was only so much interest in an album from someone who wasn't considered to be a valuable creative contributor. And when it came time to promote the record, Griff had to face journalists who questioned his lyrics for signs of potential scandal.

For instance, *NME*'s Steven Wells referenced 'Real African People Rap, Pt, 1', which contained the lines "You committed the ultimate sin / You slept with Eve / And the goddamn apple you did not receive." Was the song, which was addressed to blacks, a condemnation of mixed-race relationships? "Eve represents evil, wickedness, falsehood – all the evil and wicked things black people have indulged themselves into," Griff responded, later adding, "The apple represents pure fresh knowledge and in another sense – fruit. We didn't get the fruit that America has to offer. . . . So the so-called black American middle-class sell their values and their morals down the drain for a job in corporate America . . . That's sad."

Chuck D once said, "Flavor is what America would like to see in a black man – sad to say, but true. Griff is very much what America would not like to see." Surely, Chuck meant this as a compliment to Griff: a tribute to a socially conscious, uncompromising thinker. But *Pawns In The Game* was a reminder of Griff's (and his attitudes') deep limitations. Paying tribute to the Ayatollah Khomeini and Idi Amin alongside Miles Davis, Bill Cosby, Nat Turner and Public Enemy on the album-closing shout-out "It's a Blax Thanx", Griff seemed incapable of recognising the difference between conscientious objectors to the power elite and outright villains of liberty. He responded to a controversy by giving his critics more reason to marginalise him.

As for Chuck, he came to realise that he hadn't conducted himself flawlessly during the whole fracas. In a November 1990 interview with *Playboy*, he recounted a visit he made to Louis Farrakhan's office in Chicago while the Griff controversy was swirling. The minister's advice: "Chuck, what you got to do is, you got to lead. And if it doesn't go your way, you've got to put your foot down. For the sake of being right against what's wrong."

Chuck added, "I was trying to handle the internal situation [with Griff], but if I had the chance to do it all over again, I would have told *him* to handle it, or else." He also commented that Hank helped set him straight. "Hank will put me in my place," he told *Playboy*. "That's what happened last year. Hank said, 'Listen: Give a fuck. You're responsible for 30 motherfuckers. Family and structure are more important.'"

★ ★ ★

When Chuck D declared "I got so much trouble on my mind" at the start of 'Welcome To The Terrordome', it was easy to assume that he was referring to the fallout from Griff's comments. But that was only part of it. Before Public Enemy were defending themselves against charges of anti-Semitism, PE biographer Russell Myrie asserts, Chuck D, Bill Stephney and Hank Shocklee "had been offered a label deal by MCA". In *Don't Rhyme For The Sake Of Riddlin'*, Myrie contends that MCA executives pressured the threesome to kick out Griff – otherwise, the deal was as good as dead. And because Chuck wouldn't turn his back on Griff – unlike the other two, who wanted Griff gone – the arrangement changed, with Stephney and Shocklee co-founding SOUL Records at MCA without Chuck.

The potential MCA deal had been reported at the time. Jonathan Takiff of the *Philadelphia Daily News* noted in an article from June 28, 1989, at the height of the controversy, that perhaps one of the reasons why Chuck wanted to fold Public Enemy was that "[h]e has a tentative deal to produce other acts for MCA Records – if, that is, MCA doesn't pull out of that pact. Company representatives were seen hovering and listening carefully at the news conference last week where Chuck D announced he was ousting Professor Griff. And MCA folk are now stressing the 'tentative' nature of their agreement with PE's frontman." (Christgau's *Village Voice* piece from that summer mentioned that "Chuck D [is] talking vanity label with MCA.")

"Hank and Chuck were looking around to try to get a deal on their own with MCA at that time," Skoler recalls. "And they were told, 'We don't want any controversy. We don't want anything like this. Nothing hateful, nothing anti-Semitic.' And I think Griff was scapegoated. They kicked him out of the group, which caused a lot of controversy in the hip-hop community, because a lot of people looked at Public Enemy as a sellout at that point. Quite frankly, I think it reflected poorly on them."

Skoler feels that Chuck and the band should have stuck up for Griff: "Stand by him and say, 'Listen, we're going to stand with our friend, with our brother. This is a guy that we grew up with. You can think what you want, but he's not a hateful person and it's not what we believe. We're just going to weather the storm.' They didn't do that. They were out shopping their own deal, I believe, and it was easier to just kick him to the curb. Griff had certain beliefs, and they were kind of radical. He's been involved with the Nation of Islam, but I don't know if you consider that 'radical'. But the point is that he was a person with strong beliefs – but he was not a hateful person whatsoever."

In *Don't Rhyme For The Sake Of Riddlin'*, Myrie spoke with both Chuck D and Stephney about the MCA deal. Chuck claims that MCA head honcho Al Teller "was getting board pressure" about Griff, which is what prompted Chuck not to move forward with the deal. But Stephney refutes that: "No one ever called us and put any pressure on us at all about, 'Oh, are you guys gonna deal with Griff?' And Stephney should know – as he told Myrie, 'I was the business guy who ran everything.'"

If the MCA deal was indeed jeopardised because of Griff's actions, it wasn't the only business headache visiting Chuck. The relationship between the partners in Rhythm Method was starting to fray, too. Divided equally between Chuck, Skoler, Hank and Ed Chalpin, Rhythm Method had experienced some friction when it was discovered that Shocklee was doing projects outside of the partnership.

"We started hearing rumours," Skoler says. "'Hank is producing this record for somebody. Hank is remixing this record.' And I'm like, 'What the fuck is this? We're trying to build a company. We're supposed to put that through the corporation.' When I brought in the remix for the Ziggy Marley record ['Tumblin' Down'] for Hank, that went through us. But, apparently, he was doing things on his own and he was getting offers on his own. Rather than bring it through us, he was keeping it for himself. So, this was a problem – I felt like, 'Is this a house divided?' There was something in our corporate agreement, a best-efforts clause, that [said] before anybody could take on a corporate opportunity individually, they had to first offer it to the company."

Skoler's concern about Hank's actions increased when Rhythm was approached about a record deal from Virgin. "The music industry is very much a follow-the-leader mentality," says Skoler. "The same people – the same parasites, the same scumbags – that will never help you bake the bread can't wait to help you eat it, even though they had nothing to do with baking it in the first place. So, the same people that wouldn't have let Hank and Chuck through the door in the early days were the first ones to say, 'Oh, you guys are amazing, you're wonderful, we love you.' All of that kind of stuff and stroking their egos. So, instead of thinking, 'OK, Rhythm Method's going to be the big thing,' Public Enemy became the very big thing. We were offered to have our own record label by Virgin. It was a seven-figure deal, and we were all really happy about that – all four of us. The intention was, 'We're going to own a record company together' – not for Public Enemy, because they were already on Def Jam, but for various other artists that we were working with."

The lawyer felt that it was a great deal: each member of Rhythm would own 25 percent of this new label. And even though Shocklee's moon-lighting displeased him, Skoler felt confident that everyone was happy with moving forward with Virgin. "All of a sudden, Hank went under-ground and I couldn't reach him any more," says Skoler. "We had been having conversations with him before: 'Hank, what's going on? Are you doing things on your own?' He would say, 'I'm not.' Or 'I'm doing it, but it's no big deal. I'm just doing a favour – I'm not doing anything behind your backs.' So, we were about to sign the contract with Virgin, and I couldn't reach Hank. Chuck went on tour in Germany: I get a call from Chuck at my home at night. Chuck is like, 'Ron, why can't we get this contract signed with Virgin?' And I said, 'I can't reach Hank.' And Chuck said, 'Well, what's the problem with him?' I said, 'I don't know, you tell me – he's your friend, right?'"

After a couple of days of silence, Skoler was about to leave the office late on a Friday night when he returned to his desk because he had forgotten something. "I came back – it was, like, quarter after seven – and the phone rings. It was the lawyer for Virgin in California: 'Ron, what's going on?' I say, 'What do you mean?' He goes, 'I just got a call from a lawyer for Hank, and he said that they want to take the deal, but they want to take it for themselves, and you and Ed are out.' And I said, 'Well, that's good to know – there's no fucking way that's happening.'"

Skoler believes what transpired is that "Hank had gone to his own lawyer and said, 'Just get me out of this contract, I don't want to split it.'" There was talk of maybe giving Chuck and Hank a higher percentage than Skoler and Chalpin, but the four men couldn't reach an agreement. "There was no way to resolve it," says Skoler, "so Virgin ended up pulling the deal." Asked if Chuck had been aware of Hank's plan, Skoler seems to believe that he hadn't been. However, Skoler does say, "I think Chuck sided with Hank because he just wanted to move forward. Hank was his guy."

Lawsuits followed, Rhythm Method was dissolved, Skoler sold his rights to Chalpin, and eventually Chalpin, Hank and Chuck settled. Skoler was unhappy with some of what he calls "lies" that were spread during the lawsuits, but he's also saddened about the chance he felt they let slip through their fingers. Before the Virgin deal went south, he thought, "If we can get this record deal done, this is going to be a really big thing and it's going to be very historic. And not just in terms of money: this is going to be a very important thing, musically. This is something that I really want to be a part of, and we have a great opportunity here."

Chuck's dislike for lawyers is clear in *Fight The Power*. In a section titled 'Lawyers, No Loyalties; Accountants, No Royalties', he fumes, "I signed my contract on our low-point scale in 1986, and CDs weren't written into the contract . . . I didn't get my contract renegotiated on CDs until I got a new lawyer. I had to get a lawyer to just check my old lawyer's ass. It doesn't make sense for me to have to pay three different lawyers to all check each other." Asked if Chuck is referring to him in that swipe, Skoler responds, "I think the only bad experience he had was the lawsuit itself. Up until that happened, everything was moving along fine, and we were growing. They never expressed any dissatisfaction to me whatsoever. And, by the way, as somebody who's been in this business a long time myself, I don't like lawyers in general, either. There's a lot of lawyers in the music industry, including some of those that represented Public Enemy afterwards, that if I had shook hands with them, I'd want to count my fingers."

So, indeed, there was plenty weighing on Chuck's mind when he went into the studio to record 'Welcome To The Terrordome'. And if all that wasn't enough, he also had to shoulder the criticism that he wasn't doing enough to be a leader – an admonishment he accepted. In *Fight the Power*, he reveals that he'd been given an opportunity after Mills spoke with Griff to meet the journalist and talk about what had been said before Mills wrote the article. "I had an attitude of, 'Fuck him. I'm not talking to him if he thinks he's going to sell us out like that,'" Chuck writes. He came to regret his hardheadedness: "If it's your problem, handle your mistakes, nip that shit in the bud, and eliminate it." Instead of speaking with Mills, he let Griff and the S1Ws do it, which only inflamed the situation when Griff was confrontational with the reporter. If Chuck had swallowed his pride, maybe he could have avoided the whole PR catastrophe.

"A day or two after Chuck had fired Griff from the band," Chris Shaw says, "he came in and did a vocal for 'Welcome To The Terrordome'. I wasn't an engineer on the session, but I had to go into the room to get a cable or something. I walked in just as they started to do the vocal, and it was probably the most intense vocal I ever heard Chuck deliver. Unfortunately, it never got used in the song because the track ran out before he could finish the last verse. He did the vocal again – it wasn't quite as intense, but it was pretty amazing just standing there while he was doing it. He was obviously ridiculously angry, incredibly angry, and incredibly emotional about it. He just poured everything he had into that vocal. I mean, the second take was incredible as well, but it wasn't nearly as good as the first. Unfortunately, only five or six people heard it and can say it really happened."

No matter: the version we all know is phenomenal enough. The lyrics were written while Chuck took an impromptu road trip to Allentown, Pennsylvania. "It just poured out, exactly what I was feeling and thinking," he told *Rolling Stone* two years later. As for choosing the song's subject matter. "I knew exactly what was going to happen," he said. "I knew the first record we released then [after the Griff controversy] was going to be closely watched. I thought it was fascinating that so many people were interested in the lyrics of rap for the first time. That's what rap is about, right? Checking out the lyrics."

Incensed and passionate – "it's coming from the heart", he sings at one point – 'Welcome To The Terrordome' was the epitome of the noise Public Enemy generated so brilliantly. Culling the paranoid energy of the Temptations' 'Psychedelic Shack' and the fresh fury of the drums off of James Brown's 'Cold Sweat' – to name just two samples weaved into the mix – the song had an almost dizzying density. 'Welcome To The Terrordome' felt like a vortex, one that Chuck was desperately trying to pull himself free from.

There are two competing emotions in the song, which was apt since 'Terrordome' reflected the conflicted feelings consuming Chuck about the Griff incident. On one side, he wanted to mend fences ("God bless your soul and keep livin'" and "my home is your home"), while still being needlessly antagonistic:

> *Crucifixion ain't no fiction*
> *So-called chosen frozen*
> *Apology made to whoever pleases*
> *Still they got me like Jesus*

"The accused anti-Semitic lines were there because I knew that people would only be concerned with this one thing and not look at anything else," he said in *Rolling Stone*. "Because the whole song basically explains everything from beginning to end, but if you take a chunk out and isolate it, it may say something else. You put it in context and that's what the record is about. That's why I was very pleased with the results – I got everybody's attention to show them exactly what I meant."

Chuck may have been pleased, but prominent Jewish groups weren't, condemning the lyrics. On one hand, Chuck's gambit was clever: he was trying to write a song that articulated the need to absorb a speaker's entire message, not just a snippet. After all, this was what Chuck and Griff claimed had happened to Griff with *The Washington Times*. But on the other, the stellar wordplay – as well as "Told a 'Rab get off the rag" – only built walls between groups. If Chuck really believed that PE didn't exist to offend anyone, why spend his first post-Griff song lobbing grenades?

But for Chuck, the song was more important in terms of delivering a manifesto for African-Americans as they looked to the future. "I wrote that record at the end of '89, to signify the Terrordome is the nineties," he told *The Village Voice* in 1991. "It's a make-it-or-break-it period for [blacks]. We do the right thing, we'll be able to pull into the 21st century with some kind of programme. We do the wrong thing, the 21st century is going to be gone, there'll be no coming back."

'Welcome To The Terrordome' came to radio before New Year's, stirring up more controversy but also demonstrating the group's growing sonic sophistication. Young, who was focused on *Pawns In The Game* at the time, had been in the studio when the track was first being recorded and now realised how difficult it would be for Griff's album to compete with Public Enemy. "I knew what it sounded like already," Young says, "but I was like, 'Oh, shit, this is their single.' I was intimidated."

The song incurred the wrath of the Anti-Defamation League and the Simon Wiesenthal Center, but other Jewish leaders spoke up for Public Enemy. Most prominent of these supporters was Danny Goldberg. A talent manager who went on to represent Nirvana, Goldberg chaired the ACLU Foundation of Southern California. In an op-ed in the *Los Angeles Times*, Goldberg argued, among other things, that Chuck's crucifixion line wasn't a slap at Judaism but, rather, part of a long tradition of artists (such as John Lennon) who were using the metaphor to express their personal anguish. "Restrictions on speech have never helped minorities any-where," he wrote, disapproving of calls to censor or boycott the band. "Every gain by minorities in this country coincided with a loosening of restrictions on cultural and political speech. Every repression recorded by history has followed a clampdown on speech."

"As somebody with a Jewish name, I was really mortified when rabbis were accusing [Public Enemy] of anti-Semitism," Goldberg says today. When he wrote the op-ed, he had not yet met Chuck, but he was enor-mously impressed with the band. Furthermore, "it just seemed, to me, just so immoral and wrong and tone-deaf" to accuse the group of anti-Semitism. "I thought maybe me writing about it would be useful. It cer-tainly was useful to me in terms of saying what I wanted to say." He didn't deny that anti-Semitism was a legitimate worry in the world, but Chuck was not someone that he felt deserved such scorn. "Chuck D was an artist who didn't have a biased bone in his body," Goldberg says. "His work was positive and inclusive."

"No one in the black community gives a fuck about Jewish people," Chuck told *Playboy* in late 1990 when asked to explain what divides blacks and Jews. "The issue with black people is when do I get paid, and why are these white motherfuckers fucking with me? Black people do not separate Jews from gentiles. Really, I don't understand it."

'Terrordome' suggested the knuckle-busting temperament of the band's forthcoming album. But then again, so did the album's title. "When I walk to the 7-Eleven, I feel like I'm being watched because of who I am – a black man," Chuck told the *Chicago Tribune*'s Greg Kot during a July 1990 interview. "Sometimes I feel compelled to buy something so I won't be suspected of stealing. Blacks see the problem of racism in America very clearly because they have to live it every day. . . . Whites aren't educated about racism because they've benefited from it. *Fear Of A Black Planet* is like feeding baby food to babies – whites are babies when it comes to racism. And they won't study it unless it hits them in the face daily."

In his 1987 *Melody Maker* interview, he was even more provocative, saying, "Of course I'd like it if everybody white married somebody black and then the next generations were all black. Then there'd be no double standard, except the kind of sick, fucked-up thing black people have among themselves that makes them judge between different shades of darkness. But this integration is *never* gonna happen. So people should stick to their own. Without a strong sense of black consciousness, there's no cohesion, and no survival. The Chinese, the Jews, they stick together, deal with each other. Blacks don't."

So, *Fear Of A Black Planet*, like *Nation of Millions*, had a sort of double meaning. To PE's way of thinking, whites feared a world in which inter-racial couples produced black children – but, the band wondered, could blacks be disciplined enough to know what to do with such a future? Those tensions would pulse through the album's 20 songs: anger at white racism but also anger at black ignorance.

It was also the album where the name "the Bomb Squad" was born. Now synonymous with the production crew that oversees Public Enemy albums, the moniker was, according to Johnny Juice, something of a ruse. "The Bomb Squad name was created by Chuck to mask the fact that Hank didn't do anything [on *Fear Of A Black Planet*]," Juice says. "Everybody wanted to fucking kill Hank, but Hank was contractually obligated to have his name on it. And this is why Chuck was brilliant. How do you pacify everyone? 'OK, you guys are the Bomb Squad, and it's produced by the Bomb Squad, so everybody gets their credit, no matter who did what.'"

Juice's claim can be backed up by looking at the album credits. The album's production is credited to the Bomb Squad – Hank Shocklee, Chuck D (as Carl Ryder), Eric "Vietnam" Sadler and Keith Shocklee – but when you look at the individual song credits, Hank is nowhere to be seen. Shaw, who (unlike Johnny Juice) worked on *Fear Of A Black Planet*, recalls that Hank assisted with Chuck in determining the track order for the record. But even then, Hank was less of a force on this new album then he had been on previous records. In *Don't Rhyme For The Sake of Riddlin'*, Sadler is quoted as saying that when the band prepared to make *Fear Of A Black Planet*, "Hank wasn't talking to Griff, Griff wasn't talking to Chuck, Chuck wasn't talking to Hank, Hank wasn't talking to Keith. It was a little war going on." He also says that Keith deserves the credit for writing the music for 'Fight The Power' and 'Welcome To The Terrordome'.

But if the group was fracturing, the music wasn't. *Fear Of A Black Planet* may be one of the quintessential albums in the history of pop that reflects the tensions of its creation. But unlike, say, Fleetwood Mac's *Rumours*, which was fuelled by romantic disillusionment and egos, *Black Planet*'s turmoil was political and cultural as much as it was warring personalities. Rather than shy away from the controversy raised by Griff and their own incendiary comments in the press and on *Nation Of Millions*, Public Enemy leaned into the imbroglio, resulting in a record that, years later, still sounds like a five-alarm fire. If that wasn't enough, they were also trying to top *Nation Of Millions* while continuing that album's legacy.

"*Fear* was the second half of a back-to-back 'movement' of albums that immediately signified that rap could be as significant an album genre as rock, forcing respect," Chuck boasted immodestly in *Billboard* in 2010. "It was a musical and political statement that resonates to this day."

The album backs up his proclamations. *Nation Of Millions* includes snippets from the band's triumphant London shows to suggest the level of their cultural cachet, but *Fear Of A Black Planet* was about proving that success wasn't going to sink them. If their previous album had aimed to show that hip-hop could make meaningful full-length records, *Fear Of A Black Planet* wanted to prove PE could do it again.

"Last summer I was fighting, I was depressed, but I knew what I was doing and the group got bigger over handling the controversy," Chuck said in 1990. "People talk about controversy making a group bigger; handling it makes it bigger. If you don't handle it, you're out of here." Or, as he famously, wistfully said at the height of the Griff madness, "I was looking forward to spending the summer talking about Elvis Presley and John Wayne."

An air of cinematic drama infuses *Fear Of A Black Planet* from the start. The opening cut, the instrumental 'Contract On The World Love Jam', sets the scene, building quietly, calmly and ominously. A mixture of political speeches and news segments that hinted at Public Enemy's uncertain future, the track thrillingly suggested the album's high stakes: could the band hold together to uplift a race in danger of losing itself? The beat was stark and the tone concerned, ending on a sampled statement that was both hopeful and worrying: "There is something changing in the climate of consciousness on this planet today."

"They already had the samples laid out in the order they were going to put them in," Chris Shaw recalls about 'Contract On The World Love Jam'. "It wasn't like they were scratching their heads in the studio: 'What are we going to do to introduce the record?' They pretty much just went in and started. I wouldn't be surprised if they wrote that track before they did anything else."

And then, *Fear Of A Black Planet* exploded, the titanic 'Brothers Gonna Work It Out' riding a feverish sample of Prince's guitar solo from 'Let's Go Crazy'. Where other PE tracks were defiant and angry, quite possibly their loudest song was also their most openhearted. Rather than preaching revolution, 'Brothers Gonna Work It Out' was a beautiful distillation of the self-sufficiency Chuck responded to in the preaching of the Nation of Islam. An anthem of black unity, the track found Chuck extolling African-American history, property and business ownership, responsible fathers, and self-respect to end, as he called it, the status of "so many of us in limbo".

Backed by a dynamic chorus of Chuck and Flav singing "Let's get it on" back and forth to each other, the intensity rising with each chant, 'Brothers Gonna Work It Out' reached a glorious crescendo in its final verse:

In 1995, you'll twist to this
As you raise your fist to the music
United we stand, yes divided we fall
Together we can stand tall
Brothers that try to work it out
They get mad, revolt, revise, realise
They're super bad
Small chance a smart brother's
Gonna be a victim of his own circumstance

If 'Terrordome' worried about blacks in the next century, 'Brothers Gonna Work It Out' laid out the plan for success. It remains one of PE's most inspiring songs, fully aware of its makers' flaws but determined to fight through them to find a better tomorrow. We're now far past 1995, but Chuck's bold glimpse into the future still feels forward-looking:

positive without collapsing into 'Don't Worry, Be Happy' platitudes. It was a peaceful rally with the mayhem of a riot.

"Keith basically wrote that song," Shaw says. "That's an awesome track. I just remember putting it down, I was like, 'Uh, are you sure you've got the clearance to do "Let's Go Crazy?"'" Shaw also reveals the song features one of Hank's few on-record appearances. "He's the whispering [chorus] vocal, 'Brothers gonna work it out,'" Shaw says. "That's Hank with laryngitis." He laughs. "Hank showed up at the studio one day, his voice was shot. And they were like, 'Oh yeah, we got to use that.'"

With around 150 to 200 samples used on *Fear Of A Black Planet*, the album was even more of a sonic tapestry than *Nation Of Millions*. And like its predecessor, it was conceived with an eye toward how one track segued (or collided into) the next one. "This album also built more on thematic moods than anything," Chuck wrote. "I had saved samples and snippets, and gone through at least 100 hours of listening to samples, tapes and records to use on the album."

The album consisted of 20 tracks, but the band took care to consider pacing. The stern, forceful 'Brothers Gonna Work It Out' moved into Flav's '911 Is A Joke', a comical but ultimately serious criticism of emergency medical technicians' slow arrival into poor black neighbourhoods. "It responded to the non-response of services in our community," Chuck said on *Tavis Smiley* in 2007. "I gave Flavor the title. I said, 'You got a year to write this.'" The bedlam of '911 Is A Joke' segued to an interlude, 'Incident At 66.6 FM', which highlighted a real radio interview Chuck gave to host Alan Colmes, with angry callers commenting on how offensive they find the band. (There is one supporter, though, who gets the final word.) Then came the raging 'Welcome To The Terrordome'. Loud then subdued, incensed then funny, thoughtful then reactionary, major statements then palate-cleansing intermezzos: *Fear Of A Black Planet* hung together like a conversation – a debate, really – between the voices within Public Enemy. Perhaps the cleverest of these segues was the end of 'Anti-Nigger Machine', where Chuck talks about hanging out at home "until I got a buzz", which then jump-cuts into the next track, 'Burn Hollywood Burn', which starts with a phone ringing.

"I was at the studio every day for *Nation*," Shaw remembers, "and I saw it getting bigger and bigger as it went on. *Fear* felt a little bit darker to me: the band had the whole Griff controversy and *Nation* was such a huge record – it was being labelled as this ground-breaking, career-defining moment. So, for their [follow-up], it's time for them to deliver a record that is just as good, if not better. You could sense that was going on: every song that we worked on, there was this pressure to make it as good as it possibly could be. Every song was sort of like, 'What more can we add to make it bigger? What more can we do to make it better? What can we do to make it a lot louder and noisier?'"

"*Fear Of A Black Planet* was one of the first times that hip-hop was getting scrutinised word for word and line for line on a political level," Chuck told *Vibe* more than 20 years later. "Our job was to come up with something that people couldn't find. We wanted to dazzle and amaze and deliver something totally different from *It Takes A Nation* . . . The biggest thing that Public Enemy proved in the eighties and early nineties that made us different from any other rap group was that once we found something that worked we were going to throw it away. We never repeated ourselves. That's what the rock'n'rollers did."

All of this was being done with relatively unsophisticated equipment. Nick Sansano, who was more closely associated with *Nation Of Millions* but also worked on *Fear Of A Black Planet*, says, "Technology drives the sound, you know? People ask [Public Enemy], 'What prompted you to make your sound composed of all these little snippets? How did you have such a brilliant idea?' And it's like, 'Because that's the only way we could do it.' How much sampling [time] was there on the Panasonic, which was their first keyboard? Half a second? You couldn't do it any other way. There are bands that really use the technology well, like Tangerine Dream or Kraftwerk, but for hip-hop, those guys were the Kraftwerk and Tangerine Dream. They were making the most out of nothing – that technology, everything was bad."

But despite the pressure and the sub-par technology, the *Fear Of A Black Planet* sessions had their prankster-ish moments, especially when it came to the album's samples. As Shaw recalls, the group would nix certain ones that were too obvious. But in general, the band's attitude toward samples in an era before they would be heavily legislated was "Fuck them if they can't take a joke. But they would definitely draw a line: Occasionally, there would be a sample with a full-on vocal in it and Hank would be like, 'Oh, that was great, but we'll definitely get nailed for that.'"

Still, Shaw laughs. "I can name some samples on that record that would definitely get them in a shit-ton of trouble," he says. He won't reveal specifics, but he does offer one example: in the studio, he and Eric Sadler "were laying down this sort of muffled tone" for a track. "As we were laying it down, Eric looked at me: 'White boy, you know what that is?' I have no idea. Eric opened up the filter, and as soon as it was playing full, my jaw just dropped. I was like, 'You can't do that!' He goes, 'Yes, I can – I just did.'"

As part of creating a bigger canvas for *Fear Of A Black Planet*, Chuck D's lyrical outlook broadened. 'Burn Hollywood Burn' commented on the offensive ways that blacks had been portrayed in American films. The song was a product of Chuck shooting his mouth off in an interview, mentioning that he and up-and-coming rapper Big Daddy Kane were going to be collaborating on a song called 'Burn Hollywood Burn'. He hadn't spoken to Kane about this, nor did he even have a song in mind. But the two of them, along with Ice Cube, wrote the lyrics one day at Greene Street, the track ending with an imaginary scenario where Chuck (who was not much of a film fan) is coaxed into seeing a movie at the theatre – only to discover it's *Driving Miss Daisy*, the embodiment of the patronising depiction of African-Americans that they've been condemning on the track. The choice of movies was prescient: released the same year as *Do The Right Thing*, *Driving Miss Daisy* won four Academy Awards, including Best Picture. *Do The Right Thing* was only nominated for two Oscars and got shut out of the Best Picture race. Clearly, the Academy wasn't yet ready to embrace more nuanced portrayals of blacks.

"I was dealing with the messed-up side of the film industry," Chuck explained in *Fight The Power*, "which I had studied from seeing all of the pressure Spike Lee got with his films." Specifically, he noticed the criticism that was levelled against *Do The Right Thing*, with some reviewers worrying that the movie could provoke race riots. *New York*'s David Denby wrote, "Lee's playing with dynamite in an urban playground. The response to this movie could get away from him." In fact, it was believed by some in Public Enemy that Chuck had considered ending the band so that the Griff controversy wouldn't negatively affect *Do The Right Thing*, which hit theatres around the same time.

But even 'Burn Hollywood Burn' demonstrated how Chuck had to walk the line between provocation and sensible restraint, either because he had been burned by the Griff response or because he had wised up. In Ice Cube's verse, the N.W.A. member who was getting ready to go solo targets the police, rapping, "Don't fight the power . . . the motherfucker." On the original track, Shaw says, "Ice Cube actually says 'shoot the motherfucker.' He's basically condoning shooting a cop. Chuck was like, 'I really don't want him saying "shoot" – it's going to be on me if I let that go.' We replaced the word 'shoot' with a sample of a gunshot so it's implied rather than actually stated. Chuck was constantly treading that line of how far he could push."

This doesn't mean that Chuck never slipped up. On the 45-second 'Meet The G That Killed Me', a homosexual encounter spreads AIDS to a drug addict, who eventually infects Flavor with AIDS. The track's brevity sharply illustrated the paranoia surrounding the disease – and the seeming speed of its spread. But Chuck rapping, "Man to man / I don't know if they can / From what I know / The parts don't fit" – accented by Flav's rhyme, "Oh, shit" – played into the same bigoted attitude toward gays that the band had aired during their UK interviews.

Referencing those lyrics in his 1990 *Playboy* interview, Chuck said, "Love between men shouldn't involve sex. . . . There are gays in the black community because black women are not being loved from the heart, and black men are feeling alienated. This causes people to withdraw from the normal man-woman relationships."

Elsewhere on *Fear Of A Black Planet*, he tried to redeem the criticism that he was a misogynist on 'Revolutionary Generation', which was a salute to black women. Although sincere, the song was also a bit clunky, Chuck proclaiming, "It takes a man to take a stand / Understand it takes a / Woman to make a stronger man." Still, 'Revolutionary Generation' was a clear statement of unity, although it lacked the sneaky complexity of 'Pollywanacraka', a rather devastating example of Chuck's storytelling prowess.

Adopting an everyman voice – 'Pollywanacraka' is one of the rare moments where Chuck is supposed to sound like someone other than himself – the rapper tells the fictional tale of two characters: a black woman who wants a white boyfriend (because she's tired of no-good black men) and a black man who wants a white girlfriend (because he's desiring someone who's as successful as he is). With sympathy, Chuck's narrator observes how interracial dating sows animosity in the black community, angering those who think that African-Americans interested in white partners are trying to escape or deny their heritage. There's no judgment in 'Pollywanacraka', only a pragmatic understanding that races aren't separated just by skin colour but by cultural expectations: in the song, "white" is shorthand for prosperous, responsible, upwardly mobile.

Its companion piece is the ricocheting title track, in which Chuck imagines a conversation with a white man who freaks out from suspicion that the MC is interested in his daughter, sister or wife. ("But supposin' she said she loved me?" Flav asks with provocation, his street-corner energy terrifically playing into white fear of black men as thugs and aggressors.) 'Fear Of A Black Planet' is about the immediate mistrust that black men stir because of their skin colour, but it also turns the tables, retorting in a freaky, dehumanised, sped-up vocal that "white comes from black".

The comment was drawn from the theories of Frances Cress Welsing, a psychiatrist who wrote *The Cress Theory Of Color Confrontation And Racism (White Supremacy)*. In it, she argued, "white or colour-deficient Europeans responded psychologically with a profound sense of numerical inadequacy and colour inferiority upon their confrontations with the massive majority of the world's people, all of whom possessed varying degrees of colour producing capacity." In other words, white Americans discriminate against blacks because of envy of their skin colour. She also went on to suggest, "Whites desire sexual alliances with the 'non-whites', both male and female, because it is only through this route that whites can achieve the illusion of producing colour."

"The new album is based on certain aspects of the Cress Theory," Chuck told the *Chicago Tribune*, making the connection more explicit by including the psychiatrist's theory in some review copies of *Fear Of A*

Black Planet. "And I think there's some truth to it, but it's intimidating to whites because it's so against everything they're taught in school." Furthermore, Chuck said, he wanted white listeners to question "why 100 percent of the planet isn't shared by 100 percent of the people, why white is considered good and black is bad. God didn't make those laws, white supremacists did."

'Fear Of A Black Planet' ultimately preaches peace and love among all races, but Chuck also prominently places a sample from comedian/activist Dick Gregory saying, "Black man, white woman, black baby. White man, black woman, black baby," which also plays into Welsing's theory that racism is a product of white fear that their race will eventually be eradicated by children born from interracial couples. The sample plays as both funny and chilling, Public Enemy practically taunting bigots to overreact.

"He came to Adelphi in 1981," Chuck reminisced to *The Gainesville Sun* about encountering Gregory, "and the beginning of his speech was 15 minutes of the funniest [material] I ever heard in my life. He caught our attention, everybody was cracking up and then suddenly he flipped it like this and got real serious and to the point. I'd never seen anything like that in my life." From Gregory, Chuck said he learned the value of merging though-provoking content and entertainment, which would become one of Public Enemy's greatest artistic legacies. "If it wasn't for him," the rapper said, "I don't think I could have come up with that combination."

The anxiety and reflection that Chuck wanted to spark in the listener was also within him while making the album. "At that point, he was being hounded by the press so much that there was at least three or four days where Chuck slept at the studio," says Shaw. "The studio manager had an apartment down the street – Chuck would go and take a shower there. It was pretty intense – they were kind of on the verge of breaking up, and nobody really knew what to do or how to handle the situation." Shaw wasn't privy to any conversations about band business, such as the Rhythm Method fallout, but he was aware of grumblings over finances. "There was that pressure going on," he says. "It was a little tense. Overall, it was a lot of fun [making *Fear Of A Black Planet*], but the thing was, when we were making *Nation*, we were just making it. It was a really interesting record, a really cool record, but nobody knew how big it was going to be. That record came out, and all of a sudden it's huge. Then, we've got to dive back into the studio and make another one off the back of *Nation*. Now we're not just making this really cool, interesting record – we're making a follow-up. It adds a whole other dimension and a little bit of pressure."

Attacking organised religion ('War At 33 1/3'), mainstream pop (Terminator X's instrumental, 'Leave This Off Your Fu★kin Charts'), police corruption ('Anti-Nigger Machine'), whites' resistance to providing reparations to blacks after the end of slavery ('Who Stole The Soul?') and welfare (Flav's 'Can't Do Nuttin' For Ya Man'), *Fear Of A Black Planet* also made room for an adorably dorky reggae freestyle ('Reggie Jax') and a ready-made shout-along anthem ('Power To The People'). The album probably suffers some from its massive ambitions, but the furious rush of its songs was overwhelming. For all of Chuck's earlier talk of PE only lasting two years, *Fear Of A Black Planet* genuinely felt like an album put together under the belief that this would be it: whatever Chuck wanted to say in the studio, he'd better make sure he did it now.

The album's marvellously overstuffed quality was further illustrated by the fact that Chuck had a specific request. "He was adamant that the A side and the B side be the same length, down to almost a second," says Shaw. "Back then, the medium of choice for hip-hop records was a cassette, and he wanted to make sure that when the [listener] was driving in a car and Side A came to the end, you would only get, like, two seconds of leader time – the tape would reverse, go to the leader, then hit the next track. If you had a lopsided record where there was, like, five minutes [more] on Side A, you'd have five minutes of silence before the record would kick back in again. It wasn't as seamless as possible."

Consequently, about two days before mastering *Fear Of A Black Planet*, Chuck called the studio, where Shaw and Sadler were working on a remix for another project. According to Shaw, "Chuck says, 'Hey, Side A is a minute-and-a-half short. We need to stick another minute-and-a-half of something into Side A so it's the same length as Side B.' Eric was just like, 'Oh dude, what do you want me to do?' And Chuck was like, 'I don't care, maybe a beat with some random stuff on it.' So Eric dug through the archives and pulled out something that he'd been working on."

That beat became the foundation for the buzzy, funky interlude that starts 'Anti-Nigger Machine'. "I was listening to it," Shaw recalls, "and I looked at Eric: 'You know, this isn't a Public Enemy track. It's just a drumbeat with a little bit of a guitar hit on it.' I ran to the office and I found an old AM radio, and I went to the tape library and found one of the reels that we had of Flavor Flav outtakes." These Flav reels had been created out of necessity. "Flavor was only allowed in the studio when he was doing his vocal, because he was a complete distraction," says Shaw. "Otherwise, we would get nothing done. We'd run the tape, hit record, Flavor would do a take of his vocal, we'd stop the machine, we'd be rewinding, and then he'd say something ridiculously funny. We'd be like, 'Flav, you got to put that in a song.' We'd give him another take, but he'd forget [what he'd said]. So, we had this rule of thumb: whenever Flav was in the studio with a mic on him, we would record everything he'd do out in the room no matter whether or not tape was rolling. So we amassed five or six reels of just Flavor Flav vocals because sometimes we needed ad-libs to inject into the middle of a song when he'd be out of town."

Armed with the radio and the outtakes, Sadler tuned radio static while they randomly searched for Flav non sequiturs like "Check this out" or "Well, yo, anyway" on the reels. "We did that and had the drum machine running for 15 minutes, and we recorded it all," says Shaw. "Basically, we found the best minute-and-a-half, chopped it out and tagged it onto the beginning of 'Anti-Nigger Machine'."

The creativity spilled over onto other albums. At the same time that *Fear Of A Black Planet* was being made, Sansano was working with Sonic Youth on their follow-up to *Daydream Nation*, their major-label debut *Goo*. "They loved that we worked at Greene Street, too," Sansano says. "There was no dividing line [between rap and rock groups]." The line was further erased when Chuck guested on Sonic Youth's 'Kool Thing', which became *Goo*'s first single. The song was inspired by the most unlikely of coincidences. In the same September 1989 issue of *Spin* where Leland went deep on Public Enemy's post-Griff turmoil, Sonic Youth's bassist and co-lead vocalist Kim Gordon interviewed LL Cool J. Gordon was a fan of LL – his debut, *Radio*, "was one of the things that turned me on to rap", she wrote in the piece – but she came away disappointed by the conversation.

"It was totally ridiculous for me to assume that we had anything in common," she told the *Phoenix New Times* in 1991 about LL. "That's why I tried to make the article show how elite and small the downtown scene that I come out of is. I was trying to make fun of myself. I don't know if that came across." One of the more interesting exchanges from the interview is when Gordon asked him if he's bothered that women take his picture to bed with them "and their boyfriends or husbands start freaking out". "It's not my problem," the rapper responded. "The guy has to have control over his woman. She has to have enough respect for you to know not to do those things. It's how you carry yourself." At the end of the *Spin* piece, she wrote, "It seems pretty obvious LL doesn't have many conversations with white girls like me. . . . But I have more access to his world . . . than LL will ever have to mine."

'Kool Thing' was an imaginary conversation with someone who's about to become a star, with Chuck D's vocals complementing the buzzing guitars and masterfully sculpted feedback. Sansano still recalls "seeing the track really come to life with Chuck coming in and doing the vocals. There were other [rock] bands that would use the odd sample here and there, but his physical voice has meaning." The collaboration happened spontaneously. Sansano recalls, "Kim said, 'It'd be great if we could have a rapper [on the track],' so I said, 'I can ask Chuck. He's here.' We were in A at that point, and they were in B [at Greene Street]. It wasn't a grand plan: it was, 'Oh yeah, it'd be cool, wouldn't it? Yeah! Let's see if he wants to do it.'" Chuck was game, and 'Kool Thing' was finished, with Gordon mischievously whispering at one point in the song, "Fear of a female planet."

There could have been more Public Enemy-Sonic Youth collaborations in the future, but sadly they never materialised. "I blame myself because I gave up on it," says Sansano. "I wasn't persistent enough. I was working on a collaboration where we would do a Side A/Side B 12-inch. They would flip songs: PE was gonna take a Sonic Youth song, and Sonic Youth was gonna take a PE song, and reproduce and remix it. We had a couple of meetings. I don't even remember what the [songs] were, but we even got that far. But when it got time to actually schedule people and start to work out all the business stuff, it just kept getting waylaid. Looking back, I kick myself. At the time, I was like, 'All right, well, it'll happen.' You have that youthful [enthusiasm]. I'm 51 now, and it didn't happen."

Because of all the turmoil around the making of *Fear Of A Black Planet*, it might surprise some to know that there could have been an additional obstacle. "When *Fear* was coming out, a lot of bootleg cassettes of it got out before its release date," remembers Shaw. "Fortunately, this was before the internet era, so it didn't get too far out, but a lot of people had copies. [Public Enemy] didn't feel comfortable leaving a copy of the master at the studio, so right after we finished mastering *Fear Of A Black Planet*, they made two reference CDs, which the guys in the band took, and they made two DAT copies – and they gave me one. They said, 'Chris, take this DAT and take it to your house. We trust you.' I said, 'Yeah, sure, no problem.' Well, that night, I walked home and I got yanked into a dark doorway by these two guys. One of them held a gun to my head: 'Give me everything you've got now!'"

Never having been mugged before, Shaw tried to remain calm, handing over his wallet, which had about five dollars in it. Unsatisfied, his attackers also demanded his new leather jacket, which he'd purchased on a recent trip to Italy. "As I'm taking it off, I realise that DAT is in the pocket," Shaw says. "I thought, 'Oh shit, now what do I do?' I kinda clumsily took the jacket off and handed it to them upside down, and the DAT falls out of the pocket. The guy looks down at the sidewalk at this little plastic case and says, 'What the hell is that?' I said, 'It's my answering-machine cassette: do you want that, too?' He goes, 'Aw, fuck it,' and the two of them run off, but not before they took my sneakers." Shaw laughs. "I walked back to the studio, and I just started punching the wall. Chuck and Hank were like, 'What's wrong?' I said, 'I just got mugged! They took my jacket, they took my shoes, they took my wallet.' Chuck was like, 'Oh, wait . . . didn't you have the DAT?' I'm like, 'Naw, I got that right here.' The DAT was worth 10 times more than what I gave them."

Reviews for *Fear Of A Black Planet* were mostly very strong, with even those critics who had reservations acknowledging the depth and complexity of the music. Though he noted that the band should have been more forceful in its repudiation of Griff, *Rolling Stone*'s Alan Light concluded, "Public Enemy is looking to the future, not with apocalyptic despair but with fiery eyes fixed firmly on the prize. The group's determination and realism, its devotion to activism and booty shaking, make *Fear Of A Black Planet* a welcome, bracing triumph."

Giving the album an "A" and putting it in his Top 10 for 1990, *The Village Voice*'s Robert Christgau wrote, "All preemptive strikes to the contrary, this is a much better record than there was any reason to expect under the circumstances. It's not unusually inflated or self-involved, though its brutal pace does wear down eventually, it's got a sense of humour, not just from a Flav who keeps figuring stuff out, but from Chuck, whose 'Pollywanacraka' message and voice . . . is the album's most surprising moment." He ended his write-up by suggesting, "Shtick their rebel music may be, but this is show business, and they still think harder than anybody else working their beat."

As for *Entertainment Weekly*'s Greg Sandow, he found that *"Fear Of A Black Planet* isn't Public Enemy's masterpiece. But it's a formidable piece of work, and the one pop album released so far this year that no one interested in the current state of American culture can afford to ignore."

In that year's Pazz & Jop album poll, *Fear Of A Black Planet* finished third. (*Goo* finished fourth.) 'Fight The Power' had placed number one on 1989's singles chart, while 'Welcome To The Terrordome' landed at number 10 on the 1990 chart. But Public Enemy's strong showing was even more cheering considering other acts that also charted high. Living Colour, the progressive black quartet guided by Vernon Reid's rock guitar, ended up at number five in 1990 with their sophomore album, *Time's Up*, an equally dazzling and kaleidoscopic examination of the African-American community. Interestingly, it too featured a song about Presley, 'Elvis Is Dead', which criticised fans' insistence on perpetuating the myth that the King didn't actually die in 1977. The song even included a callback to Chuck's 'Fight The Power' line "Elvis was a hero to most", but frontman Corey Glover tweaked it by saying, "But that's beside the point", opening the door to a critique of those who make money off of Presley's image and memory.

Additionally, another socially conscious rap group, De La Soul, won the 1989 album poll with *3 Feet High And Rising*, a brilliant sample-heavy record. That same year, Beastie Boys delivered *Paul's Boutique*, which could challenge De La Soul's and Public Enemy's discs for the amount of samples.

The album that landed at number six on the 1990 chart wasn't in the same thoughtful vein as those other releases. But it had the Bomb Squad's fingers all over it. Ice Cube had ditched N.W.A. and wanted to work with the PE producers for his solo debut. *AmeriKKKa's Most Wanted* lacked the lyrical depth of *Black Planet* or *Nation Of Millions* – Cube flashed a reactionary sexism and racism that Chuck never touched – but it embodied those albums' heady musical rush.

The Bomb Squad, along with Shaw and Sansano, got to work on *AmeriKKKa's Most Wanted* immediately after finishing *Fear Of A Black Planet*. Just like *Pawns In The Game* was Griff's attempt to compete with PE, *AmeriKKKa's Most Wanted* was Cube's response to what his old N.W.A. partner, Dr. Dre, had brought to that group's 1998 debut, *Straight Outta Compton*. "Dre had changed the game as far as the rugged street sort of vibe," Sadler told *Spin* in 1999. "So we had to one-up them, and do the best work we had ever done."

According to Sansano, the process wasn't that different when the Greene Street team shifted their attention from *Fear Of A Black Planet* to *AmeriKKKa's Most Wanted*. "Even when we did the Ice Cube record, the concept, the overall arc of the songs and how they would be arranged – that was always the big thing," says Sansano. "The Bomb Squad weren't like an individual-song type of production team. There was always discussion about the arc of what it would all be and how it would all work together."

"Literally, the day before we mastered *Fear Of A Black Planet*, Cube came to town and we started preproduction on *AmeriKKKa's Most Wanted*," Shaw recalls. "Ice Cube was actually at the mastering session for *Fear Of A Black Planet*. Then we did *AmeriKKKa's Most Wanted*. Then right after that, we did [some] tracks for Bell Biv DeVoe," the trio of Ricky Bell, Michael Bivins and Ronnie DeVoe who broke away from the shadow of their old band, New Edition, for a tougher sound on *Poison*. "We never stopped: it was just this nonstop avalanche of Bomb Squad productions going on at Greene Street." They rarely ever took a break. "It was funny," Shaw says, "we'd be in the middle of doing one album when another got released. It was like, 'Oh yeah, we forgot about that record — we're on this one now.'"

The quick turnaround on these different Bomb Squad productions sometimes resulted in uncomfortable situations. "The Bomb Squad had discs of song sketches," Shaw says. For Ice Cube, the producers would play the CDs to see if any of the demos piqued his interest. "At the same time, there was also a side project that the Bomb Squad had, Son of Bazerk. There was a song that they had written for Bazerk called 'Change The Style', but by accident they played Cube the basic track. Cube was like, 'I want that,' and they said, 'Oh, wait a second, we're giving this one to Bazerk.' And Cube was like, 'No, I want that track,' and there was a big fight. They eventually wound up using the same backing track for Son of Bazerk, but they utterly buried it in a ton of samples.

"So, yeah, there was a bit of overlap, but it was just an unbelievably fruitful period of Bomb Squad productions," Shaw continues. "But I think that when you work that hard that long, there's going to be burnout. And I think *Apocalypse* was the result of that."

CHAPTER FIVE

I F you owned *Fear Of A Black Planet* on cassette, you might have been tempted to think the tape broke at the end of the second side. After the album-closing 'Fight The Power' wound down, there were a couple of seconds of what sounded like an interview between a reporter and Chuck D. "Talk to me about the future of Public Enemy," the reporter said. Chuck responded, "Future of Public Enemy got a—," and then there was silence.

Had something gone wrong with the recording? No, it was Chuck fooling with us, leaving the question of the band's future up to debate. About 18 months after *Fear's* dizzying rush was unleashed, Chuck answered that question on the first track of *Apocalypse 91… The Enemy Strikes Black*.

"The album opens up where *Fear Of A Black Planet* leaves off," Chuck explained in *Lyrics Of A Rap Revolutionary*. "At the end of *Black Planet* it says, 'What's the future of Public Enemy?' And the first thing on *Apocalypse 91* is 'The future holds nothing but confrontation.'"

That was the opening line of 'Lost At Birth' – actually, it's "The future holds nothing else but confrontation" – which rides its police-siren wail, rhythmic scratching and repeated verbal snippets into lyrics about African-American disillusionment in White America. But Chuck's dismissal of listeners "sleepin' while standin' up" seemed to be a change from his usual verbal invective unleashed upon those in power. He sounded like he was addressing his fellow blacks – and it set the tone for an album that was shifting the focus of the band's attack.

In an interview with *Melody Maker's* Simon Reynolds that was published around the time of *Apocalypse 91's* release, Chuck D elucidated this new direction.

"The first album, *Yo! Bum Rush The Show*, was like, if you can't get what you deserve, kick that motherfucking door down by any means," he

125

explained. "*It Takes A Nation Of Millions* was about how there's millions of motherfuckers stopping us from getting what we need to get. And, from the black nationalist point of view, there's millions of us holding ourselves back. *Fear Of A Black Planet* talked about the paranoia of what race is – white people's problems with themselves, their misconceptions about race. The new album . . . is about how we, the black race, have double agents in our ranks who are contributing to the genocide. In order for us to get our shit in order, we've gotta get those motherfuckers. They'll just be outright destroyed, either by the positive hardcore, or by themselves."

If Public Enemy had become a sensation by crossing over to the white marketplace, by appealing to white listeners' love of rock and punk, then *Apocalypse 91* offered that audience a glimpse into the struggles within the black community. Although Chuck and Flavor Flav didn't hold back their criticism of white power structures like corporations and the media, *Apocalypse 91* is a hard, angry look at what was going on in PE's own backyard. And in what would become a running theme of their nineties albums, Chuck was asking his community to start acting its age.

"The new album's lesson is, 'No more fun and games,'" Chuck D told Reynolds. "There's no room for kids here. The black situation needs less adolescents aged over 18. Fun and games have got to be tucked to the side; responsibility and business have got to take precedence. The album deals with the whole question of what 'hardcore' means. The positive hardcore is much harder than the negative hardcore. Negative hardcore is the easy way out. Going round shooting brothers, beating them down – that don't make you hard. Gangsta rap is street, but political rap is a level above that, because once you understand the streets then you're political. Gangsta rap has lots of good stories, but it doesn't understand the structure behind those stories. If you don't understand the situation, you're gonna end up victimised by it."

It's ironic that Chuck would go after "negative hardcore" and "gangsta rap" at a time when he was friends with Ice Cube, who had helped popularise the genre with N.W.A. (To be fair, Cube had left the band by the time they put out their sexist, wildly violent sophomore release, *Niggaz 4 Life*, which dropped about five months before *Apocalypse 91*.) And soon Dre would also exit N.W.A., putting out *The Chronic* the following year, sending gangster rap into the mainstream. 'Lost At Birth' ends by proclaiming "Hardcore will never die!" but one assumes that Chuck had no idea that his vision of "positive hardcore" – socially conscious political rap – was about to be shown the door.

In that light, *Apocalypse 91* takes on an extra level of poignancy. It's the final terrific salvo from an era that didn't realise its time was ending. But the album itself also suggests the cracks beginning to form in the foundation of one of hip-hop's grandest bands. You could hear it a little bit in the music, but it was even clearer in the liner notes.

'Lost At Birth', like many of the *Apocalypse 91* tracks, was credited to, among others, Gary G-Wiz. Born Gary Rinaldo, Gary G-Wiz had been part of the PE sphere since the days of *Nation Of Millions*. A beat-maker, he started out deejaying East Coast parties in the early eighties before becoming a protégé of Hank Shocklee. "I was listening to Run-D.M.C. and groups that were breaking down barriers, bringing rap music to the forefront," he told *Billboard* in 1998 of his early musical days. In a 2011 interview that appeared on *RAPstation*, he added, "Once [Run-D.M.C.] put on [Lee jeans] and Adidas I could relate. Before that I was playing drums and played to everything on MTV. Deejaying was a natural progression into producing, though. Early production was beats I made for people around the way to rhyme to. I'd make a beat and then scratch on it and of course for that time period they primarily rhymed about the DJ anyway, so it all worked."

After years of hanging around the Bomb Squad, Gary piqued Chuck's interest with a set of beats he was working on. "One day Chuck comes through and says, 'Yo man, I'm kinda liking what you're doing out here, give me a tape,'" Gary recalled to PE biographer Russell Myrie. But because Hank and Chuck were feuding, Gary was concerned about angering or getting in the middle of the two Public Enemy principals. "Hank said it was cool," Gary recalled, "and so I said, 'Yo Chuck, here's your tape.' Chuck was like, 'Yo man, I could make an EP off this easy.'"

Initially, the plan was to put out an EP called *Afraid Of The Dark*. "I intentionally wasn't planning to release an album for a little while," Chuck wrote in *Lyrics Of A Rap Revolutionary*, "but we came up with the cuts and boom, we had an album. I guess it was what you can call a bit of artist momentum. There really wasn't any grandiose plan for this album, sorta written, recorded, and done on the run."

Apocalypse 91 also reflected a conscious choice on Chuck's part not to duplicate *Fear Of A Black Planet*, which he said "burned my brains out. Not so much the recording process, but the preparation beforehand. More than a hundred tapes of speeches, music bits, as well as research books, and the arrangements of pages and pages of lyrics."

But the decision for a more stripped-down sound might have also been prompted by other factors. Not only was the Bomb Squad taking a step back from hands-on production – they were listed as executive producers on *Apocalypse 91* – but according to Hank Shocklee, their aesthetic had been dealt a serious, unexpected blow.

In a 2011 piece for *The Quietus* commemorating the album's 20th anniversary, writer Angus Batey recalled a conversation he'd had in 2008 with Shocklee about *Apocalypse 91*'s sound. "There was a couple of things that happened at that time," Shocklee said. "One was, we had . . . I don't wanna say a robbery; but what happened was, as we were coming out of the studio, we had all our discs of every song that we'd been working on for the past four or five years with us, and it got lifted out of the studio. So we were rushed – not just to put [the album] together, but to create it, because once you lose all your data, it's very difficult to get that data back. I mean, you may get some of it back, but you'll never get the complete set. You won't even know what the complete set is, because there's data in there you didn't really know you had. So when we lost all our material, that was like a funeral for me, man. That was a very, very dark time, and it kinda stunted our growth. We never really recovered after that. We was on a roll – I was on a roll; and to lose that material set me back so hard."

Additionally, Shocklee had felt that the group had gone as far as they could. Speaking at a Seattle music conference in 2005, he admitted, "I don't know how many of you know the PE story that much, but I wanted the group only to do three albums. The group was supposed to do three albums and then just disband and do other things. Because I think that after three albums you got your message across. And I think that anything after that is kind of like you regurgitating what you've already said. And so, I wasn't involved with the group afterwards when they decided that they wanted to continue and move on and do more records and things of that nature, [and] once again, to each his own. I'm not going to tell somebody, 'Yo, you have got to stop this.' Because everybody gets paid and whatever their case may be. So me, I'm just the kind of person where I'm always looking for the next. What's the next future? What are we doing? What's going on?"

Interestingly, though, Shocklee didn't move on to producing other acts. He mostly just went off and did his own thing, focusing on soundtracks and music-biz administration. "You know something, I never got into the business to be, you know, like a record company or even a typical producer where you're constantly putting out records and products, I only wanted to do what I feel and like," he said in a 2010 interview in *Exberliner*. "And if I have a burning desire to do something, then I go after it. But it was never – even coming out with Public Enemy, you know, I was offered to produce a lot of groups, you know, everywhere from Arrested Development to Soul II Soul and things of that nature, all these groups that were coming out. And if I feel like the group didn't have a message that I wanted to communicate, I didn't really, I didn't have the impetus to, you know, get involved."

The friction within the Bomb Squad was intensified by Eric Sadler's exit from the unit after *Fear Of A Black Planet*. "It got really, really nasty," Sadler confided to Myrie. "And I'm not the type of person who can deal with friends of mine talking about other friends of mine behind their back. . . . You know what, this isn't what you guys sold me on. They told me, 'It's us against the world. It's Public Enemy, we stick together, it's our thing.'"

Little wonder that Chuck had to look elsewhere for *Apocalypse 91*'s musical beds. (Not that he let on to the outside world: when *The Village Voice* asked him if Hank, Keith and Eric were involved in the album, Chuck responded, "Hank is the mastermind of all.") One of the people he reached out to was Kerwin Young, a musician and composer who had started working with the Bomb Squad during *Fear Of A Black Planet*, serving as an assistant and gofer. He also helped out on *AmeriKKKa's Most Wanted*, keeping a log of what samples were used on the Ice Cube album. As Young, a former DJ, recalls, "I would go upstairs [in 510 South

Franklin] to where the Bomb Squad was and I would meet with Keith and let him hear my beats. And then one day, I met Eric, and Eric was, like, 'Hey, man, these guys, they talk about you behind your back, so you stick with me.' So the nights that I didn't DJ – Mondays, Tuesdays, and some Sundays – I would go to 510 and meet Eric. I was just watching him work. He would tell me, 'Push this button, push that button.' By me being around him, I was able to be upstairs a little bit more often when they had sessions."

From being around, Young got the attention of Chuck. "I had worked with Griff [on *Pawns In The Game*], and then I did Eric & Rakim's album *Don't Sweat The Technique*," Young says. "Chuck then invited me to work on *Apocalypse*, which I didn't. At the time, I was upset that the Bomb Squad broke up. I was really close with Eric, and I had a little distrust for Hank. I was young and naïve, and that was my reasoning [for not working on the album]."

So the job fell to Gary. In a separate interview with Ron Maskell of the *This Is Not A Test* podcast from April 2013, Young stated, "If you ask Chuck, Chuck will tell you that Gary saved the whole situation by taking the helm and doing *Apocalypse*." The album's production would be credited to the Imperial Grand Ministers of Funk, which consisted of Stuart Robertz, Cerwin (C-Dawg) Depper, Gary G-Wiz and a person simply identified as "The JBL". Chuck D later acknowledged that those names, except for Gary's, were all made up – a suggestion of Hank's to give off the impression that Public Enemy albums were still being constructed by a collection of beatmakers. "I would've been solely credited with producing the album," Gary told Myrie, "[but] it would've been strange for people and people would've said, 'Well, who the hell is this guy?'"

As Johnny Juice puts it today, "They know that if you think a group of people did this, it's dope. The power of the mind is phenomenal: if you make people think that something is what it is, they think it is what it is." Juice also thinks it's funny that nobody seemed to notice that most of the fictional producers' names on *Apocalypse* are taken from brands of speakers.

Chris Shaw had worked on *Nation Of Millions* and *Fear Of A Black Planet*, and he sensed that the Bomb Squad was radically changing for this new album. "They brought in Gary G-Wiz and a few other people," he says, "and these were guys who really looked up to Hank and do whatever Hank wanted." Although Shaw wasn't around for much of *Apocalypse 91*, he notes that previous PE albums had benefited from the creative friction that came from, say, Hank Shocklee's anti-music stance and Eric Sadler's musical background. By comparison, Shaw's impression of *Apocalypse 91* was that "it was the sort of thing where you're just kind of doing whatever the producer wants you to do, without too much of a fight against what should happen. . . . People should fight, and people should argue their point – like, why a certain part should be a certain way. If a person fights for a part and they're passionate about it, you're like, 'OK, well, if you really feel that strongly about it, let's use it. Maybe I'm not hearing it the way you hear it.' There was a lot of that in Public Enemy, and there was a lot of that in the studio."

The task on *Apocalypse 91*, at least judging from the finished product, was to create an album that had the fury of *Fear Of A Black Planet* without the maddening density. But it couldn't sound like a *Fear* clone. "You have to push the envelope," Gary told *Billboard*. "You don't fuel anything by making more of the same. It's important when to know to go in a new direction." That adventurousness was welcomed by PE's frontman. "Chuck has been one who always goes after the not-so-obvious track," Gary said. "He sees that uniqueness in something and can turn it into something special. He does an incredible job with things that other people couldn't touch."

One such example was the album's superb first single, 'Can't Truss It', which harked back to 'Brothers Gonna Work It Out' and its use of Prince's 'Let's Go Crazy'. But this new track had its own spear-point sharpness. Starting with an excerpt from *Roots* novelist Alex Haley about the history of slave ships, 'Can't Truss It' introduces a piercing, insistent horn and a slow, grumbling beat. "It is almost never my strategy to create with anything specific in mind," Gary once said. "A lot of [*Apocalypse 91's*] music came from a stretch of time when I was just making things and putting them aside. . . . I made the track for 'Can't Truss It' for Bobby Brown. He had just split from his producers and was looking for beats. As Chuck likes to say, people sometimes fumble tracks and Chuck picks them up and runs them in the end zone. Bobby fumbled that one."

"When you're writing an album worth of material you damn sure better come up with a story," Chuck explained in *Lyrics Of A Rap Revolutionary*. 'Can't Truss It', he said, described "what it would be like being captured from Africa and held hostage during the Middle Passage. . . . The track was immediately tribal, and was seized upon as a lock for a leading single for the album. Gary G-Wiz and Hank Shocklee came with a post-Bomb Squad sound, a power-funk in fact."

Beyond its undeniable catchiness, 'Can't Truss It' was a brilliant origin story of sorts for the African-American experience, tracing the people's history from the slave ship to modern-day racism in the work place and in the courts. Chuck's deep bellows paired with Flavor's pointedly angry, bratty asides were harrowing and scolding at the same time, making a compelling case for why blacks can't "love the land". These deeply mixed emotions would be articulated on a larger scale in early 2008 when Democratic presidential hopeful Barack Obama's wife, Michelle, commented that "For the first time in my adult lifetime, I'm really proud of my country . . . not just because Barack has done well, but because I think people are hungry for change. I have been desperate to see our country moving in that direction and just not feeling so alone in my frustration and disappointment." Republican critics used the sound bite to question her patriotism, but it was hard to miss the racial component of her statement: for as much as blacks have wanted to feel as if they're included in the American dream, that desire hasn't always squared with reality.

Fear Of A Black Planet saw the band become masters of the segue – one track seamlessly flowing into the next without interruption or loss of momentum – but *Apocalypse 91* is PE's most impressive in terms of its thematic unity. The same collision of one track into the next exists, but now the group was as focused on constructing an album-length essay, expounding on certain points, offering counter-arguments and eyeing a cohesive intellectual through-line.

Consider this simplified reading of the album. 'Lost At Birth' sets forward the thesis (blacks are doing as much harm to their community as anyone from the outside is), 'Rebirth' positions Chuck as a man who will reluctantly take on the mantle of being a leader to inspire others, while 'Nighttrain' imagines the black community riding the same train, African-

American individuals' fates inescapably intertwined. The song's assertion that being black doesn't alone make you an upstanding member of the community is then followed by a flashback of sorts, as 'Can't Truss It' recalls the American slave trade. But that brief digression from Chuck's central thesis quickly segues into 'I Don't Wanna Be Called Yo Niga', one of Flavor's very best songs. "The word 'nigger' has been a negative one ever since us black people were whipped off them boats," Chuck wrote in *Lyrics Of A Rap Revolutionary*. ". . . I don't like the way our community throws the word around like it's water, because it's a derogatory term." From that inspiration came Flav's takedown of blacks who use the word glibly – but, more accurately, 'Yo Niga' is a condemnation of the word's continued menace in the black community, creating negative associations both within and outside the community. Flavor's impression of a Stepin Fetchit-like buffoon is particularly biting, indicating that he recognises his role as the group's comic relief but also drawing a line between his pointed, self-aware antics and those of self-destructive fools playing into whites' racist attitudes.

'Yo Niga' rides its knowingly blaxploitation guitar riff into a scene-shifting interlude where Chuck D intones over a spare, martial beat that he's tired of "sellout niggas selling drugs", Uncle Toms, and "the projects", which he says is simply "another word for 'experiment'".

"There is nothing ever fabulous about the ghetto," Chuck said in a 2006 interview, "'cause the ghetto is forced upon you. Yes, maybe it's making sugar out of salt. But to me, the 'stay in the ghetto' mentality is to accept what the slave-master has forced upon you. . . . Maybe the world is the ultimate ghetto? But let yourself be exposed to all the [things] that the world has to offer instead of saying [that the ghetto] is only your world, and you can't go no further."

From that interlude's attack on lack of self-sufficiency comes 'How To Kill A Radio Consultant', a blistering, incredibly danceable criticism of white-owned black radio stations that ignore hip-hop in favour of more comforting sounds like Quiet Storm. "I hate Quiet Storm," Chuck told *The Village Voice* in 1991. "My wife loves that shit. I don't understand it. . . . All you fucking do is go to sleep to that shit. . . . I think a beat is better."

The criticism is then pointed outward with 'By The Time I Get To Arizona', an angry retort to the states of Arizona and New Hampshire for refusing to adopt a holiday for Martin Luther King, Jr. Then, it's back to two more community-focused attacks: the need to organise in 'Move!' and the scourge of alcoholism in '1 Million Bottlebags'. 'More News At 11' – and, more forcefully, 'A Letter To The New York Post' – critiques white media's coverage of African-American celebrities but doesn't ignore black media's complacency. In between is 'Shut 'Em Down', a rallying cry to boycott white corporations who profit from black consumers but don't do anything to help those underprivileged communities. 'Get the F--- Outta Dodge' reprimands overly aggressive white police officers before the album ends with 'Bring Tha Noize', a thrash-metal remake of the *Nation Of Millions* standout.

"Black accountability" is how Chuck D described *Apocalypse 91*'s theme to *Spin* at the time. "In [the 1991 indie drama] *Straight Out Of Brooklyn* the guy says, 'Yo, you come in and talk about the white man but you beatin' up Mama.' That's right – fuck that psychoanalytical shit. Yo, you beat down one of your own or kill them or something, you gotta pay the fucking price. Fuck what the white man did. That shit is over; well, not over, but you're just contributing to it. . . . People have to understand that you gonna have to blame yourself too. Blame him all you want, but blame yourself."

Public Enemy had previously shined a light on their community's faults with tracks such as 'Night Of The Living Baseheads' and 'Can't Do Nuttin' For Ya Man'. But *Apocalypse 91*'s attacks were the most unsparing, despairing and frustrated. The album depicted a culture beset on all sides, unable to get out of its own way.

When Chuck spoke with *Deadline*'s Nick Hasted around *Apocalypse 91*'s release, he commented on what he felt were the two Americas. "There's already separation in America," the frontman said. "There's already Apartheid. Blacks live in an area, whites live in an area. The whole key is that you want to develop your people separately. You try to build a nation within a nation, which means there's a tight network of peoples. Our people have to enhance a common bond with each other, and that's what makes a nation within a nation, and that's what makes people strong –

they have to have separate development, specifically geared for the people who are catching the most hell."

But Chuck wasn't advocating a permanent separation from mainstream society. As he put it, "It's good advice for white people, to say, 'Look, this is another way of thinking, and it's all right for you to know, because communication is going to make our relationship better. If you can't communicate or understand where I'm coming from, then there's going to be that problem of you thinking you're superior to me, based on what you've been taught.'"

This is an openhearted, inconclusive way of thinking, recognising that different cultures have their own customs and encouraging each to bring its own strengths to the table. But that attitude didn't excuse the band from the occasional misstep. Preaching the gospel of black self-sufficiency, Chuck D said on *The Arsenio Hall Show* in 1992, "The black woman has been holding up our community for so long. It's time for the black man to [do his part]," a comment that received a loud ovation from the studio audience. But describing the inspiration behind 'Move!' in 2006, Chuck tried to explain the struggles facing black women in language that seemed ignorant and misguided. "A lot of sisters won't talk to a brother that's younger than them," he argued in *Lyrics Of A Rap Revolutionary*, "because brothers that are younger haven't been taught to be a man, so he's less mature mentally by maybe 10 years, even though they may only be three years apart."

Nothing too outlandish about that, but then later he adds, "Homosexuality amongst brothers is another barrier cutting into the numbers [of available men]."

Gay men remained a blind spot in PE's self-sufficiency credo. In his passion for saluting strong, proud black men, Chuck hasn't always been as kind or open-minded about homosexuals. Grilled on this point by *The Village Voice*'s Robert Christgau and Greg Tate in 1991, he sounded defensive and foolish. "I'm not afraid of them," Chuck said about homosexuals. "I'm just not one. I'm not on that side. I'm just not on that side." He later added, "A lot of homosexuals, they call it 'out of the closet'. They use it as a badge. That ain't no badge . . . They use it as a badge, I'm telling you. What the fuck does your sexuality have to do with anything?" It's not that Chuck D is homophobe, but he fails to understand – or at least articulate – why gay men would want to promote their individuality in a manner comparable to the righteous noise of Public Enemy. Chuck's irritation in the *Voice* interview stems from his confusion about why anyone would make such a big deal out of his sexuality. "I don't come out and say, 'Yo, man, I'm a heterosexual.'"

But it's not just Chuck's problem. 'A Letter To The New York Post', one of *Apocalypse 91*'s weaker tracks, spends much of its time verbally assaulting the media, especially the titular newspaper, for reporting on a February 1991 incident in which Flavor Flav was arrested on a charge of domestic violence. He was accused of punching his girlfriend Karren Ross. The previous year, Flavor had spent a night in jail, according to *Jet*, "for failing to pay child support to the mother of his three offspring". Flavor refuted the charge, saying, "I love my kids dearly and I will never, ever, ever let them do without. I've been giving it willingly. I'm a man who takes care of home."

In 'A Letter To The New York Post', Flav also gives a shout-out to notorious tough-guy actor James Cagney, who "beat up on a guy when he found he was a fagney". Hey, it rhymes, but it's a cheap slur, and when Christgau brought it to Chuck's attention, the frontman responded, "Flavor doesn't like homos. And a lot of people say, 'Yo, man, fuck them.'" Later in the conversation, Chuck, clearly tired of the topic said, "Talking about homosexuality is almost like talking about Jews, you know, it's a waste of my fucking time. I don't spend much of my day talking about either."

A year later, Chuck was still trying to downplay Flavor's lyric. "Flavor will pick a word that rhymes for the hell of it," he said to *Spin*'s Vivien Goldman in the fall of 1992. "'Fagney' was just some shit he drummed up to rhyme with Cagney. You can put a lot of science on some Public Enemy songs, but when Flavor does it, you can't put too much science on it."

Of course, 'A Letter To The New York Post' is also distressing because of the song's insistence that the *New York Post* and *Jet*, a black magazine, shouldn't be reporting on Flav's arrest. In *Fight The Power*, Chuck looked back at the track. "In my opinion if you're in the black media, your obligation should be to present your people in the most positive manner possible," he wrote. "I'm not saying you have to paint a pretty picture all of the time, but being that black people are presented as garbage in Western society, I feel that black media has a responsibility to combat that image." As mentioned in the song, Chuck took issue in *Fight The Power* that *Jet* "didn't even do their own homework" when reporting the Flavor story. The Flav quote in the three-paragraph *Jet* story from March 11, 1991, was from an earlier *Newsday* piece: "This is highly embarrassing for me. Something that goes on personally between me and Karren has to go before the public. Am I going to deny the charge? We had a quarrel. I don't think I should be charged with what I'm charged for."

In *The Icon The Memoir*, Flav spends some pages outlining his and Karren's relationship, accusing her of having a temper and being violent. Regarding the '91 incident, Flav claims that she "got right up in my face and smacked me as hard as she could". He smacked her back, which prompted her to call the cops. "[B]y the time they got there, her face was starting to swell. She knew what she was doing, man." Flav goes on to write, "I never hit a woman who didn't make me do it to defend myself. Karren, and most of the other women in my life, had issues with anger where they would start punching and thumping on me."

Public Enemy are on solid ground criticising the way white media can offer a distorted perspective on inner-city life or rap music. That's what the sound bites of out-of-touch white newsmen like Ted Koppel and Dan Rather on hip-hop records are meant to illustrate. But 'A Letter To The New York Post' and the group members' subsequent defenses made PE seem unable to accept their own culpability, blaming an easy outside target rather than looking in the mirror.

To be fair, Flavor does acknowledge in *The Icon The Memoir* that his bandmates were "pissed with me because a domestic violence charge put Public Enemy and everything we stood for in a bad light. Everybody was telling me that I was out of control and that I needed to get myself straight." And in a 2006 interview with *Entertainment Weekly*, Flav would admit, "Quaaludes, angel dust, PCP, cocaine, crack, alcohol, weed – your boy did it all back in the days."

Those inconsistencies between word and deed also show up in the grimly catchy '1 Million Bottlebags', a takedown of alcohol companies' targeting of African-Americans. "Malt liquor has twice as much alcohol content and twice as many residues, that's to say, waste products from regular beer," Chuck told *Melody Maker*. "It's fucked-up beer, with more alcohol. Instead of making people laid-back, it makes them hostile. And it leads to a lot of black-on-black violence in America. [Alcohol companies] have massive campaigns for this shit that are targeted at the black community. Malt liquors are made by the major brewers in this country. When they put their regular beers through the filters, all the excess bullshit they push to the black community. And it's been killing motherfuckers for the longest period."

Chuck was concerned with how black celebrities, such as hip-hop figures, were being used to help promote malt liquor, essentially contributing to the poisoning of the community. That concern turned to anger when a prominent alcohol company, St. Ides, sampled his voice from 'Bring The Noise' for one of its commercials. In August 1991 – less than two months before *Apocalypse 91* dropped – Chuck sued St. Ides' parent company, McKenzie River, for $5 million. A lawyer for Chuck D, Lisa Davis, told *Entertainment Weekly*, "It's unconscionable. He has taken a very strong position against malt liquor, and these ads make him look like a hypocrite."

"Personally, I've never seen the purpose of smoking or drinking," Chuck, a teetotaller, commented to *Melody Maker*. "With other people, it's their prerogative to do what they want. . . . [But] I tell the black community, if you're gonna drink anything, at least drink what white folks drink." He reiterated that point in a separate interview, suggesting of malt liquor, "If this stuff's so great, why don't they sell it to white people?"

But Chuck's antipathy put him at odds with other rappers who were happy to be aligned with St. Ides. That included Ice Cube, a friend of Chuck's, who was featured prominently in the offending ad. Clearly disappointed in his colleague, Chuck D said in a 1991 *Spin* interview, "St. Ides is exploiting Ice Cube just like [actor] Billy Dee [Williams] is exploited by Colt 45," another malt-liquor company.

When asked by *The Village Voice* if he talked to Cube about the matter, Chuck responded, "You know, he said, 'Yo, man, just trying to get out of it.' Trying to stop it, but he's contracted. I said, 'Yo, Cube, hey, there ain't nothing against you, I mean, it's your thing, your guilt thing, but you should have had quality control.' The people at St. Ides said, 'Well, we really respect you Chuck D, you know.' I told 'em, 'I don't respect y'all, fuck y'all.'" But even Flavor had been once offered the company's money to be in an ad. Chuck recalled, "I said, 'Flavor, man, you take that shit, I'll cut you off publicly so fucking bad.'"

The furor over St. Ides was hardly the first indication that hip-hop was not a monolithic, single-minded force. If anything, it reflected an African-American community that (like any other community) has its divisions and infighting. The rifts within Public Enemy – between the Bomb Squad, between the group and Flavor over his behaviour – poignantly but also bracingly mirrored the struggles of most groups taking two steps forward while taking one step back. Chuck D's agony over a need for positive hardcore could be seen in part as a frustration that so many passionate rap groups, all wanting to speak out about the injustice around them, had such varied ways of trying to achieve their seemingly similar goals. This only made the ending of '1 Million Bottlebags' more tragic; the use of a line from *The Godfather* about selling drugs in black communities ("They're animals anyway, so let them lose their souls") indicated that corporate power was amassed to destroy them if they wouldn't unite and stand up against it.

'Shut 'Em Down' addressed that unity forcefully, Chuck D beseeching his brothers and sisters to challenge corporations that exploit black consumers without supporting their communities. As often happens with Chuck, the title came first, inspiring a lyrical theme. "It was winter time," he recalled to *American Songwriter*, "and we were trying to find some new angles. This young cat came up to me and was like, 'Yo, [DJ] Red Alert is shutting down everybody on the radio station. He's shutting them down; he shut 'em down.' I'm like, 'Wow, OK, boom, a song idea.'"

Drawing from that conversation, as well as his appreciation for basketball teams with so-called shutdown defenses, Chuck crafted 'Shut 'Em Down', where he declares his love for Nike but warns that if the company doesn't support the black inner city, boycotts may be necessary. "I really don't believe in boycotts," Chuck wrote in *Lyrics Of A Rap Revolutionary*. "I believe the best way to boycott is to build your own. . . . That's better than having a march, that shit is old, played out and tired." Still, the song brought to light the power that consumers have, voting with their dollars in the same way they do at the ballot box.

Of course, Chuck had to face accusations of hypocrisy when he later lent his voice to a Nike commercial starring Charles Barkley. In *Lyrics Of A Rap Revolutionary*, Chuck defended his involvement by saying that the track he rapped on was a Bomb Squad production "and we couldn't find any other voice that would fit." Additionally, Chuck insisted that he "had gotten a commitment from Charles' people that he and Nike would do some more things in the black community, at least be conscious, which gave me the green light to do it."

Those who would complain are perhaps expecting too much from any one hip-hop band, but it also underlined the difficult position Public Enemy found themselves in: wanting to affect change without contributing to the problems in some way. As on '1 Million Bottlebags', though, 'Shut 'Em Down' ended with an eerie reminder of what African-Americans were facing. Incorporating what appears to be a scripted passage from a fictional Ku Klux Klan member, the song concludes with the voice of a good-ol'-boy Southerner announcing, "I'd like to express our deepest gratitude at the destruction of the inferior nigger race, and I'm especially pleased to report it's destroying itself without our help. To all you gangs, hoodlums, drug-pushers and users, and other worthless niggers killing each other, we'd like to thank y'all for saving us the time, trouble and legality for the final chapter of ridding y'all off the face of the earth. Your solution to our problem is greatly appreciated." The chilling, repugnant racism made PE's message plain: the more that blacks contribute to their own destruction, the easier it is for them unwittingly to create the KKK's fantasy scenario.

Released in October of 1991, *Apocalypse 91* remains the band's highest-charting album, peaking at number four in the US. It was also PE's third in a row to go platinum, doing so in about two months. And although it finished number two on the year's Pazz & Jop poll – the group's second-highest placement – *Apocalypse 91* didn't receive unanimous positive reviews.

Writing in the *Chicago Tribune*, Greg Kot (a fan of the band) observed that the album "is a sonic screamer that climbs in the listener's face from the opening note – a droning police siren – and lets up only occasionally". But despite praising *Apocalypse 91*'s sound and message, he did contend that "several tracks lack venom . . . or rehash tired complaints. . . . Even great bands don't always make great albums, and it's too early to write off Public Enemy. But it looks like it'll have to wait at least until the next album before it can reclaim the hip-hop throne."

The New York Times' Jon Pareles was full of praise but also noted, "Significance can weigh down a band, making songwriters didactic and overly deliberate; look what happened to Bruce Springsteen. Yet significance can also help performers grow up faster and think harder. Both happen on Public Enemy's fourth album." Calling *Apocalypse 91* "a high-level holding action", Pareles declared that the record "shows the competition how to create agitprop that goes beyond sloganeering."

Put simply, the critics felt that an air of familiarity hovered over *Apocalypse 91*, even if it generally was a stunner. No *Nation Of Millions*, no *Fear Of A Black Planet*, but who else in rap was getting close to producing one of those, either? Even Christgau, in his straight-A review of *Apocalypse 91* acknowledged, "Strong top to bottom, it could peak higher." Public Enemy were competing with their own lofty standards.

Even some who worked on *Apocalypse 91* recognised that it was made in a different environment than previous PE records. Chris Shaw, who mixed the police-brutality tale 'Get the F--- Outta Dodge', had been heavily involved on *Nation Of Millions* and *Fear Of A Black Planet*. But because of a busy schedule, he wasn't able to help out on the new record as much. "At that point, the staff at Greene Street had changed," he says, "and so the younger staff did a lot of that record. [*Apocalypse 91*] was done at a bunch of different studios – I just happened to be there when they did that one track, so I just worked on that one. [Public Enemy] were with different producers, different people. There was some friction between the band, the label, their management, and there was some internal things going on between Eric, Keith, and Hank and stuff like that. So that record kind of got a little bit more fractured. I don't think [*Apocalypse 91*] was as continuous a vision as their previous two, if you know what I mean. It was much more disjointed as a result."

The band aggressively planned the album's singles and videos. Which is where Eric Meza came into the picture. A Los Angeles-based video director, he had recently shot clips for N.W.A. ('100 Miles And Runnin'') and Ice Cube ('Dead Homiez') when on a trip to New York he was introduced to Hank Shocklee.

"At first, I didn't know who Hank was," Meza recalls. "Hank said to me, 'You did N.W.A. and Ice Cube? I want to work with you.' At that time, Public Enemy's getting a little more heat – they had worked with Spike and done 'Fight The Power', big record. Hank said, 'We're coming out with a big album, the label is totally [behind] it. They're going to go with these big white directors, but we want to go with a really good black director, and you're the one we want to go with.'"

Months passed without Meza hearing another word from the band. "All of a sudden," the director says, "I get a call from Hank: 'We got a single, we're ready to do this video. The budget is $125,000' – which is, at that time, for a rap video, a lot of money. You know, $125,000 was what you [spent on] really established major acts. Michael Jackson was doing $200,000–$300,000 at the time, and then eventually more. When [a label] was spending $100,000 on a video, that meant it's a serious act."

The video was going to be for 'Can't Truss It'. According to Meza, "Hank says, 'I have this vision of the old slavery days – the plantation days aren't really that different than what happens in today's society. We've gone from one plantation to another plantation, which is the factory worker. [They're] both a form of slavery, more or less, because people can't really progress into becoming everything that the American Dream is.' So, I'm like, 'Say no more.' I got the vision, like that, in my head. I was so inspired from his conversation, I just started writing. Music video treatments are like a page-and-a-half, two-page max. I wrote a five-page treatment. I wrote an outline for the whole video, shot for shot."

Bear in mind, Meza did this without hearing the song. He turned the treatment over to his producer to find the two central locations – a ranch and a factory – and began casting. "I got the music the day before we shot," he says, "which is extremely unusual." The Porsche he was driving at the time didn't have a CD player, so he and a friend, General Jeff of the one-time hip-hop group Rodney-O & Joe Cooley, took the CD to a local Best Buy so that he could hear 'Can't Truss It'. "I'm just praying that the music goes with these visuals that I'm shooting tomorrow," recalls Meza. "And I put it on and it's perfect. It's perfect. I mean, it couldn't be more perfect. After it's done playing, I'm hyped. I turn to General: 'What do you think?' He says, 'They just changed all of rap.'"

The shoot for 'Can't Truss It' was two days, and the narrative drew parallels between America's slavery past and its blue-collar present. The lynching of a slave is mirrored by a Rodney King-like beating of a black driver by police officers. Meza followed his treatment, but Flavor Flav's improvisations were quickly added to the mix. It was the hype man's idea, for instance, in the slavery sequences for him to start grabbing all the money being waved during the auction scenes. But Meza got a sense early that Flav was going to be a wild card. "I sent somebody from the office to pick him up at the airport," Meza says, "so here comes Flavor off the plane dressed like whatever. 'I got to get my bags.' So they're waiting for his bags, and he's dressed with the clock and the hat – he was always in character. Everybody's there waiting for his bag, and Flavor's only bag comes down. It's a basketball. He had checked a basketball."

Not even in a bag?

"Just a basketball. He couldn't walk off the plane with it – you've got to be in baggage claim to get Part Two of the joke." Meza laughs and shakes his head. "It's brilliant."

Pleased with how the shoot for 'Can't Truss It' went, Chuck D turned to Meza after the second day of filming and said, "I guess you're wondering what the next one's going to be? 'By The Time I Get To Arizona'. I'd like to do a video that shows the triumphs of Martin Luther King." Meza responded, "Cool, great, let's do it."

During the *Apocalypse 91* writing stage, at one point the lyrics for 'By The Time I Get To Arizona' appeared with the music for 'Shut 'Em Down'. "I was writing a lot of songs," Chuck told *Spin* in 2011. "My anger was focused on Arizona and New Hampshire refusing to honour the King holiday. It was so much of a smack in the face that I said, 'Well, this needs to be addressed.'" At the time, Public Enemy were touring with the English rock band Sisters of Mercy. "I was coming in the studio, visiting, then heading back on stage in some city," Chuck recalled. The song was written in June '91, built around the groove from 'Two Sisters Of Mystery', a 1974 cut from the funk-rock collective Mandrill. As Chuck later wrote, "The track set a mood like 'Black Steel'. . . . In the song I depict us as taking a plane trip with the S1Ws and we're going to knock these politicians off [who won't support a Martin Luther King, Jr. holiday]."

The title was inspired by the Jimmy Webb tune 'By The Time I Get To Phoenix', which had been covered by, among others, Isaac Hayes. But while working on 'By The Time I Get To Arizona', Chuck demonstrated to Gary G-Wiz how fond he was of the musical left-turn. "I was just thinking, from a musical standpoint, how can we make this more powerful," Gary G-Wiz recalled to *Spin*. "We had already recorded the thing to tape and I remember Chuck saying, 'Let's erase the middle.' It was like, 'Uh-oh.' Then we had this big gap . . . when it first happened, there was no going back, you're just recording over all tracks on a multi-track."

For the song's striking middle section, they turned to a wailing organs-and-screams sample from the Jackson 5 track 'Walk On', which highlighted the sense of bedlam, catharsis and revolution that had been bubbling under in 'Arizona'. At that stage of PE's career, 'By The Time I Get To Arizona' was the closest the group had come to approaching the soul-stirring sound of world-weary gospel. And like 'Black Steel', it had a stunningly cinematic sweep to it. No surprise that Chuck and Hank had clear ideas about the video.

"Hank calls me," Meza says. "'OK, I got this concept. I want it to be like there's this military force – Public Enemy is this crew of assassins. We see them setting up the plot for an assassination, and then they go to Arizona and they assassinate the governor.' Now for me, who's trying to do every video like a small film, this is great. With '100 Miles And Runnin'' they were running from the cops, there were shootouts, so this is great. I said, 'But what Chuck wants to do is show the life of Martin Luther King as a civil rights activist.' And Hank said, 'Can't we do both?'"

In Chuck D's memoir *Fight The Power*, he remembered the video's genesis a little differently: "Eric Meza . . . said to me, 'Do you want to do some shit that's going to be worth something?' I said, 'Bet.' He said, 'We might only get it shown once or twice.' I said, 'Bet. I want some shit that will get the point across on one showing.'"

And so, like with the 'Can't Truss It' video," the clip for 'By The Time I Get To Arizona' crosscut between two eras: in this case, the civil rights movement of the sixties (in black-and-white) and the present day as Public Enemy plan to kill Arizona lawmakers (in colour). There's a grim, procedural quality to the video as the indignities visited upon African-Americans, including an actor playing King, are juxtaposed with the S1Ws training for their bloody vengeance. What was missing, though, was Flavor Flav.

"It's another two-day shoot," recounts Meza, "and the first day was with Public Enemy. Flavor arrives on set and gets a call that his son just came down with some really weird temperature. They've got him submerged in ice, ambulance is on its way and they're probably going to have to do a spinal tap. He's like, 'Get me on the plane, I got to go home.' And that's when you see Flavor become serious – there's no jokes. And then, like, boom, boom, boom, he was gone to the airport. Everything stopped and he was gone."

As far as the shoot went, Flavor's absence wasn't crucial since he doesn't feature prominently on the track. But another obstacle almost derailed the video before Meza even got on set. Hank Shocklee received a worried call from someone at Columbia Records, which oversaw Def Jam. The executive had read the video treatment and was angry about the content. "Hank called me [after speaking to Columbia] and said, 'It was like somebody was calling me to say I just gave them AIDS, man – you just felt this anger coming over the phone.'"

According to Shocklee, the Columbia exec was asking, "Have you read this thing?" And the truth was, Shocklee hadn't. "I was nervous," Meza says. "[The label] told him, 'You better read this because they're about to shoot this. We got to stop this – they can't do this.' So Hank got in the car – he's living in Jersey, got in the car like half-dressed, drives into Manhattan, runs into the office." When Shocklee arrived and read the treatment, he rendered his opinion: "This is exactly what we want to do."

Still, even some people at Meza's production company were worried about the video treatment's violent content. One person told Meza, "You can't do this, this is murder. You're involving murder." Meza's response was, "Well, you know, it's fiction, and in this fiction, somebody's got to die." Another of Meza's partners commented, "People could come and burn down this office." Meza had a unique way of looking at the situation: "I told him, 'If they burn down this office, we'll be doing Michael Jackson videos tomorrow.'" Meza laughs at the memory. "I was surprised the office didn't get burned down and [the partner] did it."

Meza even had a conversation with Russell Simmons about the video. "He says, 'What is this video you just did for Public Enemy?'" remembers Meza. "He said, 'Do you actually shoot the governor of Arizona in this video?' I said, 'No, Russell, we don't shoot the governor – we shoot the senators. We blow up the governor.'" Meza laughs at the distinction between the two forms of assassination in the clip. In fact, the label had been queasy about the idea of even blowing up the governor, but Chuck D told Meza to leave the shot in. ("Let the label scream," Chuck instructed Meza.) Still, Meza was concerned that Simmons might be displeased. As the director recalls, "Russell said, 'Public Enemy is saying they want a Martin Luther King holiday by any means necessary. It's controversy. We don't have a problem with controversy. End of subject.'"

Filmed in December '91, the 'By The Time I Get To Arizona' video aired a total of one time on MTV, in January of the following year, immediately causing a ruckus. "Everybody just jumped on it," Meza says. "I'm getting these calls from Columbia: 'Record sales are [booming]. *The New York Times* is doing a feature on the video. The president is commenting on it. It's going to be on Ted Koppel's show tonight.' And it's, like, 'Damn, over what?'"

Koppel's late-night news show, *Nightline*, hosted Chuck on January 20 to talk about the controversy generated by the video. Specifically, the show's fill-in host, Forrest Sawyer, wanted him to answer the charges others had levelled against the clip and the group. "[The video] shows several of that state's officials being killed for refusing to adopt Martin Luther King's birthday as a state holiday," Sawyer said at the start of the segment. "The group Public Enemy calls it 'a revenge fantasy', but many who gather to honour Dr. King today call it a disgrace to his memory."

Chuck, beamed in from Hamburg, where Public Enemy were touring at the time, asserted that African-Americans were "tired of being disrespected" and that a King holiday "is the least amount of respect blacks can get in this society." As for the charge, levelled by fellow panellist Clarence Page, a columnist for the *Chicago Tribune*, that Public Enemy were simply trying to stir up controversy to provoke sales, Chuck responded, "We sold [albums] to our fanbase right from the first week." He saw the video as a way "to raise dialogue", not send *Apocalypse 91* back up the charts. Page also contended that the clip only perpetuated a cycle of violence, which provoked Chuck to say, "Violence in our neighbour-hoods is caused by a lot of things – lack of education, lack of the right information, lack of self-respect . . . not the amount of violence [in rap videos]."

"I did the interview . . . at five o'clock in the morning because of the six-hour time difference," Chuck recalled in *Fight The Power*. "I was trying to prepare myself, but there really is no way to prepare for an interview at five-thirty in the morning. . . . I wasn't nervous but I may have looked nervous because the hearing device that I had to put in my ear, which was supposed to stay in my ear while I talked, for some reason kept slipping out." As for Page, Chuck's harshest critic on the panel, the frontman wrote, "the last thing somebody truly black wants to do on TV is make themselves look bad in front of another black person. . . . [W]hen I talked to Clarence Page I was cordial. . . . I'm not with arguing on TV with another black person. A lot of times when somebody is on TV who repre-sents rap they come across looking uncivilised, to the point where the only thing a viewer gets out of it is ignorance."

Months before the 'By The Time I Get To Arizona' video hit, Chuck D had been interviewed by *Rolling Stone*'s Alan Light, and he was explain-ing his philosophy about hip-hop and its media representation. "Rap is media control," he said. "Everything else in the world about the black situation comes to you from another perspective." In the article, it was clear Chuck studied how media portrayed rap – and, by extension, his community. Recalling the firestorm that greeted Run-D.M.C. after a riot broke out before one of their shows in 1986, which some in the media used to question rap's moral decency, Chuck said, "That's what really sparked me to get into [studying the media] – if they ever came after me with that shit, I could go head to head."

As a side note, Meza also experienced this negative attitude toward rap and its message. "Rap artists and rap directors, anybody associated with the music were racists," he says about the assumptions made. "I went to an event [in the early nineties]. I was invited by some members of the country club here in Hollywood – big private event. They had this comedian get onstage. He started talking about rap music. He said, 'Every time I hear it, all I hear, no matter what they say, is 'Kill whitey, kill whitey, kill whitey.' And everybody was applauding. [I was] like, 'Get the fuck out of here.'"

Repeatedly, Chuck was questioned about promoting violence, even in a fictional scenario, to salute a leader who had preached non-violence. Appearing on *The Arsenio Hall Show* in 1992, Chuck was asked by Hall how King would have felt about the video. "He would have been upset to see himself get shot, first of all," Chuck responded, to applause from the crowd. "If Dr. King would have dodged the bullets, he would have had a different point of view. . . . Dr. King was one of my heroes. We might not share all of our philosophies as people, 'cause we're all people, and everybody thinks differently . . . but this is the way *I* think."

In November 1992, Arizona voters approved the Martin Luther King holiday. The following year, New Hampshire lawmakers created a state holiday called Civil Rights Day, but it wasn't until 1999 that the state's voters finally approved a Martin Luther King holiday.

Apocalypse 91 had been Chuck D's attempt to address his people while also letting the white establishment know that he hadn't stopped paying attention to the oppression he saw around him. The sentence that appears over and over at the bottom of the album cover is "Justice evolves only after injustice is defeated," a maxim that applies to both white and black.

But for all of Chuck's hope that the album would promote positive, constructive hardcore hip-hop, a musical shift was occurring around him. In the January 23, 1992 issue of *Rolling Stone* that featured Public Enemy, there was also a profile of a new band from Seattle that had started moving into the mainstream. In their own way, Nirvana, like Public Enemy, were rebelling against the status quo, their album *Nevermind* not just bringing grunge to the top of charts but also articulating the anger and alienation that a lot of suburban kids felt. And much like the young bucks coming up in hip-hop to challenge the elder statesman Chuck D, Nirvana's leader, Kurt Cobain, wasn't even 25, practically a kid, although clearly an artist of incredible depth. "The most anti-authority guy in the band is Kurt," Nirvana bassist Krist Novoselic told *Rolling Stone*. "The most anti-authority guy I *know* is Kurt. He'll be the one to walk up to people and scream, 'Why? Why? Why?' . . . Kurt's the guy out there yelling at the top of his lungs."

That yelling would give voice to the new decade's punk spirit, replacing bands like Public Enemy as the primary source of musical protest. But the shifting tides could also be heard on *Apocalypse 91*. The album's final track, 'Bring Tha Noize', was a remake of the *Nation Of Millions* cut, enhanced by the metal riffs of Anthrax, who were name-checked on the original.

"I checked out my first heavy metal show back in '87," Chuck D once said. "Anthrax was on it. We had some common acquaintances . . . I thought they was cool. They had the hip-hop tip, that feel." The rapper noticed that hip-hop and metal shared certain outsider tendencies, and certainly PE's use of Slayer on 'She Watch Channel Zero?!' indicated that they understood how the two sounds could coalesce. And for their part, Anthrax had incorporated rapping into their 1987 cut 'I'm The Man'.

When the possibility of the two bands remaking 'Bring The Noise' first surfaced, Public Enemy were initially sceptical. Speaking to *The Village Voice* in 2011, Anthrax drummer Charlie Benante said, "Chuck wasn't into it at first. Then we sent him over the track and then he said, 'This is slammin'. I gotta be a part of it.'"

"When they suggested it, it bugged me out," Chuck told *NME* in 1991. "It was boggling my mind! I was saying, 'C'mon, you guys! You could handle all the vocals on your own!'"

The two bands went on to tour together, a rap/rock and black/white pairing that was then pretty novel, although not for Public Enemy, who would tour with bands as diverse as Sisters of Mercy and U2. When PE played with the latter in Phoenix after *Apocalypse 91*, the group performed 'Lost At Birth' and then 'By The Time I Get To Arizona' – and then they left the stage as a form of protest for the state's refusal to give King a holiday. "I had the blessings of Bono to do it," Chuck said to *Spin*. "He just punched me in the chest and gave me a pound. The crowd was kinda pissed off. It was a U2 crowd, but there was a large contingent that was really interested in seeing us." But Chuck understood that young white audiences, opened up by 'Walk This Way', were receptive to hip-hop's message. "It's a changing environment," Chuck told *Rolling Stone*, "and we've got to be ready for the change. There's a lot of white kids knowing more about African-American culture now than black kids. Everything that starts in this country usually comes from a black source, then transcends to hip white, mainstream white, then out across the world."

But white kids weren't just getting turned on to rap because of its "exotic" sound. Chuck correctly saw hip-hop and metal also sharing an outsider status. "I think that within the white family structure there's a communication gap growing up," Chuck said during the summer of '91 when Public Enemy and Anthrax were touring. "There's been one in the black family for years. The parents don't know what's going on with their kids. Well, you say, 'Fuck it! I'm making my own rules because I'm not getting enough love, care and concern.'"

That angst in the audience was reflected in the popularity of 'Bring Tha Noize', as well as in the rise of Nirvana and grunge. But it also would spark a rise in rap-rock in the nineties, kick-started by another band, Rage Against the Machine. Releasing their self-titled debut in the fall of 1992, the Los Angeles-based quartet were vocal Public Enemy fans, with lead singer Zack de la Rocha rapping and singing his socially conscious lyrics and guitarist Tom Morello coaxing scratching-like noise from his instrument. "[Their work] was both revolutionary sounds and revolutionary lyrics," Morello said of Public Enemy in 2013. "One thing I've always taken to heart is there's a Chuck D lyric, 'The rhythm, the rebel.' I always took that to mean that the music you're playing can be as revolutionary as any words that you sing on top of it."

Public Enemy's golden age was ending – not that anyone realised it. On the season premiere of *Saturday Night Live* on September 28, 1991, Michael Jordan hosted and Public Enemy was the musical guest. There were also appearances by Spike Lee and Jesse Jackson. The band performed twice, and both songs were electric. On 'Can't Truss It', Chuck D prowled the stage, Flavor Flav gyrated with a live-wire energy and the S1Ws moved with martial precision, the most touching, stirring moment coming when Chuck and Flav joined hands and moved in unison, singing their lyrics back and forth at each other, a show of unity that belied some of the behind-the-scenes friction. Then for their second song, Chuck D first asked for three seconds of silence to honour Miles Davis, who had died earlier that day. "Without him, there would be no us," he said, and then the band kicked into 'Bring The Noise'.

Three years after its initial release, the song already sounded like a classic, and with Public Enemy performing it on *Saturday Night Live* in New York City, there was a homecoming feel to the proceedings – not to mention further proof that rap was successful in removing its stigma as a fad, or an art form that couldn't slay live. In that moment, as Chuck growled and Flav freaked, Public Enemy were producing the most amazing music out there. At that moment, they seemed like America's greatest band.

CHAPTER SIX

"THIS is not an album."

In the liner notes for *Greatest Misses*, Public Enemy's 1992 sorta follow-up to *Apocalypse 91*, those five words appear. It wasn't a slice of postmodern head-trip, their equivalent of René Magritte's painting *The Treachery Of Images* ("This is not a pipe"). It was Chuck being honest about how the compilation of new tracks and remixes of old songs should be perceived.

"The record label wanted us to do a greatest hits album," he recalled in *Lyrics Of A Rap Revolutionary*, "and the way that I am, I'm one of those people who if you tell me to go left I'll go right." Chuck thought it was too early in PE's career to think about such a retrospective, so he decided to go another way. "[W]e had some tunes laying around and I wanted to remix records that were not hits, just to be different, just to be stubborn," he wrote. "We decided to come up with an anti-concept record."

Public Enemy may have been celebrated for their taut, engrossing albums, but *Greatest Misses* seemed oddly disjointed, lacking the anger and urgency that had powered the band's earlier highlights. But that was also the point. "This is not an album" was Chuck's way of suggesting that fans shouldn't think of *Greatest Misses* as a proper PE joint but, rather, a digression or even a side project. Its first half was devoted to unheard tracks, while its second half focused on remixes of songs that, notably, weren't radio smashes the first time around. Calling the album *Greatest Misses* wasn't false modesty: Chuck seemed to be indicating that we should think of it as a mere pit stop so the band could refuel before the next salvo.

Unfortunately for him, some reviewers used *Greatest Misses* as an opportunity to slag off the band. Writing in *Spin*, critic Danyel Smith used most of her word count to complain about *Apocalypse 91*, writing, "The empire that promised the apocalypse delivered a few well-lobbed, grenade-like distractions instead." She opened her review with: "I'm wondering if it's true what they're saying: that Public Enemy is falling off big time, fell off with 'Bring Tha Noize' and the whole Anthrax collaboration. I'm wondering if it's true that PE is rapidly losing its black audience because brothers and sisters are thinking that if PE's rhetoric is so thrilling and accessible to greater Caucasian America, then maybe PE's shit is just wack." Finally, Smith turned to *Greatest Misses*, an album that, the writer opined, "beg[s] the question, 'Why?' Why is it an album? Why the soporific remixes (six!)? Why does not one song from the new side inspire thought beyond the cursory?"

Other reviews were more positive, or at least less fuming, but Smith's seemed to speak to a sense of worry and disappointment that long-time Public Enemy fans felt. "The whole thing is stagy, lacking fire," Smith concluded. "I want my old PE."

★ ★ ★

The year 1992 was one of challenges and transition for Public Enemy – not to mention hip-hop and the African-American community.

It began with the release of PE's 'By The Time I Get To Arizona' video and its immediate fallout. In April, a jury in Los Angeles found police officers not guilty of beating a local man named Rodney King, even though there was videotape evidence of the assault. This verdict set off days of riots that started in a section of the city then known as South Central.

The area, which had also experienced rioting in 1965, became famous in American culture because of its name-check in hip-hop tracks and for being the setting for filmmaker John Singleton's 1991 inner-city black drama *Boyz N The Hood*. Suddenly, what might previously have seemed like alarmist, fictional reports about the violence and poverty of South Central now felt like prescient warnings. In the process, South Central became synonymous in the popular imagination with America's struggles with racial strife and gang violence. This explains why, in 2003, the Los Angeles City Council would vote unanimously to change the name to South Los Angeles. "We believe this action will go a long way toward changing attitudes and how people view this community," Councilwoman Jan Perry, who spearheaded the measure, explained at the time.

In such an environment, gangster rap acts like N.W.A., Ice Cube and Ice-T were given more respect from news outlets that may have previously dismissed the music's violent content.

Reflecting back on the riots from the perspective of 20 years, Ice Cube told *TheGrio*'s Courtney Garcia, "You could feel the tension, could feel the heat in the community. Feel people getting fed up. You know? The police really had carte blanche in our neighbourhoods till [N.W.A.] did the song 'Fuck Tha Police', then people really started to actually look at what they were doing. And then the Rodney King incident came out . . . we had been talking about this all along, that it was happening."

Not surprisingly, gangster rap's West Coast sound was imbued with a perceived urgency and authenticity in the aftermath of the riot. Dr. Dre, Cube's former bandmate in N.W.A., went solo and released *The Chronic* at the end of '92, capitalising on the era's sense of menace by popularising a steely gangster-rap aesthetic through hit singles like 'Nuthin' But A 'G' Thang'. This wasn't the fiery rhetoric of Public Enemy, though: these were remorseless first-person narratives that felt like reports from the front line of minority oppression and black-on-black crime. If Chuck D hated the word "projects", albums like *The Chronic* gave the ghetto a grim, romantic, cinematic grandeur that made the inner city feel like the Wild Wild West.

At the same time, though, there was a rise in hip-hop music that preferred an intelligent, more introspective form of self-expression. Neneh Cherry followed up her acclaimed 1989 album *Raw Like Sushi* (and its gold-certified single 'Buffalo Stance') with the distinctive, searching hip-hop of 1992's *Homebrew*, a personal collection of songs about love, commitment and motherhood. In August of that year, Black Sheep performed on *The Tonight Show*, becoming the first rap act to play the late-night institution. Also in '92, the musically diverse collective Basehead put out *Play With Toys*, which combined rap, funk and even honky-tonk. Beastie Boys moved away from the sample-rich *Paul's Boutique* to return to their punk roots for the instrument-laden *Check Your Head*. And most prominently, an Atlanta band called Arrested Development released *3 Years, 5 Months And 2 Days In The Life Of* . . ., which preached social consciousness, gender equality and an end to the worship of gangster culture. Tellingly, the album title referred to the length of time it took the group, led by the charismatic vocalist Speech, to land a record contract – no doubt an unsubtle commentary on the struggles that positive, articulate hip-hop faced in the gangster-rap era.

Electric, diverse, exciting and idiosyncratic, these progressive '92 albums suggested that the musical map wasn't ruled alone by gangster rap, but it didn't suggest where Public Enemy fit in. They weren't gangsters, but they also didn't have the kaleidoscopic musical flair of a group like Basehead.

But Public Enemy weren't just facing a changing musical landscape. In May of that year, band associate Sister Souljah, who appeared on 'By The Time I Get To Arizona' and was identified in the *Apocalypse 91* credits as "Sister of Instruction/Director of Attitude", became a media sensation for some unfortunate comments. Speaking to *Washington Post* reporter David Mills, the same man who interviewed Professor Griff, Souljah was promoting her solo album, *360 Degrees Of Power*, and she was talking about the riots. "Rodney King is only a symbol of a million other black men that have been beaten – brutalised by the police – who didn't have what we thought was the benefit of having it on videotape," she said. "Rodney King is only a symbol of a criminal justice system that leaves 25 percent of [young] African men in this country in prison or under court supervision." When Mills said that watching the riots on television only strengthened a collective belief that the police are essential to protect the world from criminals, she responded, "Black people from the underclass and the so-called lower class do not respect the institutions of white America. Which is why you can cart out as many black people on television as you want to tell [them] that was stupid. But they don't care what you say. You don't care about their lives, haven't added anything to the quality of their lives. And then [you] expect them to respond to your opinions, which mean absolutely nothing? Why would they?"

But it was the next moment that changed Souljah's life forever. Mills asked if it was wise for people to riot, and she said, "Yeah, it was wise. I mean, if black people kill black people every day, why not have a week and kill white people? You understand what I'm saying?"

Few did, and it became part of the conversation in that year's presidential election. During an event in June in Washington, D.C., presidential hopeful Bill Clinton criticised Jesse Jackson's Rainbow Coalition for hosting an event where Souljah appeared. "I defend her right to express herself through music," Clinton said, "but her comments before and after [the] Los Angeles [riots] were filled with the kind of hatred that you do not honour." He then quoted her Mills interview, as well as comments she made the previous year about never meeting "any good white people". "I know she is a young person," Clinton continued, "but she has a big influence on a lot of people. . . . We all make mistakes and sometimes we're not as sensitive as we ought to be. And we have an obligation, all of us, to call attention to prejudice wherever we see it. . . . We can't get anywhere in this country pointing the finger at one another across racial lines."

In truth, both were speaking a truth. Sister Souljah was expressing the frustration of blacks who believed they couldn't trust white Americans. Bill Clinton was expressing the notion that fostering racial division would only exacerbate the problem. But Clinton's comments created a piece of political gamesmanship subsequently referred to as "a Sister Souljah moment", which is when a candidate publicly rebukes a position held by his or her party's extreme wing. The media would use the phrase repeatedly in the early 2010s in reference to the Republican Party's internal wrestling with the deeply conservative Tea Party faction inside its ranks. In 2013, *The Washington Post*'s Chris Cillizza wrote a story entitled "Do Republicans need a 'Sister Souljah' moment?" (One wonders if Cillizza knew that his newspaper was crucial in inventing that terminology.)

Sister Souljah, who was born Lisa Williamson, told *Spin* in the fall of '92, "I think [Clinton's] intention was to make me into a Willie Horton, a campaign issue, a black monster that would scare the white population . . . to the polls." Horton was a criminal who, while out of prison in the mid-eighties as part of a Massachusetts furlough programme, raped a woman. During the '88 presidential election, George H.W. Bush used the Horton case to attack his opponent, Massachusetts governor Michael Dukakis, and paint him as soft on crime. "I am *not* Willie Horton," Souljah said. "Clinton never realised that I'm a strong, independent black woman who would fight him and expose him for the idiot that he is."

Souljah wasn't alone in being criticised that year: Ice-T's metal side project Body Count released a song called 'Cop Killer' that drew protests from police organisations and conservative actor Charlton Heston. Weary of the controversy, Ice-T's label pulled the album and removed the offending track before reissuing it. Asked by *Spin* if her label had given her any problems because of her comments, Souljah responded, "Well, Sony is a white-run corporation that is owned by Japanese people. Sister Souljah's album, *360 Degrees Of Power*, alters the fabric of white society and the thought processes about the fabric of white society. So there has been no shipment of additional records or attempt to elevate me to a higher level by Sony. Because, clearly, they're seen as threatened in their way of life, threatened as any white person in America who sees somebody revealing the practices that they use every day to control and exploit African and Latino people."

The Souljah controversy, paired with the less-than-monumental *Greatest Misses*, couldn't help but give off an impression that Public Enemy weren't at the top of their game, producing so-so music and sideswiped by internal issues. Seen as a leader in the black community, Chuck wouldn't declare who he was going to vote for in that year's presidential election, presumably in part because of Clinton's securing of the Democratic Party's nomination. "I'm not telling," he said in that same issue of *Spin* in a separate interview when queried about whether he'd vote. "I can't tell you right now. I can only vote when I'm confident. . . . This year, voting is making more sense to me locally." Speaking about the country as a whole, Chuck said, "White people's biggest fear is a race riot situation, and black people feel that they have nothing to lose."

A few years later, he revealed that in the 1992 presidential election he wrote in former football star Jim Brown's name as his choice. That didn't surprise anyone who had heard the opening cut from *Greatest Misses*. On the horn-tinged 'Tie Goes To The Runner', which touches on the LA riots and the forthcoming presidential election, Chuck declared "Our blood from the bullet/Not ballot I vote for Jim Brown." The song lacked the headlong rush of PE's usual album openers, and other new cuts felt like the leftovers that they probably were. But 'Hazy Shade Of Criminal', powered by its repetition of the robotic phrase "rebel bass", rode a tight, minimalist groove to question the inequality of treatment for different criminals, wondering why a murderer and rapist like Jeffrey Dahmer was allowed into court without handcuffs while boxer Mike Tyson was in lockdown in Indiana because of a rape charge.

To drive home the point, Chuck D released the 'Hazy Shade Of Criminal' 12-inch with a photo from the thirties of two black men hanging from a tree while a large white crowd looks on. The picture was from Indiana, the same state that tried the Tyson case. "My mother had a book in our house called *The Movement*, and that picture was on the third page," Chuck explained in *Fight The Power*. "I was always shocked when I would look through that book as a child. It's an image that has stuck with me ever since."

Discussing the song on *The Arsenio Hall Show*, Chuck said that he didn't want to talk about the specifics of the case but that "the Indiana jury was like, 'Well, let's get this nigger. . . . We've got a prime opportunity, he's between a rock and a hard place. We gonna get him no matter what.' . . . The whole thing of getting Mike Tyson happened to be bigger than the actual case." As for equating the lynchings with the Tyson case, Chuck argued, "So many brothers and sisters is hanging by the rope of a justice system that's been corrupt from its root, people ain't even second-guessing it."

Greatest Misses was certified gold in November shortly after Clinton was elected America's 42nd president. But the record exposed tension between the band and their label. Deriding what he called Def Jam's "trendiness, cliquishness, and bullshit" about the project, Chuck wrote in *Fight The Power*, "That was the beginning of my drama and problems with Def Jam, because it was once a company that was innovative and transcended the form of hip-hop. When they started following other trends is when I started not wanting to be a part of that camp any more."

This wasn't much revealed in the press, though, unless you read between the lines. When *Spin* asked Chuck and Hank Shocklee about when PE's contract with Def Jam ended, Shocklee declared, "We're in it for life!" Chuck added, "We're one of the builders of that whole place . . . It's the house that LL built and that we put electric fixtures to."

Those tensions, along with others, would only continue as the band prepared for their official follow-up to *Apocalypse 91*. But like *Greatest Misses*, their next record didn't satisfy critics. And PE paid for it.

★ ★ ★

It wasn't that Chuck hadn't warned us. In his 1992 interview with *Rolling Stone*, the frontman said of *Apocalypse 91*, "This one isn't as dense [as *Fear Of A Black Planet*], as creative soundwise as the last. The next one is probably going to be some crazy, very experimental, gone shit."

Muse Sick-N-Hour Mess Age was a defiant change-up after the knuckle-busting sweep of *Fear* or *Nation Of Millions*. "Chuck wanted a live album," remembers Kerwin Young, who was one of the crucial contributors to *Muse Sick* alongside Gary G-Wiz and others. "He wanted live instruments, he wanted a live drummer. I brought my bass in and played on some cuts. Chuck put out a call for producers. Larry Walford responded. [Producer] Easy Mo Bee, that was the first time he worked with Public Enemy. Working with Chuck, we went through a lot of audio samples from the Stax collection, some from Richard Pryor and Eddie Murphy's movie *Harlem Nights*. Chuck wanted it to be a narrative thing. We got sound bites from a civil rights documentary. He mapped it all out. Every project Chuck ever did, he kept this huge sketchbook. He would sketch out every song: the lyrics, the format of the song, the structure. When he's in the booth doing vocals, you're in the control room with the schematic of the whole song. We also had the schematic for the whole album, how he wants to piece it together."

"[W]ith the Bomb Squad . . . we developed techniques with machines and live elements," Chuck D said in a 1994 interview with *Mixmag*, sounding more like a band leader than a rapper. "Now it's more recruitment of people that have pretty much developed their own musical standards and techniques. I pick and choose the most innovative things and arrange it. As chief lyricist and arranger of this particular group, I will pick alternative stuff. I'm usually the guy that would pick stuff that no one would pick."

Muse Sick didn't pioneer hip-hop's move away from samples to live instruments. Vernon Reid had played on *Yo! Bum Rush The Show* and instrumentalists popped up on *Apocalypse 91*. And two years before *Muse Sick*'s release, the pop-rap superstar Hammer followed up his enormously successful *Please Hammer Don't Hurt 'Em* – which featured the 'Super Freak'-biting mega-hit 'U Can't Touch This' – with *Too Legit To Quit*, which eschewed recognisable samples for a funk-band feel. But Chuck D's instinct to embrace the live-in-the-studio feel was shared by Young, who had grown up as a musician utilising samples but had tired of them by the early nineties.

"1994 was a turning point to where Chuck wanted to go," Young says. "And it was also a turning point where I wanted to go in music. That same year, I was starting to get away from using samples. I was using more live instruments, I started composing. Where Chuck was going, we were on the same page. We had a conversation one day, and he asked me, how do I envision the future of music? I said these exact words: 'I see the things that are existing now are gonna die. What'll be the new innovation is getting back to live instruments.' Chuck just looked at me and didn't say nothing. We're both happy that we made that choice at that same time."

"We wanted to borrow from soul, blues, gospel and rock'n'roll elements and blend them into something we can call our own," Chuck explained to *Time* around the album's release. "And make it faster."

Of course, the move was also precipitated by the crackdown on sampling. Around 2002, Chuck D and Hank Shocklee spoke with *Stay Free!* about the challenges they would have faced if they tried to make *It Takes A Nation Of Millions* in the current environment. "It would just be very, very costly," Shocklee said. "The first thing that was starting to happen by the late eighties was that the people were doing buyouts. You could have a buyout – meaning you could purchase the rights to sample a sound – for around $1,500. Then it started creeping up to $3,000, $3,500, $5,000, $7,500. Then they threw in this thing called rollover rates. If your rollover rate is every 100,000 units, then for every 100,000 units you sell, you have to pay an additional $7,500. A record that sells two million copies would kick that cost up 20 times. Now you're looking at one song costing you more than half of what you would make on your album." He also explained the difference between the two types of copyright: publishing and master recording. "The publishing copyright is of the written music, the song structure," Shocklee said. "And the master recording is the song as it is played on a particular recording. Sampling violates both of these copyrights. Whereas if I record my own version of someone else's song, I only have to pay the publishing copyright. When you violate the master recording, the money just goes to the record company."

Chuck added, "Copyright laws pretty much led people like Dr. Dre to replay the sounds that were on records, then sample musicians imitating those records. . . . Dr. Dre changed things when he did *The Chronic* and took something like Leon Haywood's 'I Want'a Do Something Freaky To You' and revamped it in his own way [for 'Nuthin' But A 'G' Thang'] but basically kept the rhythm and instrumental hook intact. It's easier to sample a groove than it is to create a whole new collage. That entire collage element is out the window."

In the post-collage era, *Nation Of Millions* or *Paul's Boutique* would be too cost-prohibitive to consider. In their 2011 book, *Creative License: The Law And Culture Of Digital Sampling*, authors Kembrew McLeod and Peter DiCola explain that an album like *Fear Of A Black Planet*, in the modern era of sample clearance and royalty payouts, would actually lose Public Enemy more money the more successful the record was. "The prices for all of the samples – multiple samples on each track – simply exceed the artist's piece of the recording-revenue pie," they wrote. "Public Enemy would lose an estimated $4.47 per copy sold. . . . The total amount of debt incurred for releasing [*Black Planet*] . . . would be almost $6.8 million." For what it's worth, using the same estimates, McLeod and DiCola deduced that *Paul's Boutique* would have created almost $20 million of debt for Beastie Boys.

Not only did copyright laws put the kibosh on rampant sampling, it also made those earlier hip-hop songs difficult to incorporate into later tracks. As McLeod explained to *The Atlantic* in 2011, "If you wanted to sample, say, 'Fight The Power' by Public Enemy – well, that song contains 20 samples. You'd have to get permission from Def Jam, which owns the sound recording rights, and then Public Enemy's song publisher. Then you'd have to go to the other 20 song publishers and get permission to use the song – it creates kind of a domino effect. This licensing logjam is only going to get worse and worse and worse as people increasingly sample the recent past, since that recent past is already a collage. It just becomes impossible to do all these clearances."

Consequently, a new kind of paperwork started coming into the recording studio: the sample-clearance form. "Back in '93 or '94," engineer/producer Chris Shaw remembers, "[those forms] became *de rigueur*, even with rock bands or any band that had a sampler in it. That happened after lawsuits started coming down fast and furious; everyone started making sure they had documentation. It's now standard operating procedure: I sign a document that says, 'I haven't contributed any samples to this record.' It's so if the label gets sued, they can throw all the blame on me."

Earlier Public Enemy albums had revolved around a singular thematic purpose: *Apocalypse 91*'s exploration of black self-destruction, *Fear Of A Black Planet*'s dissection of white panic. *Muse Sick* didn't have such an easily definable thesis, revisiting earlier tropes while also moving into new lyrical terrain. But what stood out at the time – and what certainly stands out now – about the album is its bitter resignation. Anger and hope put in appearances on *Muse Sick*, but the songs often bubble over with a sense of weary despair.

Surrounded by two bottles of malt liquor, a Ku Klux Klan member and a vindictive-looking white politician meant to resemble former Louisiana House of Representative member David Duke, who was previously a Grand Wizard in the KKK, the album cover's central figure, a skeleton, has a gun pointed at his own head. "The album cover explains the state of the black situation when the album was released," Chuck would later say. The figures behind the skeleton were "laughing because we're destroying ourselves".

In this way, *Muse Sick* was a spiritual cousin to *Apocalypse 91*, but Chuck's world view had been shaped by another of 1992's most crucial moments, at least for him personally. In December of that year, Chuck and Flavor took their first trip to Africa. Chuck devotes a chapter in his memoir to the experience, and it's one of the most affecting passages in *Fight The Power*. Visiting Egypt, Ghana and Nigeria had a profound effect on the frontman. "Going to Africa made it clear to me that we as a people, around the diaspora, have been oppressed and exploited to the benefit of European countries and their people," he wrote. The group went to holding cells for Africans who were sent to America as slaves. They played in front of 50,000 people. And Chuck was struck by a continent that didn't seem to have much control over its future.

"Today Africa is heavily dependent on other countries for technology, investment capital, and physical and human capital," he wrote, later adding, "African resources . . . have been drained away from Africa for the express benefit and enrichment of other parts of the world." Chuck saw in Africa the same struggles he saw in the African-American community back home. "The bitter part of Africa was seeing the exploitation, and all the forces that were in Africa to keep it from being what it could really be. . . . In America as well as Africa and every place on the planet where black people exist, we must realise that we have to save ourselves and stop relying on other people to come up with great answers for us. We have to save ourselves."

So when it came time to approach *Muse Sick*, Chuck D decided on a very loose concept-album approach, imagining that the songs were being beamed to the listener from the year 1999. "In this future," Chuck wrote in the album's liner notes, "'ex'-Klan leaders sway the public and become President. Europe and America join in brotherhood, and refine their racist grip over the so-called 'third world'." Environmental catastrophes run rampant across the globe, killer plagues are commonplace, but "people continue to be brainwashed, thinking that things are better than ever, because white nostalgia has become an easily acquired mind drug".

It was a doomsday scenario with no romantic fatalism attached. Little wonder that *Muse Sick* sounded so grim and desperate, even its pun-filled title tortuous and laboured rather than stirring or clever. A nod to the O'Jays' seventies hit 'Message In Our Music', the title *Muse Sick-N-Hour Mess Age* encapsulated Chuck's belief that he was living in calamitous times, hoping his songs could provoke change. It's worth noting this verse in the original song: "We wanna look around / In our neighbourhoods / Get your information / From this means of communication." But the bleakness of the material, no matter the warmth that the live instruments brought to the proceedings, suggested that we'd already reached a point of no return.

Perhaps Chuck knew that he was going to deliver the band's most divisive album. When *Muse Sick* begins, we hear the crackle of a needle touching vinyl, a conscious nod to the album's throwback sound. But if you rewound the CD, you'd stumble upon a hidden track. Known as 'Ferocious Soul', the song finds Chuck growling for 90 seconds over a skeletal drumbeat and disembodied female gospel vocals that sound like eerie ghosts. "This is gonna be some ol' different shit," he warns the listener, and from there he proceeds to let fly with some rather amazing get-off-my-lawn invective. "We are not created by MTV," he brags, later advising that he doesn't want anyone, white or black, "calling me nigger". Dissing blunts and 40s, he closes the track by yelling, "Don't fuck with me!" Gloves off, the official opening track, 'Whole Lotta Love Goin On In The Middle Of Hell' sketches out the album's New Year's Eve 1999 conceit, riding a rollercoaster ruckus of scratching, cowbell, guitar, beats and funky seventies bass. It was comparable to other vertigo-inducing PE openers, with Chuck and Flav punching and jabbing their lyrics, but not quite as memorable as what had come before.

That would be an unfortunate theme throughout *Muse Sick*: songs that paled in comparison to past high-water marks. It wasn't that the songs weren't good – many of them were (and still are) superb. It's that they weren't perceived by the public to be good enough.

In part, that's because *Muse Sick*, like *Yo! Bum Rush The Show*, was an album that began a particular phase in Public Enemy's career. But where *Yo! Bum Rush* was a debut that still fit into recognisable hip-hop styles of the time, *Muse Sick* was exploring its own thing. That learning curve was reflected in Young, who had returned to the fold for *Greatest Misses*, working closely on 'Tie Goes To The Runner'. He ended up mastering the compilation. "It was just myself and the engineer there," Young says. "A class from Columbia University came to observe the session, and here I was, 21 years old, and they're asking me questions. And I was able to answer them, you know? I knew what was happening; I knew what I was doing."

But although he and Chuck agreed on *Muse Sick*'s direction, Young was still a young guy, figuring out things on the fly. "During the project, I was, like, 'Man, this is different,'" he says. "Because we had a drummer, we could tune the drums up and play with some drum samples and tune them to the drums and see what kind of sound I could get. My composition skills at that point weren't the greatest. I was still – well, I'm always a student – but I was learning new things and experimenting."

He was a quick study, though. Young had learned how to mic live instruments working on outside projects, and by following Gary G-Wiz's example, he also figured out how to work with Chuck D in the studio.

"Chuck is a man of many takes," Young says. "He would do 30, 40 takes – no exaggeration. Maybe 40 takes of a verse – one verse – and maybe 25 takes of [just] a few lines. He wants to have the right inflection because he's got that baritone voice. He's completely meticulous about his vocal projection, articulation and intonation. And he's so critical: he's, like, 'Sleek, how'd that sound?' And I'm like, 'It's OK, it could be stronger.' And you do another take, raise it up a notch. And I'm like, 'Man, this guy can go and his voice never tired. Wow, we can actually push him.' When Gary would come in the studio, I saw how Gary and Chuck worked. Gary worked on *Apocalypse* and knew how far he could push Chuck, so I took note of that: 'Chuck has no limit.' In the studio, he's a producer's dream."

Chuck's baritone, of course, dominates *Muse Sick*, but it's a rawer instrument, perhaps in keeping with the tracks' comparably unvarnished sound. What's forgotten amid the power of *Nation Of Millions* and *Fear Of A Black Planet* is how finely sculpted they are as sonic totems. It would be inaccurate to call them "slick" or "polished", but they have a precision that's flawless. If those albums were arena rock of the highest order – and that's a gross simplification, of course – then *Muse Sick* felt closer to punk or grunge, its rough edges left intact. This handmade quality gave the album a shockingly lo-fi, brickbat feel with its call-and-response choruses and spare instrumentation. Tracks like 'What Side You On?' and 'What Kind Of Power We Got?' were rude, intentionally musically crude and accusatory, while a melodic interlude like 'White Heaven/Black Hell' had the smoothed-out sadness of a seventies R&B ballad.

In turn, Chuck sang more in the style of a rock vocalist than a rapper, focusing more on groove and feel rather than tight cadences. On the lead single, the bouncy, infectious 'Give It Up', the frontman bragged, "I just rap and don't sing 'em," but even here on a more traditional hip-hop track there's a strain in his voice, as if he's got no time to worry about stunning wordplay in order to get his message across. "People like to say it's preachy," he once wrote about 'Give It Up', "but that's not what I try to be. . . . [E]ither you say something or you say nothing. . . . I've never measured a persons [*sic*] intelligence by the amount of money they made."

His comments underline one of the song's main messages, which would be *Muse Sick*'s as a whole: the gangster era has to end. "No gangster lyin' / I'd rather diss presidents," he declares on 'Give It Up', planting his flag in a musical environment in which *The Chronic* had helped spawn a rap goldmine and a new approach to hip-hop's lyrical content. In Dre's wake came successful West Coast gangster rap albums from 2Pac, Warren G and Dre protégé Snoop Doggy Dogg. Meanwhile, the East Coast saw acclaimed records from Nas, Wu-Tang Clan and the Notorious B.I.G. History has tended to simplify this rap subgenre, painting all its practitioners as thugs glorifying violence, crime and drugs. History also tends to forget the hip-hop groups of the time who preached social consciousness: not just Arrested Development but also Digable Planets, A Tribe Called Quest and others. But after the ascension of bands like Public Enemy and De La Soul, the flourishing of gangster rap seemed like a coarser, less intellectually stimulating new development.

That's not to discount some ground-breaking classics like *Illmatic* or *Enter The Wu-Tang (36 Chambers)*. But gangster's generally more sensationalistic attitude can be summed up by musician Steve Linsley, who worked on *Yo! Bum Rush The Show*. Recalling his time in the studio on *Yo! Bum Rush*, Linsley says, "There wasn't a lot of that kind of bullshit, which really set [Public Enemy] apart from other rap record recordings. I mean, they were all business. There's a real party culture around recording in rap music. The gangster stuff – I mean in LA, I've worked on records where you're in rooms that were, literally, body-to-body. You're mixing a record or recording in this environment. It's, like, 'Oh my god, I'm mixing a record at the height of the most raucous party.'"

Considering Chuck's trip to Africa and the profound emotions it stirred, one can imagine how frustrated he must have been to return and see that gangster rap was being embraced while his own band's relevance was questioned. In subsequent years, Chuck has made his feelings about gangster rap clear. Speaking in East Liberty, Pennsylvania in 2007, he said,

"Usually, people who do gangster rap aren't from it. . . . If you're rapping now when you used to sell drugs, then you probably weren't good in your former career." In the late nineties, he sued because of the use of his lyric "1 2 3 4 5 6 7 8 9" from 'Shut 'Em Down' in Biggie's 'Ten Crack Commandments', which counted down the crucial rules to live by as a drug dealer.

It wasn't just copyright infringement that was claimed, though; Chuck also sued for defamation. "Chuck D had an excellent reputation for his public support of non-violence and anti-drug-use campaigns throughout the country," the lawsuit said. Additionally, it was asserted that 'Shut 'Em Down' was "not about drugs but rather about empowering young black persons through peaceful non-violent and non-drug using means". The suit was eventually settled, but Public Enemy manager Walter Leaphart insisted that it wasn't the use of 'Shut 'Em Down' that so angered the rapper. "You've got Chuck D doing a count on how to be a better crack dealer," Leaphart said at the time. "And Mr. Chuck is very anti-drugs, as we all know."

Speaking about Biggie to *HipHopDX* in 2012, Chuck said, "I thought he was a good performer. But I think Puffy had a lot to do with that training and developing, and that's something that's overlooked. And when it came down to Big, I think Puffy was just as much of an important figure in his development as Big was with his ability. . . . I rank him high. People said he's the greatest ever, I said only a kid would be fascinated. And I wasn't a kid."

Chuck had been older than his peers from the beginning of Public Enemy. But *Muse Sick* was when he went grumpy-old-man on the competition, for better and for worse. Shouting out James Brown and Sly & the Family Stone, using live instruments and easing up on the sampling, Chuck was defiantly out of step with musical trends, a retrenchment positioned as a kind of thematic purity.

Rather than being "hard", *Muse Sick* was proudly messy. 'Hitler Day', which complained that the celebration of Columbus Day was offensive to blacks, jumped out of the speakers with screams, metal guitars and frenzied scratching – Chuck's so mad he's yelling his lungs out to be heard over the din. 'Race Against Time' had a double meaning, indicating both an urgent countdown and a people's struggle to reverse its tragic history – and in a nod to the Chambers Brothers' '68 hit 'Time Has Come Today', the song careens between slower and faster sections, running the risk of toppling over at any moment. 'Bedlam 13:13', a treatise on environmental peril, rocks and rolls with high-pitched squeals and scratches. According to Young, it was one of *Muse Sick*'s most challenging tracks. "[Co-writer and co-producer] Larry Walford was very meticulous – he was never satisfied with the mix. He was concerned with the drum sounds. We did a few sessions in Queens and then came out to Long Island and did them over. We did a lot of A/B-ing out in his car so he could get that right." And in the two-part 'Live And Undrugged', saxophones and keyboards crash into impassioned background wails and funky live drums, finally ending with Chuck D bellowing his band members' names, the album title and the group's black-and-white moral code: "Right versus wrong / Good versus evil / God versus the devil." This wasn't boasting, though: Chuck's words were desperate, almost out of breath, enunciated as if this was his last, best chance to reach the listener.

But the album's apex was 'So Whatcha Gone Do Now?' Once asked why he never wrote love songs, Chuck replied, "'You're Gonna Get Yours' was my love song, man. It wasn't that that 98 was all there – barely had four wheels, man. But that was my motherfucking shit." But he has also claimed that he views 'So Whatcha Gone Do Now?' as a love song going out to "my brothers out there killing themselves in gang violence". Although the music isn't particularly romantic – the keyboards and drums merge to create an unsettlingly minimalist tone – 'So Whatcha Gone Do Now?' has a noticeably compassionate, melancholy spirit that's rare in the Public Enemy canon.

Starting with a whispered chant "rap, guns, drugs and money", the song despairs of black-on-black violence, gangster rap's glorification of the behaviour, and the industry's exploitation of the musical trend. On an album where Chuck mostly hectored and scolded, 'So Whatcha Gone Do Now?' is where he growls, albeit with palpable sadness lodged in his throat. This wasn't a knockdown anthem like 'Brothers Gonna Work It Out' or 'Fight The Power', but it wasn't meant to be: the news was too grim and the future too bleak to waste time on fiery rhetoric. 'So Whatcha

Gone Do Now?' was never going to halt the rise of gangster rap, but it was Public Enemy's beautiful, principled protest.

The album's rawness also seemed to spark something in Flavor. Less the jester than on previous records, he sounds positively unhinged, covering the Last Poets' spoken-word-with-musical-backing 'White Man's Got A God Complex' for the paranoid, electric 'Godd Complex'. Chuck later complained that Public Enemy didn't get partial writing credit for the new version, which is credited on *Muse Sick* only to original writer Alafia Pudim. "[T]hey took everything, all publishing . . . We thought that was self-centred and greedy," he wrote. "Usually there should be some kind of split or consideration." On 'What Kind of Power We Got?' Flav tears into political callousness toward the poor while Chuck backs up his "main man", supporting Flavor during trying times. Those difficulties were expressed more overtly on 'I Ain't Mad At All', where Flav did, in fact, sound pretty mad, bitching at cops slapping cuffs on him and disrespecting him.

"We booked sessions from 10am to maybe 3pm," Young recalls, "but Flav could only get in there at, like, 11pm. So we'd go from 11pm to three in the morning. . . . The engineer's burnt out, I'm burnt out, and we're only doing ['What Kind Of Power We Got?']. We spent a whole lot of time doing one song, 'cause Flav just kept changing his mind – he wants to do this, he wants to do that." Young laughs. "I'd never worked with him before, so that was a test of my patience. You have to treat him like this is your little brother. He's just energetic: let him get down what he wants, and then help him enhance it. Give him ideas, but allow him to be the creative one. Start piecing his ideas together to help him formulate it. He played everything on that track. I just produced the session and gave him ideas – what works and what may not work."

Asked how it was to be in the studio with Flav, Young says, "I got some Flavor Flav stories, but you know . . ." His voice trails off, as if he's holding something back. Pressed on the topic, Young only responds, "They're not flattering. I may save that for my [autobiography]." Working with Chuck was very different than collaborating with Flavor. "It's all in his head," Young says of Flavor. " 'Hey, man! I've got this song I wanna do!' He had an idea from one of Maceo Parker's tunes, so we just started:

169

he got on the organ and played; he got the drums and played; he got on the bass and played. He brought his children in one night and had them do background vocals. That was great [but], man, one song took, like, three weeks."

Flavor's creative flourishes and rambunctious behaviour were still front and centre. Young fondly tells the story of the day Flavor dropped by the studio and started doing spinouts out on the snow-lined street in his Ferrari. But his legal and addiction problems were also apparent. By '93, he was deep into crack. As Flav writes in *The Icon The Memoir*, Karren's success in gaining full custody of their children "made me not care about getting clean. . . . I was smoking and smoking that crack. That was my escape, man, and I escaped every damn day."

The problems got so serious that, one drugged-out night, he became convinced that his neighbour was secretly housing Karren and the kids. Paranoid, Flavor forced his way into his neighbour's apartment with a gun, desperately searching for his family, and then chased the man down into their complex's crowded lobby. "I don't remember anything other than him backing out of the building," Flavor wrote. "I don't remember firing at him. All I remember after that was me going back upstairs and putting my gun away."

The cops arrived and arrested him. He served three months in prison and when he got out went to Betty Ford. "I been to rehab like four or five times," Flavor mentions in *The Icon The Memoir*, "and none of that shit ever worked for me." The problem, he said, was that once the treatment ended, he would return to the same environment where the problems first happened. "I did the rehab thing, came back home, and started getting high."

And then there was the time Flavor was shooting the 'What Kind Of Power We Got?' video with Eric Meza. "Flavor got arrested on that video," Meza says. "That video wasn't finished."

In the clip, Flavor plays a lot of crazy characters, including a short-order cook, a waitress and a traffic cop. Meza cobbled enough footage to put together the video, but Flav got arrested halfway through the shoot. According to Meza, "It was all bullshit. His kids and the mother came to the set, and there were people who were hanging around who came up and were taking pictures of Flavor and his kids. Flavor's like, 'No, no, don't take pictures of my kid. Don't do that.' And this woman tried to take another, so Flavor hit her camera. She called the cops: 'Flavor Flav assaulted me.'"

Meza says that when the police showed up, he explained what had happened and the cops were sympathetic. "But then one of the cops goes on his computer and said, 'There's a warrant out for Flavor.' We're, like, 'What?!' Flavor said, 'I already went to court for that. That whole thing is settled.' The cop says, 'Yeah, but it's still here. Sorry, we got to take you in. We believe you, but this is the way it goes.' And they took him away in handcuffs."

When the album came out in August of 1994, *Muse Sick* was greeted with the band's most negative reviews to that point. However, it's inaccurate to say that the album was panned across the board. For instance, *Chicago Tribune*'s Greg Kot, who had been a little tepid in his praise of *Apocalypse 91*, was effusive about *Muse Sick*: "In contrast to *Apocalypse '91*, which found Public Enemy straining to fend off the West Coast onslaught of Ice Cube and N.W.A., *Muse Sick* is as bold and bracing as any hip-hop record released this year. Whether the band will regain its position as a cultural force . . . is problematic. But at a time when hip-hop seems to be drowning in gangsta clichés, Chuck D's stentorian baritone sounds more authoritative and high-minded than ever. For every poorly conceived idea – his conspiracy theories sound more malnourished by the album, and his anti-drug preaching rings hollow in the wake of sidekick Flavor Flav's recent legal troubles – there are a half-dozen provocative ones."

But none of the positive reviews that praised the band's evolving sound and continued passion will loom as large as the deafeningly negative review *Rolling Stone* ran in July. Written by hip-hop critic Touré, it opened with this devastating paragraph:

"I guess by now we should be used to watching black heroes die in public. Six years ago, *It Takes A Nation Of Millions To Hold Us Back* revolutionised hip-hop, and Chuck D became a hero. Now the political consciousness he ushered in has been bum-rushed by the shoot-first ethic of gangsta rap. *Muse Sick-N-Hour Mess Age* is his response to that new order, but PE is no longer the force it was. Flavor Flav's public drug problems have destroyed the group's position of being beyond reproach. The absence of producers Eric Sadler and Hank and Keith Shocklee from the Bomb Squad and Chuck's advancing age – being 28 in hip-hop was an asset, being 34 is not – have shoved the group far from the music's creative edge. The result is a poorly conceived, virtually unlistenable album that's as definitive a hip-hop moment as *Nation* was – but for all the wrong reasons."

He pulled no punches from there, declaring Chuck's rhymes weak and accusing the band of attacking their critics rather than focusing on making great music. Touré specifically went after 'I Stand Accused', which includes the lyric "fuck a critic" and suggests that if a critic is murdered, "Guess the crew did it." Musically, it's one of *Muse Sick*'s steeliest cuts, but its bitching tone felt unnecessarily petulant. Sure, some people felt Public Enemy had lost a step by the mid-nineties, but they remained one of the most acclaimed hip-hop units of the time. Most groups would kill to get PE's great press.

Part of the shock of *Rolling Stone*'s two-star pan was that it arrived several weeks before the album's release due to *Muse Sick*'s pushed-back drop date. But the other shock was the magazine's generally respectful tone toward major or popular artists seemed to have flown out the window in this case. The anomaly of the *Muse Sick* takedown was even more apparent when, two years later, *Rolling Stone* was embroiled in controversy when Senior Editor Jim DeRogatis saw his negative review of *Fairweather Johnson*, Hootie & the Blowfish's follow-up to their blockbuster *Cracked Rear View*, get killed in favour of a more positive notice. DeRogatis was soon fired, saying that publisher Jann Wenner is "a fan of bands that sell eight and a half million [albums]".

Touré's review wasn't the only negative one from a major publication: *The Source* also dissed it, a development Chuck predicted in *Muse Sick*'s hidden opening track. But *Muse Sick* was the first all-new Public Enemy album not to end up in the Top 40 of Pazz & Jop's critics poll, landing at number 60. The group hasn't cracked the Top 40 in the poll since.

Despite some good reviews, *Muse Sick* signalled the moment that the culture removed Public Enemy from their high pedestal.

"Good review or bad review, people are going to buy the album when they hear good things popping off of it month by month," Chuck told *The New York Times'* Neil Strauss in September of that year. He then said, "I'll let you in on a little secret. The advance tapes that I issued to critics, I intentionally took bass out of the tapes." Strauss contacted Touré and *The Source's* James Bernard to see if they noticed any reduced bass. Neither critic did. "It was just a bad album," Bernard told Strauss.

Nick Sansano, who worked as a recorder and mix engineer on part of *Muse Sick*, had been around much more often for *Nation Of Millions* and *Fear Of A Black Planet*. Talking about the work on *Muse Sick*, he says, "It was a different thing. There was a new member, Gary G-Wiz, and it was less of Hank, Keith, Chuck and Eric in the studio bouncing around having great ideas and Flavor jumping in and being a foil. There was a workflow energy that was amazing. In conjunction with the studio and the personnel at the [Greene Street] studio and the two rooms going, it was like a little hip-hop Motown in a way. It was a great environment. Then [with *Muse Sick*], it was more straight-up 'We have these new songs, we'd like you to mix them.' It was just a little bit more – I don't want to say 'corporate', that's not the right word – but it was a little less energy, a little less of that environment. It was no less supportive or sincere, but it wasn't that youthful sort of 'We're gonna change the world' energy."

The songs he mixed, including 'Give It Up', were recorded digitally – among the first batch of PE tracks recorded that way, according to Sansano. "The digital system they used was affordable – it was reliable, consistent," he says. "It didn't sound all that great, but it worked. When I got those [recordings], I said, 'My recommendation is the first thing we do is we get out of the digital.' So, even though they recorded everything digital, I literally transferred everything to two reels of analogue tape, to 48-track analogue, and then mixed and processed off of the analogue, because it was too clean. It didn't have all the artifacts of analogue recordings, which change from day to day, because electricity changes from day to day. If you listen to, like, 'Brothers Gonna Work It Out' and then you listen to 'Give It Up', there's a huge difference in everything: in size, in clarity. One's got that kind of frenetic lo-fi aesthetic, as they would call it today. 'Give It Up' is mixed on a really big, fancy Neve console under really nice conditions – alone, quiet – and it kinda sounds that way, you know? I like the song: it's a nice blend of gospel and hip-hop, and it's got a good spirit about it. But it's a different energy."

A diminished critical standing wasn't PE's only problem. In early 1994, Def Jam was in the process of being acquired by Polygram. In *The Men Behind Def Jam*, writer Alex Ogg notes that Russell Simmons was forced to put Def Jam on the market because it was "$17 million in the red", a problem quickly alleviated when PolyGram acquired half the label for $35 million. In an article in *Billboard* from November of that year, the acquisition was announced, with PolyGram head Alain Levy saying, "Def Jam is a vibrant label. I'm looking forward to seeing what they bring to the PolyGram culture by their very presence." In the same piece, Simmons was quoted as saying, "I'm excited about our new relationship with Poly-Gram. The deal process took a long time, but [PolyGram has] demonstrated their commitment, enthusiasm and support."

Simmons had wanted to get Chuck on board early with this acquisition, including the rapper in a meeting with PolyGram early that year. "Russell and [Def Jam executive] Lyor [Cohen] knew that it was important for me to be there in order for them to sell Def Jam as a burgeoning record label to the people who were now bailing them out of the hole," Chuck told writer Stacy Gueraseva for the book *Def Jam, Inc.* After Def Jam and Poly-Gram came together, though, Chuck's relationship with the label brass changed. "Somehow, Russell and Lyor said they didn't have to respect my musical judgment any more, because basically I was over with," Chuck told Gueraseva. "That was the attitude. . . . I knew no one [at PolyGram], no one knew me, and there was a whole different set of rules. It was like being traded to another team."

Speaking with writer Jason Gross in October 2000, Chuck D elaborated on his frustration. "In 1994, when I delivered *Muse Sick-N-Hour Mess Age* . . . it was time for me to leave. One of the things that made we want to leave was the fact that Def Jam went from Sony to PolyGram, they were sold. I thought that Public Enemy and LL Cool J were integral parts of Def Jam's existence and that we at least deserved 2 1/2 points of the deal. We didn't get it and all that talk of us being family was just bullshit. I said, 'Fuck that, I'm outta here. Find me a taxi and execute this contract.'"

Chuck might have also blamed the new label situation for *Muse Sick*'s commercial performance. It did go gold and it's the last PE album to do so. "We all believed in that album," Julie Greenwald, who was Head of Marketing at the time, told Gueraseva. "We spent a lot of money on that project. Like a million-dollar rollout. Put them on a huge promo tour across the country, organised in-stores, all these great things. Their album was coming out, and you didn't want them to get caught in the cold 'cause we were switching companies."

Probably no amount of money would have made a difference. 'Give It Up' became the band's first (and only) single to hit the *Billboard* Top 40, peaking at number 33. And yet *Muse Sick* couldn't escape the stench of being a disappointment, rather than a shift in musical direction.

Not that Chuck cared. Looking back at the album in 2011, he said, "We used a lot of organic sounds. In retrospect it was a strong record. But people have robotic tendencies especially at that time. Just because one style was in, that doesn't mean that Public Enemy had to follow the Pied Piper leading a bunch of children in the river."

And to Chuck's credit, the band's future was embedded within the album, not just in its sound but also in how later collaborators would respond to its risk-taking.

In the summer of 1994, David Snyder had just dropped out of college and was living with his parents in the Midwest, spending most of his free time wondering when the new Public Enemy album would come out. "PE is such an important group to me: to my musical tastes, to my upbringing, to my development as a person," he says today. "With *Muse Sick-N-Hour Mess Age*, I was at the record store weekly to see if it had come in. If I didn't get to the record store, I would ask my friend, 'You going to the record store?' One day, I'm looking through this *Source* magazine, and there was a full-page ad: the PE logo with a silver background and it said, 'July 4th. What Side You On?' I was so excited. I was like, 'Fuck yeah, man! This is so great!'"

The album was delayed until late August, which Snyder discovered when walking into the record store to buy his girlfriend the new Prince disc and realising that *Muse Sick* had come out the same day. "It's Tuesday, August 23, and my girlfriend at the time, it was her birthday," he recalls. "We were going to a blues festival that night, and I wanted to run home and listen to [*Muse Sick*], but I couldn't. I had to change to get ready to take my girlfriend out, and I'm trying to make a dub of it for the ride, but I didn't have time to do it. So I take my girlfriend to dinner, and I'm so excited about [*Muse Sick*] that she's like, 'It's my birthday and all you give a shit about is a PE record.'"

Unlike others who didn't care for *Muse Sick*, though, Snyder flipped for it. "It was fucking great," he said. "It was something that I needed at that point in my life. I got into hip-hop hardcore around '87, '88. I was raised on a lot of different stuff, but hip-hop just really spoke to me. When *The Chronic* came out and changed the face of everything – everyone seemed to be talking about getting high all the time – I was just, like, 'Come on, this is so stupid.' I didn't smoke, I'm allergic to it. [*Muse Sick*] came out and it was a different sound, but Chuck still was doing his own thing, and that really spoke to me. It was, like, 'OK, yeah, it's different, but it's still the same. This is PE. It may sound different, but it's still PE.' [The negative reviews] pissed me off something fierce. I was just like, 'You missed the point.' The Roots were coming out, and they did live drums, but [reviewers were] complaining about a drum solo on 'What Side You On?' Like, what the hell is wrong with you?"

Snyder would be able to share his enthusiasm for Chuck soon enough. Public Enemy fans probably know him better by his musician name C-Doc and for his key contributions to subsequent PE recordings.

But *Muse Sick*'s greatest legacy is probably none of its traditional songs but, instead, a three-minute interlude near the end that consists of an answering machine message.

"We were done with just about everything" on the album, Young remembers, "and Chuck said, 'Hey, I wanna add this.' It was just a segue; it was spur of the moment." It was a voicemail from Harry Allen discussing the shifting media landscape that had been inspired by a 1993 article in *Musician*. "The technology is changing, the way people use information is changing, how they get information," Allen says in the message. "The whole process is going toward decentralisation – that is to say, 'You don't have monopolies on us any more.' . . . What we're talking about ultimately is shifting away from [how] this music is distributed." Allen rambles a bit, but the point is clear: he's touching on how cheaper means of record-making and the ascension of the Internet will cataclysmically alter how the music industry functions. Considering how disillusioned Chuck was with his situation at Def Jam and PolyGram, Allen's words must have hit like a lightning bolt.

"I had a SP-1200 in the studio," Young says. "I just made a programmed beat right there." The resulting track, 'Harry Allen's Interactive Super Highway Phone Call To Chuck D', didn't appear on the back of the CD case with the other song titles, although it was listed in the liner notes. Still, the interlude felt like a hidden track, a light digression, a respite from *Muse Sick*'s dire assaults. Now, it can be heard as a prophecy of what was to come: both for music and for Public Enemy.

CHAPTER SEVEN

O N Saturday, July 15, 1995, Public Enemy were playing the Phoenix Festival in Stratford-upon-Avon, busting through killers like 'Whole Lotta Love Goin On In The Middle Of Hell', 'Welcome To The Terrordome' and 'Bring The Noise'. After wrapping 'Black Steel In The Hour Of Chaos', Chuck D took a minute to address the crowd. He told everyone that there was only one race, the human race, and he introduced himself and his bandmates. But then he said, "This [is] the news. This might be the last performance you ever see [from] us, because it's time to do bigger and better things and take on greater challenges to build a world of hip-hop and rap."

The audience groaned. Chuck then said the band's final show would be in 10 days. "It's time to build hip-hop to be the way other musics are: rock'n'roll, blues, jazz. . . . We took it performance-wise to no level that anybody ever took it before as a group, and we're only joined by Ice Cube and Ice-T as far as cutting into the edge of music history, taking it around the world. So we'd like to thank you for all the years."

The group then launched into 'What Side You On?' and finished the final 40 minutes of their set. When their time was up, Flavor Flav announced he was going to hang out at the festival's bungee-jump spot.

Some might have wondered if Public Enemy were hanging it up. But Chuck just wanted to reconceive the band's live attack. "We did take [a] hiatus between '95 and '97, but that was just off the road, that's all," he told *Antigravity* in 2007. "We just had to figure out a new way to do shows. By tour [number] 36 I'd gotten kinda tired of the whole process, and of not being able to give to the show more than the vinyl could give. We had to step it up."

"I couldn't see no growth in [touring] and something had to change," he commented to PE biographer Russell Myrie. "I had to be away from Public Enemy for a second as far as the touring thing. It was just becoming the same thing and I was trying to figure out, what did I need to do with Public Enemy to be different?"

Meanwhile, Flavor was having more problems. With the group on hiatus, Flavor writes in *The Icon The Memoir*, "Occasionally, I still sold drugs, but not so much selling was happening . . . I was using waaayyy more than I was selling." He bought a motorcycle and almost immediately wrecked it, requiring $4,000 in repairs. Once he got it back, he revved it up to 160 mph in a 35-mile-an-hour zone, smacked into a stopped trash truck and broke his collarbone and arms. If he hadn't been wearing a helmet, he would have been killed.

Chuck used his downtime more productively. To start with, he was now living in Atlanta. "I think it's the best place for black people in this country," Chuck D once said about the city. And with a new base of operations, he sought to diversify himself in the same way that rock artists made themselves visible in the culture through different platforms. Soon, he'd be a staple on the lecture circuit. And he plotted his first solo album.

"I believe in solo projects, but I could never detach myself from Public Enemy because it is me," the frontman said during a 1999 *Yahoo!* online chat. "To detach myself from PE is like taking an arm off, I'm not going to do that. What I tried to prove with my solo project is that you can still be in the group – I still worked with the same people. And I can [enlist] new people to come on and add to the fabric of what we originally created."

Autobiography Of Mistachuck might have felt like a Public Enemy album in some regards – after all, it was anchored by Chuck's bruising voice. But its tenor was different, more monochromatic than a PE release. Flavor Flav didn't appear and, consequently, *Autobiography* didn't have his unpredictable spirit. Chuck's solo album was filled with hard tales unencumbered by comic relief or lightness.

Familiar names like Gary G-Wiz, Larry Walford, Kerwin Young and Eric Sadler lent their production muscle to the project. "We did some work in Long Island and some work in Atlanta, Georgia," Young says. "It was a different process – I was working with just Chuck, and we didn't have a Flav. It was just like doing a PE album, but Chuck wanted a different sound. He wanted more of a soulful sound and some blues – he wanted to tap [into] this different element."

In a *Billboard* interview from August 1996, Chuck described his solo effort as "an extension of PE's agenda. [However, it] is more groove-oriented, more based on feel. Whereas PE was based on taking [creative] chances, this solo record takes less chances, because I don't think a whole lot of heads are ready for a lot of innovation. But yo, I could rock the same grooves anybody else could, but with more power!"

When Flavor Flav incorporated DJ Mr. Magic's diss of Public Enemy near the start of 'Cold Lampin With Flavor', it was a call to arms for the band to assert their dominance. *Autobiography Of Mistachuck* similarly opens with a slam. As the album begins, we hear snippets from a conversation in *Clockers*, Spike Lee's 1995 crime drama, in which some characters are sitting around discussing the rap artists they like. "Chuck D is the bomb," one declares, which draws a sharp rebuke from his pal. "Nigga, get the fuck outta here! Chuck D ain't shit! . . . How the fuck [you] gonna say Chuck D is the hardest rapper? That nigga ain't never shot nobody. . . . I ain't buying no shit that ain't hardcore." The bull session was Lee's way of illustrating how some young black men felt about "positive hip-hop" – Arrested Development was also ridiculed – in an era when criminality was embraced as a sign of being hard. Wu-Tang Clan and 2Pac were held up as rappers worth praising.

Chuck used that conversation as an impetus to launch into 'Mistachuck', a grumbling, soul-tinged putdown of all those who doubted his prowess. Stirring and confident, 'Mistachuck' was the sound of a proud veteran reminding the youngsters about his sizable legacy. On the track, he takes aim at what he calls "Big Willie", a soulless black artist dependent on chasing trends. He continued the attack on 'Free Big Willie', which borrows the melodic line from the Isley Brothers' 'Ain't I Been Good To You' for its assault on New York governor George Pataki, New York City mayor Rudy Giuliani and any hip-hop artists who traffic in gangster or big-player clichés.

"'Big Willie' is a false illusion of power and wealth," Chuck explained in a *Props* interview at the time, "and it's an attitude that is projected by people within [the] industry over the commonplace black person. With this false illusion, a lot of people are gravitated to getting things quick and not trying to look at the heart of the matter of learning the profession and

doing the 'ugly work' involved and just not think about the pretty benefits. . . . [W]hy flaunt what you got in front of someone else who doesn't
have? . . . Just because you're able to get into the house, don't be a house
Negro and show off to everyone else in the field."

Autobiography Of Mistachuck's album cover featured the heading "Report
from the commissioner . . .", and it was apparent that Chuck D saw himself
as an elder statesman of hip-hop. For better or worse, his solo album was
almost a series of lecture topics: on TV sensationalism ('Talk Show
Created The Fool'), on black pride ('But Can You Kill The Nigger In
You?'), on the crookedness of record labels ('Paid'). His voice still a fear-
some weapon, Chuck tried to prove that positive hip-hop still had its
place, but like with *Muse Sick*, *Autobiography* didn't break ground.

This is not to diminish the album's considerable strengths. Tracks like
'Endonesia' and 'Paid' found Chuck engaged in the sort of posse tracks
Public Enemy never attempted. (Dow Jonz and B-wyze guested on the
former; Melquan and Kendu appeared on the latter.) And on the smooth
funk of 'The Pride', he looked back at his upbringing, viewing the turbu-
lent sixties and seventies from the perspective of the African-American
experience. In his brief review of the album, *Spin*'s Eric Weisbard dismissed the song as "a sixties nostalgia trip [that] might as well be Billy Joel
singing 'We Didn't Start The Fire'". It's a funny line, especially since
Chuck does list historic figures and events in a similar laundry-list style,
but he's far less hectoring and reactionary than Joel was.

As for 'But Can You Kill The Nigger In You?' he took a dark look at an
African-American community that had turned its back on the prospect of
a brighter future. And he was backed up by Isaac Hayes, who played a
chilly keyboard part and sang about the importance of blacks getting
literate and educated about their history. 'But Can You Kill The Nigger
In You?' had the same weary tone of Hayes' *Hot Buttered Soul* – albeit
without that album's flair for the dramatic musical flourish – which wasn't
surprising considering what a massive fan Chuck was of the R&B legend.

"That was the recording joy of my career," Chuck told *Props* about
working with Hayes. "Me, being a black music fan, I listen to Isaac Hayes
every day, especially myself being a fan of his work as a songwriter at Stax
Records. Isaac Hayes was surprised that I knew so much about him. . . . It

was like an older brother/younger brother type thing." For *Autobiography*, Hayes was listed as "Special Guest Producer". "[On 'But Can You Kill the Nigger In You?'], Isaac played the keys, the chords and went into the studio and then I rapped on it. Soon as I did, I asked him to sing a little part in it. So he sang that section at the end. To be produced by Isaac Hayes, shit! . . . That's one thing about solo situations: it allows me to do experimentation that I couldn't do in a Public Enemy album."

On tracks such as 'Generation Wrekkked' and 'Underdog', Chuck wasn't so much trying to make a case for his style of hip-hop as he was proudly declaring his independence from trend-chasing. But while he was cutting the album in 1995, the cultural landscape was reflecting hip-hop's growing dominance. The Notorious B.I.G.'s debut, *Ready To Die*, arrived. Wu-Tang members Raekwon and Ol' Dirty Bastard released well-regarded solo albums. Coolio's 'Gangsta's Paradise' was on its way to going triple platinum. It was part of the soundtrack to the would-be inspirational inner-city drama *Dangerous Minds*, in which Michelle Pfeiffer plays a tough-as-nails teacher who turns minority children onto poetry with Bob Dylan lyrics.

Most striking of all was English musician Tricky, who had recently exited Massive Attack, unveiling *Maxinquaye*, which cemented the arrival of a new genre known as trip-hop, which brought together rap, electronica and even some elements of funk and blues. One of *Maxinquaye*'s premier cuts was 'Black Steel', a cover of the *Nation Of Millions* song 'Black Steel In The Hour Of Chaos', replacing the Bomb Squad's clatter for a bubbling, almost reggae-influenced sound that eventually segued into distorted guitars. Martina Topley-Bird's deceptively dispassionate vocals, matched with the hypnotic arrangement, made the story of a jailbreak feel like a stoner's lament for systematic, institutional racism. It was disconcerting but also dazzling, a cocky new artist boldly updating an old song.

"Public Enemy taught me things," Tricky said in an interview with *Self-Titled* from 2013. "Chuck D educated me, and made me want to seek knowledge. Lady Gaga is not gonna make me wanna do that. Neither is Rihanna or Justin Timberlake." And in a 1996 profile of Tricky in *Spin*, Chuck had some kind words for the emerging talent. "He's cool people, you know?" Chuck said. "Tricky's in a typical situation where he's got one foot in the hood and one foot in his career, trying to figure out how to balance it all."

Outside of hip-hop, one of 1995's most visible African-American cultural events was a gathering held in Washington, D.C. on Monday, October 16 that was spearheaded by Louis Farrakhan, among others. Though officially dubbed "A Holy Day of Atonement, Reconciliation and Responsibility," the event was more commonly known as the Million Man March, which hoped to bring together a large cross-section of black men for prayer and reflection on their role in their families and communities.

Because of Farrakhan's involvement, the Million Man March drew criticism, which extended to charges of sexism since his call for "a million sober, disciplined, committed, dedicated, inspired black men" seemed to be excluding women. Though most of the speakers were male, poet Maya Angelou, civil rights activist Rosa Parks and Malcolm X's widow Betty Shabazz all addressed the crowd.

Farrakhan did nothing to quash detractors' claims that he was anti-Semitic when, days before the march, he gave an interview to Reuters in which he said, "Many of the Jews who owned the homes, the apartments in the black community, we considered them bloodsuckers because they took from our community and built their community." Adding fuel to that particular fire, he went on to assert, "When the Jews left, the Palestinian Arabs came, Koreans came, Vietnamese and other ethnic and racial groups came. And so this is a type, and we call them bloodsuckers." Event organisers wanted the march to counteract negative media images of African-American men, but Farrakhan's comments risked driving wedges further between different racial and ethnic groups. Indeed, some prominent African-Americans took Farrakhan to task. John Lewis, a member of the House of Representatives who was heavily involved with the civil rights movement of the sixties, told CNN, "I don't want to be associated with or identified with anything that tends to demonstrate signs of racism, bigotry or anti-Semitism."

Autobiography Of Mistachuck was being made around the same time, and Young's memories of working on the album are forever intertwined with the march. "I remember being in the studio with [engineer and mixer]

Bob Fudjinski," he says. "Chuck and everyone [were] going to D.C. I stayed back in the studio and was mixing some of the songs with Bob, watching the Million Man March on television."

Chuck supported the Million Man March not just by attending but also lending his voice to two tracks on *One Million Strong*, a compilation album that was released the following month. But he continued to speak out about the gathering's importance years later: on the documentary *The Million Man March – The Untold Story* from the early 2010s, Chuck was one of the talking-head interview subjects. Addressing some of the criticism at the time, the rapper commented, "A lot of people said, 'Why couldn't it be a Million Family March?' Or, 'Our sisters weren't included.' That was a whole bunch of hype that was blown up by the media expecting *any* little thing to go wrong – or wanting, maybe, any little thing to go wrong. It was a perfect day. . . . It was necessary for us to be there to show the solidarity amongst black men."

Chuck's solo album was released in October 1996, a little more than a year after the Million Man March, but Spike Lee hit the one-year anniversary with his Million Man March-themed road movie *Get On The Bus*, which opened in theatres on October 16. One could feel the influence of the D.C. gathering on the album – or, at the very least, the artist's continued commitment to some of the same issues that had been at the centre of the event. This was especially true on 'No', a slice of laid-back saxophone and funk guitar in which he let fly with a series of items and attitudes that he rejected, including pork, absent fathers, drugs, misogyny and "East Coast/West Coast beefs". It could have been a mission statement for the Million Man March's positive message of self-sufficiency. The track's music was inspired by a panel Chuck attended at Howard University. "At the end of the lecture this white kid named [Mark] Harrison came up to me with a tape of some of his beats that he wanted me to check out," Chuck recalled in *Lyrics Of A Rap Revolutionary*. "While driving back from Washington, D.C. to New York we were listening to his tape and he had the track that we used for this song on there."

When *Autobiography Of Mistachuck* hit stores, it didn't come out through Def Jam. Instead, Mercury released the album. In an interview with *Billboard* a few months before *Autobiography*'s release, Chuck explained that he had made a deal with Russell Simmons to "go elsewhere in the universe with my solo situation". (In *Don't Rhyme For The Sake Of Riddlin'*, Russell Myrie asserts that another reason why *Autobiography* was a Chuck solo album was that Def Jam didn't want him releasing the record under the Public Enemy moniker. "[T]hey were preventing me from operating in the building," Chuck is quoted as saying in the book. "I knew that Polygram had bought half of Def Jam. What's gonna stop me as a black guy from using the building? What, you gonna kill me 'cause I'm smart?")

"I've been at Def Jam for 10 years," Chuck later told *Props*. "When I went over to Mercury, it was actually the first record company that I ever signed to. Def Jam to me was like always a street hustle. I first got signed by Rick Rubin, and after Rubin left at '89, I dealt directly with Sony. I never dealt with Def Jam. Def Jam moved over to Polygram in 1994 and it forced me to deal directly with Def Jam. . . . People thought when I signed with Mercury, it was because Def Jam was there. Hell no! I had a bidding war of eight labels."

Chuck opted for Mercury no doubt in part because it was run by Danny Goldberg, who had written the *Los Angeles Times* op-ed defending the frontman's 'Welcome To The Terrordome'. Goldberg had been chairman and CEO of Warner Bros. Records before taking on those two titles at Mercury in 1996. In the *Billboard* interview, Chuck referred to him as "a visionary, not a reactionary".

"He did a solo record that Def Jam didn't want," Goldberg recalls, "and I was happy to put it out because he was Chuck D. I welcomed whatever he wanted to do creatively. Whatever issues he had with Def Jam – they thought it wasn't commercial enough or whatever they thought – [my feeling was] if Chuck D wants to do something, I want to be supportive."

"My dealings with Mercury for the solo LP have nothing to do with Def Jam," Chuck told Tricky in a conversation between the two artists that was published in the December 1996 issue of *Vox* magazine. "Def Jam is not sophisticated enough and they can't always understand that this is about fun, it's about art. It's not about pop-chasing. They can never tell me what to do. I find joy in doing the unexpected. They're like: 'Chuck! What makes you tick?' I'm like: 'What makes me tick is something you don't understand.' I'm a normal, regular human being, but when I'm making lyrics or verses up, I don't know what the fuck it is. It's almost like I'm already naturally high and crazy. I dare to wonder what weed would do to my ass."

Goldberg, who's now president of GoldVE Entertainment, an artist management company, says he doesn't remember the particulars of a bidding war for *Autobiography*. "I was running a major label," he says. "Major labels were bigger than they are today. I had 150 people working for me, I had to make my quarterly numbers, and I was juggling a lot of different things. I just remember there came a time when I was asked whether or not I wanted to put Chuck's solo record [out], and I said yes immediately. I don't think I even heard anything or had to hear anything. I was honoured to be of use to him."

Asked if the perception that Public Enemy had lost a step concerned him commercially, Goldberg responds, "I think that there were people that would have looked at it that way, and there were people that would have been concerned that the production have a commercial producer or try to have a hit single and that kind of a thing. I respect people who would think that way, but that wasn't where I was coming from. I looked at him as being a long-term career artist the way I looked at certain rock artists such as Neil Young or Bob Dylan or Leonard Cohen. [They] have their ups and downs, but you support people like that because, over time, they're going to come up with important things culturally, rather than subject them to the kind of A&R scrutiny or the mathematical analysis of what their last record sold, which one has to do with the majority of artists. . . . [With Chuck] I just figured, 'This is a chance to be supportive to someone who's a genius, and whether [or not] this record does great, it's a relationship-builder.' Although I'm sure it cost some money, it wasn't a crazy deal – it wasn't millions of dollars."

Goldberg does acknowledge, though, that a similar thought process – ignore the sales statistics, cultivate the relationship – would be harder to justify in the current industry climate. "The record business could afford those kind of decisions then," he says. "Today, with the reduced record business and reduced sales, it's much harder to make those kind of statements with artists, unless it's [at] a lower amount of money. I knew [Public

Enemy] were commercially not at a peak. But I've seen this in my observation of rock'n'roll. Eric Clapton was hot, then he was cold, then he was
hot again. Same with Dylan. Certain types of artists can get cold, but
because they're so talented and meant so much to their fans, they get
second, third, fourth, and fifth chances – whereas a pure pop artist who's
just dependent on hit songs doesn't earn or get those kind of other
chances. To me, Chuck D was always in the category of career, long-time,
long-term talent."

The Mercury marketing people seemed to agree. In the August '96
Billboard story about the album, the label's product manager, Kim Green,
told the trade paper, "We're working with the fact that Chuck is much
more than a recording artist. We're trying to tap into the people who care
about his mind, politics and what he represents as a voice." But even
Green seemed to know the challenge *Autobiography* faced on the charts.
"[T]he heads who used to love Chuck are now much older, and the new
heads are checking for [younger, harder rappers] like Wu-Tang Clan,"
Green said. "[But] the beats on the album are great, so they'll [hear] that
Chuck's coming with phat* music and, hopefully, join the party."

Autobiography Of Mistachuck spent a solitary week on the *Billboard* 200,
landing at number 190. 'No' peaked at number 90 on the Hot R&B/
Hip-Hop Songs chart. The reviews were what you might expect for a
seasoned, acclaimed artist: respectful but also a bit dismissive. "Working
here with producers Gary G-Wiz and Eric 'Vietnam' Sadler, Chuck
successfully reinvents the sound he defined with Public Enemy, slowing
the beats down and introducing stylish R&B elements like sampled horn
parts and vocal choruses," Anthony DeCurtis wrote in *Rolling Stone*. But
he also noted the predictability of Chuck's lyrical pursuits, printing out the
connection between 'Talk Show Created The Fool' and 'She Watch
Channel Zero?!' "It's time for this 'incredible rhyme animal' to go on a
fresh hunt," DeCurtis concluded.

In a 2000 interview, Chuck seemed to blame radio's shrinking playlists
in part for the album's commercial disappointment. "If the radio stations

---

* This, by the way, will be the only instance in the book where Chuck or Public Enemy's
music will be referred to as "phat".

gotta tell people, 'Yo, go and check this out 'cause we got paid X amount to play what Chuck put down' . . . that's just wack and corny," he told reporter Dean Engmann. "I thought I did a job with *Autobiography Of Mistachuck* that had some elements on there that radio could have picked up on, but I wasn't paying them a dime. Now, if I would've gotten Mercury to pay them, they would have been playing it four to five times a day until the money ran out. To me that's corny."

Interestingly, what might have been the most memorable element of *Autobiography* was that it represented the first appearance of Professor Griff on one of Chuck's records since his exodus from Public Enemy. Griff co-wrote 'Horizontal Heroin', a 100-second interlude about the evils of drugs in the form of back-and-forth voicemail messages.

"There is a possibility of a reunion," Chuck told *Props* when asked if Griff might return to Public Enemy. "Me and Griff have been working here and there for the last four years. There wasn't a problem with me . . . Public Enemy is like 25 to 30 people in a working environment. He had some problems with the situation, which he left on his own. He's come to grips with some situations. I would like to see him work with Public Enemy, I didn't want to see him go at that particular time."

Goldberg, who had disapproved of Griff's *Washington Times* comments in his *LA Times* op-ed, says that he wasn't bothered by the rapper's appearance on *Autobiography*. "I trusted Chuck D," he says. "There's real problems in the world. There is such a thing as anti-Semitism. There are people that really deface Jewish cemeteries and beat up people with yarmulkes in the wrong neighbourhood. [Comments by] Farrakhan and Professor Griff, to me, were not in the same category. I felt Chuck was a moral person [who] worked with Jews, worked with non-Jews, worked with Muslims, worked with atheists. . . . [In the *LA Times* op-ed] I didn't mean to say that Professor Griff should be permanently ostracised. I believe he paid a price for [his comments]. I'm sure he learned something from it. He's got his own issues as an artist [but] I love Chuck D and believe in his morality without any reservation at all."

By summer of 1997, Griff had officially been brought back into the fold in Public Enemy. In a *Vibe* article from the time, Chuck said, "Reinstituting Griff was a natural thing. There were some discrepancies and in time they were cleared up." In the same piece, he dropped hints that the band was back in the studio working on their follow-up to *Muse Sick, Afraid Of The Dark*. A two-month tour was also being planned. "There's a lot of people right now that's waiting to hear from us," Flavor Flav told *Vibe*. "I just want to deliver back to my peoples."

Unfortunately, when people heard from Flav during this period, it was usually bad news. Two months after the release of *Autobiography Of Mistachuck*, Flavor was arrested in the South Bronx for carrying two pounds of marijuana. He had been riding a bike when the police stopped him, believing he was carrying a weapon in his prominently bulging pocket. Instead, it was the weed.

While PE fans waited for this new record, Chuck D put out *Fight The Power: Rap, Race, And Reality*, a memoir co-written by Yusuf Jah, in the fall of 1997. Rather than a straight autobiography, the book was divided into chapters to discuss different prominent topics, like the beginnings of Public Enemy, his time in Africa, the inspirations behind (and brouhaha over) *Apocalypse 91*, and his opinions about "Black And Jewish Relationships". Sometimes affecting, sometimes defensive, always forcefully rendered, *Fight The Power* was a Public Enemy album without the music, which is to say that it could be longwinded without always being compelling. Throughout the book, he also offered his lists of favourites, such as "Top All-Time Deejays", "Ten Emcees That Make Me Say Damn!" and "Favourite Journalists".

As part of Chuck's diversification effort, he also started his own label. In March 1996, *Billboard* reported the formation of Slam Jamz Recordings, which would be financed by the Columbia Records Group. Chuck told *Billboard* he wanted Slam Jamz to be "a minor-league farm system" that would "try to make the hardest records possible while taking the most chances. We're not trying to capitulate to popular tastes and [are] hoping to strike the iron with our own particular style." As part of the label's mission, Chuck announced that Slam Jamz would avoid putting out albums, instead focusing on singles and EPs.

He also spent time developing two TV programmes: a talk show called *Rap Live With Chuck D* and *Inside The Rhyme*, which Chuck once described to *Vibe* as a "combination of *NBA Inside Stuff*, *WWF Wrestling*, and *Entertainment Tonight*." "I'm running for commissioner of this shit," he told *Vibe*. "Hip-hop is gonna be interpreted through a structure that I'm building." Nothing came of either project.

In the epilogue for *Fight To Power*, Chuck D recalls, "In 1995, my then-accountant told me that my concentration should be as an artist and that it would be difficult for the public to accept me as anything else. Bullshit. I considered this bowing down to an insane level of nigger shit, whereas the white boys make, take, and become anything they want. I saw this as a prime opportunity to become a spokesperson and advocate fighter for this art form to keep the culture bandits in check."

He was an MTV correspondent during the 1996 Republican National Convention, famously encountering long-time senator Strom Thurmond and asking him if he wanted to address "the MTV generation and black people in the inner city". The senator's response was that he believed in equal opportunities for all people. "Has that always been your philosophy?" Chuck D asked, alluding to Thurmond's history as a one-time segregationist. "Times have changed and I've changed with the times," Thurmond responded.

Chuck was at the forefront of a changing media landscape, not just because he was a rapper doubling as a reporter but because he bore witness to the ways that the burgeoning internet was going to shift how the world disseminated and absorbed information. Covering the convention for the *Chicago Tribune*, reporters V. Dion Haynes and Vincent J. Schodolski noted, "Thanks to miles of fibre optics, hundreds of computer terminals and a vast array of satellite dishes, the 1996 Republican National Convention was the first such gathering to begin to exploit the potential of the information age. On alternative networks, through different newspapers and via the vast regions of cyberspace, there are possibly more ways than ever before to plug into the convention."

In May 1997, it was announced that Chuck had signed on to be a commentator and correspondent for a new cable news channel called Fox News that would eventually overtake CNN as the country's most popular. "My fault with the media before was that they weren't well-rounded," he explained at the time. "They were limited and unbalanced. I can definitely make changes within by kicking the door down." Ironically, Fox News used the motto "Fair and Balanced" for years, although it soon became clear it was more of a mouthpiece for conservative values, trumpeting the GOP agenda and promoting Republican candidates. In the early years of the 21st century, Chuck would air serious grievances with Fox News on his band's albums.

While Chuck was trying his hand at other pursuits, hip-hop was in crisis. On September 13, 1996, a month before *Autobiography*'s release, Tupac Shakur was gunned down in Las Vegas, dead at the age of 25. After Shakur's death, Chuck publicly questioned whether the slain rapper had faked his death, citing the fact that he was supposedly killed on Friday the 13th as part of his reasoning. Chuck eventually gave up such speculation, instead focusing on hip-hop's loss.

"Tupac was a reflection of these times," he told *Props*. "Unfortunately, he will go down as the James Dean of this particular period whether for young black or white kids. I think the media picked from the downside of Tupac instead of his beautiful upside. Too many times, brothers are not given the two roads to take equally, the high road and low road. The low road is much wider, much bigger and more lucrative than the high road many times. That road was more beneficial to Tupac . . . that's unfortunate."

Chuck had taken pride in suggesting to Ernest Dickerson, the director of the 1992 crime drama *Juice*, that he cast the young Shakur as one of the film's stars. As part of the Bomb Squad, Chuck helped produce the movie's soundtrack, which went gold. He had known Shakur since the man's days in Digital Underground. "[*Juice* was] his first acting role," Chuck told *Vlad TV*. "The next movie Tupac did was *Poetic Justice*" – a romantic drama starring Janet Jackson directed by John Singleton – "[and] he really played a more positive character." Chuck seemed sad, or maybe disappointed, recalling the rapper's acting career. "At that time, you had so much people that wanted him to just be that thug gangster that they thought that Pac fell off in the movies," because of *Poetic Justice*, Chuck said. He pointed to the fact that Shakur's follow-up to *Poetic Justice* was the crime drama *Above The Rim*, a movie Chuck doesn't seem to have much fondness for. "[People] was like applauding the fact that he was 'back'," Chuck said. "I was like, 'His life ain't a movie, man.'"

Because of a heightened West Coast/East Coast feud between Death Row Records (which housed Tupac, Dr. Dre and Snoop Dogg) and Bad Boy (the home of the Notorious B.I.G. and Puff Daddy), Shakur's death was seen as an escalation of the bad blood – a fear that only grew when, six months later, Biggie was murdered in Los Angeles.

Neither rapper's murder was ever solved, fomenting suspicion in the African-American community and music industry. But it also seemed to be a line in the sand for listeners who had grown tired of gangster rap's glorification of violence. Biggie, who had been a crack dealer for a time before turning to hip-hop, sang eloquently about the struggles to escape poverty, but he also made his name by being a memorable memoirist of the criminal life with its kill-or-be-killed reality. Just weeks before his death, with his second studio album, *Life After Death*, about ready to drop, he told a *Los Angeles Times* reporter, "There's nothing that protects you from the inevitable. If it's going to happen, it's going to happen, no matter what you do. It doesn't matter if you clean up your life and present your-self differently, what goes around comes around, man. It's crazy for me to even think . . . that a rapper can't get killed just because he raps. I'm stupid for even thinking that it couldn't."

It had been 10 years since PE's first release, which had shown little interest in the materialism and bloodshed that had quickly become two of the music's major selling points. By '97, Public Enemy were discussing a new record, but it was amid a landscape where their style of political hip-hop seemed hopelessly passé. They didn't have the melodic flash of an exciting new group such as the Fugees, and like their contemporaries in De La Soul, whose '96 album *Stakes Is High* worried over rap's commer-cialisation, they seemed to be retreating into a stripped-down, bitter sound that was more reactionary than revolutionary. It would be inspiring for Public Enemy to right the ship with their next album. But that isn't quite what happened.

CHAPTER EIGHT

B Y the late nineties, Spike Lee had established himself as a prolific, varied director, moving from politically charged biopics (*Malcolm X*) to warm family dramas (*Crooklyn*) to comedies (*Girl 6*) to documentaries (*4 Little Girls*, about the murder of four Alabama children in 1963). Showing a flair that has long been his hallmark, he zipped from one project to the next. In '99, he looked back with interviewer George Khoury on his output over that decade, which saw him moving away from writing original screenplays and instead developing other people's material.

"I look for original voices, people with something to say," he explained. *Malcolm X* had initially been set up for Norman Jewison to direct. *Crooklyn* had started with a script by his sister Joie and brother Cinqué. *Clockers* was written by crime author Richard Price, based on his own novel. As for *Get On The Bus*, "I got this phone call to do this film about 12 men going cross-country on a bus to the Million Man March," Lee recalled. "And I had time to write that with a very fine writer, Reggie Bythewood; he wrote that. And then this is where my beautiful wife, Tonya, stepped in, and she said, 'Spike, you need to write an original screenplay. I've missed your voice.' At first I said, 'What is she talking about?' And then I saw she was right as usual. I checked the top of my mind and saw that the last orig-inal screenplay I had written was *Jungle Fever* – which I did back in 1990. So it was like seven years since I had written an original screenplay. And that's how *He Got Game* came to be."

Lee had long been a basketball fan. He was an infamous fixture courtside at Madison Square Garden rooting on his hometown New York Knicks for years, and his early fame was tied in part to his Mars Blackmon Nike commercials with NBA legend Michael Jordan. "I never met anybody like that character," Lee told ESPN columnist Ralph Wiley in 2001 about the motor-mouthed Blackmon. "[He came] [a]ll from

imagination. The bike messenger, hoop fan, seer, who was 'kinda small'
. . . but who loved the Knicks, Bernard King's game. Probably a lot of
Mars was me . . ."

No wonder, then, that he had been deeply impressed with *Hoop
Dreams*, a 1994 documentary about two Chicago teens, William Gates and
Arthur Agee, who are trying to become professional basketball players.
One of the landmark films of the nineties, *Hoop Dreams* used these young
men's quest as an examination of race, greed, poverty and the role of sports
in American society. A few years after *Hoop Dreams'* release, Lee came on
board to executive-produce a TV remake, but nothing ever came of it.
The filmmaker told Wiley that *Hoop Dreams* "is the best basketball film
I've seen. Even though it was a documentary, it had a great dramatic arc, a
fine narrative twist, and was so real. Just goes to show, you can make it up,
but you can't make it up as well as life."

He Got Game provided Lee a chance to tell a basketball story, and it was
clear that he took inspiration from the documentary, and not just because
the director gave Agee a cameo in the film. *He Got Game* is about Jesus
Shuttlesworth, a high school prodigy who is being courted by several of
the country's powerhouse basketball universities. Jesus' father, Jake, hasn't
seen his son for a few years because he's been in prison, but the warden
arranges to let the convict out early if he can convince his boy to sign with
the warden's alma mater. The problem is that Jesus wants nothing to do
with his father, who accidentally killed Jesus' mother.

While Lee was developing the idea, he knew who he wanted to play
Jake. "Some parts have been written for people," he said to actor Delroy
Lindo in 1999. "I wrote *He Got Game* for Denzel, wrote *Mo' Better Blues*
for Denzel." *He Got Game* was their third collaboration, but Washington
wasn't the only familiar name attached to the film.

Afraid Of The Dark was meant to be Public Enemy's formal return after
their retirement from touring. Expected in the fall of 1997, the album
never materialised. Instead, the group came back together, along with the
Bomb Squad, to do a companion album to Spike Lee's film. Despite
Chuck's misgivings about Def Jam, it was better that he was focusing on
music than on some of his other endeavours. In February 1998, he
co-starred in *An Alan Smithee Film: Burn Hollywood Burn*, a witless,

cameo-studded Hollywood satire in which he and Coolio played indie filmmakers Leon and Dion Brothers. (That's right: they're the Brothers brothers.) In *Fight The Power*, Chuck recounted how he got involved in the comedy. "On a recent film that I was trying to get the composing job for," he wrote, "the music supervisor asked if I would play one of the parts in the film. I never thought I would end up acting, but one night while I was visiting the set . . . Whoopi Goldberg, Sylvester Stallone and Jackie Chan all told me in the same night, 'Just try it. You have nothing to lose.'"

The movie was a commercial bomb, but it did generate some wonderfully vicious reviews. "*An Alan Smithee Film: Burn Hollywood Burn* is a spectacularly bad film," Roger Ebert groaned, calling it "incompetent, unfunny, ill-conceived, badly executed, lamely written, and acted by people who look trapped in the headlights." "[B]urning is too good for such a wretched fiasco," the *Los Angeles Times* critic Kenneth Turan opined. "Only a surgical nuclear strike could suitably destroy what has to be one of the most enervating comedies ever made. More sluggish and not nearly as entertaining as the world of Hollywood moviemaking it nominally satirises, *Smithee* is more painful and dispiriting to watch than anyone could possibly imagine. If this truly is, as the film's tag line claims, 'The Movie Hollywood Doesn't Want You to See,' Hollywood has rarely done the world a bigger favour."

Chuck also did some music for the film, and when he was asked by *The A.V. Club* in 2001 if he was interested in doing more acting, the rapper responded, "I'm more interested in doing film scores and dominating that field in the urban hip-hop area. Doing what Stanley Clarke has done for jazz scores. That's more important to me than the acting part. I will throw the acting in if I can get [to compose] the score."

He Got Game gave Chuck a chance to hone his talent for material that lined up with his own lyrical interests. Like Lee, he was a long-time basketball fan, working in references to players like Charles Barkley in his lyrics almost from the beginning of Public Enemy. But also like Lee, he didn't watch the game blindly, understanding how the racial and economic inequality that affected America as a whole also infected the game he loved. When the filmmaker approached him about the project, Chuck didn't hesitate.

"When I was small I wanted to be a sports announcer, and for years I had a lot of sports analogies inside my head that I wanted to use if I ever became a sports announcer that I never could use within a Public Enemy song," Chuck wrote in *Lyrics Of A Rap Revolutionary*. "So when the *He Got Game* project came along I jumped on it like a raccoon on an old roof."

Or, as he said at a press conference before the album's release in the spring of 1998, he was an ideal candidate to write songs for a basketball movie because, "There's not a motherfucker in hip-hop who knows more about sports than me."

Initially, however, Lee hadn't thought of Public Enemy for the sound-track. The director told MTV News, "We knew we wanted a rap group to do all the songs for the film. A Tribe Called Quest was a consideration, that couldn't be worked out. Then I said, 'Well, how come I didn't think of PE?' And it was stupid on my part." But there was another reason he hadn't immediately thought of PE. "I had been told, or I read, Public Enemy was no longer together and had disbanded," Lee said. "But I did not want to take no for an answer. I talked to Chuck, then with Hank Shocklee, and the guys reunited."

The soundtrack album didn't have a tight concept. "I was raised in the days of Isaac Hayes' *Shaft*, Curtis Mayfield doing *Superfly* and other artists doing entire soundtracks for films," Chuck recalled to *Vibe* in 2011. "And Spike Lee approached us in that same way." Several of *He Got Game*'s songs touched on basketball or the film's Coney Island setting. And as a whole, the soundtrack could be seen as an extension of Chuck's *Greatest Misses* cut 'Air Hoodlum', in which he grinded over a slow beat, telling the story of a high school phenomenon known as Mickey Mack who wins a championship for his college team but then hurts himself, left with no options since he never pursued an education. 'Air Hoodlum' had been inspired by true events. "[T]here a lotta cats who were studying ball over books," Chuck once wrote. "Realities were overlooked. One cat who was all Long Island and one of the [state's] best high school players was cracked out, drunken, and homeless eight years later. I saw a system use and abuse this brother and spit him back on the streets. . . . [T]here was one just like him for almost every black neighbourhood." Though neither of the young men of *Hoop Dreams* ended up with such a horrible fate, it was clear that 'Air Hoodlum' was addressing a similar scenario: institutions profit off the hard work of underprivileged kids, tossing them aside when they no longer serve a monetary purpose.

"I had the most fun with ['Air Hoodlum'] because it was an aspect of exploitation I hadn't focused on before," Chuck said to *Vox* in 1992. "Racism exists every day and discovering its many faces isn't easy. People look for me to give them a different Public Enemy story but I'll tell the same story the same old way. Racism never changes so my answers never change. I don't start controversy for its own sake. I talk about alternative viewpoints. They might think I'm offensive. That remains to be seen."

Little wonder that Chuck saw a similarity between aspiring basketball players and the hip-hop game. On *He Got Game*'s opening track, 'Resurrection', Chuck makes some noise about a "label switch", casting Public Enemy in the role of an aging superstar wanting to prove he's not out of the game yet.

In that light, the album was meant to be a grand reunion of PE alums working together for the first time in for ever. But the spirit of reconciliation and resurrection didn't play out so smoothly.

"*He Got Game* was about how a group of guys can make an album in three days," Kerwin Young says. "We did that whole album in three days." According to Young, who worked on tracks for the record, "Hank was given the task of doing the album the previous year for some undisclosed large amount of money – and all he had to show after a year was one song." Young lived nearby Chuck, and one night he got a call. "Chuck calls me up and says, 'Sleek, we got a problem. I need you to come to my house. We're having a big meeting.' I walk over to his house, and there's Chuck, [producer] Abnormal, Gary G-Wiz. Chuck says, 'Hey, look, we have an album to do for Spike's new movie. . . . You guys need to get working on this ASAP.'" As Young recalls, they only had a few days to work on the basic tracks Chuck had in rough form if they were going to be included in the movie.

Even if Young exaggerates – or is mistaken – about the timeframe, *He Got Game* was beset with chaos. In an MTV article from the end of March 1998, less than a month before the album's release, reporter Chris Nelson writes that he spoke to a PE publicist who said that song selection and track listing were still being completed and that mastering wasn't yet finished. In *Don't Rhyme For The Sake Of Riddlin'*, Russell Myrie quotes Chuck as saying the album was "bittersweet. Sweet in the way it brought teams back together to handle a particular record and the record was definitely good. But not all the teams worked together with each other because there were factions that were apart from each other." The frontman also says that it's the only PE album to cost more than $1 million to make. "If it was up to me," Chuck said, "I'd have given Def Jam a record for $90,000. . . . I'm still unclear how and where the money was spent."

Chuck's lyrics didn't follow the movie's plot. Instead, he bobbed and weaved, bringing in KRS-One to guest on 'Unstoppable' and incorporating 'James Bond Theme' for 'Game Face', minimalist songs about PE's continued relevance. But then there was 'Is Your God A Dog', Abnormal's steely production and Johnny Juice's piercing scratching combining with Chuck's complex thematic linking of basketball, the music industry and black crime. Shifting back and forth between the three topics, the rapper argues that entertainment becomes a way to distract the consumer from noticing the dark realities around him. Even worse, the celebration of black athletes and musicians creates an impression that there's no other way for African-Americans to succeed. "Rap or play ball," Chuck bellows. "Do the game or duck the drive-by."

Johnny Juice, who had exited the group in the late eighties, was recruited by his old friend Eric Sadler, who had also moved on, to return for *He Got Game*. "Had nothing to do with Chuck," Juice says. "Eric Sadler was asked to come back 'cause the Bomb Squad was supposed to come back together. Eric wouldn't work with Hank, so what they did was they split up tracks. Eric was like, 'I'm not producing anything, but I'll be a production coordinator.' Eric had this team of producers and one of them was this guy Abnormal, who did a bunch of songs. Eric just wanted me scratching and stuff. I was only supposed to scratch on two little records, that was it – we were, like, in eight studios in two days."

Another Abnormal production, 'Super Agent', seemed to be a sequel to 'Air Hoodlum', looking at the talent agents who represent the athletes. In perhaps a nod to the real-life player who portrayed Jesus in *He Got Game*, Ray Allen, Chuck imagines the song's new recruit being signed to the

Milwaukee Bucks – Allen's team. From there, 'Super Agent' paints a dark picture of the NBA as a modern-day slave trade, name-checking the league's commissioner, David Stern, as the "auctioneer" leading the draft of new players. Chuck touches on the film's father-son dynamic – specifically, Jake's life in prison – but 'Super Agent' is more interested in the mindset that creates *He Got Game*'s scenario. The so-called "super agent" (and, by extension, the NBA in general) visits the projects to pick the best prospects, who either have to develop their skills at universities (which exploit their talent without paying them) or make the jump to the pros (where they're controlled by owners and agents until they get injured or see their skills diminish). Like 'Air Hoodlum', 'Super Agent' is a cautionary tale about the downside of professional sports, in which big business survives long after the kid who's pinned his entire future on hoops gets put out to pasture.

"I'm an older person so I watch [sports stars] as professionals, for the thrill of the game, rather than sticking to a team," Chuck said in December 1992. "Sports is one big fucked-up business. It's mega, mega, *mega* bucks. I'm trying to challenge black athletes to speak up for the 'hood rather than make their cheque, go home and satisfy white America's wants and needs with their physical skills instead of their intellectual abilities."

The Wu-Tang Clan-esque 'Politics Of The Sneaker Pimps' is built around skeletal beats and what sounds like a guitar loop, opening with a quote from the film: "Jesus is the best thing to happen to the game since the tennis shoe was invented." And Wu-Tang member Masta Killa showed up to do a verse on the album's opener, 'Resurrection'. With 'Politics Of The Sneaker Pimps', Chuck shines a light on endorsement deals for shoes, which then become coveted items in the inner city – so much so that kids kill each other for them. 'Politics Of The Sneaker Pimps' is a follow-up of sorts to 'Shut 'Em Down', which condemned Nike's lack of interest in supporting the projects while taking their money. The new song offered a front-row perspective of a player landing a sponsorship agreement with a shoe company, reflecting on how cheap the shoes are to make overseas, even though the company sells them for a huge mark-up in the States. Calling out not just Nike but also Adidas, Reebok, New Balance and Fila, Chuck shows how endorsement deals are just another way that corporate America exploits black stars, marketing their coolness for profit. All the while, the unnamed narrator has to hope that a debilitating knee injury doesn't end his career, forcing him to turn to drug-dealing, a similar fate to the sad former ball player in 'Air Hoodlum'.

Chuck saw a parallel to his line of work. As he recalled in *Lyrics Of A Rap Revolutionary*, "I had reached a point where I was selling more Starter jackets and Pittsburgh Pirate hats." When he wore a St. Louis Cardinals hat in the 'By The Time I Get To Arizona' video, "Major League Baseball sent me a letter requesting that I . . . not wear their hats in the video. . . . This was in 1991, when most established business situations did not want the connections with hip-hop that they cherish today."

Understanding that hip-hop was a brand as much as an art form, Chuck formed his own fashion line, Rapp Style, in the summer of '92. Featuring high-tops and shirts, Rapp Style wasn't meant, in the words of Chuck's father (and business partner) Lorenzo Ridenhour, to "make a political point". As Chuck told *Spin* at the time, "I'm looking at getting into merchandising worldwide. I look at it as being bigger than sports, because it's international. Rappers are selling so many things the sports guys are selling. We've sold more, but the sports guys don't give a fuck about us, so I wanted to set up my own, even if it meant failing for two or three years. I know that if I keep on doing it, I'll be all right."

Rapp Style never took off, but that didn't stop others, like Jay Z's Rocawear, which began in 1999, from becoming profitable, influential fashion entities. "[W]hen you look at the Rocawears . . . and others that have partnered other backers," Chuck wrote, "it's clear that established businesses realised that they couldn't stop [hip-hop's rise], so they joined it."

Kerwin Young oversaw 'House Of The Rising Son', an homage to the Jesus Shuttlesworth character. "I had an a cappella that Chuck gave me," Young recalls, "and I was working with an Akai DL4, so I synched it up in my Akai, laid the track. I got my mother to come upstairs and do a vocal – I had her say, 'house of the rising son'. I recorded my saxophone so I could have some added noise. I just recorded a bunch of stuff I could get. I went to Gary's house and laid a bass line from his keyboard. I did take a sound bite from the Who's 'Won't Get Fooled Again', but I thought I could get away with not having to pay for that. I had to give a percentage to Pete

Townshend, unfortunately, but [I only had] one day, and there was a sound I wanted, man."

The rush of completing the album may have contributed to its spare sound, but it also made *He Got Game* stand out from other Public Enemy records in one important regard. "It's pretty much close to the albums that followed it," says Young, "but it doesn't have the vocal interludes that all of the other Public Enemy albums have. That's the one thing that's missing – we didn't have time to find those things. We didn't even think about that – we were, like, 'We need to get songs done. Interludes, screw all of that.' Had the album started the year prior, when it should have, you would have ended up with a Public Enemy album of immense proportions produced by, probably, Hank, Keith and whoever else. Gary would have probably been involved with it, but I wouldn't have been on that album."

"It was supposed to be a reunion situation," Gary told biographer Russell Myrie, "but Hank basically said up front, you know, 'It's gonna go down this way and everyone's gonna . . .' I just don't think it went over well with everyone. Everyone's thinking something different and it ended up being more of a broken-up situation than an inclusive situation."

"It was a cluster-fuck," Juice says. "Everybody was all over the place and nobody really liked each other or wanted to talk to each other. Hank already developed this reputation for really ripping people off, so a lot of people didn't wanna work with him."

Young produced 'House Of The Rising Son' and the album-closing coda by Professor Griff called 'Sudden Death', spending the rest of his time assisting other producers. "It was nonstop working," he says. "We didn't get any sleep. Not only were we doing the music during these few days, we had to negotiate contracts. [We had to do] a lot of shit – too much shit."

While Young, Gary G-Wiz and others were working on the East Coast, musician and producer Jack Dangers was tackling another *He Got Game* track in California. The leader of the electronic-flavoured dance-rock group Meat Beat Manifesto, Dangers had been approached to finish a rough demo Chuck had. He had not worked with the rapper before, but "I was a big fan [of Public Enemy] ever since their first record," Dangers says. "I think they'd sort of fallen out with Hank Shocklee or whoever it was they were working with in the studio, and I was available to sort of fill in and finish off this last track. It was just an opportunity, really, and I jumped at it."

Dangers' memory is that he had about a month to complete the track. "It was just Chuck's vocals and a very sort of basic framework," he says, "which I more or less completely dumped and started from scratch. . . . There was no guitar work on it, and the beat was like a drum-machine beat. It was very, very sparse, and it wasn't produced at all. Just a blueprint, really. But what I liked was that we were allowed to do anything we wanted to do to it."

He collaborated with Danny Saber, a guitarist and producer who later teamed up with Dangers in a short-lived duo called Spontaneous Human Combustion. "I did all the drums and all the sampling," says Dangers about the PE cut, "and Danny did all the guitar work on it. We worked together at the Record Plant in LA – just me and him in the studio. I finished it off at my studio in San Francisco." Dangers laughs. "When it was all done, I had an awful time trying to convince the guy at Def Jam that there wasn't any samples in it. We didn't nick anything [but] it was supposed to sound like samples from something else. [The Def Jam rep] started mentioning certain tracks from classic seventies records – some of them I had heard and some of them I hadn't. It was very odd, very paranoid behaviour but, I suppose, sort of understandable at that time. 'Oh, that's too good – it must be from something else': that's the attitude, you know? But that was about the only thing [Public Enemy] said: not to use any samples."

The track became 'Go Cat Go', *He Got Game*'s de facto finale before Griff's 'Sudden Death' epilogue. Highlighted by raging guitars, it's the most rap-rock song on the collection, Chuck sounding like he's sprinting to the finish line, furiously throwing out references to different TV networks and even ESPN's flamboyantly excitable *SportsCenter* anchor Stuart Scott and his "Booyah!" catch phrase. "He's definitely my favourite lyricist," Dangers says about Chuck D, "because he had a political angle. 'Go Cat Go', it's got that line – 'White man's burden / Be a black man's dream' – which is one of my favourite lyrics he ever did. So, I made sure there was a drum break on that bit." And it's terrifically executed, giving the couplet additional power. 'Go Cat Go' might be Chuck's most ferocious vocal performance on *He Got Game*, and Dangers and Saber gave it combustible music to match.

But it's not the song most identified with the soundtrack album. That, of course, would be the title tune: a moving, melancholy song about trying to persevere in the face of harsh obstacles. When Chuck met with Spike Lee to discuss *He Got Game*, the filmmaker presented the frontman with what Chuck called "a small postcard of references that he needed me to make in ['He Got Game'], which helped me tremendously as a writer to make a cohesive song." Some of those words were "ball players" and "contracts". 'He Got Game' "signified my most consistent, thorough writing on one theme," he declared in *Lyrics Of A Rap Revolutionary*. "I wasn't just writing about basketball, but the hypocrisy of the sports game and making parallels and comparisons of the thin line between the sports trade and the slave trade."

Those parallels were laid out as well on 'Super Agent' and the gospel-inflected 'What You Need Is Jesus'. But in 'He Got Game', he went in a more poignant direction. Where Chuck usually hurls fireballs, 'He Got Game' caught him in a moment of genuine confusion, even doubt. "What does it all mean / All this shit I'm seeing?" he asks early on, admitting "My wandering got my ass wondering / Where Christ is in all this crisis." Backed by Flav, he goes into the chorus, which questions the whole notion of "game": an ineffable confidence or talent, whether it's for hoops or life in general. As on much of the *He Got Game* album, Chuck wants us to see through that lie on 'He Got Game':

> *I got game*
> *She's got game*
> *We got game*
> *They got game*
> *He got game*
> *It might feel good*
> *It might sound a little somethin'*
> *But fuck the game*
> *If it ain't sayin nothin'*

The song drew much of its strength from a prominent sample of the guitar melody from 'For What It's Worth', the 1967 Buffalo Springfield hit written by Stephen Stills. A song of social protest that asked listeners to open their eyes was repurposed for a new era, and Stills appeared on the new track to sing some of his indelible lyrics from the original. ("There's something happening here / What it is ain't exactly clear.")

"It brings it to a different society," Chuck told a roomful of reporters that April when discussing the title tune, which he hoped "upgrades" the Buffalo Springfield landmark. Later in *Lyrics Of A Rap Revolutionary*, Chuck expounded, saying "[T]o be on a track that is known as a classic you'd better say something that bridges the new idea and the old theme well. I really felt that God was with me that day I was writing those lyrics because I don't think all the lyrics came from me."

And what convinced Stills to collaborate with Public Enemy? "I started out playing black music and blues, so, of course, I'm gonna follow what the brothas is up to next," he explained to *Entertainment Weekly*. At the time of the song's release, he was actually working on a rap song of his own. "I've gotta live with it for a while," he cautioned. "It might be completely ridiculous. But it's very difficult to do, I can sure as hell tell you that. Anybody who thinks [rap is] stupid or simple oughta try it."

On one level, 'He Got Game' seemed strange because it was such a blatant usage of an older, famous song – the sort of thing that less-admired rappers like Puff Daddy or Hammer would have done. But after the initial shock wore off, what became clear was that 'He Got Game' was one of Public Enemy's most mature anthems, a sincere way to build bridges between generations in a way Chuck had never tried before.

Speaking of Puff Daddy's blatant biting in relation to 'He Got Game''s appropriation of 'For What It's Worth', Chuck D addressed what he felt was the difference in a *Rolling Stone* interview from 1999. "I think when somebody like Puffy does a 'Missing You' with a Sting, for 'Every Breath You Take', he paves the road in society to make something like that less corny. Not to say we would have been afraid to try it. I mean if he knocked down the barrier, maybe we could obliterate it."

"'He Got Game' was a lost moment," says Danny Goldberg. "I mean, that song could have been a hit. For whatever reason, Def Jam didn't think it was, and maybe it wasn't a hit on Hot 97. But to me, that song is as good as any Public Enemy song ever. That's a somewhat underappreciated song in their canon."

It wasn't that Def Jam didn't try to put some muscle behind it. Spike Lee shot a video for the song, which was the first single from the album. In March of '98, the group was in New York City with the filmmaker working on the clip. During a break from shooting, Chuck talked to MTV News about the soundtrack. "Spike Lee wanted to do something different with the movie soundtrack," he explained. "He kind of got tired with the way soundtracks were treated for movies, especially urban flicks, with various artists, and sometimes the artists doing a song that doesn't even mean anything to the movie, and 10 years later he said, 'Why not try something different?'"

But while the shoot was going on, there was tension behind the scenes. "Flav didn't want to be on the video set if Griff was there," remembers Young. "They had a beef. The day of the video, I'm like, 'Damn, man, come on!' These guys hadn't worked with Griff since '89, but I had been working with him all along. I didn't know about these issues from being on the road and just personal stuff."

Also during that video shoot, Chuck told a reporter, "This project, here, has been an internal and external hell" – referring, presumably, to the entirety of the struggle of reuniting the fractious members of Public Enemy.

Flav was also mad at Def Jam at the time. As he describes in *The Icon The Memoir*, he was broke – the IRS had frozen his assets, he claims – and he was too ashamed to ask for help from his bandmates. So he approached label head Lyor Cohen for assistance. "I went into his office," Flav writes, "and I told him straight up, 'Lyor, I need some money. . . . My kids need diapers, milk and all that shit. I need some money to live on, man.'" Cohen declined, which infuriated the artist. "Here I am, signed to Def Jam as a solo artist and with Public Enemy, and I can't get a dime?"

According to Flav, Cohen said "that the label wasn't going to advance me a dime until they got more work out of Public Enemy. . . . [T]hey were advancing all this money for the new Public Enemy album and there wasn't any more coming until it came out and they saw how it did, financially."

Flav acknowledges that he probably looked frightening when he met with Cohen. "I'd been using crack for over 10 years," he writes, "and by then I was starting to look like a crackhead, naw'mean?" The more he tried to convince Cohen, the more resolute the executive was. And the label refused to put out his solo album. "No album meant no cash," Flav writes, "and I ended up living in an environment that kept me around drugs."

The singer lashed out at Cohen and the label on his *He Got Game* contribution 'Shake Your Booty', a dancy number that's fun but disposable. According to Flav, he included the lyrics "Fuck Lyor" and "Fuck Def Jam", neither of which appears in the final version. However, there is a moment during the second verse where the vocal is noticeably muted, which might have been where the lyrics were. Flav claims that Cohen heard the "Fuck Lyor" line and said, "Take it out or we won't put the album out."

When the film *He Got Game* opened in May 1998, it received strong reviews, with critics calling it one of Lee's best fiction films in several years. They also noted the mixture of Public Enemy's new tunes and older pieces from deceased composer Aaron Copland, which gave the drama a poetic grandeur that juxtaposed with the rap band's harsher sonics. As comparative literature and film professor Krin Gabbard argues in *Black Magic: White Hollywood And African American Culture*, Lee had already pulled off this trick once in *Do The Right Thing* by mixing Public Enemy's abrasive 'Fight The Power' with his father, Bill Lee's, jazzy score.

Speaking to *Entertainment Weekly* in 1998, Lee talked about that juxtaposition of hard and soft, anger and sweetness. "I know people think that's insane," he said, "but that's the music I listen to. I play Aaron Copland and Public Enemy and the Beatles and John Coltrane and Steely Dan and Busta Rhymes and Dinah Washington and Ella Fitzgerald and Patsy Cline. I don't make distinctions – just the music I love and the music I hate."

Public Enemy received solid reviews for *He Got Game*, which was generally considered their best since *Apocalypse 91*. It's an imperfect but focused album, lacking the undeniable genius of the band's early days but repositioning some of Chuck D's familiar diatribes into a new, fresher context. Then again, maybe it's miracle enough that the album even happened. In a chat with AOL users after the film's release, Chuck was asked how he'd rate the soundtrack. "I would give it an 8," he responded, presumably on a scale of 1 to 10. He said he was basing his score on "the short amount of time we had to make it."

A final note on the absurdity of the period. The *He Got Game* album cover is the only one in the PE canon not to feature the band's iconic bull's-eye logo. The familiar stencil of the group's name – "Public" on top of "Enemy" with a thick line in between – appears, though. This was not PE's idea. In a piece for *Vibe*'s August 1998 issue, band confidant Harry Allen explained that Disney, which released the film through Touchstone Pictures, nixed the crosshairs logo. "We decided, from a corporate stand-point, that we had some problems with their logo," a senior vice president of publicity for Buena Vista Pictures Marketing, told Allen. "It's a violent image."

Dealing with Disney about the album cover, Chuck said to Allen, was "the low point of the project". In exchange for removing the logo, Public Enemy were allowed to use the movie's artwork, including the prominent picture of Denzel Washington that ended up on the cover. A similar image was the centrepiece of the movie's poster. "Def Jam wasn't putting up anything toward marketing, so we decided to replace the target with Denzel," Chuck said. He laughed and added, "For the first time, maybe PE can get the elusive black female audience."

He Got Game spent 10 weeks on the charts, getting as high as number 26. The movie, which was the number one film in the US on its opening weekend, was one of Lee's highest-grossing, ending up at about $21.6 million.

★   ★   ★

"Everybody looks at this like it's kind of weird. My lighting technician told Queen Latifah about it. She was like, 'What's up with Terminator? What's he smokin'?'"

It was a few months before *He Got Game* was coming out, and Terminator X was speaking to *Vibe*'s Corey Takahashi from his farm in Vance County, North Carolina. He was discussing his side business, one of the strangest in pop music: raising African black ostriches. "It's considered a red meat," explained Terminator X, who pointed out that the exotic delicacy had a lower fat content than chicken. "They're like big chickens, as far as taking care of them. They graze on grass like cows, but you have to give them pellet seed too."

Though still part of Public Enemy, Terminator X had been considering his options after a 1994 motorcycle accident sent him to the hospital for a month, his legs badly injured. "When he got home," Young recalls, "I went to his house and visited him. We were like family – I'm just glad he was alive, you know? When they mentioned how fast he was going . . . that overpass is stone he smacked into, he was just going fast. I had lost a few friends to motorcycle accidents, but for him to survive, man, that's a blessing."

But after *He Got Game*, Terminator was essentially done with the group. Or as he puts it in an email, *He Got Game* was "[t]he last album I had input on". In *Don't Rhyme For The Sake Of Riddlin'*, it's suggested that Terminator left because of a dislike for touring. According to Russell Myrie's biography, after PE had finished touring at the end of 1998, Chuck reached out to the DJ to discuss road plans for the following year. When Chuck finally got in contact with Terminator X, "He said he 'kinda wanted to come on tour and kinda didn't,'" Chuck said. "And then he just said that was it, which left us kinda like, 'OK, now what do we do?'"

Terminator X refutes that version of events. "I loved touring in the US," he responds via email. "I loved touring overseas . . . BUT, I didn't like being so far away from home for long periods of time while overseas. I loved performing onstage. I just didn't like being so far away from home. To me . . . it felt like I may as well have been on another planet. It was too expensive to call home from overseas at that time and there was no [FaceTime] or any of the things we have now. So I felt cut off from home. That is not part of the reason I left the group."

So what was the reason? "To make a long story short, and to keep from 'putting all my business in the street', I will say that I was monetarily pushed out of the group," he writes. "Any self-respecting person would have left just as I did. It's the same old story as always. Egos and bands don't mix." The DJ also suggests that tensions during the making of *He Got Game* contributed to his departure. "There was a rift between Hank

Shocklee and Chuck during the *He Got Game* album," Terminator writes. "I don't know the details because I was a business outsider. I found out later that Chuck felt that I sided with Hank Shocklee and I think that is why I was treated badly at the end of my time with PE."

From Terminator's perspective, his exit was in part precipitated by the fact that his involvement in the group had decreased as Public Enemy went along. "Yes, the PE album process definitely evolved over the years," he says. "There was no 'Bomb Squad' on the first album. . . . For the most part I had little say in the making of the PE albums." In fact, Terminator confirms that he "was never on the PE contract. . . . I was only a full member in the public eye but when it came to the business end, I was always left out. I was always promised to be included later but never was."

"Hank Shocklee, Bill Stephney and Chuck were the major players," Terminator says, in regards to who masterminded the early albums. "Once in a while I was tossed a bone [by] using one of my tracks. In the early albums I was there for a lot [of] studio time. But as time went on I was left out more and more. I was called in to do scratches for songs. There were songs that I was not even given a chance to scratch on."

Unlike Chuck's claim that Terminator surprised them by wanting out, the DJ says that his choice to leave PE was met with indifference by his fellow band members. "[T]hey didn't even ask me why I left," Terminator writes. "No effort was made to get me back." Now looking back on his time with the band, he sounds proud of their achievements, if still a little disappointed how it all played out. "I had a good run with PE and it was a great experience," he writes. "I loved the shows the most. But I think the bad things keep me from missing it." Asked if he keeps up with the band's albums since his departure, he admits that he hasn't. "Why? I'm not exactly sure. I think it's because I have moved on with my life . . . and PE isn't a part of it."

Terminator was still part of the line-up for the group's next album – Chuck D even name-checked him in a song – but he was already plotting his post-PE life. In a 2013 interview, he made it clear that he had no love for an industry he viewed with contempt. "The music business is like the worst street in the worst neighbourhood you can think of," he told

WHO?MAG TV. "You can be robbed, pimped, hustled, misled and everything else if you don't realise where you are. Someone said to me, 'The music business can break your heart.' They couldn't have said it any better. I didn't want anything to do with it. I didn't know where I was then."

Incidentally, he's no longer raising ostriches. "My family is raising goats now," he writes. "The ostrich thing didn't work well. Goats are doing much better. I am not involved with it any more though."

CHAPTER NINE

EVEN while finishing *He Got Game*, Chuck D was looking ahead to the group's next album. In the liner notes, there appeared this: "Prepare yourself for *There's A Poison Goin On* in the fall, yet another album, another sound before 1999." That message didn't prove completely correct – *There's A Poison Goin On* didn't come out in the fall of '98 – but it did represent a different aesthetic from the band. The album isn't remembered for that, however, although it should be. Instead, it's known mostly for the way it came to fans.

He Got Game was the final album Public Enemy made for Def Jam. Chuck was ebullient about the split. "I finally murdered my contract," he said with a laugh while talking to *Perfect Sound Forever*'s Jason Gross. Later, he added, "A lot of people said, 'It seems strange that you're not on Def Jam any more. How do you feel?' I say that I feel like a black man in 1866, trying to figure out what the fuck I do with my freedom."

It's not uncommon for an irritated artist to gloat about being rid of a label that didn't understand his genius, especially when it seemed that the artist's commercial and creative peak had passed. But Chuck's braggadocio wasn't just empty patter. Years later, he claimed that Def Jam had offered him a contract worth a million dollars to stay. "What the hell is a $1 million contract when you don't have control of your shit?" he asked *Billboard*. "That $1 million is never going to be spent by you. It's going to be spent on your behalf by someone who's just pressing buttons and pushing numbers. And at the end of the day, you've got what? Because they've spent your money trying to make their profit while you're working on a percentage."

His aggravation might also have something to do with the financial situation surrounding *He Got Game*. In *Don't Rhyme For The Sake Of Riddlin'*, Chuck says, "I wasn't in charge of that record and it still affects me today, it affects my royalties."

But while other artists moan about label interference, at least Chuck was a trendsetter in how he addressed the problem. The rapper had become convinced that the future of music wasn't in traditional record labels but, instead, this developing technology known as the World Wide Web. He met with different companies about distributing *He Got Game*'s follow-up, coming away most impressed by a label veteran, the sort of old-school executive one would assume might be the last person Chuck would want to partner with.

Before Al Teller ran CBS Records, Columbia Records or MCA, he earned two engineering degrees from Columbia University, later moving on to get his MBA from Harvard. "I was at Columbia [University] for most of the sixties," he recalled in an interview with *This Week In Music*, "and I was down in Greenwich Village with friends of mine from Columbia, and we would see some of the greatest artists in the world passing through the clubs down in the Village. . . . But I never thought that there was a business attached to this. It was just being a fan." That changed after he partnered with the consulting firm McKinsey & Company while at Harvard. He was assigned to work with CBS Records, which had hired McKinsey. "Walking into the CBS building and turning off the elevator bank and rounding the corner to head to the office for my first meeting there, I heard music coming out of the offices," Teller said. "I looked inside, there were guys wearing T-shirts . . . and I knew instantly, 'This is me. This was what I had to do.'"

His first music job was as the assistant to powerful mogul Clive Davis in the fall of 1969. Five years later, Teller was his own label boss as head of United Artists Records. The combination of technology and artistry, the mixture of business and passion, drove him. And his engineering background gave him an advantage over some of his competitors.

"I was always interested in technology and always keeping up to date with what was happening," he told *This Week In Music*. "I certainly knew about the internet early on . . . Even when the CD first came about – some old engineering-school classmates and I were sitting around in a bar one night, and we were talking about how the CD was not only a new physical format for music but it planted the seeds of what was to come many years later. Because once you could represent music in a binary fashion, you're talking the language of computers. We had a signal-processing engineer with us at the bar, and he said, 'Hey, once it's on a computer, we can move it from one computer to the next.'"

That conversation, by Teller's recollection, was in 1983 or '84. "I was really, totally convinced that, one day, the entire music business as we knew it in its pre-internet form − all of those functions were going to migrate and be mapped onto the internet, on the online space. And I wanted to be part of that."

The notion that computers were going to be the future of music − not just in the studio but also for distribution − was Teller's constant refrain. In March 1994, *Billboard* published his essay about the commercial prospects of MCA, where he was chairman. Teller sounded confident about the label's potential growth, but he ended with this warning: "The industry's number one priority as a whole is to emerge from the new technology fray with an improved ability to deliver software to each and every consumer across the globe."

"I probably sounded like Paul Revere on steroids," he admitted on *This Week In Music* when talking about the meetings he would have with his fellow major-label bosses. "I kept saying, 'The internet's coming, the internet's coming, the internet's coming. We need to do something about it. We need to get ahead of this, because if we don't get ahead of this, we're going to get wiped away by it.' It fell on deaf ears."

Instead of leading the charge to prepare the industry for the coming storm, Teller soon found himself out of a job. In November 1995, he was fired from MCA, replaced by Doug Morris, who himself had just been sacked by Warner Bros. "I've never seen the music industry in a greater state of flux than right now," Teller commented to Chuck Philips of the *Los Angeles Times* after his removal. "But I've had seven very exciting years at MCA, and I leave knowing that the company is in good hands with the new management."

In February 1999, Teller made it clear that he remained serious about the Web being the business's future. That month, he announced that he was starting a company called Atomic Pop, which would market and distribute bands online. "We plan to break artists online and migrate a number of record company functionalities online," Teller told Philips.

"Because we will be web-centric, our cost structure is going to be radically different than that of the major record labels. We intend to create a very different financial landscape that will be appealing to artists."

One of those artists it appealed to was Chuck D. "Al Teller was the first and last person I spoke to once I decided to go with the internet" to release *There's A Poison Goin On*, the singer told *Billboard* in the summer of 1999. "In between, there were about 25 other companies, but they leaned too heavily on either technology or music. Al just had the right combination in his approach. We were a perfect match in our vision, and I've had a good experience working with him in the past." Teller, of course, was at MCA when the possibility of a label deal for Chuck, Hank Shocklee and Bill Stephney was floated in the late eighties. "We both think of the music in interactive terms first, then move it into the offline world," Chuck continued.

The rapper had been thinking in interactive terms when he planned the release of a remix album, *Bring The Noise 2000*, which the band would put on its website. But when Public Enemy tried to do so in the fall of 1998, the label bosses blocked them. Chuck expressed his annoyance on PE's home page, writing, "Today Polygram/Universal or whatever the fuck they're now called forced us to remove the MP3 version of *Bring The Noise 2000*. The execs, lawyers and accountants who lately have made most of the money in the music biz are now running scared from the technology that evens out the creative field and makes artists harder to pimp. Let 'em all die . . . I'm glad to be a contributor to the bomb . . ."

"Major record labels are like dinosaurs," he later told *Wired*. "They move slow. Our album *Bring The Noise 2000* was slated for a March '98 release, but PolyGram slept on it. So we released it in MP3 on our supersite. Why not? Our fans wanted the music. And we believe in the technology. We didn't sell the tracks, so to us it was the same as just making more promotional copies."

The industry, sensing what this new digital revolution could trigger, panicked, blocking artists from putting their music online. Public Enemy weren't the only band slapped by its label: around Christmas 1998, Billy Idol and Beastie Boys both saw some songs pulled from the web. In the case of Idol, he reportedly was annoyed that his label, Capitol, wasn't going to release the album he'd just finished, and so he approached a new-ish site, MP3.com, to preview some of the rejected tracks. But Capitol, which was working on a deal with Idol to get him out of his contract, was supposedly angered by the MP3 leak and threatened to end negotiations if he didn't remove the songs. "Capitol said the [contract] exit deal hadn't been finished, even though everyone knew it had mainly been negotiated but hadn't been signed," a source told Chris Nelson from MTV News. "[Idol is] effectively being told, 'You're dropped, but you can't do what you want anyway.' It's really a weird place that they've put him in."

These other artist disputes only emboldened Chuck. "It's the chicken coming home to roost," Chuck said to *Wired* about the Beastie Boys and Idol situations, "the levelling of the playing field, the little man getting his chance. Soon you'll see a marketplace with 500,000 independent labels – the majors can co-opt all they want, but it's not going to stop the average person from getting into the game. Today a major label makes a CD for as little as 80 cents, then sells it wholesale for $10.50 so retailers can charge $14 – that's highway robbery. They were able to pimp that technology. Well, MP3 is a technology they can't pimp." As for music executives' concern that online music will only contribute to piracy, Chuck responded, "To the pirates, I say the more the merrier. Success comes from the fans first – if someone is going to pirate something of mine, I just have to make sure to do nine or 10 new things. I mean, you can't download me."

Chuck was inspired in part by noticing that his daughter, who was 10, was discovering new artists online. For the rapper, who never enjoyed a lot of radio airplay, the idea that there was this new technology that could get his music out, without the hurdles that traditional radio presented, must have seemed like a godsend. "There's incredible, diverse talent," Chuck told *Wired*. "But the way radio, retail, and record companies govern the music is wack – playola, payola, and censorship turn artists into one-track ponies. . . . Instead of just depending on a song and a video, the net will bring back live performances. Artists will be able to release a song every two weeks, instead of waiting six, seven months for a label to put it out. A band can become like a broadcaster."

Public Enemy's deal with Atomic Pop guaranteed the band 50 percent of the gross profit from *There's A Poison Goin On* – that number was usually closer to 10 percent at a traditional label – and Chuck would maintain ownership of the master recordings. His rationale was summarised in two lines from the *Poison* track they put up online as a free download, 'Swindlers Lust': "If you don't own the master / Then the master own you." Essentially, if an artist has control of his masters, he can dictate how they're used in the future.

As one example of the importance of owning your masters, the pop-metal band Def Leppard decided that they weren't happy with the digital royalties they were getting from their label for their old hits. So, in 2012, the band rerecorded smashes like 'Pour Some Sugar On Me' with a fidelity that made them sound like the originals and then blocked their record company, Universal, from using the originals on platforms like iTunes or in movies and ads. Since Def Leppard owned their masters, they had the right to redo the songs and enjoy a higher royalty rate. Chuck D would no doubt have appreciated Def Leppard frontman Joe Elliott's sentiment about not feeling bad for the label. "We bought that building in the eighties [because of all the band's hits], and they treat us like shit," Elliott told *The Hollywood Reporter*. "We've become irrelevant to the label, so we're putting on the battle armour."

"Public Enemy and Atomic Pop is like a partnership, whereas the music business is more like music *employment*," Chuck told *NME*. "It's different from the same old game. Yes, it's capitalism, but it's like socialistic reform of the music purchase process."

Landing Public Enemy was a coup for Atomic Pop, which had previously signed New Wave legends Blondie, punk-rockers L7, and Wu-Tang Clan's RZA. Beyond releasing music, Teller's label also wanted to sell items like cosmetics and comics. (With L7, Atomic Pop developed a video game featuring the band members.) "Never underestimate the true music fan who's always eager to hear new things, always eager for new information about the artist," Teller told MTV News. "When a fan gets into a particular artist, there's no such thing as too much."

Online distribution also had the advantage of requiring fewer costs. There was no longer a physical item that needed to be made, nor was there a need to ship that item to a store. With *There's A Poison Goin On*, the album would be available online first but then sold as a CD in traditional outlets like record stores and malls. These lowered costs would mean that a label such as Atomic Pop could sell the album for a lower price than their old-fashioned competitors could. And with artists enjoying a higher percentage of each album sale, they would see bigger profits than if they signed with a traditional label. "Change is inevitable, and everything is about to change," Chuck D said to *The New York Times'* Neil Strauss. "Once one record goes through this, it's the shovel in the dirt."

Label executives could see the shovels everywhere. In April, around the same time as the Public Enemy deal with Atomic Pop was announced, alt-rock superstar Alanis Morissette made plans for a new tour, which would be sponsored by MP3.com. The site would also, reportedly, offer Morissette a financial stake in the company. Tom Petty got into a dispute with his label, Warner Bros., after he offered his new single to MP3.com for download. And soon we saw statements like this from corporations such as Warner Bros.: "While we are happy that MP3.com has found a way to work cooperatively with Tom Petty & the Heartbreakers to promote the legitimate sale of their music, Warner Bros. Records Inc. does not endorse the dissemination of its copyrights through any unsecured digitally distributed format." The music industry still wasn't heeding Teller's warning: it was trying to fight an insurmountable tide.

But revolutions rarely run smoothly. In *The New York Times*, Teller acknowledged that "People are going to have to be patient" when it came to downloading the record from the web, estimating that it might take up to three hours for some consumers. In a separate piece for the *Times*, Neil Strauss related his troubles with downloading *Poison*: "As I write this, three days have passed, I have spent 12 hours on the computer, I may or may not have spent $16 on my credit card for the $8 album and only moments ago I had the hard-earned privilege of hearing the first of its songs." And some at the traditional labels weren't convinced that an entity like Atomic would really usher in an era of greater artistic freedom. "The artist takes all the risks and pays for everything," Lawrence Kenswil, the head of MCA Inc.'s Universal Music Group e-commerce division, said to *Forbes*. "All [Atomic] does is post the files on the web. And for that they take a 50 percent cut? That sounds like a bad deal to me."

But when *Billboard* ran a front-page story in early May discussing the controversy surrounding MP3s, it was clear that, despite the fears of piracy, some in the music business saw the internet as an opportunity to reach listeners in a new way. "The technology companies . . . have the community," one anonymous exec said, "and they have the money to move things forward. It's frustrating, because we just want to break our bands. . . . The internet is the only place [a new artist] will get exposure – and we are limited in what we can do." A label president told *Billboard* that an unspecified new band would be putting out its album by MP3. "This record never had a chance to be heard when it was originally released," the president said, "because it was shut out by radio. Making it free won't lose us any money, because there is no money to make on the record. But it will enable us to build interest in the next release."

Such sentiments echoed Teller's own reasons for getting into the business in the first place. "I loved the idea of participating in the process that would take a fabulous, unknown musician to major public hero," he once said about his drive during his early days. "I loved the challenge of finding artists and taking them to the fans. . . . There are only two permanent aspects of the music business: artists who create music, fans who want it. The challenge of the business, however that business is constructed at any point in time, is to connect those two constituents in the most efficient and effective way."

Before anyone heard a minute of *There's A Poison Goin On*, it was a landmark album simply based on the fact that it was being distributed in a new way. But the album was also novel because it found Public Enemy approaching record-making with a different set of tools. As Flavor Flav told biographer Russell Myrie, "Put it this way: Chuck was somewhere and I was on the other end. Chuck would do some shit, and send it. I would listen to what Chuck did, take whatever parts that I wanted, put my parts on it, then send it back. The chemistry of that album was slightly different."

The passing back and forth of digital files would become the standard operating procedure for PE afterward. Granted, it had been a while since the tight, in-the-studio feel of *Nation Of Millions* or *Fear Of A Black Planet*, but *There's A Poison Goin On* formally started the tradition of Public

Enemy albums coming together in parts. Gone were the gospel choruses and booming samples of *He Got Game*. Gone was the live rock'n'roll vibe of *Muse Sick*. In their place was a slinky, insidious, almost paranoid energy. In interviews, Chuck described *Poison* as a "combination of Redman meets Pink Floyd meets Rage Against the Machine meets Chemical Brothers". Around the album's release, Chuck was quoted as saying, "Anybody who knows anything about Public Enemy knows that we've never made two records alike. It's a blessing and curse. The topics are relevant. They follow the line of Public Enemy discussion. Sonically, yes, there's dense layering, but it's gonna be different."

What was also different were the credits. "Beats created, conceived, hacked and demolished by Tom E Hawk," the liner notes said. When *The Stranger* queried Chuck about the identity of Hawk, the rapper responded, "Tom E Hawk is a guy who works on the Mountain. That's all I'm allowed to say. . . . Too much emphasis is put on producers. We started that [with the Bomb Squad], but it's gotten out of hand. So we're ending it. Every time we put out an album it's [like], 'Who produced it? Who produced it? Who produced it?' I'm like, 'Did you listen to the record?'"

Reviewers listened, and mostly liked what they heard. But there was a perception in some of the reviews that the band was trying to reclaim some of its lost cultural relevance. Howard Hampton's *LA Weekly* review opened this way: "If any pop group wants to commit career suicide, there's no better blueprint than Sly & the Family Stone's 1971 classic *There's A Riot Goin' On*: all junkie smiles, bad-news bulletins, slow-death jams and yodelling space cowboys. The crucial difference between that and Public Enemy's doom-struck homage *There's A Poison Goin On* is Sly and Co. had a career to throw away, while PE has already been pretty much consigned to the ranks of the has-been/washed-up. But failure, desperation and irrelevance seem to have opened up Public Enemy's paranoia even as the music's gotten bleaker, trickier and more intense."

"A decade after they reinvented hip-hop, Public Enemy no longer bring the media noise the way they once did," wrote Greg Kot in *Rolling Stone*. "But after a falling-out with their long-time label, Def Jam, PE are now once again wearing redwood-size chips on their shoulders." Kot's review concluded with the assessment that *Poison* "suggest[s] that a little midlife crisis is just what PE needed."

There's A Riot Goin' On was a personal, bleary depiction of the sixties' fading idealism. *There's A Poison Goin On* was Chuck's way of crafting a similar epoch-defining statement. But rather than looking back like Sly Stone was, he had his eyes fixed on an uncertain future. The album opens with the instrumental 'Dark Side Of The Wall: 2000', which, as it's described in the liner notes that accompanied the album's 2004 rerelease, was meant to chronicle "the countdown to a 'terrifying future'" that included fears of a Y2K bug that would wipe out computers worldwide and create mass hysteria. Much like 'Welcome To The Terrordome' articulated Chuck's fear for the African-American community in the nineties, *Poison* was an anxious response to the new century.

But unlike earlier albums, *Poison* wasn't so much a statement about black America as it was an attack on society at large. "We're always going to try to be topical so we always pick topics that are going to be different," Chuck explained to *Perfect Sound Forever.* "There's different topics for every album and different sounds on every album. It's inevitable. The larger detail remains the same though – I'm always fighting something." With *Poison*, he was fighting racism, war and (in '41:19') police brutality. But the record got its prickly tension by channelling the pre-millennium anxiety that was swamping the culture. In the buildup to 2000, there was excitement regarding this new century, but there was also a lingering dread. Most prominent of these worries was Y2K, the shorthand for a belief that certain computer programs would fail on January 1 if the way they recorded the date couldn't adjust for a new millennium, perhaps because some programs only accounted for the last two numbers in a four-digit year. This sparked fears that crucial systems, such as air traffic control computers, would collapse, throwing the world into chaos.

But the change from 1999 to 2000 nonetheless held an almost euphoric sense of apocalyptic dread, perhaps best encapsulated by Prince's hit 1982 anthem '1999', which made the cusp of a new century sound both transcendent and cataclysmic – a huge party to celebrate the end. (The chorus: "They say two thousand zero zero / Party over / Oops, out of time / So tonight / I'm gonna party like it's 1999.") And in the music business, the spread of MP3s signalled a similar mixture of hope and apprehension, pointing toward a future that promised great change and possibility but also a fundamental shift in how the industry operated.

Poison doesn't overtly address that shift except for the anti-radio rant 'Crayola' and the anti-label closing track 'Swindlers Lust', but the album's minimalist beats and electronic instrumentation couldn't help but seem to tap into the era's high-tech anxiety. Making that connection isn't so much of a stretch considering that, after *He Got Game*, Chuck swore that his next album would be distributed online. Even before including 'Interactive Super Highway Phone Call' on *Muse Sick*, the singer had long been intrigued by the possibility of the internet. "I was first introduced to the internet in 1991 with a Terminator X record," he told *Billboard* in July of 1999. "We used it as a different way to handle interviews. Since he was a DJ, he was not a verbal person. The computer let him speak with his hands." And as with 'Interactive Super Highway Phone Call', it had been Harry Allen who had suggested to Chuck that he use the web to promote the DJ's solo album, *Terminator X & The Valley Of The Jeep Beets*.

Especially in retrospect, *Poison* feels like the sort of album that reflected how the internet would change our lives. It's a record of random observations pulled from headlines, varied cultural influences and the sorts of ranting message boards that you stumble onto at two in the morning. *Poison* is buzzy and impatient where previous PE records stomped and shook with compelling force. It's as if we can hear our attention spans shrinking as we listen to it.

That's not meant to sound glib or dismissive: even its title suggests that *There's A Poison Goin On* wanted to address the ways that we were becoming more interconnected thanks to the web. Chuck's revelation of how globalisation creates more have-nots became the inspiration for *Apocalypse 91*'s 'Shut 'Em Down'. On *Poison*'s 'World Tour Sessions', he marvelled at his band's ability to tour the planet, only to discover that injustice and inequality were everywhere. The wonder of cutting-edge science was treated as a grim nightmare in 'First The Sheep Next The Shepherd?': Chuck imagines a frightening scenario when cloning becomes a reality. And in the album liner notes, there are several mentions to the songs being jammed with lots of ideas, a symptom of an era in which information overload had reached new heights. For example, 'Kevorkian' recalls Jack Kevorkian, a doctor and euthanasia activist prominent in the nineties, for a condemnation of how governments legally kill people.

Also worth remembering: Chuck was going to turn 40 in 2000. Always an older head in the rap game, he was certainly feeling his seniority by the time of *Poison*. After the album's release, a journalist asked Chuck where he saw Public Enemy's standing in the hip-hop world. "Elder statesmen," he replied, "legends. But not just people who sit on their laurels. Public Enemy is like the Led Zeppelin of rap music but kind of more intact because we don't have a John Bonham," Zeppelin's drummer who died in 1980.

And like some older people, Chuck indulged his reactionary, paranoid side. While 'First The Sheep Next The Shepherd?' freaked out about cloning and abortion, 'Do You Wanna Go Our Way???' ripped on Def Jam, gangster rap and inner-city crime, with Chuck bragging that his flash-in-the-pan competition could focus on the 100-metre dash – he was busy training for a marathon. The song ended with what sounded like unsettling horror-movie dialogue: "*Please*, be quiet! They'll hear us!" And on 'Crayola', Chuck forgoes lyrical complexity to snarl and scream about the payola he observes in commercial radio.

But unlike loony conspiracy theorists gumming up the comments section of your favourite website, Chuck retained control of his faculties, even sounding rejuvenated. *He Got Game* sharpened his lyrical thrust because he was able to use sports as a microcosm for the social ills he saw elsewhere. The opposite proved true on *Poison*: a larger perspective enriched his assault. Take 'LSD', whose title, according to Chuck, stood for "lawyers should die" (or "lawyers suck dick") – and, indeed, there are a few venomous lines directed at power brokers such as accountants and attorneys. Chuck made his feelings more explicit in *Fight The Power* when he wrote, "I detest the system of white lawyers, agents and accountants dominating the music and sports industry. . . . Entertainment law is not like real law. Real law is more stable and the environment is built around it. Entertainment law can shift at any time."

Backed by a quietly percolating beat, Chuck on 'LSD' also touches on the 1995 Oklahoma City bombing ("Truck fulla fertiliser / Blowin' up the spot / Think it's terrorism . . . / Surprise they home grown / And one of your fuckin' own"), compares himself to Nirvana frontman Kurt Cobain, who took his own life in 1994, and declares that he's in it for the long haul ("Rather try at 37 than die at 26"). Like the best of *Poison*, 'LSD' stealthily skips around from topic to topic, absorbing current events and drawing parallels between disparate items. Most Public Enemy songs feel like news bulletins, but *Poison* counterbalanced its lyrical overload with the band's sparest music, giving the songs the equivalent of the arid post-apocalyptic landscapes we recognise from movies like *Mad Max*.

Chuck and his team weren't hiding in their bunker, though. 'Last Mass Of The Caballeros' opened with what sounded like the theme music to a forgotten Western, while 'Kevorkian' incorporated the gnarly, grimy energy of trip-hop. Promoting the album, Chuck used the same over-blown rhetoric wielded by most artists trying to hype their latest release. "The album is like no other rap and hip-hop album," he declared to MTV News, later adding, "This is the most aggressive music imaginable." But on *Poison*, Public Enemy didn't want to be louder than a bomb: these songs were as quietly menacing as that nagging fear that won't let you go to sleep at night.

A perfect example is Flavor Flav's '41:19', about Amadou Diallo, a twentysomething immigrant from Guinea who was slain by officers of the New York Police Department in February 1999. He was unarmed, and the song's title refers to how many shots were fired and how many times Diallo was hit. Spare and insistent, '41:19' finds Flav in inspired form, lamenting the killing but also noting how quickly such atrocities are forgotten, especially by those in power: "Your kids miss you when you're gone / But life still goes on / You think they give a fuck?" It's a minor marvel of responding to a tragedy without drowning good intentions in overblown theatrics. By comparison, Bruce Springsteen the following year started performing a new song, called 'American Skin', that, although heartfelt, stumbled over its own melodrama. When NYPD officers pro-tested the Boss's song, Springsteen had Flav's support. "Bruce Springsteen, he sees the picture," Flavor said in the summer of 2000. "Can't no one blame a man for seeing reality the way that it is. And y'know what? I'm with my man all the way."

Springsteen and Public Enemy intersected in unexpected ways again on 'I', which was also known as 'Eye For An Eye'. It's that rare storytelling song from Chuck D as he plays a nameless, homeless narrator walking through the inner city, seeing the scars of crime and disrepair all around him. "I was influenced by Bruce Springsteen's 'Streets Of Philadelphia'," Chuck told Amazon.com. "Especially the video, when he walks through the streets of Philadelphia for the movie *Philadelphia*. . . . I'm walking through the streets of the 'hood, and not only do I not recognise the 'hood, I don't recognise myself! The whole concept is that, in society, there are a lot of things happening to people that we don't even notice. And these are poisons, and if you know anything about poison, you know poisons can take you over unknowingly. And there are a lot of poisons in the environment, and people are being killed slowly in the process. This is the real 'Killing Me Softly'," which might have been a reference to the 1996 smash cover of 'Killing Me Softly With His Song' that helped propel the innovative hip-hop group the Fugees and their singer Lauryn Hill into the mainstream.

In Springsteen's Oscar-winning song, the main character laments, "I was unrecognisable to myself / I saw my reflection in a window / I didn't know my own face." The same malady affects the narrator in 'I': he looks in the mirror and doesn't recognise the face staring back, a physical embodiment of the spiritual isolation he feels after years of expecting more from himself and his community. The film *Philadelphia* chronicled the plight of a gay attorney (played by Tom Hanks, who won a Best Actor Oscar for the role) dying of AIDS, but in "I" the death sentence is the ghetto itself, a permanent prison that traps the narrator and all those around him. At the song's end, the narrator "escapes", sort of: he gets his throat slit by muggers.

"I was influenced strangely enough by the walks I used to take through Roosevelt, Long Island back when I was around 19," Chuck wrote in *Lyrics Of A Rap Revolutionary*. "I would just take long walks trying to figure myself out. . . . As I'd take these long walks I'd be looking around and thinking, 'I don't want to be that. I ain't trying to do that.'" In *Lyrics*, he mentions that Springsteen's video didn't square with his own recollections of walking through the inner city. "There are some abnormalities in a regular walk through the neighbourhood when you're black," Chuck wrote. In 'I', that included the presence of drug dealers, malt liquor ads, preachers and pimps talking to one another, broken bottles and snack bags littering the street, mentally ill vagrants, and unemployed black men looking for work or resigned to stop trying. The first-person reportage wasn't just a new wrinkle from Chuck, it was a revelation – one, sadly, he hasn't tried much since.

Naturally, much of the attention surrounding *There's A Poison Goin On* centred on its online release. But the album's finale, 'Swindlers Lust', generated some unexpected controversy. After Public Enemy were forced to remove *Bring The Noise 2000* from their website in early 1999, Chuck responded by posting 'Swindlers Lust', a bitter, slinky kiss-off that compared the modern music industry to the slave trade, condemning the "vultures of culture" who for decades exploited black artists such as blues musicians, soul singers and rappers.

On its face, the song was a catchy, somewhat familiar gripe about the sleaziness of the business. But Chris Nelson of MTV News saw the song as perhaps targeting Jewish music executives. "Recently, I asked Chuck D if he was concerned that 'Swindlers Lust' would attract new allegations of anti-Semitism," Nelson wrote. "The track, after all, levels charges of graft and greed against an industry in which Jews have played a significant role (among the many labels founded or run by people of Jewish descent are Blue Note, Chess, Geffen and the hip-hop imprints Def Jam and Loud). To some, that might teeter perilously close to the ugly stereotype of Jewish people as money-hungry."

"I'm a wordsmith," Chuck D said to Nelson. "I knew I was going to raise some attention. There was no harm intended towards anyone." In the same interview, he suggested, "The truth is the truth. Black people have been blindsided by all [types of people], including black people. I think it's a hell of a title. People gotta check out the song and tell me whether I'm right or wrong."

About the title: part of Nelson's concern stemmed from the fact that the name 'Swindlers Lust' seemed to be a reference to *Schindler's List*, the Oscar-winning Holocaust drama from director Steven Spielberg. *NME* brought up this charge to Chuck D, who responded, "People might say,

'How could Chuck D play around with Spielberg's creation?' But I'm like, 'Why the fuck not? He's not God!'"

Nelson contacted the director of media relations for the Anti-Defamation League, Myrna Shinbaum, to get her response to the track. "We listened to 'Swindlers Lust' and found no apparent anti-Semitism," she said. "ADL believes it is just as important to say what is not anti-Semitism as what is."

But the issue didn't go away. In June, Abraham Foxman, ADL's national director, sent a letter to Al Teller to condemn 'Swindlers Lust' and its accusation that Jews were responsible for, in Foxman's words, "the plight of financially underprivileged blacks". In particular, he took issue with the lyrics "Mo dollars mo cents for the Big Six / Another million led to bled claimin' they innocence," which he charged was a reference to the Holocaust's killing of six million Jews.

This, paired with the fact that Chuck and Professor Griff had recently formed a side rock band called Confrontation Camp, a play on "concentration camp", didn't sit well with Foxman. ADL, Foxman wrote, would "exercise our First Amendment rights by standing up and calling this unambiguous anti-Semitism". In regards to the alleged allusions to the Holocaust, Foxman declared, "We don't have the luxury to play games. The gas chambers at Auschwitz did not begin with bricks. The gas chambers began with ugly words, hateful words, and they were permitted to evolve into bricks because people found excuses for them." Foxman's letter also complained about the song's mentioning that Chuck's enemies "own the banks". "[C]ontrolling banks and controlling the industry have been classical canards of anti-Semitism fed . . . into the black community," he wrote.

Atomic Pop released a response, pointing out that the so-called "Big Six" lyrics weren't about the Holocaust but, in fact, a swipe at the six major record labels of the time. The "million" was a nod to the Million Man March. Chuck also went on the offensive. On the band's website, he wrote, "I knew some assholes would blindly attack me in the dark. In the beginning, I claimed there were swindlers in all shapes, colours and sizes and left it at that." He also told MTV News that he wanted an apology from the ADL. Foxman was unmoved: "If he didn't intend it to be anti-Semitic, fine," he responded to MTV News. "I welcome that. But in light of where he's coming from, or where he came from before, this is not a time that I should apologise to him."

All in all, it seemed like a rather overblown fracas. If anything, the song could be criticised for Chuck's proud boast that "Chuck don't suck no dick", a needlessly coarse and homophobic way to express his unwillingness to compromise his artistic principals. But pretty soon, the music business would become consumed with matters far more urgent than whether a rap artist may have offended a particular group.

★   ★   ★

In the July 1995 issue of *Wired*, Al Teller was interviewed about his belief that the internet was the future of music. "The internet, and online interactivity in general, is going to have a profound impact on the music business," he said. "So few people in the music industry want to deal with that concept. You have huge resistance to the net throughout the record industry. Some very major players dismiss it as a silly notion." At the time, Teller was part of the National Information Infrastructure Advisory Council, a programme overseen by then-Vice President Al Gore. Its mission, in essence, was to advise on policy regarding how the internet – or, as Gore called it, the "information superhighway" – should be monitored and regulated. And one of the council's focuses was how to handle the question of copyright on the web. "[We're] in the process of drafting our principles regarding copyright," Teller told *Wired*'s John Battelle, "but it's a slow, tedious process. There are extraordinarily complicated questions and issues involved. We encounter opinions that range from complete copyright anarchy on one hand to intense copyright-protection belief on the other. And that entire range of opinion is represented on the council," which included representatives from radio, cable television, and telecommunications companies.

In October of 1998, Congress passed the Digital Millennium Copyright Act as a way to enforce longstanding intellectual property laws in this new online world. One of the act's first tests was Napster, an online service that allowed users to trade songs online for free through their computers. Shawn Fanning and Sean Parker, two guys in their late teens, started the company on June 1, 1999. By September, record companies were taking serious notice of Napster.

Music critic Jessica Hopper was working as a publicist for bands when Napster arrived on the scene. "I remember labels being really frightened, really scared and frantically trying to find a way to stem albums being file-shared – and it was impossible to do so, all efforts were in vain," she told *The Daily Beast*'s Alex Suskind. "Some artists were just happy to have their music out [but] the labels were just wringing their hands."

Fanning, with his omnipresent baseball cap and short-sleeved T-shirts, became the skate-park, punk-rock face of Napster's insurgency. In the 2013 documentary *Downloaded*, he explained that what drove him to the web initially was an absence of connection to his Massachusetts family or classmates. He wasn't a very confident young man, but computers seemed to offer him an escape. "Going online and finding people who had the same interests . . . your reputation was your own," he says in the film. "It was not about, like, how well off your family was, or how well you dressed, or how well you spoke, or body language. It was about the merit of what you were saying. And I think that, for me, was intoxicating."

Within nine months, Napster had found plenty of people who shared an interest in downloading songs: the company had 20 million users by March 2000. A month later, Metallica sued Napster – as well as colleges such as the University of Southern California and Yale – charging them with copyright infringement. On Metallica's website, the band's drummer, Lars Ulrich, posted a statement that said, in part, "We take our craft – whether it be the music, the lyrics, or the photos and artwork – very seriously, as do most artists. It is therefore sickening to know that our art is being traded like a commodity rather than the art that it is. From a business standpoint, this is about piracy – taking something that doesn't belong to you; and that is morally and legally wrong. The trading of such information – whether it's music, videos, photos, or whatever – is, in effect, trafficking in stolen goods."

By that point, Napster was already facing a lawsuit from the Recording Industry Association of America. Rather than speeding up their efforts to produce a legal form of online distribution, the labels attacked upstarts who had figured out how to create a legally questionable alternative.

Responding to the Metallica lawsuit, Napster's acting CEO, Eileen Richardson, said, "We regret that the band's management saw fit to issue a press release – and to file a lawsuit – without even attempting to contact Napster. . . . Many bands who have approached us, learned about Napster and how to leverage what we offer, understand the value of what we do."

Metallica weren't the only artists who despised what Napster represented: Dr. Dre and Nine Inch Nails' Trent Reznor also called the service theft and, like Metallica, Dre sued the company. But one of Napster's early proponents was Chuck D. That was hardly a surprise: by the end of 1999, he had started Rapstation.com, an online radio station that, as he once put it, was "a super-multimedia network on the web providing music, concert, video, radio information, and interaction worldwide to a starving rap audience." Ever since *He Got Game*, he'd been actively thinking about a new career path beyond traditional labels. Napster suggested possibilities to him.

"I'm pro-file-sharing," he told ABC News in the spring of 2000, "and I think file-sharing is the process that Napster specialises in, and you have tons and tons of situations [that] are going to join the process. . . . [T]he government is looking at file-sharing like they can stop it and they just can't. They're stopping one company, and I think that's shortsighted of the industry, but I don't really give credit to the industry for being too smart anyway."

Around the same time, he also wrote an editorial in *The New York Times*, arguing that "We should think of [Napster] as a new kind of radio – a promotional tool that can help artists who don't have the opportunity to get their music played on mainstream radio or on MTV." But where other artists complained about theft, Chuck insisted that services such as Napster could also help a band's bottom line. "Artists can profit more from the internet," he said in his ABC News interview, "but at the same time they shouldn't have delusions of grandeur of creating their art for the standard industry price. Artists usually make their art because the industry dictates the standards for the amount they should make their art for. Therefore, a lot of the artists are in the position of trying to recoup what has already been spent on their behalf. And now as far as the internet is concerned, it gives each artist the ability and the advantage to control every aspect of [their art]."

Chuck also memorably appeared on *The Charlie Rose Show* alongside Ulrich to debate the merits of Napster. Watching the broadcast now, it's striking how correct both musicians turned out to be – in certain ways. Chuck expressed the pragmatic point of view, which is that services like Napster had fundamentally changed how consumers would get music. And rather than fight that reality, like Metallica were, he chose to embrace it. "I think it's beneficial to trigger off the enthusiasm of what's taken place," he told Ulrich, later adding, "There are so many ancillary areas that you guys control that you won't be able to download that they gotta come to you for." That, in a nutshell, is what became of the music industry: individual artists used the web to connect with fans through social media, making money not on album sales but through concert revenue and other outlets, such as licensing songs to movies and TV ads. And when Rose questioned Chuck about making something artistic, whether it be an album or a movie, and then watching users download it for free, the rapper responded, "I can't have the accountant's mentality of counting what wasn't there in the first place. 'Accountant mentality' is, like, [*adopting the voice of an executive*] 'You could have had . . .' Now, the terrain is totally different."

But Ulrich wasn't wrong when he challenged Chuck's belief that the Napsters of the world were doing this out of the goodness of their heart. They had financial backers, just like record labels do, the drummer said. "If the record-company bosses don't take the money, then the internet people are gonna – somebody's gonna profit off this," he said. "And if it's not the artist, then you're profiting illegally." After the lawsuits were settled and the smoke cleared, the music industry eventually figured out how to distribute its wares online, whether through iTunes or on subscription services such as Spotify. Indeed, the terrain is totally different, but the labels were essentially able to assert some sort of control over this new digital wilderness.

Although Chuck and Ulrich disagreed about Napster, the rapper has maintained a respect for Metallica. In a 2012 interview with *The Nervous Breakdown*, Chuck responded to a comment that he has never stuck to the same blueprint, branching out into other areas than just hip-hop. "We learned that from the rock guys," he said. "Never repeat yourself and expand your territory in the world into as many places as you can get to. Those were not really hip-hop traits." Asked to name bands whose example he emulated, Chuck responded, "A lot of the rock guys. Look, Metallica started out five years before us and they came across as a group that didn't give a fuck what you thought about them." Chuck laughed. "Most people in rap music and hip-hop come from black neighbourhoods and black communities and you want to be loved; you want to be respected, but you want to be loved and ask people to support your art. You wanna do all those things. It takes a lot of nerve and a lot of guts to say, 'Well, this is what it is, whether the fuck you like it or not.' But it's principled and it's passionate. It's very opinioned. [Metallica] didn't just rebel for the sake of rebelling – it's very focused. And I think that's the attitude of where we were coming from."

By the summer of 2001, Metallica and Dr. Dre had resolved their legal issues with Napster. At that point, the company had been legally blocked from continuing its business, so the settlement was seen as a step toward Napster finally being embraced by the industry once it made some changes. "We await Napster's implementation of a new model which will allow artists to choose how their creative efforts are distributed," Ulrich said in a statement announcing the settlement. "It's good that they're going legit." The following summer, Napster filed for bankruptcy protection. Soon after, it was a forgotten novelty item, replaced in the cultural consciousness by other sites like Facebook, which was supported by Parker in its early days.

Chuck's advocacy for Napster made sense. A man whose music was built on the brilliant appropriation of preexisting songs and sounds, he probably had little patience for the argument that file-sharing was theft. And on *Nation Of Millions*' 'Caught, Can We Get a Witness?' he articulated that anger at those who would dare send him to court for stealing beats. "Sampling basically comes from the fact that rap music is not music," Chuck once said. "It's rap over music." To the cynical and the sceptical, Chuck D's support might have seemed like a chance to raise his profile at a time when Public Enemy were far from the limelight. Or perhaps he wanted to strike back at the labels that had screwed him over. But on *The Charlie Rose Show*, he swore that his intentions were quite simple. "I don't have that typical American entrepreneurial spirit that would probably, you know, land me in a nest egg," Chuck said. "I've always been that way."

In September 2000, Atomic Pop laid off the majority of its 25 employees amid reports that the company had no more funding. "The core of our model was that we were going to buy digital rights for artists and promote them online, market them online," Teller would say later about Atomic Pop's mission. So why didn't it work out? "My passion for this vision overwhelmed my logic in a certain way. In retrospect, we were just too early. We had to invent everything ourselves." But he would also cite two major factors that conspired to doom Atomic Pop. One was the bursting of the internet bubble around 2000, which saw promising dot-com companies rise and fall in equally spectacular fashion. "The venture-capital window came down pretty hard," Teller admitted. But the other was companies like Napster. "The peer-to-peer file-sharing services, Napster and MP3.com, really dealt us a mortal blow," he said, "because our model was we would pay for these digital rights. The [Napster] model was, 'Everything on the internet is free, so it's there for the taking.'"

There's A Poison Goin On was the only album Public Enemy released through Atomic Pop. After 'Swindlers Lust' fades out, a spoken-word piece from Professor Griff fades up. "Welcome to the end of the beginning of this world – his world – as we know it," Griff intones. Was he talking about the 20th century? Or the music business?

CHAPTER TEN

WHEN Public Enemy put out *There's A Poison Goin On*, it had the unfortunate honour of being the first PE album to fail to make the *Billboard* charts. The chances are that this was because the record was initially released online, but Chuck also blamed it on brick-and-mortar stores that were irritated by the unconventional distribution strategy. "That album was basically banned when it first came out because major retailers were mad that we offered it strictly online," he would say in 2003.

There was, of course, another possible explanation. Where once Public Enemy had been at the forefront of the cultural conversation, now they were behind the curve, largely forgotten about. But if the group had any concern about the potential loss in visibility, they didn't let it show on their next album. If anything, Public Enemy doubled down on their particular path, saying goodbye to the mainstream to go their own way.

Where *Poison* anticipated the possibilities of the web as a means of digital distribution, *Revolverlution* demonstrated how the internet was opening up channels of communication between people in different parts of the world. Around *Poison*'s release, Chuck liked to advertise the fact that it was the first album from a major artist to be commercially available online. By comparison, *Revolverlution* might have been the first crowd-sourced album, the band collaborating with their fans in a meaningful, unprecedented way. On *Nation Of Millions*, Chuck had wanted to prove that hip-hop was an international art form. With *Revolverlution*, he'd prove it yet again.

The album would also begin the frontman's peculiar tendency of writing long, somewhat rambling essays in the liner notes. Somewhere between manifesto and unfiltered rants, these essays – grammatically nightmarish and sometimes riddled with typos – sounded like they came from the mind of a true believer making his case for his cockeyed vision of hip-hop's future. In the *Revolverlution* essay, Chuck mocked a music business "nuked by the digital age, the mp3 . . . a biteback from the labels selling the cd to save the music companies in the first place". In response, he explained, *Revolverlution* was constructed in a novel new way that threw out the old conventions of what an album should be. "[I]n 2002," Chuck wrote, "a 12 track album should be considered outdated, more supply than the demand because theres [*sic*] so many albums out there, especially 12 new songs from a new group. 12 new songs from an old or classic group is just as intolerable. These albums are too long and even if they're great, one must remember that a new disc can never beat out a groups [*sic*] prime time disc, because the eras can't be carried over and the prime disc is still competing in the same record rack."

And so, *Revolverlution* was a mixture of live versions of classic PE songs, remixes of old album cuts, leftovers and new tracks. And unlike the new-and-remixed *Greatest Misses*, which was divided neatly into halves, *Revolverlution*'s hotchpotch wasn't separated into sections. Instead, the tracks were all jumbled together, as if the listener had ignored the properly arranged track list and hit "shuffle".

Speaking to radio host Davey D after the album's release in 2002, Chuck explained that he was trying to reflect the times. "You ask a young cat which cut that they like and they'll say, 'Well, I like track nine,'" the rapper said. "They don't even try to figure out the title. . . . So we wanted to put something together that was a combination that some new heads will bop to and some old heads will say, 'Oh yeah, I know that.' That is what is gonna keep my CD in there. It is very hard to keep albums in the CD rotation. It is very hard to get albums played from cut one on down to the last cut. So you gotta programme an album like a radio show. . . . People want to hear compilation albums with a lot of different things, so we made a compilation of ourselves."

Chuck had always been insistent that the internet could be a new, freer form of radio, so it was understandable that he'd be thinking like the host of a radio programme when sequencing *Revolverlution*. After all, radio is how he got his start. Plus, the album's reach back into the archives made sense when you consider that Public Enemy were celebrating their 15th year as a group. Indeed, Chuck makes several mentions of the anniversary in *Revolverlution*'s liner notes.

For the frontman, such landmarks weren't a sign of age but, rather, longevity and endurance. In an interview around the release of *Muse Sick-N-Hour Mess Age*, he reflected on the fact that he was (at the time) 34, which was old for the rap game. Did he feel sensitive about that fact? "I think it's something that should be used as a plus-side," Chuck responded. "Now we're in a society that looks down on age. . . . With age should come wisdom. Experience should help you. It's a brave new world out there. Being 34 is something new for a rap artist. . . . Very few people [can] talk about, 'How does rap feel at 34?' . . . This is *new*. I think with hip-hop, we should have something that's always new and exciting. Other than just a new artist, we should have new ideas, too."

Rap itself is a celebration of making something new out of the old, and *Revolverlution* was simply PE's latest embrace of that edict. For years, the band had reintroduced old sonic elements from their past songs into newer tracks – a callback to an indelible Flavor Flav line, the 'Let's Go Crazy' sample from 'Brothers Gonna Work It Out' reintroduced in 'Can't Truss It' – which created a sense of continuity over the years between disparate albums. Those repeated musical bits are as iconic in their own way as the Public Enemy logo and graphic. With *Revolverlution*, Chuck took that strategy to the next level, making an album where the past, present and future coexisted.

Revolverlution's 21 tracks were collected from different sources, spearheaded by different individuals. One of them was Amani K. Smith, also known as Burt Blackarach. The songwriter and producer had met Chuck D and Gary G-Wiz while they were working on the theme song for the short-lived Jessica Alba TV show *Dark Angel*, a series on which Smith was a composer.

"Gary and I formed a partnership and started composing and doing a lot of projects together," Smith recalls. "So any work that came either one of our way, we would share with each other and just knock it out, whether it was a television show or producing songs for artists. So when that PE album came up, Gary and I made a bunch of music. Chuck would come over, and we'd play him some stuff. He'll just start writing ideas down and get hyped on stuff. He'll then come back the next day or two and have really strong ideas."

Smith co-wrote and co-produced three of the album's nine new songs, but just as importantly he was with *Revolverlution* from the beginning, assisting Gary G-Wiz in Los Angeles and being what he calls the "cheer-leader" of the record. "Griff had songs, Juice had songs, but eventually [all the songs] came over to us," Smith says. "We were compiling [*Revolverlution*] together under Chuck's instruction on what songs he wanted. The process is that he's working on an album, he's already got a concept in his head, he's written lyrics, he's got some songs he's done with certain people and he's seeing what flows together. As that process is building, we're interjecting songs in between them."

In other words, this trial-and-error process was very different than the approach taken on PE's eighties records, where the band came into the studio with a clear roadmap.

Asked if Chuck articulated what *Revolverlution*'s thematic thrust would be, Smith replies, "I think all of his concepts tend to be similar in that there's some sort of hypocrisy going on and we need to stand up for ourselves." Smith, who's also produced hip-hop acts like Method Man and Busta Rhymes, says that for Public Enemy "you're always trying to make aggressive music that captures 'fighting against the system' or 'fighting for what's right' or not putting up with [the status quo]. That's always been my approach with Chuck. As you start making stuff like that and presenting it to him, it starts to just fall into place. Ultimately, it all has the same type of vibe: you're not coming to him with a smooth R&B track – you're coming to him with something loud and forceful and in-your-face."

The pull of the past influenced the take-a-stand mantra 'Put It Up', which Smith says was inspired in part by the *Autobiography* song 'No', although its chanted, anthemic chorus also calls to mind *Apocalypse 91*'s 'Shut 'Em Down'. Smith says, "We were trying to make a certain type of track for the album. For 'Put It Up', we were trying to get that kind of skippy-beat feeling but make it aggressive at the same time. I got a lot of people saying, 'Oh yeah, man, that reminds of that Dilla track, "Give It Up",' but the choruses are not similar."

For '54321 . . . Boom', Chuck D's latest broadside against the music business, Smith and Gary G-Wiz were given the title and instructed by Chuck to build a track around it. The song is a slinky, echo-y number in which Flavor's "What ya all want?" chant is repeated alongside anxious scratches, an off-kilter beat and some ghostly keyboards. It sounds like the song is trapped inside the haunted house where the now-deceased record industry used to reside. Even now, Smith can't quite explain how the minimalist, edgy tune came about. "I don't know, music is interesting, man," he finally says. "You hear something and you start searching for sounds to lay on top of it."

Smith was also partly responsible for a Flavor track, 'Can A Woman Make A Man Lose His Mind?'. The song, essentially a lighthearted, in-offensive take on the old "women: can't live with 'em, can't live without 'em" cliché, was remixed by Smith and Gary. "Those lyrics were on a different track," says Smith, who calls his revamped version "my favourite song on the record – I think that song is so underrated". Without wanting "to shit on whoever produced [the original version]", Smith contends that "it wasn't mixed well. There was nothing distinct to it. It was just really boring. It sounded kind of amateurish." For the remix, he decided to emulate the sound of Nice & Smooth, a rap duo whose sound was encap-sulated within their name. Says Smith, "They had this certain kind of feel to them that I was trying to capture for 'Can A Woman Make A Man Lose His Mind?' I was trying to make it a little more upbeat and a little more fun – a little more tongue-in-cheek-ish."

Meanwhile, in Long Island, Johnny Juice produced and co-wrote 'Gotta Give The Peeps What They Need'. David Snyder, a beatmaker and filmmaker who worked on *Revolverlution* as an archivist, remembers, "That record has a funny story. Griff did the original, but he based it around 'Whole Lotta Love' by Zeppelin, so that record was going nowhere," because it would be too hard to get permission to use the sample. "So, Juice got ahold of the a cappella for ['Peeps'] and totally rearranged the record and then did the version that ended up becoming the single. Juice re-entered the fold in a big way with that record."

Juice's return to the band and the mending of fences happened in acci-dental fashion. One day, he had to go to Walmart to buy a microwave. "I'm in line," Juice recalls, "and I hear, 'Mr. Rosado'. Chuck was buying stuff because his toilet was fucked. So we talked for a little while."

Juice estimates that his work redoing 'Gotta Give The Peeps' took about four hours. "As soon as I heard [the original], I said, 'You know what this needs? Some congas,'" Juice remembers. "See, I'm Puerto Rican, I like that shit. Public Enemy has a distinct lack of percussion – the irony being that they're supposed to have this 'taking it back to Africa' approach. But I'm like, 'Yo, I'm gonna make some shit that sounds like some Fela Kuti shit, but really stripped down and gritty.'" Before Juice rescued 'Peeps', Chuck had written the song off as a lost cause. It ended up being *Revolverlution*'s ass-shaking opener.

Additionally, Juice manned the boards for 'Get Your Shit Together', the album's most overt reference to the recent 9/11 terror attacks. "Governments, fundamentalists," Chuck declares, "But how you gonna / Kill the innocent? / Between terrorists and CIA hit lists." But the frontman sounded just as wary of the looming invasion of Iraq, which would begin the following year: "Be careful what you ask for / War is hell and hell is war." And in another example of Chuck drawing on PE's past, he adds, "Seen four planes kill everyday folks / Guess 911 ain't no joke." In a surreal twist, the band would sometimes have to explain in later years that '911 Is A Joke' wasn't a reference to the September 11 attacks. In December 2009, the *Washington Post* actually had to issue a correction to an article about PE that erroneously claimed that the band believed 9/11 was a joke – or, to use the language of the time, an inside job concocted by the US government. "The song refers to 911, the emergency phone number," the correction helpfully stated.

Several memorable albums that touched on the terrorist attacks were released in 2002. Some were mournful and self-consciously sweeping (Bruce Springsteen's *The Rising*), some were personal (Sleater-Kinney's *One Beat*), and some were made before 9/11 but were embraced by unknowing listeners who perceived the songs' sadness as emblematic of the era (Wilco's *Yankee Hotel Foxtrot*). By contrast, *Revolverlution* doesn't feel like any of those kinds of 9/11 albums, even though images of towers falling and planes crashing appear on 'Get Your Shit Together', a song about man's thirst for vengeance and living with the stark new normal of a country under siege. But rather than dwelling on grieving for 9/11's victims, *Revolverlution* is fixated on what's next for America: the spectre of a war that many in the country don't want.

Which brings us to the most important contributor to *Revolverlution*. Since he returned to Public Enemy on *He Got Game*, Professor Griff had mostly served as a supporting voice, a gruff vocal cameo and spoken-word aside. On *Revolverlution*, however, he dominates, serving as a co-conspirator to Chuck. Griff co-wrote and produced the blazing title track, the closest thing Public Enemy had come to the anxious energy of the peak Bomb Squad years in quite a while. Somewhat recalling the locomotive fury of 'Brothers Gonna Work It Out', 'Revolverlution' finds Chuck barrelling over the racism and sexism peddled by other rappers, smacking down "Bush shit" – a fun little play on then-President George W. Bush's name – and laying out one of the group's finest mission statements:

> *I don't give a damn if you bounce to this*
> *I don't give a damn if you shake to this*
> *But I give a damn that you overstand*
> *Revolverlution*
> *The rap superman*

'Revolverlution' was hard rock accented by actual rock musicians. Guitarist Khari Wynn and bassist/guitarist Randy Glaude played on several *Revolverlution* tracks alongside Griff. Kerwin Young, who worked on *Revolverlution* at Chuck D's Atlanta studio, says, "I remember when Khari joined the band and first came to the studio. Griff was the one who would recruit people. Griff was the master genius at just finding talent and bringing it into the fold. Khari as a guitarist – man, he can't read music, he's like Hendrix. But the sounds that he hears and how he plays is, like, damn." There had been a thought that maybe Young would be the group's bassist, but he admits, "I couldn't keep up with this guy."

And although he'd been part of PE for a few years, DJ Lord (a.k.a Lord Aswod) also shined on *Revolverlution* and was another Griff find. Beyond his turntable work, Lord also co-wrote 'Revolverlution'. "I relocated to Atlanta in 1999," Young says, "and when I got down there, Griff had brought DJ Lord to the studio. He was doing some things that I was like, 'This guy's the shit!'"

Lord's emergence in Public Enemy hadn't been easy. Growing up outside of Philadelphia, he moved to Savannah, Georgia before relocating to Atlanta in the hopes of being discovered. "I got started listening to my cousin Bernard in Philly," he said in a 2013 interview with *myRNB* when asked about his DJ roots. "He did all the block parties in Philadelphia. We would have family reunions, and I would come back to Philly, sneak in his room and try to DJ on his set. He would come knock me out every time!" Lord laughed. "I figured it out once I got my own set. From watching him and getting motivated by DJs like Grandmaster Flash, Mix Master Ice, Jazzy Jeff . . . I just took it upon myself to learn the art, starting with second-hand turntables and harassing my mom to buy pawn-shop turntables."

His arrival in Atlanta didn't exactly portend great things were in store for him. "[I was] doing my Foot Locker and Radio Shack thing – yeah, two jobs in the same mall, upstairs and downstairs (start the day looking like Clark Kent and leave looking like Superman in black and white poly-ester stripes . . .)," Lord once said in an email interview about his pre-PE days. Fortunately for him, Griff was friends with Lord's roommate. "I was doing my whole 9-to-5 thing, man – getting dressed, putting on my tie, and headed out the door," he recalled to *myRNB*, "and [my roommate was] like, 'Yo, man, Griff called me. Public Enemy needs a DJ.' I totally thought he was bullshitting me. . . . Come home that night – 9.30, 10 o'clock – Griff is in the living room. . . . 'Yeah, I'm Griff. Terminator X is retiring, we need a DJ for our upcoming *Poison* tour. Can you handle it?'"

At first, Lord struggled in PE, too star-struck to do the job properly. But he soon got the hang of it, determined to stop emulating Terminator X's style and instead focusing on his own. And he clearly didn't want to reach out to Terminator for guidance. When asked if Lord ever got in contact with him, Terminator X emails in response, "My first time meeting DJ Lord was during [PE's] Rock and Roll Hall of Fame [induction]."

Not only did Griff assemble much of the team that was now part of the Public Enemy extended line-up, his militant outlook informed *Revolverlution*. "Professor Griff, in the Atlanta studios, has just stepped up unbelievably so," Chuck declared in a promotional interview connected to the album's release. That wasn't hype: Griff might be *Revolverlution*'s MVP. Chuck D is often praised for his "fiery rhetoric", a clichéd compliment meant to suggest the anger and power of his voice. But there's also inspiration and community in there as well, a sense that he's a born leader you'd follow anywhere. By contrast, Griff is a firebrand or a ranter: he doesn't want to win you over to his side as much as he wants to bulldoze you over with the point he's trying to make. Griff's rhymes are less about flow than they are about blunt force. But that lack of subtlety proved necessary on *Revolverlution*: at a time when many Americans were dazed by 9/11, Griff and Public Enemy demanded that listeners snap back to attention.

Griff wrote, produced and sang 'Now A'Daze', a stomper that frames the future as a grim choice between two options: ballots or bullets. "Shit, damn right I'm vexed," Griff snarls at one point, later practically getting apoplectic when he asserts, "Some of you motherfuckers don't have a goddamn clue." It's a song about revolution that doesn't offer any half-measures: 'Now A'Daze' is the sound of a street protest that could get violent at any moment. A punishing keyboard line serves as a kind of hook, and a chanted chorus helps brighten the darkness some, but 'Now A'Daze' nonetheless stands as one of PE's most unapologetic tirades about the powerless rising up.

Griff brought in his fellow rock musicians for the metal-edged 'What Good Is A Bomb', another *Revolverlution* track that was practically a Griff solo joint. Starting with Vietnam and fast-forwarding to the Bush adminis-tration's attack on Afghanistan after 9/11, the song, which ends the album, decries America's interventionist attitude. With a paranoid edge, Griff criticises governments that suppress the will of the people, whether it's in the form of repealing civil liberties or staging coups in other lands to advance their own interests. Without mentioning the Patriot Act, the ordinance signed into law in October 2001 by Bush that allowed for a broad expansion of what the US government could do to investigate its citizens and invade their privacy, 'What Good Is A Bomb' pinpoints the disillusionment and anger felt by many in 9/11's aftermath. But further-more, the song articulated the inherent inequality of war: the powerful force those on the lower rungs of society to fight their battles. Over speed-metal guitar and twitchy scratching, Griff presciently envisioned where America was heading for the next decade in Afghanistan and Iraq. Endless war, insidious government overreach, creeping insecurity: 'What Good Is A Bomb' puts all these unpleasant realities in its crosshairs.

But probably the most famous *Revolverlution* song was 'Son Of A Bush'.

Produced by Griff, led by Chuck and backed by Griff's assembled rock musicians, the song strongly opposes assassinating W., but it has no compunction about railing against him and his father, former President George H.W. Bush. "He's a son of a bad man," Flavor taunts on the chorus.

Chuck noted in *Lyrics Of A Rap Revolutionary* that the song's origins trace back to before W.'s presidency, when Bush was governor of Texas. A man on death row in Texas contacted the rapper, which helped inspire 'Son Of A Bush'. During Bush's six years as governor, the state executed 152 prisoners, an unusually high rate. (Between 1976 and August 2011, Texas executed 472 prisoners. The state with the second-highest number of executions during that time was Virginia, which killed 108 prisoners.) "In [Bush's] years as Governor it was like a killing machine," Chuck wrote. "It was like a reign of terror. I kind of compare George Bush to Josef Mengele, the infamous 'Angel of Death'. This song talks about that tenure and . . . him being the president with that type of heartlessness."

Taking aim at Bush's party-boy youth ("Fulla cocaine / Froze the brain") and his reputation as a serial-executioner ("Killed 135 at the last count / Texas bounce"), Chuck relished the opportunity to lay into this family one more time. When Public Enemy were starting out, they were living through the Reagan years, in which George H.W. Bush was vice president, seen as a man who would continue Reagan's policies if he became president. He would be elected to that position in 1988, just a few months after *It Takes A Nation Of Millions To Hold Us Back* was released. "We've always found a struggle to fight against," Chuck said in a 2000 interview. "People always want to cheer for the underdog." And in W., he'd found a worthy struggle.

Frustratingly for Chuck, though, he often felt alone in this struggle. "I think a lot of people in the rap music community are robots and puppets, who do as they are told," he said in a 2002 *Billboard* interview. "Where in the past, they were rebellious to certain things and they had a mind of their own. So, it's not so much the hip-hop or rap community, it could be the black community in general. Being a person who is a world traveller, I've seen that America has had an arrogant foreign policy . . . So, I decided to make a statement about it."

If *Revolverlution* had stuck to new songs exploring the political ripple effects of 9/11, it might have been a better-remembered album. But *Revolverlution* also contained several remixes, including one of 'Gotta Give The Peeps What They Need' that was overseen by Oakland-based militant rapper Paris. Unlike Chuck, who had refused to suggest assassinating W., Paris had advocated the killing of George H.W. Bush on his 1992 track 'Bush Killa'. The 'Peeps' remix came together online, Paris contacting Public Enemy's message board about wanting to collaborate and Chuck reaching out to him. "Brothers came together from East to West and got it done through the new technology of the Internet," Chuck explained proudly in an interview in the fall of 2002.

The album's other remixes, which were of older PE tracks, featured collaborators who weren't nearly as high-profile as Paris, but their means of reaching the band weren't that dissimilar from his. According to Smith, Chuck's concept for the remixes was "giving producers across the world an opportunity to have their shine, try to build a career for themselves." The group put a cappella versions of four songs on their Slam Jamz website and encouraged users to come up with their own tracks. "The contest was, 'If you remix this, you [might] be on the next Public Enemy album,'" Smith says.

The a cappella tracks were downloaded, according to Chuck, more than 11,100 times, generating approximately 463 remixes. An impressive turnout, but that also meant someone had to listen to them all. "There was never any, like, sitting session between all of us," says Smith, "but I know that everybody heard a lot of submissions, and I know that there was a filter process." In an interview for the book *The Art Of Digital Music*, Chuck said of the remix contest, "I think we had the world's first record company with a virtual staff. About 50 people, many of whom I've never met, evaluated the . . . mixes by making their top 10, top 20. And that's how we scaled down to pick the four winners."

Smith's memory is that "there was a lot of really bad stuff" amid the glut of entries, "but there's some talented people out there, and you know there's some gems. You know these people are doing things that you're going to listen to and be like, 'Holy fuck, that is dope! How did they do that?' You get inspired."

The remixes that landed on *Revolverlution* included 'By The Time I Get

To Arizona' redone by Mike Sapone, who has subsequently produced albums for bands like Taking Back Sunday and Brand New. 'B Side Wins Again' was transformed into industrial rock by Scattershot, a duo consisting of Jeff Snyder (no relation to David Snyder) and Ryan Smith. "Their mix was like sonic shrapnel," Chuck D said in *The Art Of Digital Music*, "going about five or six different places but still sharp enough to win." In later years, Jeff Snyder co-founded an experimental-music label, Carrier Records, and is a director of the Princeton Laptop Orchestra, whose website explains that "each laptopist performs with a laptop and custom designed hemispherical speaker that emulates the way traditional orchestral instruments cast their sound in space. Wireless networking and video augment the familiar role of the conductor, suggesting unprecedented ways of organising large ensembles."

Meanwhile, a DJ from Vienna who calls himself DJ Functionist took 'Shut 'Em Down' and gave it a nervy, dancy vibe. Besides producing, he also DJs across Austria, Germany and Switzerland.* And 'Public Enemy No. 1' was dismantled by the Jeronimo Punx, who made his remix in Buenos Aires. In *The Art Of Digital Music*, Chuck praised the new 'Public Enemy No. 1' as "a combination of club, hip-hop, and house," which no doubt pleased the rapper, proof that his band's music could transcend genres and remain relevant.

Not one of these remixes is definitive or will replace fans' fond memories of the original. But that seemed beside the point. As long-time Public Enemy fan Robert Christgau noted in his *Village Voice* review of *Revolverlution*, the remixes simply "accentuate what's most extreme and inaccessible", in the process preserving the familiar, hooky elements and adding new layers of noise, distortion and sonic muck that require the patience to dig through – sometimes rewardingly, sometimes not. Collectively, the remixes showed the global reach of hip-hop and PE's place in the vanguard of internet collaborations.

Alongside these remixes was intriguing marginalia, such as audio from an interview Chuck gave right after performing 'By The Time I Get To

---

* DJ Functionist is now based in North Carolina, posting similarly aggressive revamps of tunes like Pharrell's 'Happy'.

Arizona' in Phoenix when Public Enemy were part of U2's Zoo TV tour. Plus, there was an extended clip of the phone conversation that kicks off *Fear Of A Black Planet*'s 'Burn Hollywood Burn', revealing how Flavor improvised his responses to Big Daddy Kane. Rarely has a rap album featured a demo of what is essentially a skit. And Flav is hilarious throughout it: you can understand why he cracked Kane up.

"I think [*Revolverlution*] was a way to stay current and compete with what was becoming popular that other artists were doing," Young says. "It was just to have extra stuff for the PE fan. They didn't have anyone at the record label telling them what they couldn't do. So, they wanted to just offer more."

With the exception of a few interludes that were labelled 'Public Enemy Service Announcement #1' and 'Public Enemy Service Announcement #2' from the early nineties – these advised that you stay in school, stay away from drugs and celebrate black culture all year round – the final set of extras were live versions of 'Miuzi Weighs A Ton' from the fall of 1999 (shortly after DJ Lord joined the group) and two performances from 1992: 'Fight The Power' and 'Welcome To The Terrordome'. David Snyder, who would soon become known to PE fans by his nickname C-Doc, selected the live tracks. It wouldn't be long before C-Doc was more than a PE archivist: he would quickly prove to be the greatest example of what could happen when the band reached out to their fans.

In an interview with *Stay Free!* about *Revolverlution*, Chuck said, "We have a powerful online community . . . My thing was just looking at the community and being able to say, 'Can we actually make them involved in the creative process?' Why not see if we can connect all these bedroom and basement studios, and the ocean of producers, and expand the Bomb Squad to a worldwide concept?" But where the album's remixes brought unheralded producers to a larger audience, creating an online talent show of sorts, the group's courting of David Snyder constituted a more permanent collaboration.

In the late nineties, Snyder was in his mid-twenties. He had grown up loving film. "My parents got a video camera when I was, like, 10," he recalls, "and that whole summer, my brothers and my friends and I would make these little movies. Any time I had to do a school project, I'd ask my teachers, 'Can I make a movie instead?' My teachers were cool about it." He'd also work on music videos, hoping to somehow parlay this passion for filmmaking into a career.

He went to film school for a year and a half, but he had to drop out. "I ran out of money," he says. This didn't discourage his filmmaking dreams, but he'd also become interested in music: "I had a little sampler and a four-track recorder." He'd been a lifelong Public Enemy disciple after getting *Nation Of Millions* as a kid and had even made his own remixes of Chuck's solo track 'No' and *Muse Sick*'s 'Give It Up'.

But his future came into focus when he noticed a post from Chuck on Public Enemy's website. "He was talking about leaving Def Jam," Snyder says. "I think it was the whole *Bring The Noise 2000* situation: Chuck wanted to post a track once a week until the whole thing was available, and Def Jam threatened to sue him. He was pissed, and he wrote something about looking for a new home. For some reason, I felt compelled to email him. I said, 'What about Ruffhouse? They're a Sony imprint, and you guys were on Sony. That might be a good fit.' They still had Cypress Hill, and I think they were putting out the Kool Keith record at the time. I emailed him from my home email address – I didn't really check that email all the time. I just sent it out there thinking, 'OK, I'll just throw this out here.'"

To Snyder's shock, he discovered that Chuck wrote him back. The email waited in Snyder's inbox for three months. "He said something like, 'Yeah, Ruffhouse would be a good fit, but we've got some other options,'" Snyder recalls. "It was a short, simple email – 'Thanks for writing' – but it was the coolest thing ever. I thought, 'Wow, this is great.'"

Shortly after, Snyder ventured to a hip-hop conference in Cleveland where Chuck would be a featured speaker. He introduced himself to the rapper, who surprised Snyder by remembering him from his email. Snyder says, "He looked at me and he goes, 'C-Doc, what's up, man?' Like we're old friends, like we hadn't seen each other in 10 years or something." Despite the annoyance of Snyder's girlfriend, he spent several hours with Chuck, talking about everything from *There's A Poison Goin On* to the potential of Slam Jamz and the future of online distribution. Snyder went to Public Enemy shows in Pittsburgh and Philadelphia, giving Chuck a

CD of his remixes, which the frontman dug. Soon, they would start talking on the phone every once in a while.

"It was a crazy time because technology was changing and the music industry was on the verge of changing," Snyder says. "Chuck was in the middle of it all. He had a debate with Lars Ulrich, and I remember screaming at the TV: 'This guy doesn't understand! He doesn't get it at all! Chuck, you're right, man!'"

Excited to be part of this new internet revolution, Snyder would send Chuck remixes that the rapper would put on the band's web radio show. "Looking back, the music wasn't very good," Snyder admits, "but it was something – it was a start. I had been doing music for a while, but I was making the transition to the computer, and it was a different thing. I was getting my bearings."

Chuck was as well. Curious about starting up a virtual hip-hop group, he enlisted Snyder to team up with other PE fans online. "How that all started was Chuck and Griff had done a guest spot on a Vanilla Ice record [2001's *Bi-Polar*]," Snyder says. "Vanilla Ice was doing the rock thing at the time, and Chuck and Griff were doing Confrontation Camp. Everybody on the Enemy Board [PE's message board name] was all, 'Chuck, why are you doing songs with Vanilla Ice? Fuck this guy.' Somebody said to him, 'If you can do a song with Vanilla Ice, why don't you do a song with somebody like C-Doc?' Chuck responded and said, 'Sure, I'd love to do a song with C-Doc.'" This new band, including Snyder, also featured musicians from the UK, San Francisco, New York and Flint, Michigan. "Chuck called us the Impossebulls," says Snyder, "because we were doing what was previously thought impossible. He was a major label artist collaborating online with his fans."

Obviously, all of this was exciting and unbelievable for a guy who grew up worshipping Public Enemy, but these collaborative endeavours weren't enough to make a living for Snyder. "I was delivering pizzas at the time," he says. "I was working nights. I didn't have a cell phone, and Chuck called me at the pizza shop – he called the house, and my girlfriend said, 'No, he's at work, I can give you the number.' He'd call the shop and I had to ask my manager, 'This is Chuck D from Public Enemy. Do you mind if I talk to him?' And he was like, 'Dude, talk to the man. What are you asking me permission for? What are you, nuts?!' So, I'm talking on the phone and people are taking orders around me for an hour and a half. But, yeah, it was so exciting: I'm producing some records with Chuck on 'em, and we're putting out singles on Slam Jamz. And the Impossebulls were doing what we were supposed to do: we'd think of a record, we'd cut it, upload it to the internet, and then people could download it."

When it came time to select the live cuts for *Revolverlution*, Chuck turned to Snyder. "That was the first [Public Enemy] album I got a credit on," says Snyder, clearly proud of the fact. But for C-Doc, it wasn't just about the credit: it was that he was working with his heroes. "I tell Chuck and I tell all the guys: 'I will do anything I possibly can to help preserve and further your music and your legacy.' I care about it, you know?" To show he cared, he volunteered to take over as the band's sequencer on future albums. "I liked *Revolverlution*, I like the new records on it, but I didn't love the sequencing of the album. I thought it was just kinda thrown together haphazardly – maybe there was more thought put into it, I don't know. But when I got the opportunity, I was like, 'Look, I'll do it. Whatever you guys wanna do, or if you want me to be involved, I will be involved because I really give a shit. I care about how you guys are presented, and I always want PE's best foot forward.'"

Revolverlution came out through Koch in July 2002 and reached number 110 on the *Billboard* chart. Some reviewers understood and appreciated what Chuck and his cohorts were trying to achieve with the album's seemingly schizophrenic personality. *Pitchfork*'s Sam Chennault declared, "[T]hey have largely prevailed with *Revolverlution* by revamping the very structure of how we digest music. One can only hope that their ability to examine the relationship between themselves and their audience will be infectious, and that other hip-hop crews will pick up where the group left off." Meanwhile, *Vibe*'s Joe Schloss lamented, "Like the web technology that spawned it, this collection of current and classic material is a decidedly mixed blessing." At its best, *Revolverlution* suggested the far-reaching possibilities of the web to connect people. And at its weakest, the album hinted at the rise of static and incoherence that the internet's global reach could produce. Rather than providing sharper focus on our world, the web risked being a cacophony of myriad voices and attitudes.

One of the biggest disappointments with *Revolverlution* was that audiences didn't get to hear 'Psycho Of Greed', a jittery diatribe about the increasing corporatisation of America, Chuck and Flav bouncing between "cycle of greed" and "psycho of greed" in the chorus. Unfortunately, the track couldn't make the album because of a dispute about the use of the screaming sitar noise from the Beatles' 'Tomorrow Never Knows', off *Revolver*, the album that helped inspire *Revolverlution*'s name. The Griff-composed track simply would have cost too much in order to license the sample, which annoyed Chuck, who for a time tried to insist that 'Psycho Of Greed' and 'Tomorrow Never Knows' just happened to sound similar in parts. "Where does it stop?" Chuck asked in a *New York Times* interview. "Does a lawnmower company copyright its sound? Does a Macintosh copyright its sound when you hit the keyboard? I don't think you can copyright sound. You can copyright compositions. But nobody invents a sound."

Maybe. But on *Revolverlution*, Public Enemy tried to show that a band could reinvent their old sound by dreaming up new schemes.

CHAPTER ELEVEN

I N the fall of 2002, Public Enemy were on tour supporting *Revolverlution*. Not every member was there, though: Flavor Flav was in jail because of a parole violation. According to Flav's autobiography, the hype man had 68 moving violations at the time of his incarceration. He had been sentenced to a year in jail in September 2001, just a few days after the 9/11 attacks. The night before 9/11, Flav recalled, he had smoked crack in his home, having just returned from Atlanta to work with Chuck D on 'Can A Woman Make A Man Lose His Mind?' for *Revolverlution*.

Beyond missing the PE shows, Flav also lost his Bronx apartment while in jail. When he was finally released, he was homeless and penniless. "I was back at my mom's house . . . 41 years old and all messed up," he wrote. "I didn't have a girl, I didn't have a gig, and I didn't even have an apartment. I'd been to rehab at least four different times, and I was still a fucking addict." Finally, at a stage where he says he was "broke, addicted, alone and angry", he talked to Chuck and Hank Shocklee.

According to Flav, Shocklee offered a radical idea for how to turn his life around: move to Los Angeles. It wouldn't be the first time Flav had tried leaving New York as a way to escape his demons, but previous stays in Chicago and Houston had proved fruitless. However, LA appealed to Flavor. "I told myself that I wasn't coming back until I got on TV or in a movie," he remembered thinking. "I told myself I wasn't coming back until I got myself a house in LA and another one in Las Vegas."

By 2003, the Public Enemy name had lost plenty of its lustre: the band hadn't enjoyed a hit single or an acclaimed album for about a decade. Still, Chuck D had remained a respected figure on the lecture circuit, and his populist stance in support of Napster had earned him plenty of goodwill among audiences. But Flavor's career was in a serious nosedive. Never an equal partner when it came to mic time on PE albums, he saw his long-awaited solo album, 1999's *It's About Time*, go unreleased. "If an album is recorded but never officially dropped, does it make a sound?" *Entertainment Weekly* asked him in 2008. "Yeah, it still makes a sound – in my own car," Flav responded. A tabloid figure who'd become more punch line than court jester, Flavor was hoping for a fresh start flying out to LA. Thankfully, the change of scenery did help him get clean. And then reality television came calling.

Flav had a meeting with Chris Abrego and Mark Cronin, who created VH1's hit programme *The Surreal Life*, which stuck a bunch of forgotten celebrities together in a house. They proposed the rapper join the cast of the forthcoming third season. Flav resisted – he didn't like thinking of himself as a has-been – but the executives suggested he talk to Hammer, who'd been part of the inaugural season. According to Flav, Hammer, who was long removed from his *Please Hammer Don't Hurt 'Em* stardom, told him, "Great things can happen for your life after the show. It happened to me, man, and it could work for you, too."

That was enough to convince Flav. "I am an entertainer," he explained to *The Daily Beast* in 2011, "and my job was to bring good entertainment to television and that I did." The chief entertainment of *The Surreal Life 3* was watching the exploits of Flav and Brigitte Nielsen, the *Rocky IV* co-star who at one time dated Sylvester Stallone. The two began a tawdry affair on the show, which aired during the summer of 2004. "It's like a bird being in his nest, baby," Flav once said about laying in Nielsen's bosom. "Hell, yeah! And guess what? You just want to stay there till momma bird comes around with the worms and feeds you." The show was a smash, and soon he and Nielsen spun it off into 2005's *Strange Love*, which focused on their unlikely love affair. Not everyone was convinced that the romance was real, however. Former *Full House* star Dave Coulier, who was on *The Surreal Life 3*, told *The New York Times* that their fling had started out genuine but subsequently became "a cartoon of itself . . . I don't think it's believable".

As an attempt to dissuade doubters, Flavor told the *Times*, "Whatever y'all saw between me and Brigitte was all real, nothing phony. That's why they call it reality TV." Perhaps realising that his argument wasn't airtight, he added, "Well, OK, there's a lot of people that do act phony on reality TV, but not me and Brigitte."

Television fame, no matter how tacky, had been something Flav had dreamed of as a kid. "Never thought it would happen," he told *Vibe* in early 2005. "Now I feel that my life is starting to change over from music into television." What made the success of *The Surreal Life* and *Strange Love* particularly galling was that, in comparison to the integrity and tough wisdom of Public Enemy, these reality shows seemed like mindless, cheap exploitation: the kind of tomfoolery that the band would rightly ridicule as distracting people from the social horrors around them. Even Flav seemed to understand that such shows were fluff – his interest was merely mercenary. "*The Surreal Life* was a good thing," he said in a *Billboard* interview in late 2004, "but it was just a vehicle. My main purpose moving to Los Angeles from New York in the first place was to switch over into television. I'm happy to have been part of the biggest and highest-rated show VH1 has ever had. I have goals I want to reach, so hopefully TV can help me reach them."

And what did his bandmates make of the reality sideshow? "Chuck and Griff thought their boy Flav was a little nutty," Flav admitted in a 2006 interview with *The Guardian*. "I snuck surprises on them. I should really have talked to my group. But at the end of the day, it's me who lays down with my stuff, not Chuck and Griff."

Not that Flavor had completely given up on music: in the same *Billboard* piece, he insisted he was working on a solo disc. "I'm going independent right now," he said. "Right now, I'm going to release it. I will spend my own money to press it up until someone picks it up. I don't want to sign with another record company. All companies I sign to make money off of me. Now it's my turn to make some money off of me!"

But Flav also spent his newfound 15 minutes talking up Public Enemy's forthcoming record. "It's really almost done," he said. "Honestly, this album is way better than our most recent albums." This wasn't the critical consensus when *New Whirl Odor* came out in the fall of 2005.

★   ★   ★

Crawling along the bottom of *Revolverlution*'s front cover were the words: "A Trilogy Within A Trilogy Within A Trilogy Within A Trilogy". In interviews, Chuck indicated that *Revolverlution* represented three different aspects of Public Enemy – new tracks, live tracks and remixed tracks – but he also envisioned *Revolverlution* as the first of three records, with *New Whirl Odor* planned as the second release in the series. But according to Chuck, Koch (which released *Revolverlution*) baulked at the idea. Instead, the label put out a collection of PE remixes, *Bring That Beat Back*, in 2006 and reissued *There's A Poison Goin On* with bonus remix tracks.

"[T]he focus at that time was to combine the new studio songs with remixxes [*sic*] and live songs for the remaining two albums," Chuck wrote in the *New Whirl Odor* liner notes. But because of a "distribution limit", he had to reconceive *New Whirl Odor* as well as the trilogy's final instalment, *How You Sell Soul To A Soulless People Who Sold Their Soul???*

Consequently, *New Whirl Odor* was a more conventional release: all new songs, no remixes or live cuts. But Chuck didn't want to repeat the strategy of earlier Public Enemy albums. "This album is a revisit to warm sound," he told *American Songwriter*. "People hear a warm sound with nice bass and feel that." Chuck also conceived *New Whirl Odor* as a way to further encourage collaboration, albeit in-house this time. "All of our producers . . . had to [accept] the philosophy that they should share, and know what everyone was doing," he said. "They also passed around their works to each other. It was a double-checking establishment . . . I'm against having one producer captain an entire album."

"None of us were in New York any more," Kerwin Young says. Around the time of *New Whirl Odor*, "Griff had relocated to Atlanta, Chuck was in Atlanta, and Chuck moved me down to Atlanta. Gary was in LA. So we were no longer in close proximity with each other. The chemistry was different: we were shuttling files back and forth digitally, using email, [being] on the phone. It's a different process. In the studio, I had my process, Griff had his process – I would help him arrange his songs and track them out, and Chuck would come by with his lyrics. He'd send [songs] to Gary, and Gary would do post-production. It was a lot of back and forth like that."

With *How You Sell Soul To A Soulless People Who Sold Their Soul???* being supervised by Gary G-Wiz, *New Whirl Odor*'s tracks were overseen by (among others) Abnormal, Professor Griff, Johnny Juice and David "C-Doc" Snyder. But Chuck's hope for a utopian, Motown-like production line for *New Whirl Odor* didn't play out as smoothly as he might have liked. According to Snyder, "The [other] producers weren't turning in tracks on time. The album was dragging out, dragging out, and Chuck was getting pissed."

Juice has thoughts about why Chuck's grand plan didn't quite pan out. "Chuck read about Motown and the assembly-line-production thing, so Chuck thinks Juice will start a record, give it to Gary, he'll add on and finish it," says the DJ/producer. "That works in theory – it worked with the Motown sound because every one of those fucking dudes was a genius. [But] I'm not handing my drum track off to a guy that really can't play keys because you think that he should be the next person that does something to it. I can physically play drums as well as programming – I also can play keys and I can play bass. I'm not gonna hand over my song to somebody that can't play bass unless I'm supervising it."

Nevertheless, when the tracks eventually arrived, they in some ways emulated the raw, punishing tone of *Muse Sick*. Where *Poison* was stripped-down and *Revolverlution* more of a jumble, *New Whirl Odor* had a grimy, grim tone, the music as gnarly as the canisters of hazardous chemicals depicted on the Paul Stone-designed album cover that were labelled "AIDS", "Radiation" and "Mad Cow".

"Chuck never picks beats that are the same from one album to the next," Juice said in a 2005 interview with O'Reilly Media. "He's always going with what sounds new and different from the last time. He actually picks a lot of what we call 'ugly beats' around here – beats that disrupt him in a certain deep kind of way."

Talking about *New Whirl Odor* now, Juice admits, "A lot of the things I did on those records were fucking outtakes that I didn't wanna use. Chuck used them anyway. I was upset at that. I'm like, 'Come on, Chuck.'" According to the DJ/producer, there was a whole batch of other tracks that he wanted Chuck to consider, to no avail. "Later, he'll hear a song I did for somebody else and be like, 'Damn, you should've given me that music,'" Juice says. "I'm like, 'Dude, I did give you that music. You didn't do anything to it, so I gave it to them.'"

In the same O'Reilly Media interview, Chuck pointed to the group's use of a 30-year-old Portastudio four-track recorder as a crucial component to crafting Public Enemy tracks. "Soul is a beautiful accident in musical terms," Chuck said. "Sometimes, when you're reaching for the stars, you should dig in the dirt, too. That's what we do with our old Portastudio, man: we dig into the dirt. You've got to be as honest as you possibly can with your sounds."

Recent PE albums had tried to keep pace with the times through the use of remixes, but *New Whirl Odor* was proudly out of touch. The instrumental 'Either We Together Or We Ain't' recalled the beat-driven minimalism of 'Security Of The First World'. On 'Makes You Blind', Chuck name-checks Ray Charles and Stevie Wonder. 'Check What You're Listening To' paid homage to Run–D.M.C.'s DJ Jam Master Jay (who was murdered in October 2002) with old-school scratches and stern loops. On 'What A Fool Believes', Chuck fumed over a rock arrangement that took a page from eighties metal and punk, while also tipping its hat to seventies soul. The interlude '66.6 Strikes Again' draws from the same radio interview with conservative host Alan Colmes that was used on *Fear Of A Black Planet*'s 'Incident at 66.6 FM'. Times had changed, though. Chuck recalled that when Public Enemy used Colmes' voice on *Black Planet*, the host tried to sue, "but NBC, who owned the broadcast, felt it would be a waste of time". For *New Whirl Odor*, the band had to get permission from Colmes and give him a songwriting credit. Even the most striking cut, a collaboration with Moby called 'MKLVFKWR', wouldn't have felt out of place on the techno musician's nineties discs.

If all that wasn't enough, the album's production sonically evoked the old and the ragged. Speaking with *Remix*, Juice mentioned, "Sometimes, I'll even try to make it sound more like a record and less like a band. I'll record the band into Sonar [a recording software], mix it down the way I like it and then export it to a four-track cassette deck, like a Tascam Portastudio, to make it sound grimy. Then, I'll play that back into the analog inputs in my machine, and boom – I've got myself a loop with tape hiss and everything. And if it gets to the point where I want it to be real grimy, I'll take a mic and put it up to the speaker and play it back."

Referencing the title of a Temptations song, Chuck would say that *New Whirl Odor* was meant to reflect the fact that "the world is a ball of confusion". Speaking to *The Guardian* while the band was touring Stockholm in June 2006, the rapper said, "The album is a global warning against the weapons of mass distraction. They could be anything: a video game, a religion. What are they distracting you from? Thinking."

Even if musically *New Whirl Odor* harked back to earlier eras, thematically it was very much the product of its times. Bush and the Iraq War, which had been launched due to a false belief that Iraqi strongman Saddam Hussein had weapons of mass destruction, were frequent talking points in the lyrics. "Where do we start with these guys?" Chuck said of the Bush administration in an interview with *The Progressive*. "The first thing I would like to say is that to be truly American and represent American ideals you need to consider yourself a citizen of the world. American policy has gone contrary to that ideal. The Bush administration is bent on making the world submit to 'Americanism' instead of becoming a member of the world community."

Chuck had long been critical of commercial hip-hop, but building off of *Revolverlution*, the new album also condemned the art form for abdicating its responsibility as a voice for the voiceless during those politically charged days. "The powers that be are trying to meld, shape and corral the culture of hip-hop into another speaking voice for the government," he complained in *The Progressive*. "They have exploited hip-hop and some of the culture around it – magazines, videos, etc. – to recruit people into the military."

Even if that's an exaggeration, the truth is hip-hop in the early 21st century had mostly ignored social consciousness to pursue other lyrical terrain. It's not that there weren't any examples of popular protest. In the fall of 2004, shortly before Bush won presidential reelection over Democratic nominee John Kerry, Emimen released 'Mosh', an anti-war tune. And in the wake of Hurricane Katrina, which devastated New Orleans and the surrounding area in August 2005, infuriating those who accused the government of being slow to respond, Kanye West appeared on a televised benefit concert. With the cameras trained on him, he declared, off the cuff, "I hate the way they portray us in the media. You see a black family, it says, 'They're looting.' You see a white family, it says, 'They're looking for food.' . . . George Bush doesn't care about black people." It was shocking, in part because such outspoken commentary had seemingly vanished from mainstream rap.

Public Enemy get in our face during a June 1997 photo shoot in London. DAVID TONGE/GETTY IMAGES

Chuck D signs a copy of his memoir, *Fight the Power: Rap, Race, and Reality*. In the book, he recalled the band's early days and discussed the fallout over the Professor Griff controversy, while also sharing his thoughts on gangs, black media, lawyers and accountants.

RAYMOND BOYD/MICHAEL OCHS ARCHIVES/GETTY IMAGES

Beastie Boys' Adam Yauch, Mike Diamond and Adam Horovitz pal around with Chuck D. Yauch, who died in 2012, recalled hearing Public Enemy's 'Rebel Without A Pause' for the first time. "It was just unlike anything I had ever heard before," he wrote. "It blew my wig back."

JEFF KRAVITZ/FILMMAGIC, INC./GETTY IMAGES

In 1998, Public Enemy headlined the Smokin' Grooves Tour, which also featured Cypress Hill, Busta Rhymes, Wyclef Jean and others.

DARRYLL BROOKS

Shortly after the October 30, 2002 shooting death of Run-D.M.C.'s Jam Master Jay, Chuck D spoke at a press conference in which it was announced that a coalition of musicians, executives and organizations would team up to offer financial support for the slain DJ's family. FRANK MICELOTTA/IMAGEDIRECT/GETTY IMAGES

DJ Lord salutes the crowd during a Dublin show on April 13, 2003. Filling the shoes of Terminator X proved daunting at first, but Lord eventually became comfortable in the role. (The two DJs didn't meet until Public Enemy were inducted into the Rock and Roll Hall of Fame in 2013.) GETTY IMAGES

Flavor Flav and Brigitte Nielsen share a moment at the VH1 Big In 2004 Awards in Los Angeles. The two started dating after meeting on the reality show *The Surreal Life*.
LAURA FARR/ZUMA/CORBIS

DJ Tim Westwood chills with Chuck D at the 2005 MOBO Awards in London. JOHN ROGERS/GETTY IMAGES

Public Enemy perform as part of Rock the Bells on July 28, 2007. BRYAN BEDDER/GETTY IMAGES

In July 2007, Flavor Flav was the guest of honour at his very own Comedy Central Roast. Here he is with his mother Anna Drayton, who died on New Year's Eve of 2013. STARTRAKS PHOTO/REX

Professor Griff, Chuck D, Adam Yauch and Walter Leaphart (Public Enemy's manager) attend a 2007 New York screening for *Public Enemy: Welcome to the Terrordome*, a documentary about the band. JAMIE MCCARTHY/WIREIMAGE/GETTY IMAGES

Chuck and Flavor get ready for the 2008 VH1 Hip Hop Honors, which featured a tribute to De La Soul.
JEFF KRAVITZ/FILMMAGIC/GETTY IMAGES

In the spring of 2009, Public Enemy (including Flavor Flav) performed at the Coachella Music and Arts Festival.
JOHN SHEARER/WIREIMAGE/GETTY IMAGES

Flavor Flav does a little cooking at his restaurant, Flavor Flav's Fried Chicken, which opened in Clinton, Iowa, in early 2011. Thirteen weeks later, the store closed, with Flav and his business partner, Nick Cimino, blaming each other for Fried Chicken's failure.
KEVIN E. SCHMIDT/QUAD-CITY TIMES/ZUMA WIRE

Flavor Flav speaks from the podium in Los Angeles, California, on April 18, 2013, as Public Enemy are inducted in to the Rock and Roll Hall of Fame, becoming only the fourth hip-hop act to be enshrined. KEVIN WINTER/GETTY IMAGES

Still louder than a bomb: Flavor and Chuck rip it up at the 2014 New Orleans Jazz & Heritage Festival.
TIM MOSENFELDER/GETTY IMAGES

"These are inevitable destinations for artists like Eminem," Chuck said about 'Mosh' in *The Progressive*. "Where else can you go with respect to the work, lyrics and message of the music? If you are past high school age, you can get by with saying very little the first or second time around. However, after a while you know you are going to have to say something beyond high school stuff. Eminem has talent, and his talent is the thing that influences many young people who would have never gone anywhere near rap."

On *New Whirl Odor*'s bluesy 'Preachin' To The Quiet', Chuck made his grievances with contemporary hip-hop known, ridiculing the cultural craving for celebrity. Chuck raps, "In these rich-or-die-tryin' times / Y'all see the greed I see / Got these cats whipped by TV," a clear knock on *Get Rich Or Die Tryin'*, the 2003 multiplatinum debut from gangster rapper 50 Cent. Two years later, a fictionalised version of Fiddy's pre-rap thug life was made into a movie of the same name. "Rap has become a sad reality," said Griff, referring to the film, which received negative reviews, especially for 50 Cent's monotone acting. "50 Cent comes out with a movie that's a step-by-step instruction in how to be a thug. And sells it to children?"

But Chuck was equally vocal, although not on *New Whirl Odor*, about his disappointment with Jay-Z, who had famously retired from hip-hop with 2003's *The Black Album*, only to return a few years later. "If you had to look in a book for the definition of a rapper you would probably see a picture of Jay-Z," Chuck said in 2005. "He is the chosen one right now." But that wasn't meant as a compliment. "Someone like Jay-Z does have a timeless quality," Chuck acknowledged, "but it's much different than ours. You can look back at something like 'At The Hop' by Danny & the Juniors or the music that was on *American Bandstand* in the fifties and sixties. It was the emergence of rock in the suburbs – without its teeth, let's say. You will get the same thing out of Jay-Z with the street-hustler mentality of the late nineties. It won't be able to resonate far beyond that, but it's something that will go on with just a different person telling it. When it comes down to Public Enemy and the Clash or Bob Marley . . . you can play the music now and it's like, 'Damn, what the music is saying is just as important today as it was when they recorded it.' It also becomes a powerful historical document of a particular time of struggle and resistance.

But this is maybe the purpose of artists like Public Enemy – speaking truth to power – while artists like Jay-Z represent the escapism of that time."

And that, perhaps, was the great value of PE's early-2000s records. Though musically less inspired, these albums sincerely engaged with the state of the world. Albeit imperfectly, PE captured the ugliness of the national mood as war, partisanship and anxiety – *Could the terrorists strike again?* – seeped into our consciousness. Records like *New Whirl Odor* weren't pretty or exhilarating. How could they be?

Chuck's disdain for escapism reared its head most prominently on 'Makes You Blind', a soul-inflected cut that rails on thug rappers and Xbox. And in a nifty little rope-a-dope, Chuck shifted from hit rappers to corporate control: "It ain't Eminem / It's M and M and M / McDonald's, MTV and Microsoft / Can't you see / They got the young strung at a cost." It called to mind a comment that Chuck made during an interview for *Muse Sick* when he was asked about whether he was still as hungry as he was when he started out. "No, I'm not hungry about making the best rap record in the world," he answered, taking the long view. "What I'm hungry for is snatching these companies and hoping that hip-hop can hold onto what it builds. I'm hungry in a different way at a higher level. Before, a hamburger was enough – now, I want the restaurant. . . . Having a Top 10 record, does that make me hungry? I've had that before, done that. Have I put out *Takes A Nation*? . . . Did it already. What can I do now?"

New Whirl Odor, like its immediate predecessors, was Chuck's attempt to figure out what the next step would be for Public Enemy in an era that didn't care too much about Public Enemy. "Rap comes from the humble beginnings of rebelling against the status quo," he told *The Progressive*. "Now, rappers have become the status quo themselves. You can't rebel against the Queen and then become the Queen yourself." But *New Whirl Odor*'s lyrical and musical conceits didn't offer enough that was fresh or innovative. No matter what one thought of Jay-Z, 50 Cent or Eminem, they were taking hip-hop and introducing new twists to the genre. Especially in the case of Jay-Z and Eminem, the music stirringly melded autobiography, braggadocio, vulnerability, menace and humour in a way that became those artists' distinctive signature.

Meanwhile, a group like the Atlanta-based Outkast were radically shifting the landscape of what hip-hop could be, embracing Southern soul and psychedelic elements. Chuck sounded incredibly petty in his annoyance that Outkast's bold reinvention on each new album was praised when, to his mind, Public Enemy helped pioneer the concept in hip-hop. "That was our motto, like the rock'n'roll credo: never repeat yourself," he claimed in an interview with *Tastes Like Chicken*. "That was our whole thing, and it still is. A lot of people that follow hip-hop, they didn't get that whole pattern of going about albums until Outkast came along. Then all of a sudden people was like, 'Oh, wow!' You know? People didn't know that that was our thing. So when we took a different approach with each album, it was even abandoning what we did with the previous album, and some people just thought, like, 'Well, they lost the sound.' How the fuck you gonna lose a sound that you created?"

And this is to say nothing of the new century's most impressive artist, Kanye West, who miraculously bridged the gap between the intelligent introspection of indie/backpacker hip-hop and the broad appeal of Top 40 pop. Public Enemy cohort Paris, who would become more intimately involved with the group on their follow-up to *New Whirl Odor*, once complained, "Why do music without taking on challenges? . . . [I'm] one of those guys that can actually make music and also write lyrics. Today, they talk about Kanye West, but Paris was the prototype and has been doing that for years. In fact, Paris was Kanye West before Kanye West existed." Chuck and his ilk would sometimes get huffy about rap's young turks, but just because newer acts didn't sound like Public Enemy didn't mean they had forfeited their artistic integrity in the process.

On 'New Whirl Odor', Chuck declared, "I flock to refugees / Who flock to me / The Roots, the Coup / And kick aside the genocide and the juice." It was a slap at gangster rappers like Snoop Dogg, who had a hit with 'Gin And Juice', but it also was a salute to bands who Chuck saw as like-minded soldiers in his struggle. But both the Roots, with their dazzling mix of rock and R&B, and the Coup, whose frontman Boots Riley celebrated Communism and delivered a superb combination of hip-hop and funk, were outpacing and outclassing the backward-looking Public Enemy, even though both bands acknowledged their debt to the classic Long Island crew.

The reality was that *New Whirl Odor* wasn't going to change people's perception of Public Enemy as an over-the-hill band. Even Chuck's flow in some ways suggested a man reaching back into the past. Johnny Juice, responsible for what he calls the "New Orleans funeral" sound of 'Preachin' To The Quiet', says, "Chuck has a habit on my songs to rhyme-talk. He don't really have a flow or a cadence – I started calling him 'the hip-hop Paul Robeson' because you're sitting there with a freaking smoking jacket on and a pipe and you're just talking and shit."

But that didn't mean Public Enemy couldn't still surprise. 'MKLVFKWR' was created for *Unity: The Official Athens 2004 Olympic Games Album*, a compilation that featured plenty of ballads and covers like 'Knockin' On Heaven's Door' by Avril Lavigne. By contrast, 'MKLVFKWR' was a siren-like rallying cry to reject war and respect peace. The song title was a shortened form of 'Make Love, Fuck War'. "When I went to Russia," Chuck explained to *Mother Jones*, "you look at them [Russian] letters and go, 'What the hell?' Someone told me they're offshoots of the Greek language, it made all the sense to me. So the statement I was saying all last year when I was touring throughout the world was: 'Make love, fuck war.' And I said, 'Well you could actually say, "Make Love Fuck War," and say it without saying it.'"

The song was a collaboration between Moby and Public Enemy, with Moby providing the music. In 2013, Moby told *The Quietus* about the first time he heard PE in the late eighties. "I remember . . . thinking, 'How did they do this?' Because they've basically made punk rock hip-hop, the sounds they were using, the way they were distorting bass lines, it was a lot of the same ways industrial records were being made but they were making hip-hop. It was so revolutionary."

Perhaps not surprisingly, then, when Moby finally got to work on a track with PE, "I was trying to go for that late-eighties Bomb Squad production sound," he recalled in 2004. "A few of my friends said, 'Wow, it sounds really dated.'" That comment made Moby laugh. "I said, 'Well yeah, that's the point.' I didn't want to make some kind of Neptunes-ish, slick R&B track with Chuck D on it. I wanted to make something that sounded like a building falling down."

He succeeded. The techno artist's songs have often dabbled in dance-rock, so his approximation of *Nation Of Millions*-era PE wasn't too much of a stretch. Dynamic and striking, 'MKLVFKWR' found Chuck and Flavor in fine form, juiced by the uptempo rhythm. It's not only one of *New Whirl Odor*'s highlights, it's probably Public Enemy's best antiwar tune.

"The song is a request that being a citizen of the world should transcend nationality in the name of peace," Chuck once said. This notion of being "a citizen of the world" had become important to him ever since visiting Africa in the early nineties. In *The Progressive*, he blamed Bush's jingoistic demeanour for "[pushing] America into a corner. So, rather than trying to humbly mix with the rest of the world, we are forcing ourselves upon it. We seem to create conflicts with everyone." While speaking with *Right Wing News*, Chuck commented, "I think people are people and human beings are human beings. I look at myself as being a citizen of the world and I think art and music bring human beings together . . . But, I also think governments have always had a historical tendency to split people up, categorise them, and put them in compartments. So, I'm not really for that as much as I'm for the beauty of music and culture."

But *New Whirl Odor*'s standout song is its finale. Snyder made it a habit that, when he heard PE were working on a new album, he'd send Chuck ideas for tracks. "I wasn't setting out to make the longest PE song in their catalogue," he says, but that's what happened with 'Superman's Black In The Building', a nearly-12-minute blues-funk tune that's the closest the group ever got to the stoned, weary resignation of *There's A Riot Goin' On*.

The track's origins came from Snyder scanning Public Enemy's message boards. He recalls, "Somebody said, 'I'd like to hear a new PE song like "Shut 'Em Down", something with really big drums.' I was like, 'Yeah, that'd be dope. I'm gonna make that record.' And so I sat down and started writing the beat. It totally didn't end up sounding like 'Shut 'Em Down' at all." Still, Snyder liked what he'd come up with and sent it to Chuck. The producer heard back within about 10 minutes: the rapper loved it and was already working on lyrics. Initially, Chuck had one idea for the track, but a week later he connected with Snyder to let him know he'd switched gears. "The original title was like, 'Now Black Superman's Back In The

Building','" says Snyder, but after the song was mixed down, Chuck decided to streamline the title a little.

Chuck had actually envisioned 'Superman's Black In The Building' as the first single for *How You Sell Soul To A Soulless People Who Sold Their Soul???* He knew the song was special. "A lot of our collaborations, I'll send him the beat, he'll record it and send it back, and then I'll mix it from there," Snyder says. "The only record we did together in the studio was 'Superman'. We rented a studio in Cleveland – he was doing a lecture, and after the lecture we went into the studio and worked on it a couple of hours that night. He really was working that record." Snyder laughs. "Chuck's funny because sometimes he'll give you three takes. He'll be like, 'Yeah, that's cool. Go ahead, work some magic.' But if he's really digging the record, he'll work it." That night in Cleveland, "he kept doing take after take. He was like, 'You want another one, Doc?' I'm like, 'It's up to you.' And he goes, 'Hey, I'll give you another one.' It just depends on the record."

But after Gary took the helm of *How You Sell Soul*, the decision was made to move 'Superman's Black' to *New Whirl Odor* and feature it as the lead single. Still, Snyder couldn't stop fiddling with the song. "I tried changing up the time signature," he says, "and I thought, 'Wow, that's kinda cool.' I called Chuck and said, 'Hey, I got a crazy idea for this song. You mind if we make it a little longer?'" Snyder's inspiration to make an extended track that ran beyond the normal length of a single came from the music he was listening to at the time: old Isaac Hayes records and Chicago albums. "They had all these 12-minute, 13-minute songs," he says. "I'm like, 'Well, let's mess around with that.'"

The final version of the song demonstrated how deftly Public Enemy could transcend the perceived strictures of hip-hop. 'Superman's Black' has the feel of a Windy City blues club, different generations of African-American musicians coming together as gospel, blues, spoken-word, funk, jazz and hip-hop find common ground.

The song's *coup de grâce*, though, was the inclusion of saxophone played by the legendary Gene Barge, who had played with or worked alongside luminaries such as Ray Charles, Muddy Waters, James Brown, Little Richard, the Rolling Stones and the Chi-Lites. A staple of Chess Records

and a fixture of the Chicago music scene, Barge was born in Virginia in 1926, being drawn to music at a young age. "The saxophone was the instrument, coming up, that had the sound closest to the human voice," he once told *Virginia Living*. "It was the one with the impact. It was the featured instrument in the band, so that was the one you wanted to play."

Barge's graceful sax lines elevate and embolden 'Superman's Black'. And it came about one late night in a Chicago studio. Craig Bauer, an engineer, producer and mixer who had worked with Kanye West early in the rapper's career, supervised the session. "I can remember it very clearly," Bauer says. "Chuck arrived first. To be honest, I had no idea what to expect, [considering] Public Enemy's material and knowing sort of their vibe. I was pleasantly surprised at how unbelievably nice he was, down to earth and just genuine."

The session consisted of just Bauer, Chuck and Barge, and there was little discussion beforehand about what the saxophonist would do on the track. "We had a brief conversation," says Bauer. "We played the track a number of times, and Chuck actually just let him try out a number of ideas and work through some stuff. Mostly, he left it up to Gene – what he wanted to do, how he wanted to do it. Chuck would give him yeas or nays, but he didn't give tons of direction. I deal with guys in the jazz world, and you get a lot of musicians that have a holier-than-thou vibe when they're told to come in for a session. Gene was nothing like that. It was a very collaborative process between all of us, frankly."

Lyrically, the song contains a familiar trope of Chuck's, reminding listeners that he's been part of the rap game for a long time. But the faintly melancholy tenor of the music (accented by Barge's sax) makes his boasts seem more exhausted than defiant. Even Flav's snickering laugh offers little comfort. And four minutes in, the pace slows down, saxophone laments and gospel-girl wails starting to come to the fore, duelling for dominance alongside a lonely juke-joint riff and a far-off abbreviated guitar solo. In turn, Chuck switches from rapping to testifying, seemingly free-styling about heaven as an elevated level of consciousness rather than a final destination. It's a poignant, heartfelt monologue that condemns materialism as a trap and offers that self-knowledge and perseverance are life's true rewards. "Being able to meet life's struggles head on / Head on / Head on / Without compromising your soul," Chuck argues, is real strength. Then at the seven-minute mark, Chuck steps away from the mic, letting the scratches, wails and riffs carry the song the rest of the way, the MC only returning to shout-out his crew and repeatedly intone "That's heaven."

C-Doc was right: 'Superman's Black In The Building' ended up sounding nothing like 'Shut 'Em Down'. But the richness of its sound, the scope of its ambition and the daring of its suite-like construction made it a comparably stunning song.

"I remember reading a review somewhere [of *New Whirl Odor*]," Snyder says, "and the guy didn't really care for the album. But he really liked that song. And he said, 'It's a shame that they didn't use this song as the starting point for the album instead of finishing with the album, because if they would have started it here and went where this song goes, it could have been something really adventurous.' And I was like, 'Wow.' I didn't think [*New Whirl Odor*] was terrible, but that was kind of the idea [with 'Superman's Black']: get adventurous."

As an insight into the song's sonic mission, Snyder mentions that Chuck often compares hip-hop to other black art forms like jazz or blues. "It's all just stories," C-Doc says. "Hip-hop is so young compared to everything else: how can you say it's one thing or another? Grandmaster Flash is still doing it. Whodini still tours. Doug E. Fresh tours, like, 220 days of the year. That's awesome, that's incredible. So how can you say what it is and what it isn't? Chuck says a lot, 'People want to pigeonhole it, but you can't.' When Chuck turns 70, they might not be doing the prototypical Public Enemy show, but I can see Chuck hitting the stage and doing something different, reinterpreting his songs into something else."

As proof, Snyder points to the baNNed, PE's live rock band that includes guitarist Khari Wynn. When Chuck decided to retire PE as a live act in the mid-nineties, part of his plan to reinvent their onstage attack was to bring in musicians to give the old tunes new dimensions. "They reinterpret all the songs into something else: funk, soul and stuff like that," says Snyder. "There's a lot of potential [in hip-hop]. I don't think people see that, for whatever reason: they want to pigeonhole it. And that was part of the thinking behind 'Superman's Black In The Building' being 11 minutes long."

Regardless, *New Whirl Odor* didn't make much of a dent with the public. The album failed to chart on *Billboard*, the second of the band's last three records to earn that unhappy distinction. And the reviews, sometimes quite correctly, pinpointed the album's flaws. *Billboard*'s Bill Werde wrote that *New Whirl Odor* "showcases the group's classic sound" but that "there is not much new ground here. As he has for years, Chuck takes aim at a government that tries to keep the have-nots sedate ('Makes You Blind', 'New Whirl Odor'), sell-out black role models ('Preachin' To The Quiet', 'Revolution') and the suckers that fall for it all ('What A Fool Believes'). The problem is, no one seems to care any more. Chuck D called rap 'the black CNN' when PE burst onto the scene in the late eighties. Today, the kids are watching MTV. Their loss."

Werde doesn't give any ink to *New Whirl Odor*'s highlight tracks 'Superman's Black In The Building' and 'MKLVFKWR', but he's essentially correct about the album's limitations. As *Spin*'s review suggested, "Chuck D has struggled to nuance his preaching for a shrinking choir, so this admirable record powers down to rote rhetoric too early." Or, as *Pitchfork*'s Sean Fennessey put it more harshly, "There's a fine line between deflating institutional bullshit and a curmudgeon's condescension. PE fell prey to the latter years ago." Fennessey concluded, "It's no fun disliking this album, but it's no fun to listen to, either. If you align yourself with Public Enemy, you'll be thrilled with all the shouting and sloganeering. But that's precisely what they should be combating: homogenisation, T-shirt politics, musical uniformity. Instead they get closer to Fiery Cover Band status."

The criticism didn't just come from record reviewers, though. Some questioned Chuck after it was announced in September 2005 that Public Enemy would be releasing *New Whirl Odor* exclusively for its first month through the superstore Best Buy. For the store, the rationale was obvious: as record sales continued to decline in the download era, a Best Buy could leverage exclusivity as a way to attract customers to other items. And certainly a retailer such as Best Buy, which sells everything from CDs to big-screen televisions to appliances, was better positioned than traditional record stores like Tower Records. In a December 2005 issue of *Billboard*, an article entitled "Retailers Work Toward Digital Future" explained how stores had to rethink their sales strategy for the web. "We need to start the migration from a record store to an entertainment lifestyle store," said the senior vice president of corporate development at Musicland, which for a time was owned by Best Buy. More and more, music was becoming just another commodity.

Chuck pitched his partnership with Best Buy as a smart, progressive move. In a press release that accompanied the announcement, he said, "I have long sought to find a way for independent companies such as my SLAMJamz Records to hold onto their artistic integrity while at the same time get a chance to reach many of the masses from highly visible places. We appreciate the opportunity to have our new album positioned alongside those from major record labels, expanding opportunities for not just our group but for other small companies in our genre. We thank Best Buy for this position to create these new avenues." Around the same time, an anonymous source told *Billboard*, "This is an opportunity in the best interest of Chuck and the group to promote positive music in as broad a stream as possible."

This is a valid argument. At a time when major labels were shrinking and investing less capital in hip-hop acts that were on the margins, the Best Buy deal gave Chuck visibility he couldn't achieve through more traditional means. But the partnership also meant that Chuck was cozying up to the big companies he detests in his lyrics. It couldn't help but feel hypocritical, especially when the frontman had long advocated that artists should embrace the internet as the future – one in which selling albums was less important than reaching out to a broader range of fans across the globe. As one unnamed merchant groused to *Billboard*, "Mr. Chuck D says, 'Everything should be on the web for free unless it's my CD and I get a big fat cheque from Best Buy.'"

But such contradictions have always been at the heart of music-making. How does an artist present himself as a populist who prizes his integrity and independence while, at the same time, earning a living? Chuck has been inconsistent in his attitude toward retailers. He was happy to put out *There's A Poison Goin On* online initially as a middle finger to traditional record stores, but *New Whirl Odor* seemed to be a reversal of that position.

In 2014, Chuck D was named official ambassador to Record Store Day, an annual spring event in which independent stores sell limited-edition items from participating bands.

"I come from DJ culture," he said about his association with Record Store Day. "We DJs recognise the importance of records and the importance of music culture. Independent record stores have enhanced the curation of records and music as it's matured. The stores we musicians were influenced by are places that breathed life into us as music-makers, as well as music collectors. And that's why the survival of record stores worldwide is so important."

Chuck didn't sound like a romantic getting misty about the past, though. "Everything is there on the internet – everything," he said. "But if you don't know how to read the internet and interpret what's there, then it's useless. The record stores are our curators. They're GPS systems to guide us through what's out there on the internet – they help you into understanding what is what. . . . Independent record stores must be able to spread their wings and to show their flexibility, and also keep the soul and the thrill of it all. It's beyond just going to a record store and getting vinyl: it's about going there and being able to pick up content, data, collectibles, lifestyle, relevancy."

Relevancy was an urgent issue for Public Enemy. *New Whirl Odor* was a decent stab at it, but its follow-up would prove to be their most significant record of the new century. To that point, anyway.

CHAPTER TWELVE

CHUCK D was speaking with writer Tamara Palmer, reminiscing about the music of his youth. "I don't know if you can get a better time of songwriting than 1964–1974," he was saying. "It's when we had a war, we had assassinations, we had confusion. But the music clarified a lot of different things that weren't said in the news and in society itself."

Their conversation was in connection to *Rebirth Of A Nation*, Public Enemy's 2006 release. In the 21st century, PE had made music that addressed their era's war and confusion: *Revolverlution*'s 'Son Of A Bush', *New Whirl Odor*'s 'MKLVFKWR'. But it wasn't until *Rebirth Of A Nation* that the band produced an album that in its entirety seemed to capture the bitterness and disillusionment of the Bush presidency. It's a record that didn't necessarily clarify the post-9/11 world, but it certainly gave voice to the rumbling discontent of those angry about the Iraq War and the president's record of incompetence and wrongheaded macho swagger.

It's also the Public Enemy record that had the least input from its founding members.

A few months after the release of *Revolverlution*, Chuck visited KPFA in Berkeley, California, to do an interview. On the air, he was asked about working on the remix of 'Gotta Give The Peeps What They Want' with Paris, a Bay Area rapper and producer. The two men had first met in the early nineties around the time that Paris dropped his first record, *The Devil Made Me Do It*. "I recall that Chuck liked my video producer on my single 'Break The Grip Of Shame'," says Paris by email, "which led to them using the same company for their 'Anti-Nigger Machine' video. I had a cameo in that, too." *The Devil Made Me Do It* advocated social-consciousness accented by hard beats, which would put it in Chuck's wheelhouse. Paris emulated the West Coast sound of N.W.A., but he also had a knack for the melodic hook that was reminiscent of his Bay Area contemporary MC Hammer. Paris and Chuck had lost touch over time, but after Paris reached out during the making of *Revolverlution*, they renewed their friendship. Pleased with Paris' contribution to the 'Gotta Give The Peeps What They Want' remix, Chuck was planning on guesting on the rapper's forthcoming album, *Sonic Jihad*. "I can't explain how thankful I am for Paris, who is always a warrior and detonating verbal bombs," Chuck told KPFA's Davey D. "I am more than happy to be involved with whatever he does."

Unbeknownst to Chuck, Paris's next project would deeply involve Public Enemy. Shortly after the KPFA interview, Chuck met with Paris, who told him he wanted to do an album for the band. As Paris later recalled, Chuck was open to it. "[Chuck] said 'My time is short, so the only way this is gonna happen is if you do the work,'" Paris told writer Anil Prasad of *Innerviews* in 2006. "So, I ran with that and wrote all the parts, completed all the songs and forwarded him the completed tracks to learn."

In the past, Chuck had rejected the idea of having one producer helm a whole PE album.* Johnny Juice recalls, "I once asked Chuck to do a whole album and he told me, no, he doesn't believe in that. Then I told him, 'Let me write a whole album including the lyrics.' Chuck said, 'No, I'm not interested in that.'" But with *Rebirth Of A Nation*, something changed for the frontman.

"When Paris approached me about doing something together, what manifested out of that was me saying, 'Let's take on a challenge that not only you would do the music for but also write the lyrics and put together a [Public Enemy] album as you see it in your mind,'" Chuck explained to *Billboard*. "'Be Prince or be Kanye West on this one.' It has an entirely different feel that is West Coastal, which deals a little bit more in the element of music and funk, as opposed to just beats."

In pop, it's common for the top stars to work with of-the-moment producers and songwriters in order to keep their sound cutting-edge. Rockists complain that such a tendency reduces stars to little more than pretty packages, but the mass audience doesn't mind: they're buying into a

---

* Part of the reason *Apocalypse 91* was credited to fake producers was to mask the fact that Gary G-Wiz had done so much of it.

persona that's fairly mutable. By comparison, the great singer-songwriters such as Bob Dylan or Neil Young are celebrated because they've chronicled their lives and bared their souls through their own musical and lyrical expression. They, too, may have worked with buzzworthy producers to update their sonic architecture, but these artists' fans value them because of a sense of authenticity, integrity and continuity.

That might explain why *Rebirth Of A Nation* surprised some PE fans. Although it's billed on the album cover as "Public Enemy Featuring Paris", it might be more accurate if it read "Paris Interprets Public Enemy". *Rebirth Of A Nation* is a Public Enemy album, but it's also a tribute album of sorts: one artist's attempt to pay homage to another. "The overall concept for me was to celebrate the group's legacy in an updated way," Paris says. "I suppose the project is current and retro at the same time, as there are numerous nods to key elements in their past works throughout."

That's not to say that Paris is unreserved in his admiration for the group. "I first heard PE when I had a radio show while in college in the late eighties and was given their first record by [onetime Def Jam rep] Dave Funken-Klein," remembers Paris. "I couldn't stand *Yo! Bum Rush The Show* at first, but it eventually grew on me. I was much more on the Cool J and Rakim page back then. Once *It Takes A Nation* dropped, it was over, though. I was hooked." As for his feelings about the group before working on *Rebirth Of A Nation*, Paris says, "I know that I've always dug PE for their highlights, and to me they're a group that runs hot and cold. When they're just going through the motions and not really motivated, they suck ass. But when they're on, they're *on*. Like most of us, I guess."

As for Chuck, who was already mapping out the next Public Enemy album, the Gary G-Wiz-supervised *How You Sell Soul To A Soulless People Who Sold Their Soul???*, he felt no compunction about handing over the reins to an outside songwriter and producer. Writing in *Rebirth Of A Nation*'s liner notes, he explained, "As a big fan of music, I know about the time when Chess Records, the great Chicago blues label, had the owner Leonard Chess' son Marshall assemble an album for the great Muddy Waters." He wondered if the same thing could be done with a Public Enemy album: "[I]t would be interesting to go back to the retro flows I did 15 years ago, but someone with the skill, trust and commitment would have to do it."

Chuck was quite comfortable having that someone be Paris, whom he told PE biographer Russell Myrie "is the only cat that I know who could actually write a Public Enemy record". But he didn't just want a carbon copy of the PE aesthetic. "I can always push myself to write something I didn't write before," he said to Palmer, "but you really can't change yourself . . . Therefore I think a lot of artists could afford to have other people write for them and just put this rap ethic bullshit down that it's taboo."

Most of Public Enemy's 21st century albums harked back to the band's late-eighties/early-nineties period, recycling lyrical or musical hooks from classic tracks. So if *Rebirth Of A Nation* isn't unique in that way, what does make it stand out is that it's another person's idea of what a PE album could still be. It was the work of a man whose music had created even more controversy than PE's. On Paris' second album, 1992's *Sleeping With The Enemy*, there was a track called 'Bush Killa' in which he imagined assassinating President George H.W. Bush. "It was a record that had a lot of anger and spoke directly in response to conditions that existed in our community, and the neglect and lack of attention that was paid to us except during the election year," Paris later said about 'Bush Killa', which arrived the same year as 'Cop Killer', Body Count's attack on police brutality that advocated offing corrupt cops. Both artists were on Warner Bros., which faced massive pressure from groups who condemned the songs. For Body Count frontman Ice-T, it meant eventually reissuing the album without the controversial song. For Paris, "Warner Music for the most part shut me down. I ended up putting that record out on my own and it damn near went gold."

In the late nineties, Paris stepped away from music to focus on a career as a stockbroker, returning to his birth name Oscar Jackson Jr. "You have to have more than one iron in the fire, because nothing is promised," he explained to *SF Weekly* in 2003. "It's the guerrilla way: hands-on, adapt, survival tactics." But the election of Bush's son, George W. Bush, in 2000 and the 9/11 attacks inspired Paris to return to music. In October 2003, angry at the direction of the country, which had invaded Iraq earlier in the year, Paris put out *Sonic Jihad*, an album whose cover depicts a plane on a collision course with the White House. Public Enemy appeared on a remix of the track 'Freedom', which decries abusive cops, economic inequality and America's hawkish foreign policy. An uneven, raging album, *Sonic Jihad* set the stage for what Paris would bring to *Rebirth Of A Nation*.

Paris has stated that his rapper persona is a different version of himself, so it was perhaps fitting that to make a Public Enemy record, he had to think like that group's frontman. "When we did *Rebirth Of A Nation*," Paris once said, "I basically had to become Chuck in order to understand his cadence, different intonations and things he had done before. His particular style really influenced me when I was first starting out, and I wanted to capture some of those classic Public Enemy elements on this project."

"It was kind of different," Chuck D told *HipHopDX*'s Paul Edwards about the *Rebirth Of A Nation* creative process, "but he kind of wrote in a way that was reminiscent of earlier work that I've done. He had great substance in the writing of the words and when he did the flow, he based it off of what I did before. He laid a guide vocal – it's really a total science how he put it together, he's almost like a scientist-slash-musician."

Asked today about his approach in mimicking Chuck D, Paris says, "I recorded all of his vocals originally, and did my best Chuck D imitation so he could see exactly what I was going for. There was a specific snapshot in time that I was trying to emulate, so I wanted to be sure we were all on the same page." That "snapshot in time" was PE's golden era of the late eighties, and since Chuck D gave no instructions about the album's direction, Paris decided to channel his favourite moments from the band's past. "I did listen a lot to what I consider to be their best works, which helped shape my vision for what I wanted the album to be," he says. "Lots of 'Night Of The Living Baseheads,' 'Prophets Of Rage' and 'Anti-Nigger Machine' references, if you can catch 'em."

Those references are most apparent on *Rebirth Of A Nation*'s 'Hard Rhymin'', which echoes lyrics from 'Prophets Of Rage', to say nothing of that *Nation Of Millions* cut's frenzied scratches. Elsewhere, you can hear the influence of 'Anti-Nigger Machine''s rhythm and lyrical cadence on 'Plastic Nation', a diatribe against women's fascination with cosmetic surgery. The album's acknowledgment of that bygone hip-hop era was further emphasised by the appearance of old-school and socially conscious guest vocalists like Kam, MC Ren, Dead Prez and onetime PE associate Sister Souljah. This, too, was Paris' idea. "I wanted to provide a unified front by having some of the best conscious heavy-hitters in hip-hop on board as a show of solidarity," he explains.

If West Coast rap was a response to hip-hop's East Coast origins, then *Rebirth Of A Nation* is Paris trying to imagine a Public Enemy record that married the two sounds: a West Coast artist heavily indebted to an East Coast legend. For instance, the album-opener, 'Raw Sh★t', evokes the bomb-dropping salvos of earlier PE discs, but its icy keyboards and lack of burning-rubber beats suggests a deceptively laid-back, sun-splashed menace. And the picture the song paints is horrifying: a country still reeling from the fallen towers of the World Trade Center, devastated by economic stagnation and the strangulation of individual liberty.

"This project was really a merger of our styles," Paris says. "I don't sample – ever – so everything I was trying to accomplish or emulate, I had to play. That approach provides a very different, very crisp first-generation studio slickness to the sound of a project, which I felt this project merited." Despite calling back to earlier PE sonic or lyrical moments – such as 'B Side Wins Again''s "make it hardcore" for 'Make It Hardcore' – *Rebirth Of A Nation* is less musically dense, substituting a steely austerity for the Bomb Squad chaos. Paris says, "My production aesthetic is much cleaner [because of the lack of sampling]. I have a much more defined approach to song structure and format. I'm still very much from the 'Intro, verse, chorus, verse, chorus, bridge, verse, chorus-till-fade' school. I don't think PE is as much."

The straightforward aesthetic does little to belie Paris' sense of outrage. When asked about the album's themes, he says, "Really just commentary on popular culture and the slow commercialisation and cultural demise of hip-hop. We tried to cover it all: reality shows, plastic surgery, the state of affairs in politics, war, everything." Paris didn't just mastermind the album, though – he also contributed the occasional vocal. Where Chuck D bellows, Paris barks: the juxtaposition of the two voices wasn't as pleasingly different as Chuck's steel and Flavor Flav's goof, but as a result *Rebirth Of A Nation* felt like a double-barrelled assault.

All PE albums are angry, but *Rebirth Of A Nation* is particularly aggrieved. As Paris suggests, the record is mad about the ongoing Iraq War – the album's liner notes decry "racist wars and murder for profit" – as well as Fox News' blind cheerleading of the administration's policies. But it's also angry about the public's fading respect for Public Enemy. In the title track, Paris utilises scratching, guitars and even a snippet of 'Bring The Noise'. In the lyrics, Paris gives Chuck D and Professor Griff the chance to reassert their cultural supremacy while scolding ignorant and self-destructive rap artists. Chuck has never been shy about declaring his righteousness, but the fact that his words came from Paris gives them an added urgency and emotion, as if he wasn't speaking just for himself but for all the band's fans.

Those words and beats were written by a man unafraid to give his heroes some tough love. In an interview published around *Rebirth Of A Nation*'s release, Paris praised Public Enemy but also noted, "They have put out a lot of stuff that to me has been suspect, like fan remixes and shit like that. Things like that made the weight of the legacy not as heavy as I thought it might be at first. I knew if I put the record together and did the best I could do given my abilities that I could do them justice."

That criticism extended to Paris' feelings about Flav. In the mellow, despairing 'Coinsequences', Paris takes the lead vocal, counting down all of the world's ills, which include racism, terrible schools, the Patriot Act and a societal infatuation with celebrity and so-called "reality" television. Along the way, he growls, "No love for the Enemy with video play / But they give Flav a show to take the focus away / From the realest group ever made, whaddya say?" The artificiality of pop culture wasn't just corroding the world outside Public Enemy, Paris was saying – it was corroding the group from within.

Paris had a point. By 2006, Flavor had moved on from his cringe-worthy adventures on *The Surreal Life* and *Strange Love* to become the star of *Flavor Of Love*, a show where a group of women would compete for the rapper's affections. By this stage, Flavor had thoroughly embarrassed himself in much the same way that another music legend, Ozzy Osbourne, had with his dopey reality show *The Osbournes*. Stripping away these artists' aura of mystery or danger, the shows turned icons into jokes.

Flavor's laughing-stock status was only cemented by his confession in

The Icon The Memoir that he was already in a serious relationship while filming *Flavor Of Love*. "I wasn't really looking for love, man," he wrote. "I'd already found it. . . . I had met this great girl, and I knew I wanted to be with her, but the show meant that I had to entertain all these other girls and pretend like one of them would be my girlfriend at the end." In his book, he explains that before *Flavor Of Love* started filming, he met Liz Trujillo at the 2004 American Music Awards. "It was love," he writes, "almost from first sight." The first season of *Flavor Of Love* ran in early 2006, with the second season arriving less than six months after the finale of season one. The third and final season aired from February to May of 2008, with a Comedy Central roast airing in 2007. In fact, a photo of Flavor smiling while sitting on his roast throne adorns the back cover of *The Icon The Memoir*. This TV sideline made Flavor the most visible member of Public Enemy in the new century, but it was the sort of vulgar, cynical celebrity that seemed unbecoming of a group that preached self-respect.

It also didn't help matters when *Flavor Of Love* co-creator Mark Cronin explained to *Vulture* in 2014 how the producers were able to find willing women to participate on the show. "When you take a group of people, take them away from their homes, take away their cell phones and television, and their phone calls are bugged – and there's this one guy who shows up and decides whether you'll get to eat a nice dinner tonight or whether you're going to be in a limo with him – it's like Stockholm Syndrome and they become very quickly caught up in it," he explained. "You'll actually even see that when somebody gets eliminated from one of these shows, they kind of snap out of it very quickly. Like they suddenly realise, *What was I thinking?*"

When Chuck D was asked by a reporter for his opinion of Flavor's reality shows, he was polite. "That's what Flavor does," Chuck said. "You don't expect people to sit around and go to a college lecture with Flavor lecturing like myself. I lecture at colleges, Professor Griff writes books, Flavor does TV and happens to be a hell of a visual character. . . . We're all one family so that's what that is. As long as he doesn't get hurt or doesn't hurt his family, I'm good."

In a January 2008 interview with *The Starting Five*'s Michael Tillery,

Chuck D responded to the question "What do you say to those who say Flav is a minstrel?" by answering, "Flavor Flav has always been the same person. He's never changed. He does his own thing without Public Enemy. When he's in a Public Enemy context it's no different than the family . . . You know how black families are. They always got that one character." Chuck laughed. "If white folks don't understand, we even had a president who understood that: Billy Carter. Remember Billy Carter? He put so much heat on the president. But at the end of the day he still was family."

Chuck again addressed – and rationalised – Flav's TV stardom in *Lyrics Of A Rap Revolutionary*. "The beautiful thing about what Public Enemy did for Flav is that it rescued him from his prior demons in the hood," he argued. "He became addicted to fame, and that's why I didn't have the problem with his TV series as cats thought I would. I just didn't want any malicious acts upon his family seen. I guess I can live with Flav addicted to fame as opposed to drugs anyday."

In some ways, it seems that Chuck has taken the same approach with Flavor as he did with Griff in the late eighties, insisting that his hype man speaks for himself, not the band. Thankfully for Chuck, Flav's antics never reached the level of controversy that Griff's did, which nearly sank Public Enemy. Instead, Flav's have been a nagging, ultimately harmless nuisance, slowly chipping away at PE's standing without ever seriously jeopardising it.

If Paris' thoughts on the matter weren't clear enough on 'Coinsequences', he removes any ambiguity when questioned point-blank about Flavor. "His situation is tragic to me, if only because he comes from Public Enemy and he should know better," Paris writes in an email interview. "Is his bullshit a reflection on the group as a whole? Sadly, yes – he has tainted their legacy somewhat. While it's true that they've been inducted into the Rock and Roll Hall of Fame, it doesn't change the fact that he is a coon. Shit is what it is, I'm not gonna sugar-coat it. He's shameful and continues to get a pass, but he's coonin', straight up."

Even *Rebirth Of A Nation*'s 'They Call Me Flavor', an entertaining variation on the typical Flavor Flav track, underlined the rapper's lack of focus on his musical career. "I had no interaction with Flav throughout the entire process," Paris says. "I pieced that song together, line-by-line, from a tape of his ramblings." Later, Paris notes, "I don't think Flav likes me at all based on shit that he's said that's gotten back to me. Doesn't really matter though, 'cause it's all fake hugs and smiles when he sees me."

On one hand, it's hard to be too critical of Flavor Flav. His segue to TV star was inspired by a move to the West Coast in which he was determined to kick his drug habit and escape some of the temptations of his New York hometown. In 2011, Flav told *The Daily Beast*'s Marlow Stern, "All I had was $142 and a cellphone and this was like the middle of 2003 when I left New York and went to LA to pursue a television and movie career." In another interview from that time, with *PopEater*, the hype man claimed, "I was spending $2,600 a day, for six years, every single day [because of my drug habit]. I don't know how much that is but if you did the math, wow, I went through a lot of money."

Reality television undoubtedly tarnished his image, but it padded his bank account and, according to Flav, helped save his life. Still, it drew barbs from other African-American entertainers, most notably comedian Chris Rock who did a joke about Flavor's minstrel routine in his 2008 stand-up special *Kill The Messenger*. Talking about the importance of voting for Barack Obama – not because he's black but because he's a worthy candidate for president – Rock said, "Hey, I love Flavor, loved him for 20 years. I love the *Flavor Of Love* show, I think it's quite entertaining. But Flavor Flav must be killed. In order for black people to truly reach the Promised Land, Flavor Flav has to be shot. These are important times! We got a black man running for president! We don't need a nigger runnin' around with a fuckin' clock around his neck and a Viking hat on his head! 'Not this year, Flav, put a suit on, nigga, put a suit on.'"

"When you make a joke that said, 'I would pay the legal fees for anyone who kills Flavor Flav,' if someone came to do that for real, what about my kids?" Flav said in response. "Now, they're out of a father. It's good to be a comedian, but you should only go so far with your jokes. You do have people out on the street who could try that for real. Do I hate Chris Rock? No. I'm just disappointed in the joke that he told about me. To this day, I would accept his apology, give him a hug, and congratulate him for still being so successful."

With Public Enemy, Flavor Flav harnessed his high-pitched whine as a weapon that irritated and provoked in equal measure. He was the vocal equivalent of the Bomb Squad's screeching, aggravating samples. His was never meant to be the voice of consciousness – that honour belonged to Chuck – but Flavor's ability to parlay his manic energy and goofy persona into a lucrative reality-show career threatened to drive a permanent wedge in the public's mind between his work with PE and this new, coarser persona. *The Surreal Life* and *Flavor Of Love* may have rescued Flav from a dark time, but risked reducing him to the has-been he feared becoming.

Not that Flavor Flav's counterpoint couldn't still provide sparks to a Public Enemy track. He's just as galvanic as Chuck D on 'Hard Rhymin'', a message of renewed purpose that disses "crap rap" and those blind to Bush's tyranny. On 'Rebirth Of A Nation', Flav's bratty patter is sprinkled throughout, a reliable vocal hook to offset Chuck and Griff's pit-bull strike. However, the fact that Flav gives a shout-out to Terminator X, even though he's not on the album, does suggest the heavily nostalgic quality to the proceedings. And on 'Rise', where Chuck bemoans "fake gangster quotes" and the commercialisation of materialistic rap music on MTV and BET, Flavor urges his frontman to greater heights. If you didn't know better, the push-pull of their voices felt like old times.

Still, Paris minimises Flavor's contribution to *Rebirth Of A Nation*. "Flav didn't have any impact on the project's creation," Paris states. "I flew out to Long Island and recorded Chuck and Griff in-studio for all of their contributions. . . . I had to piece all of Flav's vocals together from a tape of babbling bullshit that Johnny Juice gave me, though. He wasn't available because of his reality show shenanigans."

David Snyder, who's known Flavor Flav for about a decade now, praises his generosity and love for family. Still, he admits, "Flavor, because he's so giving, he'll sometimes surround himself with people he probably shouldn't surround himself with. It's like, 'This guy's just a common opportunist' or 'This over here is just a bad situation, dude, stay away from this.'" Snyder mentions Flav's annoyance about the group assigning Griff to babysit him when PE were starting out. "He feels kinda disrespected sometimes," C-Doc says. "He's like, 'I don't need babysat.' But it's like, 'Yeah, Flav, you do – you can't always be left to your own devices.'"

Paris' desire to invigorate the Public Enemy brand on *Rebirth Of A*

Nation saw the rapper/producer reimagining recent PE efforts to winning effect. On *There's A Poison Goin On*, Chuck D's 'I' was a despondent view of an underprivileged black man walking through an urban metropolis beset with economic disparity and crime. On *Rebirth Of A Nation*, Paris revamped the track and renamed it 'Invisible Man'. "I simply made a new music bed that reflected the mode of that song within the context of the rest of the album," says Paris. In the process, he gave the track a post-apocalyptic vibe: the spare keyboards provide a ghost-town quality to 'Invisible Man', making the final act of violence all the more shocking.

Likewise, Chuck D originally wrote 'Hell No (We Ain't All Right)' over Labor Day Weekend of 2005, mere days after Hurricane Katrina devastated the New Orleans area. The track first appeared on *Beats And Places*, a 2005 collection of PE leftovers, and its immediacy and urgency reflected the artist's stunned anger in the wake of the Bush administration's clumsy, insufficient response to the unfolding tragedy. Viewing the disaster as another case of America's unfeeling attitude toward minorities and the poor, 'Hell No (We Ain't All Right)' bristled with barely contained outrage. When Paris remixed it for *Rebirth Of A Nation*, the anger was slightly subdued, creating room for a righteous indignation that felt broader and more mournful. The focus was still on New Orleans, but six months later the song felt more like a lingering scar than the original track's fresh wound. And Chuck D's peeved comment that "some of y'all voted for that cat" – meaning Bush – only accrued more force.

Even Paris got into the act of revisiting old material: the album closer was 'Field N*gga Boogie', which had originally appeared on *Sonic Jihad*. But one of Paris' strongest moments was a new effort, his solo tune 'Hannibal Lecture', where he imagines driving around New York contemplating the similarities between black America and Iraq: both are under the control of a powerful elite. As Paris has suggested, 'Hannibal Lecture' is a West Coast take on a prototypical Public Enemy track, and the density of thought in the lyrics is equal to Chuck D's multifaceted assault. Plus, Paris' penchant for guitars on tracks like 'Rebirth Of A Nation' mirrors Chuck's love for the rock'n'roll instrument. "What we do is not rock music," Paris once said, "but electric guitar bridges the gap and provides a sense of urgency that's sorely needed because most current popular music isn't particularly passionate or inspiring. I like music that's ultra-aggressive. I don't think hip-hop is even worth doing if it's not. So, electric guitar is a useful component in what I do."

Unfortunately, the album's fondness for hip-hop's supposed good old days extended to a slightly sexist attitude. The appearance of Sister Souljah and the Conscious Daughters, a female rap duo who were signed to Paris' Scarface Records, doesn't entirely mitigate the existence of 'Plastic Nation', a no doubt well-intentioned lament about plastic surgery's popularity that nonetheless paints women as shallow and self-absorbed. With echoes of *Nation Of Millions*' 'She Watch Channel Zero?!', 'Plastic Nation' is less an attack on media representations than it is a finger-wagging dismissal of women's complicated relationship with beauty. There's some sympathy as Chuck mouths Paris' words about men's need to help make women understand that they're perfect without cosmetic enhancements. But the repeated chorus of female voices complaining about their figure comes across as whiny, turning these fictionalised characters into objects of scorn.

Released in the spring of 2006, *Rebirth Of A Nation* is the last Public Enemy album, to date, to chart in the US, spending a solitary week on the *Billboard* 200, peaking at number 180. Reviews were polite but dismissive, reflecting the growing critical indifference towards Public Enemy. Outside of *The Village Voice*'s Robert Christgau, who declared it "PE's best album in nearly a decade", the notices were more aligned with *The Guardian*'s Hattie Collins, who observed that "Public Enemy's politically fuelled poetics feel depressingly outmoded. The ridiculous raps of Flavor Flav, better known nowadays for rambling appearances on reality TV shows, are no longer irreverent observations, merely ubiquitous non sequiturs. The siren-heavy sonics, meanwhile, sound stale compared with contemporary hip-hop beats. Granted Chuck D is still a convincing commentator, but his resolute rants that governments are corrupt and the police are racist are of little interest to the kids."

Paris put out *Rebirth Of A Nation* through his Guerrilla Funk label, which allowed for creative independence. Explaining Chuck D's interest in letting Guerrilla Funk handle the album's release, Paris says, "He knows me, knows my level of dedication to the music, and knows that Guerrilla

Funk is wholly black-owned and operated." Still, Guerrilla Funk lacked the budget that PE once enjoyed. That was no more apparent than with the so-so Photoshop job on the album cover, which is meant to depict Paris, Chuck and Flavor hanging out in front of the Capitol Building – and when you opened the CD, the back jacket photo showed the same image, but with the Capitol on fire. Still, Paris bought ads on television and in print for the album. "*Rebirth* is definitely a high-profile project," he said back in 2006. "If it doesn't fly – at least on par with the other stuff I have going on, given Public Enemy's name and recognition – Flav's bullshit is the only thing I can chalk it up to."

Looking back on the album now, Paris remains proud of what he created. And he's held onto fond memories of PE's principals – except for Flav, of course. "Chuck is cool, and is very much into his 'elder statesman' status in hip-hop – a pretty laid-back brother," Paris says. "Griff is my folks, though. That's my man. Hella cool, no issues, no drama, just a love for the music and for the causes we all represent and rap about."

And how does he feel about the band's subsequent recordings? "PE is mainly a touring group, and I think they make music to facilitate that aspect of their careers," Paris responds. "I'm much more concerned with the actual creation of albums, so I'm more critical than most because *nothing else matters* if the music isn't 100 percent. To me, it's not about the quantity of your catalogue, but the quality. I'd like to see fewer releases that are executed with more attention to detail. I am proud of them for their Rock and Roll Hall of Fame induction, though."

Rebirth Of A Nation was an album embedded in the misery of the Bush years, and 'Bush Killa' condemned the president's father. Does Paris have an opinion about which Bush turned out to be the worse Commander-in-Chief?

"All of them are terrible," Paris writes back, "including Obama, our war-criminal, one-percent Protector-in-Chief."

CHAPTER THIRTEEN

AT the movies, the third instalment in a trilogy tends not to be the strongest. Inspiration fades, cynicism sets in, the lure of an easy pay-cheque supersedes all else. Trilogies aren't as common in the music business, but for Public Enemy, the finale was the best. *How You Sell Soul To A Soulless People Who Sold Their Soul???* topped *Revolverlution* and *New Whirl Odor* but, more importantly, established that the band's finest moments weren't behind them. For more than a decade, PE had tried to celebrate their glorious past while simultaneously demonstrating their continued relevance. *How You Sell Soul* succeeded on both fronts, rocking hard and showing the sort of effortless range and depth that once were hallmarks of their records. Chuck had long understood that he couldn't recreate *Nation Of Millions* or *Fear Of A Black Planet* – partly because he didn't want to – but with *How You Sell Soul*, he concocted an album that could at least tussle with those masterpieces.

There had been PE releases in between the trilogy, of course. *Rebirth Of A Nation* was a fine one-off supervised by Paris. There was also *Beats And Places* (a collection of leftover tracks), *Bring That Beat Back* (a remix record), and *Power To The People And The Beats* (a greatest-hits disc). But the arrival of *How You Sell Soul* in the summer of 2007 – 20 years after *Yo! Bum Rush The Show* – was a watershed moment. For once, the hip-hop legends weren't just leaning on their legacy. They were building on it.

How You Sell Soul was overseen by Gary G-Wiz, who left *New Whirl Odor* to others so that he could focus on the follow-up. He's not solely responsible for the album's hardness, but it doesn't seem like an accident that *How You Sell Soul* is one of the band's most consistent recent works, securing Gary's lasting legacy in the band in the post-Bomb Squad era.

"Gary's a very humble dude," Johnny Juice says. "He says very little, he listens. He's basically Hank Shocklee without the attitude. But Gary does have skills – he's able to produce records and he's smart, too."

How You Sell Soul's sharpened assault was also partly a product of letting its songs coalesce. It's not just that this 19-track collection is strong pretty much top to bottom – it's that its themes and moods bounce off each other, informing and strengthening individual moments along the way.

Initially, Chuck had hoped that the trilogy would be released in close succession. "He's always loved the idea of being able to cut records and put them out when he wants," David Snyder says. "He hated the fact in the old days, when he was tied to Def Jam, that he couldn't do that. When we did *New Whirl Odor*, he was still tied to a traditional distribution system, and he was pissed because he wanted to put out *New Whirl Odor* and *How You Sell Soul* [back to back]."

Still, Chuck found a way to make the most out of a situation that annoyed him. "Songs on this record were marinated and stewed like Southern cuisine itself," he wrote in *How You Sell Soul*'s liner notes. "They were waited to be finished for this 20th year [anniversary] by the team of Gary G-Wiz and [Amani] K. Smith."

As with Smith's work on *Revolverlution*, *How You Sell Soul* was a combination of the songwriter-producer coming up with tracks that inspired Chuck or working from an idea by the frontman. "You're trying to make that aggressive shit," Smith explains. "[Chuck] is the only artist you could find in the history of rap music that has not changed his direction or focus. It's always been the same type of music, same focus – he's never chased a genre or trend or money. Any other artist, this would be a different conversation. But with him, everything is, in my mind, supposed to be like 'Rebel Without A Pause'. We're all trying to recreate that sound. Putting him on a boom-bap track just doesn't seem to make sense to me. A Pharrell Williams track, it just doesn't seem like that's what he's meant to be on – or that he wants to be on. With any other artist, I'd say, 'Hey, maybe you should get on a track that sounds like this and be a little more open-minded.' Busta Rhymes has been on all types of tracks – he's open-minded to get on an R&B track, or on a rock track, or on a boom-bap track – and that works for him. But Chuck, he's the only one I can say you just can't do that with."

Smith's comment perhaps doesn't give Chuck enough credit for the shift in styles between, say, *There's A Poison Goin On* and *Revolverlution*.

But it does highlight an odd, troublesome limitation of Public Enemy: their refusal to follow hip-hop trends cemented the group's specific sound, but it also risked trapping them in a dated aesthetic, especially after the end of the Bomb Squad's era of dense, intricate productions. Talk to producers who have worked with Public Enemy since the early nineties, and you notice they all mention a desire to recreate PE's past glories, which can sometimes make the band's newer material feel like imperfect knockoffs. But although *How You Sell Soul* didn't radically alter PE's sound, it found plenty of juice in a proudly old-school approach.

"The songs on the album are tinged with a point of view that answers the need for the recognition of the power of music itself, reaching the 'soul' of folks rather than just exhibiting a rehash of a sound reminiscent of a forlorn era," Chuck commented in the liner notes, adding, "I personally think the sound is as 'soulful' as it is abrasive."

The rapper expounded on that idea somewhat when he and Griff appeared on *Tavis Smiley* around the album's release. "If you don't know what soul is . . . then maybe you should be introduced to soul to recognise it," Chuck said about the title. "We give people the option: we say, you know, 'You could support us if you want. We're still gonna do our thing.'"

On *How You Sell Soul*, Public Enemy carried themselves like icons, complaining a little less than normal about the state of hip-hop and instead focusing on what made them such a vital force in the first place. There was anger, but for once there was also inspiration. But most importantly, there were plenty of good songs. And they came from all over – most memorably from a revitalised Flavor Flav.

By the release of *How You Sell Soul*, the first two seasons of *Flavor Of Love* had already aired, and Flavor Flav's Comedy Central roast was broadcast less than a week after *How You Sell Soul* hit record stores. Flavor had also finally released his solo album. *Flavor Flav*, also known as *Hollywood*, appeared on Halloween of 2006. "This is my first and only album ever because I want it to be a collector's item," he claimed in a *Billboard* interview. "I always wanted to do a solo album but coming up through the years there's been a lot of obstacles in my way that have stopped me from being able to do so."

Kerwin Young was one of the musicians who assisted on *Flavor Flav* and remembers the arduous process of it coming out. "Yeah, [it took] a lot of years," Young says, laughing. "It took maybe, I don't know, maybe 15 years? He started an album back before I knew him. At the time when he and I did record, it was 2002. He spent a whole lot of money, man – we did this work in 2002, and it wasn't released until, what, four years later? Flav just had a lot of stuff in the can. It's hard for him to get in the studio and work on something and finish it, he's not that type of guy. Working with him on that album, he came down to Atlanta and he would sleep [during the] day. We'd start recording, like around 9, 9:30 at night – or maybe later, maybe 12 or one in the morning. We'd go from one in the morning to, like, 6am." Without specifying what he means, Young says that Flav would take breaks during recording to "go get his supplies, which he need[ed] to keep him active".

With its mixture of R&B and hip-hop, *Flavor Flav* wasn't a commercial force, despite Flav's insistence that "[i]t has music for all ages, from 10 up 'til senior citizens". But three of its strongest tracks found their way onto *How You Sell Soul*. 'Flavor Man' was obnoxiously, insanely catchy, its repetitive "flavor, flavor, flavor man" chorus an earworm you couldn't extinguish. Meanwhile, 'Col-Leepin' reprised 'Cold Lampin With Flavor' with a beat that recalled Beastie Boys' 'Brass Monkey' (or, more accurately, Wild Sugar's 'Bring It Here', which Beastie Boys sampled). Less funny, more intense than the original, 'Col-Leepin' had a rawness and danger that had been missing in Flavor's later recordings – it was as if he temporarily forgot that he was supposed to be the band's court jester, tapping into the street-thug energy of his earliest PE cuts.

But *How You Sell Soul*'s highlight Flav moment was 'Bridge Of Pain', a mournful tune he dedicated to "all my brothers locked up in the penal systems all over the world". Inspired by his time on Rikers Island, the song offered a snapshot into the mindset of a felon, devoid of the gangster glamorisation heard from Flavor's younger peers. In a 2005 *Vibe* profile, Flav was interviewed wearing the boots he was given while serving his prison sentence. "I wear them to remind me how I felt when I got there and how I never want to go back," he said.

But despite the slow-motion pain of 'Bridge Of Pain', which acknowl-edged his fading fortunes – "My career down the drain / Can't make no moves" – Flav didn't completely turn his life around, continuing to have run-ins with the law. In October 2012, he was arrested on an assault charge, accused of attacking his fiancée, Elizabeth Trujillo, and threatening her teenage son with a knife. In April 2014, he reached a plea agreement to avoid prison time.

Flavor may have alienated some of his bandmates with his reality shenanigans: at a speaking engagement in Chicago in 2009, Griff told an audience, "You know Professor Griff don't approve of Flavor Flav picking electronic cotton," condemning Flav for furthering the "niggerisation of hip-hop". But on record, Flav discovered a newfound intensity, adding teeth to *How You Sell Soul*'s balanced assault.

As to the question of whether Griff and Flav get along now that Griff has rejoined Public Enemy, Snyder says, "Yeah, they do. At the heart of it, they love each other. Griff is interesting because – all these guys are chained by their public persona, you know? You don't get to see how hilarious Griff is – you don't get to see what a funny fucking guy he is, especially when he and Flav start snapping on each other. Oh god, it's hilarious, it's ridiculous. They're family and they're friends from way back, and even though Griff publicly will speak out against Flav and his buffoonery, at the heart of it they're old friends. They just deal with each other in measured doses on the road – it's kinda like, 'OK, cool, I've had enough of you.'"

But the album also found Chuck finally successfully integrating hard rock into Public Enemy's sound. Since 'She Watch Channel Zero?!' sampled Slayer, the frontman had embraced the idea that headbangers and hip-hop heads had more in common than they realised. But too often, the band's stabs at hard rock came off as forced. That wasn't the case with 'Black Is Back', an effective slab of thick riffs and choice scratching that owed a debt to Jay-Z's rap-rock '99 Problems' from his 2003 disc, *The Black Album*.

"Don't wear throwbacks / 'Cause I'm a throwback," Chuck bragged early on 'Black Is Back', which had a monstrous swagger largely missing from Public Enemy's 21st century records. It's such an immediate fist-pumping anthem that it's surprising that it was actually a last-minute addition when the band's original idea for the track was scrapped.

"'Black Is Back' almost got cut from the record," David Snyder recalls. Originally, the riff was based on AC/DC's colossal 'Back In Black' and, according to Chuck, the song featured a guest vocal from Run-D.M.C's Darryl McDaniels. "There were big plans for that record," Snyder says. "Khari Wynn, who was the guitarist for PE, replayed [the riff]. Gary had him replay it, and they did a really nice, faithful, rocking version of that record. They were talking about touring: AC/DC and Public Enemy. We were talking doing a video. There were big plans, and it was all set to go through. But at the last hour, the last minute, some lawyer got involved and nixed the whole thing."

When it seemed that the song wouldn't be able to be included on *How You Sell Soul*, Snyder made a suggestion. "I said, 'As a backup, why don't we do another version of it? Something that's more like "99 Problems" that Rick Rubin did? Cut up the guitar and stuff like that.' Gary goes, 'Yeah, I could do that.' So when the record didn't happen, we renamed it 'Black Is Back' and we used Gary's new version of it."

Much like *Apocalypse 91*'s 'How To Kill A Radio Consultant', 'Black Is Back' shamed media outlets such as BET, MTV and radio stations that didn't have the imagination to play someone like Public Enemy. Chuck and Flav weren't pissing and moaning but, rather, boasting and taunting, regaining some of their mojo. They kept it going on 'Frankenstar', a blistering, stomping track about the emptiness of fame. As Chuck described it, the song was "grit–ghetto metal still whacking away at the fact that much of today's shrunken record labels dog-train their artists into treating their fans like crap".

"That was definitely [Chuck]," Smith recalls of the song's origins. "That was something he had that we built around. We tried really hard to make that aggressive." When Chuck first flirted with fronting a rock band with the tepid Confrontation Camp, he sounded winded and uninspired. By comparison, a track like 'Frankenstar' was enraged but energised, the musicians laying waste to their lyrical targets.

But *How You Sell Soul* didn't just rattle your skull. One of its most radical tracks – one of PE's most radical ever – was 'Escapism', a down-right soulful groove that bordered on R&B. Utilising female singers in the background, a lovely saxophone line from Gene Barge and a slinky beat,

'Escapism' was Chuck's nod to the Commodores' 'Zoom', which the rapper referred to as a "getaway song" for its dreamy melody and summertime sultriness. On 'Escapism', Chuck and Flav preached self-knowledge, dissed the ongoing Iraq War and stuck up for dismissed, once-white-hot black artists like Prince and Michael Jackson: "What has Bob, Mick, Sir Paul done for you lately?" Rather than scolding, though, Public Enemy rode the beat with a slippery charm, the duo declaring in classic tag-team fashion, "Soul is back / So flip them hits back / Damn the fashion / I wanna know where's the passion." It's the closest they'd ever gotten to a slow jam, sacrificing none of their principles or message in the process.

"That was a track [Gary and I] already had made," says Smith, who co-produced 'Escapism'. "We sent it to Chuck just to have him look at a bunch of tracks, and that's one that he pulled out that he liked." For someone who talks about a desire to write aggressive music for Public Enemy, Smith admits that he didn't think Chuck would go for 'Escapism'. "Not at all," he says. "But we really liked that track. We thought, 'Oh, this has got a cool feel to it.' That wouldn't be something normally I would send. It's so gritty and grimy, but yet it's so soulful and laid-back."

The song's spiritual soulmate may well be 'Long And Whining Road', whose title is a play on the Beatles' 'The Long And Winding Road' but whose content riffs on Dylan titles. One of a few moments on *How You Sell Soul* where Chuck aligns Public Enemy with the giants of rock, 'Long And Whining Road' utilises a spare, bluesy lick to recap Chuck's personal history and the band's legacy, working in lyrical references to everything from *Nashville Skyline* to *The Basement Tapes* to 'It's Alright, Ma (I'm Only Bleeding)' to 'All Along The Watchtower'. With calm confidence, Chuck proudly makes the case for PE's longevity, tracing their explosion on the UK tour circuit in 1987 to the divisive reaction to *Muse Sick-N-Hour Mess Age*. More than anything, the un-whiny 'Long And Whining Road' sounded grizzled, a celebration of 20 years in a cruel business.

"When people talk about 20 years, it's a benchmark in rap music and hip-hop," Chuck acknowledged on *Tavis Smiley*. "But one thing we came along understanding is that we have to be musicologists. And being a musicologist comes out of the understanding that this comes out of records." DJs like Afrika Bambaataa, Chuck said, "not only understood the record but the musicians inside the records", and Public Enemy saw it as their mission to continue that tradition of honouring the musical past. In the band's early years, that meant a direct sampling of idols like James Brown within the tracks, but on something like 'Long And Whining Road', they stood shoulder-to-shoulder beside a legend like Dylan. The simplicity of 'Long And Whining Road' lacked the brilliant rush of a *Nation Of Millions*, but that wasn't the point: this was music that felt timeless and eternal, carved in stone like the presidents on Mount Rushmore.

Chuck's focus was also on living up to the image of being a generational spokesman. On the slow-mo funk of 'Can You Hear Me Now', he rhymed, "At the age I am now / If I can't teach / I shouldn't even open my mouth / And begin to speak." And on *How You Sell Soul*, he also reached out to younger men in his community, advising them on 'See Something, Say Something' to avoid the so-called "stop snitching" ethos that had become popular in hip-hop.

As explained in the book *Snitching: Criminal Informants And The Erosion Of American Justice* by Alexandra Natapoff, the "stop snitching" movement was popularised by a Baltimore rapper, Skinny Suge, who "walked the streets of West Baltimore with a camera, talking to local residents". One of the topics his subjects discussed was "snitching", or giving information to the cops about their friends and neighbours. The people Skinny Suge interviewed "said that people 'in the game' shouldn't snitch in order to escape punishment", Natapoff wrote. "They made threatening statements, suggesting that snitches might 'get a hole in their head.' One man identified another person as a potential snitch: 'He's dead,' he rapped, 'because I don't believe he's from the 'hood'."

Boosted by the appearance of NBA star Carmelo Anthony in one of the interviews, the resulting movie Skinny Suge made in 2004, *Stop Snitching*, drew national attention. (It's important to note, however, that Anthony made no claims supporting the stop-snitching mindset.) Soon, hip-hop artists were adopting the catchphrase, including Lil Wayne, whose 'Snitch' appeared on 2004's *Tha Carter*, and Ice Cube, who included a track called 'Stop Snitchin'' on 2006's *Laugh Now, Cry Later*. And in the case of Busta Rhymes, the credo was used in real life: when his bodyguard Israel Ramirez was murdered in February 2006, the rapper refused to cooperate with the police, even though he had witnessed the crime.

"There's such animosity toward the police in some urban communities that even people who aren't afraid, and who hate crime, still feel cooperating is something good people don't do," David Kennedy, the director of the Center for Crime Prevention and Control at John Jay College of Criminal Justice in New York, explained to *USA Today*. "That's the Busta Rhymes story. He has nothing to fear. He just doesn't want to talk. His reputation would take a dive if he did."

Chuck D took umbrage, writing on the PE website, "The term 'snitch' was best applied to those that ratted revolutionaries like Huey P. Newton, Bobby Seale, Che Guevara. . . . Let's not let stupid cats use hip-hop to again twist this meaning for the sake of some 'innerganghood' violent drug thug crime dogs, who've sacrificed the black community's women and children."

The movement became so mainstream that it was covered on *60 Minutes* in 2007, with segment host Anderson Cooper explaining to America what "stop snitchin'" meant. He spoke to respected community leaders like Harlem educator and anti-violence advocate Geoffrey Canada, who had known Ramirez for years and condemned the stop-snitching philosophy. On *60 Minutes*, Canada told Cooper, "It's like we're saying to the criminals, 'You can have our community. Just have our community. Do anything you want, and we will either deal with it ourselves or we'll simply ignore it.'"

How You Sell Soul's 'See Something, Say Something' – a play on the New York Metropolitan Transportation Authority's public-safety campaign 'If You See Something, Say Something' – was Chuck's response to "stop snitching". Noting that it had been 10 years since Biggie and Tupac had been murdered, their killers still a mystery, Chuck rode a funky seventies groove to declare that "the whole town lose" when citizens don't assist bringing criminals to justice. "You see something / You better say something," he rapped, "'Cause saving something / Ain't worth sayin' nothing." In contrast to his hip-hop contemporaries, Chuck sounded rational, reasonable and mature, a man blessed with the proper perspective to see that the stop-snitching movement, although partly a response to police corruption, was ultimately shortsighted and self-destructive.

Even Public Enemy's old beef with gangster rap found fresh voice on *How You Sell Soul*. On 'Sex, Drugs & Violence', the band repositioned their argument to zoom in on the genre's corrosive effect on communities, especially the young and impressionable. Opening with a children's choir imploring rappers, "don't corrupt our minds", Chuck examined how the titular topics sell, no matter the medium.

"'Sex, Drugs & Violence', that was a concept of Chuck's from the beginning," Smith recalls. "Gary and I collaborated on the idea, and we thought, 'Well, if it's gonna be 'Sex, Drugs & Violence', let's get KRS on the track'" as an homage to Boogie Down Productions' 1992 album *Sex And Violence*. Smith and Gary decided to make the track a posse song, inviting both KRS-One and Flavor Flav to contribute verses. "The title was already there," Smith says, "but the concept was from Gary and myself: 'We should talk about the killings going on, these rappers coming up and [ending up] dead.'"

KRS-One had previously appeared on *He Got Game*'s 'Unstoppable', and he and Chuck were close. The rapper, born Lawrence Krisna Parker, had written the introduction to Chuck's book *Lyrics Of A Rap Revolutionary*, comparing the PE leader's lyrics to Psalms and the writings of Martin Luther King, Jr. But Smith had worked with an engineer, Bob Tucker, on the Temptations' 2000 album *Ear-Resistible*, and Tucker was friendly with KRS-One. "I would go over to [Tucker's] house and KRS would be over there," remembers Smith. "So, I was like, 'Shit, man, maybe we can get KRS. Let me call up Bob and see what's up.'" KRS-One immediately said yes. "When KRS came down to the studio, we told him what the concept was, and I started telling him stories of, like, the Indians having their land taken," Smith says. "He started writing his lyrics – he's quick, he's incredible. He came in and he knocked it out."

Inspired by Smith's talk of the Native American hardships, KRS-One threw in a reference to two famous Native American warriors: "We be hurtin' the least / We be workin', no seats / Bringing it to America like Geronimo and Cochise." It was a deft merging of the African-American and Native American struggle. KRS-One also cited Jam Master Jay's 2002 murder in a New York recording studio – "Once upon a time in Jamaica, Queens / An icon gets shot and no one knew what it means / It was just another murder scene" – that was a callback to Chuck's first verse on 'Sex, Drugs & Violence', which lamented that after the memorial parade for a slain rapper, people move on with their lives and forget the brutality of violent crime. 'Sex, Drugs & Violence' wasn't just a somber reflection on gun violence: Gary and Smith worked in a clever sample of Boogie Down Productions' 'The Bridge Is Over' at the moment that KRS-One boasts about his and Chuck's "old sound". This was an intelligent, thematically hefty song that also found room to salute these veterans' roots.

But, in a subtle way, the song also tipped its hat to the future: Gary recruited his young son to sing the children's chorus. "He was eight or nine or 10," Smith says of the boy. "Never sang before. He nailed it: first take, second take, third take, doubles, background vocals. Completely nailed it."

Public Enemy's heyday is rightly celebrated for its layered productions, but in the process we overlook the scope of a *Fear Of A Black Planet*, how song-to-song it ebbs and flows, creating an emotional and sonic journey that was thoughtfully planned out. Beyond having great individual songs, *How You Sell Soul* was the first PE album since perhaps *Muse Sick* that felt structured like a complete experience.

In a 2014 interview with *Billboard*, Chuck recalled, "When we first got into [the music business], hip-hop was still a singles marketplace with 12-inch records, cassette albums and maybe vinyl." The innovation of *Nation Of Millions* helped elevate rap music to an art form that treated the album as a creative expression akin to what rock acts like the Beatles and Dylan had begun pioneering in rock'n'roll in the mid-sixties. Ironically, the rise of the internet, which Chuck had embraced for its democratisation of music, also nullified the album-as-artistic-unit ethos. Granted, the CD had begun this process – now the listener could skip around, ignoring the musician's sequencing – but the web accelerated the focus on individual tracks as consumers just grabbed the songs they wanted. Public Enemy's post-*He Got Game* releases suffered a bit as a result – and remember that Chuck had purposely intended *Revolverlution* to be a reflection of the web's chaotic freedom – but *How You Sell Soul* had a coherence that the band's recent albums lacked.

David Snyder had been critical of *Revolverlution*'s sequencing, feeling it had left the album sounding haphazard. Soon after, Chuck handed over the responsibility to him, letting C-Doc sequence *New Whirl Odor* and *Beats And Places*. According to Snyder, Chuck had gotten burned out on sequencing after *Fear Of A Black Planet*. The rapper had told Snyder, "That used to be my job. In the Bomb Squad, that's what I did, but I don't really do that any more. I don't know *Fear Of A Black Planet* as songs: I know it as seconds. I had a notebook thick with sample notes and snippets and all this shit, so [*Fear*] is all, 'This happens at this second, and this happens at this second.' I know all the edits."

Since Gary had spearheaded *How You Sell Soul*, it was his job to sequence the album. But Chuck, happy with what C-Doc had done on *New Whirl Odor* and *Beats And Places*, instructed him to fly to LA to assist Gary on the new record. Recalls Snyder, "I said, 'Gary's not gonna do it himself?' Chuck's like, 'No, you go out there, you guys do it together.' That was the first time I got to actually sit down and work with Gary. It was great, 'cause Gary was a New York guy – you know, he did the *Apocalypse* record, did a lot of records back in the day. He produced one of my two favourite PE records, 'So Whatcha Gone Do Now?' I got to talk to him about that, pick his brain about that stuff. He'd tell me stories, all this crazy stuff about how they used to work and how they did the records, things like that. It was really informative – it was great, a lot of fun."

A super-fan now part of the group's inner circle, Snyder hit it off with Gary, who, he discovered, had strong opinions about how track lists should be put together. "Gary has a thing where he's like, 'Whatever the best record is, it's going first,'" C-Doc says. The only person who could veto that, naturally, was Chuck, who did just that on *How You Sell Soul*, wanting the horn-driven funk of the title track to kick off the record. From there, Gary and Snyder had to wait to see if 'Black Is Back' would end up making the album – if it did, it would be slotted second. After that was 'Harder Than You Think', a bruising number in which Flav repeats the spoken intro of 'Public Enemy No. 1', relating a story to Chuck about a conversation he had on his way to the studio. The symmetry of the two songs' openings was obvious: two decades later, Public Enemy were in the same position as when they started, having to prove the doubters wrong.

"'Black Is Back' has gotta go second – it's gotta be the buildup to

'Harder Than You Think'," says Snyder. "And once 'Harder Than You Think' hits, everything else is a moot point after that. It's so big, you know? Such a huge record. Gary has that kinda outlook on [albums]: All the great records go up front, put everything else to the back, it doesn't matter. It filters down from there."

That strategy might suggest that an album like *How You Sell Soul* is frontloaded, with all the duds near the end. But that's not the case: the album's back end contains some of *How You Sell Soul*'s finest moments, including the impressive segue between the stone-cold 'See Something, Say Something' into the legacy statement 'Long And Whining Road' into the melancholy 'Bridge Of Pain' into the stark cover of the sixties antiwar anthem 'Eve Of Destruction'. And throughout *How You Sell Soul*, interludes of about a minute each provide temporary breathers, sampling early PE songs but also harking back to golden-era intermission tracks like 'Final Count Of The Collision Between Us And The Damned', which helped give *Fear Of A Black Planet* its sense of dynamics and pacing.

Not that Snyder loves all the songs that ended up on *How You Sell Soul*. 'Amerikan Gangster', the album's other anti-gangster track, "is the only Public Enemy record that I outright hate. I don't like that record at all – I can't stand it," C-Doc laughs. "It sounds like it's a 50 Cent reject or something like that." He's not wrong: guest rapper E Dot Infinite wields a low growl that's a dupe of Fiddy's flow, and the track's attempt to channel the bullet-strewn bravado of hardcore gangster rap feels forced.

After PE wrapped production on the album, it was time to think about videos. This also became one of Snyder's specialities in the group. Despite dropping out of film school, he had maintained an interest in making films. In fact, during Snyder's early friendship with Chuck, he presented the rapper with a 16mm short he'd put together. "I gave it to Chuck and I said, 'I wanna direct a music video for you guys,'" C-Doc recalls. "He took the tape and he was like, 'OK, cool.' I think he still has the tape – I think I saw it last time I was up in New York at his place."

Snyder's chance came thanks to 'Superman's Black In The Building'. The song had been the centrepiece of *New Whirl Odor*, but it also elevated his stature within the group and their cadre of producers. "Johnny Juice, I earned his respect with that record," Snyder says. "You know, Juice and I were always cool, but I noticed Juice would talk to me in a different light after that record. Juice did two songs on that album – 'New Whirl Odor' and 'Preachin' To The Quiet' – and I thought both those tracks were great. But Juice himself said, 'No, man, nothing touches "Superman". That's the definitive track on that record.' That was huge for me."

"C-Doc is a cool dude," Juice says. "I love C-Doc – I think he's extremely valuable, 'cause he's a great video director, a decent producer and a great guy. He's real good at what he does."

When it came time to make a video for 'Superman', Snyder had established his directorial credentials by helming low-budget spots for the Impossebulls and Griff's metal band 7th Octave. As Snyder recalls, "Chuck said to me, 'Look, man, here's the deal: I'm gonna buy you a better camera, and you can do all the Slam Jamz videos and the new PE video. Is that cool?' I'm freaking inside. I'm thinking, 'All right, I got my shot.'"

The video for 'Superman's Black In The Building' was filmed at night and focused mostly on scenes of Chuck singing, random instances of crimes occurring, and inserts of a hooded crime fighter prowling the streets. It had an amateurish, school-project vibe, which even Snyder seems to acknowledge. "I watched it the other day, and it held up a little better than I remembered," he says. "[What] we were trying to do was [create] Black Superman, the rebel superhero that was gonna save the day where he could. It was supposed to be more comic book-y and more epic than it ended up being. The video didn't quite reach the aspirations that we wanted."

Nevertheless, Snyder quickly established a rapport with Chuck that made him the rapper's go-to director. "The whole reason Chuck hired me to do these in the first place was because he hates shooting music videos," Snyder says. "He'll say, 'For years, I'd be on set all day for two days for this three-minute video. It drives me nuts! You just gotta wait – it just wastes my time. But I love working with you, Doc, because you go out and we'll have a video shot in three hours.' So, yeah, I work quick, but I also like to get it right. Sometimes he can be like, 'All right, we got two hours, let's go do this.' I'm like, 'Ah, dude, you're killing me.' We can do it, but it's not gonna be quite what I want it to be. Sometimes, literally, we would just make them up on the spot – most of them were done guerrilla style. We'd have very thin permission to do stuff – just kind of 'go do it and grab it and get it done'."

Snyder laughs. "I think he loved that, too. I think he gets a kick out of it: 'Let's go shoot a video and try not to get arrested.'"

For *How You Sell Soul*'s videos, Snyder took different approaches depending on the song. For the epic rock sound of 'Black Is Back', he filmed Chuck up close with white-hot lights all around him, making him look like he was in the middle of a prizefight and a stadium show simultaneously. "It looks huge, but it was still guerrilla style," C-Doc says. Initially, Public Enemy didn't want to do a 'Black Is Back' video, but Snyder pushed them on it. He told Chuck, "I got this concept, which is Chuck in the room with the real harsh light." After filming, though, Snyder realised, "Just Chuck in the room by himself is not going to be enough." So he recruited friends and extras to be stand-ins for the rock band included in the final video, as well as a makeshift audience. Plus, he inserted footage from Public Enemy's recent show at Rock the Bells, which added to the sense of the band's brawling energy. "There were 40,000 people or whatever the hell it was there," C-Doc says, "and so it looks big. I think they actually were performing 'Shut 'Em Down,' which, tempo-wise, is close to 'Black Is Back'. In the video, they look like they're rock stars, and that was the idea."

For 'Harder Than You Think', though, the idea for the video came from Chuck. In the clip, Chuck and Flavor Flav are driving around in a U-Haul truck. "Chuck called me up and he goes, 'This is what we're gonna do: 20th anniversary. Since we sample "Public Enemy No. 1" in that record, we're gonna take it to when Flav actually said that to me and we were working that day.'" Hence, the 'Harder Than You Think' video recreates the two rappers' pre-PE existence. "My dad had the old U-Haul truck and we were hauling shit," Chuck told Snyder. "That's what the video's gonna be: we'll drive through Roosevelt, we'll drive through Hempstead, we'll drive through the area and shoot me and Flav in the truck like that day."

In *Fight The Power*, Chuck reminisced about the period before writing 'Public Enemy No. 1' when he and Flavor would make a little extra money delivering furniture for Chuck's dad's company. "One of us would drive, most of the time it would be me, because I wasn't going to sit in the passenger seat while that crazy motherfucker drove," Chuck wrote. It was during those drives that the two young men began developing their James Brown-Bobby Byrd rap routine. Specifically, Chuck's idea to have Flav talk at the top of 'Public Enemy No. 1' was born in that U-Haul truck.

Where 'Harder Than You Think' is proud and resilient, the video is nostalgic and downright charming, with Chuck and Flav goofing around, the frontman even pushing the jester in a shopping cart at a couple of points. Still, Snyder has his reservations about the clip. "I don't think the video's as big as it should've been," he says. "The song is so big, and I didn't think the video was big enough. But Chuck likes the video. It means a lot to him."

The song and the video clearly hold a special place in Chuck's heart. As he told PE biographer Russell Myrie, "['Harder Than You Think'] happened with divine intervention. G-Wiz had this track and I had this song and it was like 'boom boom boom' and it was one of those rare times when two takes was all it took." Drawing from the horns-and-guitar melody of Shirley Bassey's 1972 cut 'Jezahel', 'Harder Than You Think' salutes PE as the Rolling Stones of hip-hop, and the title (which never appears in the lyrics) has a barbed double meaning. Yes, Chuck and his crew rock harder than you think but, as Chuck told Tavis Smiley about the track, "To be progressive, proactive and positive, it's harder than you think. That don't mean that you don't do it."

Unfortunately, that doesn't mean that people want to listen. *How You Sell Soul* failed to crack the charts, unable to build off the scant commercial momentum *Rebirth Of A Nation* provided. The band's 20th anniversary didn't receive much press attention, either. If the group's name was in the press, it tended to be for extra-curricular activities. For instance, Flavor was out promoting his reality shows – and starring in his first sitcom, *Under One Roof*, which only lasted 13 episodes. Clearly, Flav was mostly famous because of his antics, not his acting ability. But then again, the man's finest role is probably Flavor Flav.

"Flav's always been a happy-go-lucky dude," says Juice, who's known him since *Yo! Bum Rush The Show*. "But [now] it's like he's doing a satire of himself. It's real weird, like he's playing himself." Snyder feels some-what similarly. "At the heart of it, Flav really loves his family and he loves people," C-Doc says. "But all that stuff gets overshadowed by the 'Flaaavor Flaaaav!' and 'Yeeeah, boyee!' and all that shit. I think he feels like he has to do it now – maybe not, that's probably just him. He likes to do that shit, 'cause he's so funny. But there's a lot more going on up there than people give him credit for."

As for Chuck, he seemed to settle into the role of a respected cultural figure who spoke out against social ills. He verbally attacked radio talk-show host Don Imus, who in April 2007 referred to African-American women on Rutgers' college basketball team as "nappy-headed hos". A few months later, Chuck offered (somewhat in jest) to become the new head of Def Jam after Jay-Z resigned as president. "After 10 years looking on the collapsing of the record industry, and upon hearing the news of Jay-Z stepping down from Def Jam, I would throw my name into the hat of somebody who understands how the hell [parent company] Universal should establish the name-brands they acquire with stockholders' money," he said at the time, later adding, "I'd show them how to make a profit, if they care. I will bring the noise. It will be interesting to hear the require-ments [for the job]." Nothing ever came of it, though, which wasn't sur-prising. It was probably just as well: after years of being the underdog, Chuck simply wouldn't look right as the boss.

★　★　★

In the spring of 2005, Chuck was giving an interview to writer and pro-fessor Hua Hsu for *Wondering Sound*. Hsu mentioned that he thought Public Enemy's recent albums had been "misunderstood". Chuck just laughed. "Well they're very misunderstood in this country," the rapper responded, "but then they're supposed to be because they're actually making a commentary on the climate. And so if you make a mockery of the climate and if you make a commentary about the climate, expect the climate not to understand, or to come crashing down on you."

Hsu asked him what he meant by "the climate". "The climate of how things are promoted on the television," Chuck said. "It's almost like the music is irrelevant . . . it's almost like the video is irrelevant. The climate

. . . is the conditions that allow you to look at the rap game and say what you gotta say about it. Either you gonna be with it, or you gonna be against it. I don't think it's healthy being against it. I can't go outside and scream at the rain. And I think that's what we do as PE – we don't rage against the climate, we rage against the machine. It's funny because I run into people all the time and they're like, 'Oh man, we need you, why don't you come out with something.'" Again, Chuck laughed. "But where are they gonna catch you? On MTV? On the radio? We have to be able to do what we did in the eighties: cling onto other areas."

Chuck was articulating a frustration shared by many long-time Public Enemy fans: the culture had moved on, unaware that the band had kept making music because the traditional outlets had shown little interest in promoting their recent work. (Though, to be fair, PE's drop in relevance was also due to putting out records that didn't capture the zeitgeist or demonstrate the brilliance of *Nation Of Millions*.) So it was interesting that the group's biggest commercial single of the new century didn't come from MTV or the radio – and that it happened five years after the song had been released.

Like the other singles from *How You Sell Soul*, 'Harder Than You Think' was a commercial stiff. But it found other ways to enter the culture. It was on the soundtrack for the 2009 video game *Skate 2* and provided the musical backing in ESPN's commercials for the 2012 Winter X Games. Then, in July of 2012, Britain's Channel 4 unveiled a 90-second spot entitled 'Meet The Superhumans'. The promo showed a group of athletes in wheelchairs or who were missing limbs as they prepared to compete on the basketball court, in the swimming pool, or on the track. Powered by 'Harder Than You Think', the images of defiant athletes were then intercut with stark, music-free shots of war zones and car accidents, suggesting the tragedies that had caused these competitors to become physically impaired. But then 'Harder Than You Think' would kick back in, showing the athletes in the present day as they determinedly train. The song, originally a statement of purpose from a veteran hip-hop group, suddenly became an anthem of resolve and defiance. "Forget everything you thought you knew about humans," a title card read near the end, "it's time to do battle."

Riveting and inspiring, the commercial was advertising the upcoming Paralympic Games in London, which would air on Channel 4 shortly after the Summer Olympics. The spot quickly became a viral sensation.

"We really didn't want to shoot around the particular physical attributes of these athletes and their disabilities," Tom Tagholm, the director of the commercial, told *Adweek* at the time. "We wanted to absolutely embrace all of that – their stance, the ways they've adapted to their sport, the ways that they use their bodies. It's very much 'Here we are!' y'know? There's no tiptoeing around anything."

With that in mind, the choice of 'Harder Than You Think' was a virtuoso touch. Even though the song has nothing to do with athletics, its rabble-rousing, populist tone perfectly matched the gritty spirit of the Games. And as the Paralympics drew closer – the Games kicked off August 29 – the song became a hit, eventually reaching number four on the UK charts. No Public Enemy song had ever peaked higher in the UK, and their last minor hit there was 1999's 'Do You Wanna Go Our Way???' Twenty-five years after invading London on tour, the band had returned with a leftfield smash, scoring their 10th Top 40 hit on the UK charts. (In the US, Public Enemy have had precisely one, 'Give It Up'.)

"The song has been a part of our show for the past five years," Chuck told *Crack* that year. "When it was chosen to be part of the Olympics, that took it into the stratosphere. Its strength was the YouTube video, which made it a theme song for these incredible athletes."

Dan Brooke, Director of Marketing and Communications for Channel 4, says that the producers tried many other songs over the footage until they turned their attention to the Public Enemy track. "I must say, we all just looked at it [with 'Harder Than You Think'] and everyone said, 'Yeah, that's the one,'" he recalls. "It was amazing because the song's got an attitude, and it's got a little bit of aggression about it. It's got a bit of a 'fuck you' quality to it, which a lot of these athletes have. A lot of them have been through some quite hard shit in their lives, and they want everybody to understand that, as athletes, they're right up there with Olympians."

The surprise renaissance of 'Harder Than You Think' in the UK didn't translate to chart success in Public Enemy's home country, but Chuck was philosophical about the track's late-blooming success. "It was a noble cause," he told *God Is In The TV* about the use of the song in the ad. "There was an explosion with that song – people were like, 'Wow, this song,' but you know, it's the same song we had five years ago. So it doesn't show that Public Enemy is back, or anything like that – the music supervisor made that possible just like Spike Lee did with 'Fight The Power' in 1989. So we appreciate it and we're very thankful for the uses of our songs because we don't get radio and all these other things." He added, "It's really funny because when we came out with the album *How You Sell Soul To A Soulless People Who Sold Their Soul???* it was the lead single and radio stations didn't even wink at it once. But when Public Enemy performed it, it became one of our best 'performing' records so we always kept it in our set."

"I think they were really kind of charmed by the success of it all," Brooke says. Asked to explain how 'Harder Than You Think' became such a huge radio hit in the UK, Brooke offers that its success was linked to the local embrace of the Paralympians' underdog attitude. "As a nation, we're quite progressive," he says. "We're quite liberal in our attitudes to people of different, diverse backgrounds, and I think people could see the strong and defiant messages that the advert was sending out about people with disability. I think people were sitting at home going, 'Yeah! Why should disabled people be any weaker or any different? They're just as good as anybody else.' You could hear that energy coming out of living rooms all over Britain. For a lot of people, ['Harder Than You Think'] is not necessarily the music that they would listen to, but it matched the message so unbelievably well on an emotional level. I mean, when we all heard it [with the ad] for the first time, we're like, 'OK, we're done, that's it. It can't be anything else. They're made for each other.'"

In interviews, Chuck will often talk about being the champion for the little guy. With 'Harder Than You Think', it took five years, but eventually everyone was singing along with him.

"That was great, man," Snyder says of the belated success of 'Harder Than You Think'. "It was kinda like, 'Oh cool, the world is finally catching up to what we knew all along. You guys are just slow.' But, you know, we'll take that."

What was even stranger about PE's increased profile was that, by the time of 'Harder Than You Think''s chart breakthrough, the band was out promoting *How You Sell Soul*'s follow-up. Actually, *follow-ups*. Chuck had initially conceived *Revolverlution*, *New Whirl Odor* and *How You Sell Soul* as a trilogy. For his next trick, he'd give us a double album that wasn't exactly a double album.

CHAPTER FOURTEEN

IN the early fall of 2012, Chuck D pondered a topic that seems to be constantly on his mind: Public Enemy's staying power. He was speaking with *Rolling Stone*'s Greg Prato, who, like a lot of music journalists, was writing a story about the band's surprise hit with 'Harder Than You Think' in the UK.

"If they played 'Harder Than You Think' on urban radio two times a day, three times a day, it would probably do the same thing here," Chuck noted. "And the thing about the UK, they blasted it through television. So that shows the power of being able to have opportunity on major media – even more so than the strength of the song."

Chuck went on: "The song was basically saying we're the Rolling Stones of the rap game," he explained, reciting a popular saw of his. Later, he added, "25 years' longevity for a rap group is uncanny, unprecedented, and you can make the statement that *Rolling Stone* and all these magazines don't speak enough about the longevity of black groups – especially a black rap group like Public Enemy, who has 84 tours in 83 countries under its belt. The song speaks to that. The song was basically celebrating the 20 years of Public Enemy in 2007, and now it just seems to be a better fit – 25 years, our silver anniversary."

The albums Public Enemy put out in 2012 even more explicitly hammered home the value of the group's longevity. Two of the group's strongest of the new century, *Most Of My Heroes Still Don't Appear On No Stamp* and *The Evil Empire Of Everything* were, to repeat a phrase Chuck used in several interviews promoting their release, "fraternal twins – not identical, but they talk to each other". Arriving a few months apart, the two records were awash in current events: the 2008 election of America's first black president, Barack Obama; the 2012 shooting of an unarmed African-American teen, Trayvon Martin; and the wave of Occupy protests in 2011 and 2012 that sought to bring attention to economic inequality. But they also had their eye on history.

"I don't remember talking about it at the time – I know we talked about it afterwards," David Snyder says. "It was like, 'This is gonna be the first new PE record in five years. It's the 25th anniversary of the group. It's gonna be the bid for the Rock and Roll Hall of Fame coming up the next year.' That was very much on Chuck's mind."

Most people who follow rock and pop know the Rock and Roll Hall of Fame's primary stipulations for an act's worthiness for inclusion: "Artists become eligible for induction 25 years after the release of their first record. Criteria include the influence and significance of the artists' contributions to the development and perpetuation of rock'n'roll." Public Enemy had satisfied both sentences, but Chuck wanted to clinch their chances with their next record.

However, he didn't want PE in the Hall of Fame just for himself and his bandmates – he saw their possible induction as a triumph for the art form as a whole. That had already been demonstrated by Chuck's happiness at inducting Beastie Boys in 2012. "It came about because they requested," Chuck told *Rolling Stone* in a separate interview, "and definitely it's an honour to do so. The third hip-hop group to be inducted into the Rock and Roll Hall of Fame," after Grandmaster Flash and the Furious Five and Run-D.M.C. "It's a very important juncture of rap and hip-hop."

"Chuck always sees [the Hall of Fame] for the bigger picture," says Snyder. "Chuck is, first and foremost, a big guy about preservation and legacy – not just Public Enemy but hip-hop. Any time he can get respect shown towards hip-hop in any kind of fashion, he's gonna do it. He's done a lot of stuff with the Rock and Roll Hall of Fame. They did that big Rolling Stones exhibit and he went – they asked him to be there, so Chuck went."

At the Beastie Boys' induction ceremony in Cleveland on April 14, 2012, Chuck D took to the podium to pay tribute to the Brooklyn trio. In his remarks, he said, "One of the most admirable qualities about the Beastie Boys is that they stayed so true to the game over the years. . . . They remind us that this is a craft . . . this is not a hustle. . . . They represent the best of the hip-hop/rap music idiom . . . especially before people took us seriously as artists." He was talking about the Beastie Boys, but he could just have easily been expressing the mission of Public Enemy and many of the hip-hop groups of the eighties who encountered derision and suspicion from the mainstream.

In January of that year, *Billboard*'s Patrick Flanary mentioned to Chuck that his band was getting close to their 25-year qualifying status. "We gotta work to get there," Chuck said in response.

But before Chuck could worry about the Hall of Fame, he had to figure out how to finance his latest album.

In October 2009, Public Enemy had announced that they would team up with SellaBand, a Dutch website that facilitated crowdfunding, a relatively new phenomenon in which filmmakers and musicians turned to fans for donations, in turn offering special incentives to those who contributed. For Chuck, a long-time proponent of alternative distribution and business models, SellaBand seemed a good fit. Planning a 2010 release for the untitled album, which hadn't even been recorded at that point, Chuck said, "SellaBand's financial engine model goes about restructuring the music business in reverse. It starts with fans first, then the artists create from there. The music business is built on searching for fans and this is a brand new way for acts to create a new album with fans already on board."

Chuck's plan was to sell fans "shares" of the record, hoping to raise $250,000 in the process. Contributors could donate at different levels: the "Believer" level, for instance, was $25 and netted the fan an "exclusive, numbered CD". At the other end of the scale, if you wanted to fork out more than $10,000, you received, among other things, an executive producer credit and an opportunity to visit PE in the studio while they were making the album.

It wasn't a success. By mid-December, the group had raised less than $72,000. In February 2010, the amount actually dropped down to around $67,000. Meanwhile, the group received criticism from some in the media, who accused them of being unrealistic with their funding goals. Flav's high profile didn't help: as *Billboard*'s Glenn Peoples put it, some fans may have been unsympathetic to PE's request for a handout. "Public Enemy's Flavor Flav is now well known for a VH1 reality series," Peoples wrote. "Clips from the show are front and centre at the group's website. Does this look like a group that needs fans' money to further its career?"

So, Public Enemy made some changes. By the spring of 2010, the band had decided to reduce their goal to $75,000. "Even through much uncertainty, the commitment and allegiance of our fans has been inspiring," PE said in a statement. "Fundamentally, true Public Enemy fans always know, respect and understand that it is our true nature to go where the path is least defined and where the risk averse will never tread. . . . [But] [w]e now firmly believe that it is time to rethink and restructure our fundraising efforts here, as well as our goals and pursuits. We have learned that the fan funding model is still not fully developed and, as a result, a $250,000 fundraising effort, while possible, will take too long to accomplish."

The SellaBand difficulties in some ways mirrored the obstacles Public Enemy had faced when they had rushed into an online-only distribution model for *There's A Poison Goin On*, their enthusiasm getting ahead of reality. But in November, they announced that they had reached their new fundraising target. "It has been a long and winding road," the group said in a statement. "We've had explosive starts, media attention, corporate troubles, media criticism, recalculations and finally resurgence. When [it's] all said and done, the bottom line is that we never lost faith in ourselves, our fans and the future of fan funding as a model."

Instead of one album, the group hatched two. "I can't remember if we were consciously aware of it at the time," says Snyder, "but I think it was partially the best-foot-forward kind of thing. *Stamp* was coming out first, and so it tended to be the more accessible record. *Evil Empire* is, you know, the redheaded, bastard stepchild, or the ugly little brother – it's the more challenging record."

Chuck told *The Nervous Breakdown*, "They sound similar – *Evil Empire* is a little more eclectic than *Most Of My Heroes Still Don't Appear On No Stamp* – pretty much very aggressively straightforward." Talking to *Rolling Stone*, he added, "They're totally separate albums, but 25 years ago, it probably would have been called a double album. And maybe 25 years ago, it would have been called an extended A-side or extended B-side. But now, in today's digital space, we thought it's very important to be able to slow the listener down. The fact that you work on something, and a reviewer or a listener listens to it on their iPod or their file in about 15 or 20 seconds, it's like, 'Wait a minute. *Slow down.*'"

It's easy to be cynical about Chuck's comments: it was he who had been passionately devoted to the digital takeover, which helped create the sped-up, easily distracted modern-day music consumer. Still, the inherent contradictions in Chuck's world view didn't keep him from delivering extraordinary music about it. In *Stamp*'s 'I Shall Not Be Moved', he declares, "What good is learnin' from some record / When y'all only listen to 15 seconds?" As a remedy, Public Enemy produced two albums where you wanted to listen beyond 15 seconds – track after track grabbed the ear, got your feet moving, made you hum along.

Chuck was particularly proud of 'I Shall Not Be Moved'. "[The title] is a slogan from the civil rights days and it's a strong-ass rap song that really doesn't care what people think about it," he said with a laugh. "There's no measurement for it. There's no expectations of it. It is what it is. It's a creature that came out of me. It's its own living self and it doesn't care what anybody thinks about it. So even when people say, 'Oh my God, what the fuck is this?' it's still its own animal, which is the way it should be. So 'I Shall Not Be Moved' measures up as a song that I've done only a few times in my career. 'Rebel Without A Pause' is one, 'Welcome To The Terrordome' is another, and maybe 'No', from my solo project, *Autobiography Of Mistachuck*, in 1996, 'Harder Than You Think' and this song. So for the fifth time I'm a part of something that I think is really crazy. And you don't plan it. It has to just happen. I totally got lucky. Look, you can have the right beat and go into the right performance, but sometimes you come up with something that came from some fucking place else itself."

Chuck laughed again. "I can't explain it all the way."

'I Shall Not Be Moved', which was written by Chuck and Gary G-Wiz, doesn't have the jackhammer propulsion of 'Rebel Without A Pause' or 'Welcome To The Terrordome'. But it's a marvel of old-school funk, utilising keyboards, hard beats, juke-joint guitars and buzzy distortion to reimagine Public Enemy as the sort of band that could have backed up James Brown. If all that wasn't enough, after a long drum outro Chuck then starts vamping over a stirring coda that's a mixture of keyboards and Flavor Flav's repeated "Yeah"s. 'I Shall Not Be Moved' didn't sound like *Nation Of Millions* – it sounded like the extraordinary records Chuck and Hank would have sampled for *Nation Of Millions*.

But even then, Snyder and G-Wiz knew that 'I Shall Not Be Moved' wouldn't lead *Stamp*. The two were once again in charge of sequencing both *Stamp* and *Evil Empire*, and Chuck had made it clear what would be the opening track of *Stamp*. As Snyder recalls, "The only stipulation Chuck had was, 'I think 'Run Till It's Dark' is probably first. That's just kinda what it feels like – I don't know where else to put it.'" Snyder agreed: "Obviously, 'Run Till It's Dark' is the jump-off. That just throws you into it headfirst."

Opening with a snippet from the 1987 Arnold Schwarzenegger sci-fi film *The Running Man* – "It's time to start . . . running!" – 'Run Till It's Dark' is an uptempo track that kicks off with Chuck quoting a statistic that 88 percent of Americans who live in cities are black, while 95 percent of Americans living in suburbs are white. "Forty-or-so-million blacks in America," he intones, before asking white listeners, "How can 13.5 percent of the population be scaring ya?" As the first track off the first album from Public Enemy since the election of a black president, 'Run Till It's Dark' sneers at the notion that the country had now entered a glorious period of post-racial harmony.

"America is still black and white," the rapper told *The Philadelphia Inquirer*'s Brian G. Howard shortly after Obama won a second term in November 2012. "President Obama won the election, [but the country] harkens back to a Civil War/North and South attitude. Thankfully, young people continue to knock down the barriers."

Boosted by Khari Wynn's slashing guitars, a conglomeration of several different solos stitched together into one seamless whole, and DJ Lord's squeaky scratches, 'Run Till It's Dark' felt like a jailbreak or a foot chase, sounding the warning for an America still in crisis. Snyder, who master-minded the track, says, "I was just kinda thinking, 'It's gotta be some really epic, classic, noisy-crazy-chaotic PE kind of shit.'" On top of that chaos, Chuck sounded off on, among other things, the Tea Party, a conservative grassroots movement advocating smaller government that blossomed soon after Obama's first presidential election. Because of the Tea Party's predominantly older, white constituents, the movement was widely accused of being racist and behind the times, refusing to accept an America in which racial demographics were rapidly changing.

Stamp can be seen as a response to the Tea Party, but it's also critical of a country's growing indifference towards its lower classes, no matter of race. In the summer of 2008, the world experienced the most severe financial meltdown since the Great Depression, culminating in the implosion of Lehman Brothers, one of the planet's largest banks, that September. The fault for the crisis was laid at the feet of Wall Street and banking executives who had gotten rich off subprime mortgages: risky home-ownership loans to individuals who couldn't possibly afford them. The popular assumption was that those who had knowingly created an economic environment where such a global disaster could occur would be punished. But that assumption was false: rather than seeing nightly news images of high-powered bosses going to prison for their actions, Americans watched the financial industry move on as if nothing had happened. In response, the Occupy movement sprang up, protesting not just Wall Street but the larger Wall Street mentality, which allowed a disproportionately small amount of individuals to hold a large percentage of the world's wealth. In the Occupy movement, this group was known derisively as "the one percent".

It's not a shock that Chuck aligned himself with Occupy, whose members gathered and often camped in public places like Wall Street. Although the protestors drew from the example of the recent Arab Spring peace movement in the Middle East, Occupy also had roots in events like the Million Man March. For Chuck, Occupy was another example of ordinary citizens standing in unity against their oppressors. "Many people thought the economy of the US would be on top for ever and continue to do extremely well," he told *Business Insider*'s Lauren DeLisa Coleman in 2011. "But when one thing does well, there is a tendency for other things not to do well. . . . Once you have people start to catch up on technology and education, they begin to start rejecting being exploited."

Occupy's spirit pervades both albums, but it's expressed most clearly on *Stamp*'s 'Get Up Stand Up', a horn-powered protest tune where Chuck declares, "Occupy if you denied / Protest songs 'cause I see wrong," later adding, "Got so much to shout about / What the one-percent is gettin' out / Recession, depression, desperation due / Never have so many been screwed by so few." But in a moment of remarkable clarity, he throws this in between those two verses: "Hope I don't end up being the same thing I'm fighting against."

With Occupy and the Tea Party in the news, a new era of grassroots protest bloomed in America, which helped make Public Enemy's spirit of revolution relevant again. As its title suggested, though, *Most Of My Heroes Still Don't Appear On No Stamp* was also about staring hard at the state of the African-American community. As with Public Enemy's best early work, *Stamp* was critical of both those inside that community and those on the outside.

The album title was inspired by Chuck's line in 'Fight The Power' about Elvis Presley. For years after, Chuck would have to explain that he didn't really think Presley was racist. "As a musicologist – and I consider myself one – there was always a great deal of respect for Elvis, especially during his Sun sessions," the rapper said in 2002. "As a black people, we all knew that. My whole thing was the one-sidedness – like, Elvis' icon status in America made it like nobody else counted. . . . My heroes came before him. My heroes were probably his heroes. As far as Elvis being 'The King', I couldn't buy that."

Stamp pays tribute to those heroes who still don't get their own stamp, with several of the album's tracks ending with spoken-word interludes that list worthy candidates, everyone from actor-activist Danny Glover to Emiliano Zapata, a leader of the Mexican Revolution of the early 20th century. The band also took a moment to pay homage to two deceased hip-hop luminaries who came up at the same time as PE: Jam Master Jay and the Beastie Boys' Adam Yauch, who died less than a month after his band's Hall of Fame induction. Public Enemy were demonstrating that the world's forgotten or underappreciated icons weren't just African-Americans, a broadening of the pro-black posture of the group's first records.

But Public Enemy's two albums didn't just focus on the underprivileged. It had been customary for PE to slam gangster rap and the materialism of mainstream hip-hop, but Chuck sharpened his attack by zeroing in on one record in particular. In August 2011, Kanye West and Jay-Z, two of rap's biggest superstars, joined forces to release *Watch The Throne*, a platinum-selling collection that often celebrated the duo's lavish lifestyles.

On one of the album's singles, 'Otis', Kanye articulated this new genre: "luxury rap".

At a time when many listeners were still suffering from the effects of the 2008 financial crisis, which had been dubbed the Great Recession, there was perhaps something perverse about listening to two rappers brag about their wealth and power. But there was also a political element to *Watch The Throne*, as two black men who came from modest means exulted in the fact that they had overcome racism and poverty to become icons. Also, Kanye and Jay-Z were aware that their millions didn't protect them from racism – or blind them from the crime and hardships around them, which was illustrated by 'Murder To Excellence', a sombre tune about the plight of African-Americans killed in gun violence, often by other blacks.

This political argument wasn't very compelling to Chuck. "I like them as rappers," he once said. "I respect their rap game but I don't respect the *game*. . . . I don't hate the player; I hate the fuck out of the game." Asked to clarify, he responded, "It's not the industry, it's the *game* – the drug game, the hustle game. I hate the fuck out of that, and I'm allowed to, you know? Jay-Z and Kanye have the right to rap about what they're rapping about. I'm not telling them to stop, but I *hate* – all caps – *hate* the game. Drug game, hustle game, street corner game . . . hate it. I'm man enough to say it."

In a conference in Barcelona in 2008, Chuck was asked if there's anything wrong with "aspirational motivations" in hip-hop. "There's nothing wrong with aspirational motivation as long as you have reality glued into it and as long as you can spread it," he responded. "If you spread the fantasy without answers for the reality, then you're bound to have side effects. . . . [T]here's a growing prison-industrial system which houses more people than any other country on the planet. They don't brag about that."

In response to his dim view of *Watch The Throne*'s fantasy world, Chuck made 'Catch The Thrown', one of his rare clever puns after coming up with clunkers like *New Whirl Odor* and *Muse Sick-N-Hour Mess Age*. Though 'Catch The Thrown' doesn't directly address Kanye and Jay's so-called luxury rap, it does vent at the rich in their mansions ignoring the suffering of their fellow citizens. "Feed the people / Fight the power / Fix the poor," Chuck sings, "but that one-percent done shut the door."

Rather than criticising the *Watch The Throne* mindset directly, Chuck targets the callousness that had crept into America's desire for more and more. "Who's gonna catch the thrown?" he asks, a plea to help those less fortunate.

But Chuck wasn't done there. On *Evil Empire*, he included a track called 'Notice (Know This)'. It, again, is a pun, on *Watch The Throne*'s 'Otis', which sampled Otis Redding's rendition of 'Try A Little Tenderness'.

"Chuck was really pissed about that Jay-Z and Kanye 'Otis' record," Snyder says. "He felt like they had an opportunity to do a tribute, and they didn't: they just called it 'Otis' and said 'featuring Otis Redding', even though they just sampled him. That really rubbed him the wrong way."

An early, shorter version of 'Notice (Know This)' was posted on YouTube shortly after 'Otis' was released as a single. Sampling Redding's take on Sam Cooke's 'Chain Gang', this embryonic 'Notice' is probably the closest thing Chuck has come to a diss track. And even then, it's not that close: "Respect to you two heroes," he sings, "but trickle-down got us less than zero." His song's depiction of a country filled with minority groups decimated by poverty and incarceration was deeply felt. And it came from observing such hardships up close.

Chuck had been made aware of the rampant homelessness in downtown Los Angeles by his second wife, Gaye Theresa Johnson, a professor at the University of California, Santa Barbara. Skid Row, which as of the summer of 2014 covers 50 blocks, had been a focus for Johnson, who had worked with the Los Angeles Community Action Network to raise awareness for the area's poor and mentally ill. Chuck was affected.

"Her associates put together an initiative and a programme and some books talkin' about the Skid Row area of Los Angeles, which is the largest concentration of homeless people in the country and the second in the world to São Paulo," he said in an interview with *Origin Magazine*. "Just talkin' about this situation the more I kept hearin' about *Watch The Throne*. Seeing that the situation of 85 percent of people on the streets are black folks. And you know, we're supposed to be in a post-racial society, and everybody's supposed to be affluent now. But I'm lookin' at this and hearin' the song in my head."

When it came time to bring 'Notice' to *Evil Empire*, the band knew they had to make some changes. "Their original version had the Otis Redding sample," Snyder says, "so they were like, 'We can't put this on the record.' There was a remix [of 'Notice'] that Chuck wanted to put on the album by these guys out of Kansas City – Chuck and I are both big fans of them. I was like, 'Oh, I wanna hear this – this is gonna be dope.' And it just wasn't. It was a big disappointment for me because it wasn't up to their usual high-quality standard."

But Chuck, Gary and Snyder all believed the track was worth saving. Gary was the one who hit upon an idea. Snyder remembers Gary telling him, "Some guy that we know digitised breakdowns of some old James Brown tracks. He just sent me this multi-track of these James Brown records. Let's play around with those." The two producers examined different bass lines and horn parts, remixing them into what would become the final track. At just over two minutes, 'Notice (Know This)' isn't one of the major musical achievements of the two albums, but its principled stand against swagger made it stick in the listener's consciousness.

"[Outsiders] look at rap music and artists in hip-hop as being as elitist as the power structures that keep them down," Chuck told *Billboard* about his involvement with Skid Row and the Los Angeles Community Action Network. "You've got organisations in your city that are trying to say and do the right thing – who are practically invisible – fighting for some media time. What other place do I have? My place in hip-hop is not to be a tycoon, making trillions with a yacht. That's not my place. My place is maybe bringing people together and me being able to identify and illuminate a cause."

In other words, it was Chuck's small way of making sure that he didn't "end up being the same thing I'm fighting against".

The two albums featured a litany of guests. Darryl McDaniels of Run-D.M.C. appeared on *Stamp*'s 'RLTK', which Johnny Juice says was PE's homage to Rick Rubin's eighties hip-hop sound. "That was my ode to the 808 drum style," Juice notes. "Me and Chuck get mad that all these young rappers that use 808s now, all their records sound exactly alike with this noisy synth. I said, 'We gotta strip it back to the old Beastie Boys-style 808 type of shit.' I wanted it to sound like it was done in '85." Elsewhere, Large Professor produced 'Catch The Thrown', rapper Brother Ali showed up on 'Get Up Stand Up', and DJ Z-Trip produced 'Most Of My Heroes Still . . .'

Snyder noticed that the added guest spots seemed to boost PE's profile among hip-hop fans, a development he finds ironic. "Hip-hop and rap music, I love it to death, but it's so fucked up," he says. "There's this pre-conceived notion – and I blame it completely on the fans – and it's that bullshit, elitist idea of what it's supposed to be. . . . On *Empire* and *Heroes*, we reached out and we got [great guests], and that gives PE some reinforced kind of stupid-ass hip-hop credentials. Like they didn't already have it."

Of course, it was also a way for Public Enemy's peers and admirers to lend support to a beloved group. Bumpy Knuckles, also known as Freddie Foxxx, had grown up in Long Island, emboldened by seeing Public Enemy perform in the late eighties, which was around the same time that he, too, was diving into a rap career. A writer and producer, Bumpy had collaborated with Chuck in the early nineties on a slow, gritty hardcore number called 'Step' for his long-shelved record *Crazy Like A Foxxx*. Recalling Chuck's impromptu trip to the studio to lay down his vocals to 'Step', Bumpy says, still in awe, "I said, 'Yo, man, I can't believe it – I'm finally going to get to do a song with my man Chuck D.' I couldn't believe he just came by himself. All I did is ask – 'I would love for you to come' – and he showed up."

Bumpy's *Stamp* track, 'Get It In', was his way of saying thanks. He'd had the track for a while when a thought occurred to him. "Every time I listened to it," he says, "I kept saying, 'Man, Public Enemy would kill this.' So I reached out to Flavor and I told him about the track. And he was like, 'Yo, send it to me, Foxxx, I'd love to hear it.' He liked it and sent it to Chuck, and they sent it back [to me] with the vocals on it."

'Get It In' is one of *Stamp*'s simpler songs – a raw beat accented by horns – but it has an unmistakable old-school vibe. Although now might be a good time to point out that Chuck hates that term. "We categorise this genre area as classic as in 'CLASSIC RAP'," he writes in the *Stamp* liner notes, "not the limited 'old school' term used for promoters to get a quick buck." Chuck, Bumpy and Flavor each deliver a verse, with Chuck focusing on corporate corruption, Bumpy mentioning that "I always wanted to be an S1" and Flav lamenting his woes, including going to jail, fighting with his lover and having tax troubles. That last admission wasn't fiction: in August of 2012, TMZ reported that Flavor owed more than $900,000 to the IRS due to the success of his reality shows.

The one downside of the albums' many featured collaborators is that the producers didn't get to watch the creative combustion in the studio, a by-product of an era in which albums are rarely created with all the participants in the same space. In the case of *Evil Empire* tracks like the militant minimalism of 'Don't Give Up The Fight' (which had Ziggy Marley) and the rap-rock of 'Riotstarted!' (with Henry Rollins and Rage Against the Machine guitarist Tom Morello, nowadays a featured member of Bruce Springsteen's E Street Band), the performers' pieces were sent in. "It's not like how it was," Amani Smith says. "You know, you're getting together and being in a room together. If you're lucky enough to get the artist to agree to work with you, she'll go to her studio at her convenience and send over what she does. That's how a lot of collabs work."

For 'Riotstarted!' Smith sent the basic track to Morello, a long-time PE fan, so that he could lay his patented DJ-scratch guitar effects on top of it. "Morello's dope," Smith says. He doesn't recall needing to give the guitarist much direction. "You're taking whatever you can get from Morello," Smith notes. "Whatever he puts on is gonna be fresh. Whatever he sends you, you're gonna be able to work with." Indeed, 'Riotstarted!' has the rabble-rousing spirit of primo Public Enemy and Rage Against the Machine, but Morello's signature guitar tones are refreshingly tempered, displaying a fluidity and restraint he doesn't always flex.

Then there was 'ICEbreaker'*, a commentary on America's punitive immigration policy. The track is over seven minutes long and features, among others, the Impossebulls. "Chuck told me, 'I wanna do shorter songs,'" C-Doc, laughing, recalls about the track's genesis. "The longest song on the album and it's supposed to be the shortest. I had the beat, and I wanted to make a punk-rap song – it's just nasty. I sent it to him, and he wrote to it, but he kept piling on the ideas." Soon, Professor Griff and

---

* ICE is the abbreviation for the US government's Immigration and Customs Enforcement department.

long-time PE associate Kyle Jason were contributing verses, as was True Mathematics, reprising his role from *Apocalypse 91*'s 'Get The F--- Outta Dodge' as the racist law-enforcement character Sgt. Hawkes. C-Doc recalls, "Then Chuck said, 'Hey, you wanna get the 'Bulls on it?' I was like, 'Be on a PE song? They're not gonna say no.'" C-Doc also recruited Sekreto, a rapper he knew whom he felt could add an important voice to 'ICEbreaker'. "He's a Mexican dude and had to deal with this shit first-hand," Snyder remembers thinking. "We should get him on the song." Sekreto raps his verse in Spanish, adding an extra level of universality and anger to the brawling, careening tune. One of his lines translated into English: "This is my accent and I'm proud of it."

But perhaps the highlight of collaboration on the two albums comes on *Evil Empire*'s '. . . Everything', a disarming change of pace for the group in which Chuck does that rarest of things: gets introspective. On the song, he looks around at his life and declares that he doesn't care about the things he doesn't have: the fancy car, the superstar status, the Grammy trophies, the million followers on Twitter. Instead, he focuses on what he does have: his health, his friends, his family, zero regrets.

'. . . Everything' wouldn't have been so striking, though, if it wasn't for its arrangement. The song is a piercingly affecting and soothing blues, with Chuck testifying like a gospel singer. It's the sound of a preacher singing to the congregation, offering comfort and reminding them what really matters in life. Or maybe it's the soundtrack to a bar as it's about ready to be closing time, the final few stragglers draining their drinks and heading off into the night. Regardless, this is probably the only PE song suitable for a slow dance.

"I don't know, I'm still baffled by it," Smith says admiringly of '. . . Everything'. "When I first heard the track, I was like, 'Whoa, this is a fucking trip. This is dope.' I was trying to figure out how he put the track together. That track is a blues, in 3/4. An old-time bluesy track – that was what the concept was. I don't know if I would say 'risky', but they just don't have a lot of cuts that are like that. But they seem to work really, really well."

According to Chuck's *Evil Empire* liner notes, '. . . Everything' "was cut deep into the night over two glasses of wine. Since I don't drink and Gary rarely does, this is a big deal here." The track was inspired by Otis Redding's 1966 song 'My Lover's Prayer', a romantic, soulful, saxophone-driven tune, the singer pleading with his lover to end his misery and let him know what's wrong. The two songs don't have similar melodies, but '. . . Everything' captures the isolation and heartfelt sincerity that oozes from every pore of 'My Lover's Prayer'. And perhaps not coincidentally, 'My Lover's Prayer' appeared on *The Otis Redding Dictionary Of Soul*, the same album that housed 'Try A Little Tenderness', which had been sampled for *Watch The Throne*'s 'Otis'.

With '. . . Everything', Chuck was "imagining if [Redding] were alive today how would he actually rap. What would he sound like? How would he bring it?" Instead of a song about despondent love, Chuck had fashioned a quiet anthem of perseverance. And because Chuck didn't have Redding's pipes, '. . . Everything' felt rugged, resilient, human – as opposed to the sound of an angel. The song's beauty came from the melancholy blowing of Grammy-nominated Gerald Albright's saxophone and a weary, gorgeous chorus from singer Sheila Brody, whose insistence that "We've got it all" felt like a warm hug, a moment of genuine compassion from a band whose catalogue rarely allowed such sentiment.

For all his lyrical prowess and inspiring stances, Chuck D focuses on the social, cultural and political in his music almost entirely to the exclusion of examining his inner life or the emotions of the everyday. "[*How You Sell Soul's*] 'Long And Whining Road' is probably the closest PE song to getting inside him and his headspace," says C-Doc, "although getting to know him, you can kinda pick up the [personal] references through the years. I just don't think it interests him to talk about 'me' all the time. That's not him, you know? He's like, 'It's bigger than just me and what I'm doing.' But he'll put little references and ideas in there: he'll say something to me and we'll laugh about it and then it ends up in a song down the road somewhere."

To illustrate his point, Snyder mentions 'I Shall Not Be Moved', which includes the lines "Paid the cost / Father Time ain't never lost, the boss." "It was originally in reference to his daughter being the boss of time," the producer says. "'Like, 'When I'm at home, I'm on her time. She's the boss of time.' That's what he and I always talk about: we're the parents, but they're the boss of time, the kid. So ['I Shall Not Be Moved'] was something where I was like, 'Oh, that's what he's talking about.'"

It's shortsighted to suggest that political music isn't "personal" in a comparable way to the confessional tone of sensitive singer-songwriters with their acoustic guitars and dear-diary poetry. But '. . . Everything' was arresting because it seemed to be Chuck lowering his guard a bit, even if it was in the service of decrying hip-hop materialism and reclaiming the legacy of a great soul singer from two artists he felt diminished it. Also, it's worth pointing out what a remarkable night of recording it was for Chuck and Gary the evening they made '. . . Everything'. After they finished that track, they decided to play around a little more, coming up with 'I Shall Not Be Moved' – which was equally ambitious and unexpected for Public Enemy, although very different in tempo and thrust.

When C-Doc approached the '. . . Everything' video, he tried three different treatments, all of which he ended up disliking. "Nothing was working," he says. "Nothing was conveying the weight of that record. Then Gary called me up: 'I got it!'" G-Wiz reminded Snyder of a video idea they'd batted around for past singles and always abandoned. "You have regular people doing regular things," Snyder says. "Just everyday people doing stuff, but they were gonna be [singing] the lyrics." The '. . . Everything' video consists of a series of shots of actors engaged in ordinary activities – fixing a car, taking pictures, exercising, hanging out with family – as the camera starts close on the actor, slowly zooming out. The characters are all talking out loud to themselves, lip-synching the lyrics; men reciting Chuck's verses, women taking over for Brody's chorus, and during the sax solo there are shots of the band members.

As with many of Snyder's PE videos, '. . . Everything' is low budget, occasionally to a fault, but it's also charming and direct in its simplicity. This wasn't the first video to incorporate the idea of having "regular people" sing a song's lyrics, but the cumulative effect of the different characters, matched with the poignant tune, was undeniably affecting. Says Snyder, "Chuck saw it and said, 'I damn near cried. You nailed it. That's it. You got it right.' That's nice – there's been [a few] videos that we've done that he called me and said that we really got it right."

The comfort of '. . . Everything' stood out as well because of its appearance on *The Evil Empire Of Everything*, which was generally a darker, stranger record than *Most Of My Heroes Don't Appear On No Stamp*. Kicking off with the scene-setting opener 'The Evil Empire Of . . .', which is introduced by a 911 call of a frightened resident reporting a strange black man in his neighbourhood, *Evil Empire* seems less concerned with legacy than it is in sounding off on the social ills of the time. The track ends with Chuck warning, "Easier to [be] misunderstood than understand this song / Beware, the youth is not youth for long / Rest in peace, Trayvon."

This was a reference to the killing of Trayvon Martin, a 17-year-old African-American living in Florida who, on February 26, 2012, was shot dead by George Zimmerman, a Hispanic neighbourhood watch volunteer who claimed he was acting in self-defence. Martin was not carrying a weapon, just a bag of Skittles. The teen's death, and the subsequent acquittal of Zimmerman on a charge of second-degree murder, inflamed the African-American community, which saw the incident as the latest deadly example of racial profiling. And for Public Enemy, the incident perhaps felt like an eerie callback to the beginning of their career when they were tempted to name *Yo! Bum Rush The Show*'s opening track 'You're Gonna Goetz Yours' in remembrance of the four black men shot by Bernhard Goetz.

For *Evil Empire*, Professor Griff focused the group's anger on 'Beyond Trayvon', mixing sound bites of news clips and talk radio with a lyrical attack on prejudice. Along with Griff and Chuck, the song's other vocalists were the sons of Griff, Brother James Norman and Andrew Williams, who were all part of the PE crew. In the process, 'Beyond Trayvon' felt like a multi-generational condemnation, and proof that Public Enemy's message was being carried on by younger MCs.

The track was co-produced by C-Doc, who had established a rapport with Griff after the two worked together on *Beats And Places*. "Griff's cool because he loves to collaborate," Snyder says. "A lot of the other producers go off and do their own thing, but Griff loves to collaborate. He goes, 'Nobody wants to work with me.' I'm like, 'I'll work with you, let's do it.' With 'Beyond Trayvon', he did the skeleton and then I did the rest

– I added all the technical stuff to it. Griff came to me and said, 'Look, I got this track, but it needs something.'"

Mimicking the *Fear Of A Black Planet* buzz saw, 'Beyond Trayvon' was the albums' strongest rebuttal to the hope of a post-racial America. But *Evil Empire*'s pessimism extended to '1 (PEace)', a chaotic hard-rock number highlighted by sampled drums from James Brown's famed drummer Clyde Stubblefield. "'Yes, we can' / It's out the can," Chuck sings, referencing Obama's indelible three-word political slogan from his 2008 campaign, and it's not quite clear if he's mentioning the phrase in jest or solidarity – or if he's expressing frustration at those trying to undermine the man's presidency.

In an interview in early 2008 – eight months before Obama's election – Chuck spoke with *The Starting Five* about the candidate's chances. He was asked why some African-Americans weren't automatically throwing their support behind the first viable black contender for the presidency. "They feel Barack Obama hasn't talked to black people enough," Chuck replied. "Black people are also smart enough to say just because you have a black face doesn't mean you get automatic love. We are at a time where words have to ring with some sort of style and substance over appearance. If I were to look at Barack Obama real quick, I would think he was somebody from the Nation of Islam. That's all right with me, but what comes out of his mouth is something where he's trying to straddle some sort of line that he's not a thug to white folk. People behind Barack Obama – even Oprah – are just giving it their best shot to make sure America feels comfortable with him not to be president, but that he can be a running mate to Hillary Clinton so people can still vote for her. He's got a presidential investment to make America feel comfortable with him as a vice president. That's probably what it takes for a black face to get up into those high ranks."

Chuck's grim assessment of Obama's chances proved incorrect, and by the time of the 2012 election, he was advocating for the president's second term. That didn't mean he had fundamentally changed his view that presidents can only do so much for the people. "I've always liked Obama the man," Chuck said in October of 2012, "but he's made to respond to how the New World Order wants him to respond. [Republican nominee Mitt] Romney's no different. Obama can't serve the black community; he can only serve the needs of people who are disenfranchised, and there's a lot of black people who are, but he's gotta serve a lot of other communities too. The president could really be more destructive than anything, so just having a president be not as destructive as some of the rhetorics of the past is helpful. George W. Bush was running roughshod all over the rest of the world." Chuck D's advice? "Young people need to understand how to vote for their local representatives before even thinking about voting for president."

Not that Chuck's support of Obama was halfhearted. Talking to *The Daily Beast* in 2013, he confessed, "I never thought I'd see a black president, like most black people. But of course when we got one, it would be when the country was in such a mess that he has to work three times as hard, which is OK. But as black people, that's what we know we must do anyway. But he won't even get credit for it. He gets nothing but grief for it while he's working much harder than the guy who had the job before him."

As for Flavor, he's all over the twin albums, but his presence on *Evil Empire* is more dynamic, both because he peaks higher there and because his problematic public profile is more on display. By 2012, the man born William Drayton had significantly blurred the line between his musical identity and his TV one. Consequently, his *Evil Empire* tracks are similarly blurry. On the propulsive '31 Flavors', Flav boasts that he's the "hype-man chameleon" who's enjoying big checks from VH1 while avoiding TMZ and the paparazzi. Not just urgent but fever-pitched, '31 Flavors' was Flav's battle cry for his continued importance as an artist, the hype man laying out his frantic schedule and myriad obligations in such a way that it's both exhausting and exhilarating.

But in the *Evil Empire* notes, Chuck would reveal that the song delayed the album's release, Flav's insistence that it be included after the deadline causing a huge fight between the two men. "The good and the bad thing about Flav is he pays little mind to the criticism hurled at him, I'm usually there to sweep the mess around PE to the world press," Chuck wrote. "Trust me, by now this is a technique, after 25 years, to let [band members] do their thing while maintaining the so called brand."

Unfortunately, Flavor was also behind 'Broke Diva', a catchy but tiresome song about women obsessed with reality-television fame. Another in the band's 'She Watch Channel Zero?!' subgenre of faintly condescending tunes about shallow females, 'Broke Diva' puts Flav centre stage as he bemoans women who are after his celebrity and money. The song condemns gold-digging without having any awareness that tawdry TV stardom helped resuscitate Flavor's career. In the liner notes, Chuck says that Flav's involvement in 'Broke Diva' "wreaks [sic] of irony", one of the rare occasions when the outspoken frontman has ever understated something.

'Broke Diva' was even harder to take after suffering through *The Icon The Memoir*, which Flav released the previous year. Juvenile and overbearing, with only the occasional moment of heartbreaking candour, the autobiography peddled Flavor's *Behind The Music* narrative as a man laid low by celebrity excess and drug addiction who turned his life around. But the book also enjoyed revelling in his sexual indulgences, including one rather distasteful passage about a trip to Paris during PE's late-eighties/early-nineties heyday in which he wrote: "I take the [five] girls to my room and we all get naked. I'm sitting in a chair while one girl is sucking my dick, and another girl is licking my balls. I'm fingering another two, and that fifth one, she's holding my [crack] pipe while I'm smoking and kissing her. I'm in heaven, naw'mean? Flavor Flav is living every man's dream."

Between *The Icon The Memoir* and *Evil Empire*, it was clear that anyone still devoted to Public Enemy would have to make some sort of peace with Flavor's contradictions, deciding that Flav was both an embarrassment and an enormously talented musician. Or, put another way, fans would have to realise that he was as flawed as just about any other artist, lending an air of compromise to a principled group, permanently tarnishing but also humanising a band that always aimed to live up to its high aspirations. One would constantly have to remember this as Flav continued to be in the headlines in subsequent years – like, for instance, on Fourth of July in 2014 when Las Vegas police confiscated more than 100 pounds of illegal fireworks from his home.

Compromise and lowered expectations are inevitable as part of the aging process, whether it's for a band or the individuals within it. On August 1, 2010, Chuck D and Professor Griff both turned 50, a milestone birthday. But Chuck wasn't willing to bend an inch or concede anything to his critics. On *Evil Empire*'s final track, 'Say It Like It Really Is', he boasts, "Who dat gonna tell y'all we too old? / But we still bold / Plus I got soul / It's my birthday / And I'm 50 years . . ." – intentionally leaving off the word "old" at the end of the rhyme, lest anyone think he's going to assign that pejorative to himself.

Age has its benefits, though. With so many hip-hop pioneers dead or utterly forgotten, Public Enemy had survived. Their commercial standing had faded, the critical hosannas for recent albums had been largely non-existent, but Chuck had figured out how to stay relevant, positioning his band as the watchdogs of a hip-hop purism that risked being swept aside by the music's growing popularity. Public Enemy gig relentlessly – Chuck always likes bragging about how many tours and how many countries PE have rocked – and they've seen their classic albums be heralded on significant anniversaries. For instance, *Billboard* spotlighted the 20th anniversary of *Fear Of A Black Planet*, and the group did special shows for *Black Planet* and *Nation Of Millions* at which they played those albums in their entirety.

However, Chuck's desire for "classic rap" to be celebrated in the culture comparably to classic rock hasn't been easy. Like other hip-hop groups that started in the eighties and feasted on samples, Public Enemy have faced challenges repackaging and rereleasing their material in the same way as, say, Elvis Costello or the Rolling Stones. On Valentine's Day 2014, De La Soul made most of their catalogue free online, an attention-grabbing move precipitated by the complications involved with trying to sell those albums through services like iTunes. If the band had wanted to make money off the records digitally, they'd have to untangle the knotty rights issues for all those samples. As Tom Silverman, the head of De La Soul's old label Tommy Boy, said in the 2011 book *Creative License: The Law And Culture Of Digital Sampling*, "It's a lot of accounting work. . . . You have to pay out on 60 different people on one album. It's quite a nightmare actually."

In the past, similar problems had made it hard for PE to sell their albums digitally. But even though they're now available on iTunes and Amazon, these records still don't get to enjoy the treatment given to totems of other genres, where a classic like *Layla* can be reissued with extra tracks and outtakes to entice consumers to buy a favourite album all over again. Or, in the case of the Beach Boys' *Pet Sounds*, a 36-minute album from 1966 can yield a four-disc box set in 1997, *The Pet Sounds Sessions*, that ran over four hours. When *Nation Of Millions* was reissued in the spring of 2014, it didn't feature any additional tracks. Kembrew McLeod, one of the authors of *Creative License*, said in a 2014 interview with *Slate*'s Geeta Dayal, "The reason why Public Enemy, the Beastie Boys, and De La Soul haven't been able to release reissues of expanded albums is because once they re-release an altered version of the actual album they have to relicense from all the sample holders, which is totally crazy."

Even Chuck seemed unenthusiastic about the 2014 Record Store Day no-extras reissue of *Nation Of Millions* by Universal, which now owned the rights to Def Jam material. "Universal is doing that," Chuck told *Creative Loafing* about the reissued album. "[For Record Store Day], I'm releasing the new Public Enemy album *Evil Empire Of Everything*. We have what's called an uneasy truce with Universal. I won't diss my own record – *It Takes A Nation Of Millions* is my 60-home-run, Babe Ruth season. I'm also not going to have Universal beat me out. *Evil Empire Of Everything* has something new to offer: it's a double LP, this is the first time it's been pressed on vinyl in the States, and it comes with a calendar for the year. . . . Come Record Store Day, that's what I'm going to be holding up."

(In November 2014 both *Nation Of Millions* and *Fear Of A Black Planet* were finally reissued as multi-disc sets that included instrumentals, remixes and alternate versions.)

Public Enemy weren't just trying to safeguard their past but also make a case for their present and future. And why not? For PE fans who have stuck with the band while the culture moved on, it can be maddening to watch younger listeners consider the group to be merely an oldies act. Thankfully, there are those preserving the music and politics of Public Enemy. Aside from militant groups like the Coup, there are also engaging one-offs, such as when a collection of Arizona rap artists recorded 'Back To Arizona', a remake of 'By The Time I Get To Arizona', in 2010 to protest that state's harsh anti-immigration bill. PE's visibility isn't as high as it once was, but because of America's unresolved racial issues and economic disparity, the band's message will remain vital, waiting for new generations to discover. It's a testament to the art Public Enemy created, but it's also a sad sign of how far we still have to go as a nation and as a world.

"Can you imagine all the people who haven't gotten turned on to Public Enemy yet?" Bumpy Knuckles asks. "You're always going to have people who understand the cries of someone who's yelling out a painful noise. They did it with Bob Marley; they did it with Tupac. They did it with all these guys who had their fist in the air for something."

★ ★ ★

Come the fall of 2012, Chuck had his eye on the announcement from the Rock and Roll Hall of Fame. In early October, the Hall listed the nominees for induction, which included two rap groups, Public Enemy and N.W.A. And on December 11, the Class of 2013 was revealed: Heart, Albert King, Randy Newman, Rush, Donna Summer and Public Enemy. Their induction, held in Los Angeles on April 18, 2013, made them only the fourth hip-hop group to enter the Hall.

"It's amazing to get the induction into the Hall of Fame now, given we never won a Grammy, never had a *Rolling Stone* magazine cover, and never had a *Billboard* Top 10 single," Chuck D told *The Daily Beast*'s Allison Samuels. "All the things that define success today, we never had. We had the influence, but not the awards to go with it. That speaks volumes about why you have to just do your thing and not worry about the other stuff. It comes when it comes."

The honour also allowed some former PE members to make peace with the past. By email, Terminator X reveals that he was initially uninterested in attending the event. "Public Enemy and the music business was like a previous life in my mind," he writes. "I had moved on from that life. I was so disconnected from this 'previous life' that I didn't even think about whether I was proud, happy or how I felt. It just didn't matter. I wanted nothing to do with those days. . . . [M]y gold and platinum album plaques, and other awards, were not on a wall in my house or office. Some of them I gave away to family, the others were in a closet collecting dust. My music equipment . . . also collecting dust in storage. I had no intention of attending the induction. Zero."

Ultimately, it was a letter from Joel Peresman, the CEO and President of the Rock and Roll Hall of Fame, that changed Terminator's mind. "[He] said that they would mail the award if I didn't want to attend but they would prefer that I attend," the DJ says, adding, "He said he had his staff do a search for info on me to get the address. I was really touched that he took the effort to look for me. So much so that I decided to go."

He didn't regret the decision. "I enjoyed the induction immensely," Terminator writes. "The RRHOF foundation is a class act that is so unlike the typical music industry environment. I enjoyed all the presenters and recipients' stories, the performances . . . everything. It was definitely strange being around PE again for the first time in so many years and all the resentment I had felt in the past. But everyone was very cordial and it went well. . . . I have opened my communication with PE since the induction. I have not necessarily fixed any issues with PE, but I have moved on."

Others had their own mixed feelings. Johnny Juice, who had been part of the group's early days, left after *Nation Of Millions* over a disagreement about credit and money, and then returned to the fold in the early 21st century. He says that he really enjoyed the induction. Still, "It means less to us – it probably means a lot to Chuck," Juice says. "It doesn't mean a lot to me because it doesn't matter. We've always been this outcast culture that you really didn't give a fuck about, so now it's almost [like], 'You're happy that, oh look, we finally get credit?' I'm finally getting credit 30 years after I did shit, and it doesn't mean much to me now, really. To be honest with you, I've done bigger things, to me, in my life. I was a Navy SEAL. Jumping out of a plane at 27,000 feet, then landing in the water and swimming five miles in the water to a beach, then hiking 10 miles, then doing some incredible shit there – and then doing the same shit in reverse – is a little bit more challenging than making a beat."

In February of 2014, Juice would again separate himself from the group, blaming the split on several factors, including issues of credit, payment and how the Public Enemy business is run. "I love Chuck, I've known him for 30 years, I've loved him like a brother," Juice says. "I was actually responsible for his house in New York – I was his house-sitter. I watched that house, I built the studio, did everything for him. But after 30 years, you realise . . . you can't tell me, 'Oh, I didn't know, I didn't know.' Chuck is not a person that doesn't know stuff."

At the LA induction ceremony, Spike Lee and Harry Belafonte inducted the band. Most groups are introduced at the ceremony by fellow rock musicians, so it was telling that Public Enemy chose speakers outside the rock'n'roll world. Like Lee, Public Enemy had used their art form to speak uncomfortable truths about black America to a mainstream white audience. And although Belafonte had a sizable music career, it was his role as a social activist that was probably just as important to the band.

From the stage of the Nokia Theater, Belafonte praised "these extraordinary artists, who for more than 25 years in the tough and sometimes heartless business of music provide inspiration to writers, musicians, poets, filmmakers but, perhaps most importantly, ordinary citizens tackling the seemingly intractable problems of our day. . . . Artists like Public Enemy are the gatekeepers of truth, civilisation's radical voice."

The band members then came up to receive their award. Griff closed his acceptance speech with a quote he attributed to Steven Biko: "Revolution is not an event, it's a process." Flavor Flav laughed and goofed around, but he also sounded humbled, appreciating the gravity of the moment. He thanked Chuck for writing such good records and for supporting him at the beginning when Def Jam didn't want him as part of the band.

Chuck then told the crowd, "This award is just not ours. We come from DJ culture, everybody. A culture that values bringing the noise from diverse messages, from a Minister Louis Farrakhan to Anthrax." He acknowledged that some may question a rap band's induction in the Rock and Roll Hall of Fame, but he was quick to remind those doubters, "Let us not forget: we all come from the damn blues."

And then he leaned in for his closing remarks. "We study the forms of music and DJ culture," he said. "People like Kool Herc, Afrika Bambaataa and Grandmaster Flash. We know the music and its history. For those who don't think hip-hop is high art, this is elements in motion. Tonight, what we are being honoured for is just not the longevity, but for skill and our craft and for the tenure earned as a group and also individuals within."

The crowd cheered.

"Rap music and hip-hop at its best, *at its best*, does the right thing," Chuck said. "So, yes, maybe there goes the musical neighbourhood, but – in salute to Harry Belafonte, Spike Lee – here comes the truth."

And just then, for a moment, they seemed like America's greatest band.

ACKNOWLEDGEMENTS

As always, I have to start by thanking David Barraclough at Omnibus who found me online five years ago and created an incredible new set of possibilities in my life.

My thanks also go out to the people who supported me during the writing of this book, offering a kind word or some general encouragement. They include Russell Brown, Justin Chang, Kory Grow, Andy Hungerford, Will Leitch, Jen Lopez, Jason Major and Dan Reines.

I'd also like to thank the friends who, when they heard I was working on a biography of Public Enemy, immediately had to tell me their stories of seeing the band in concert or running into Flavor Flav at a Halloween party where they were dressed as, of all things, Flavor Flav. Those little things really perked me up when I needed it.

I so appreciate the people who gave of their time, allowing me to interview them. I always sensed how important it was for these individuals to get down on the record how much Public Enemy meant to them. I hope I've done your voices justice.

My parents remain the best any son could ask for. My sister is the spitfire. And my wife has been my rock yet again.

And thank you for reading this book. Even if you're just reading this page to see if I mentioned you, it means a lot.

DISCOGRAPHY

Public Enemy (selected discography)

Yo! Bum Rush The Show (1987)
You're Gonna Get Yours/Sophisticated Bitch/Miuzi Weighs A Ton/
Timebomb/Too Much Posse/Rightstarter (Message To A Black Man)/
Public Enemy No. 1/M.P.E/Yo! Bum Rush The Show/Raise The Roof/
Megablast/Terminator X Speaks With His Hands

It Takes A Nation Of Millions To Hold Us Back (1988)
Countdown To Armageddon/Bring The Noise/Don't Believe The Hype/
Cold Lampin With Flavor/Terminator X To The Edge Of Panic/Mind
Terrorist/Louder Than A Bomb/Caught, Can We Get A Witness?/Show
Em Whatcha Got/She Watch Channel Zero?!/Night Of The Living
Baseheads/Black Steel In The Hour Of Chaos/Security Of The First World/
Rebel Without A Pause/Prophets Of Rage/Party For Your Right To Fight

Fear Of A Black Planet (1990)
Contract On The World Love Jam/Brothers Gonna Work It Out/911 Is A
Joke/Incident At 66.6 Fm/Welcome To The Terrordome/Meet The G
That Killed Me/Pollywanacraka/Anti-Nigger Machine/Burn Hollywood
Burn/Power To The People/Who Stole The Soul?/Fear Of A Black
Planet/Revolutionary Generation/Can't Do Nuttin' For Ya Man/Reggie
Jax/Leave This Off Your Fu★Kin Charts/B Side Wins Again/War At
33 1/3/ Final Count Of The Collision Between Us And The Damned/
Fight The Power

Apocalypse 91 … The Enemy Strikes Black (1991)
Lost At Birth/Rebirth/Nighttrain/Can't Truss It/I Don't Wanna Be
Called Yo Niga/How To Kill A Radio Consultant/By The Time I Get To
Arizona/Move!/1 Million Bottlebags/More News At 11/Shut 'Em Down/
A Letter To The New York Post/Get The F--- Outta Dodge/Bring Tha
Noize

Greatest Misses (1992)
Tie Goes To The Runner/Hit Da Road Jack/Gett Off My Back/Gotta Do
What I Gotta Do/Air Hoodlum/Hazy Shade Of Criminal/Megablast/
Louder Than A Bomb/You're Gonna Get Yours/How To Kill A Radio
Consultant/Who Stole The Soul?/Party For Your Right To Fight/Shut
'Em Down

Muse Sick-N-Hour Mess Age (1994)
Whole Lotta Love Goin On In The Middle Of Hell/Theatrical Parts/Give
It Up/What Side You On?/Bedlam 13:13/Stop In The Name . . ./What
Kind Of Power We Got?/So Whatcha Gone Do Now?/White Heaven/
Black Hell/Race Against Time/They Used To Call It Dope/Aintnuttin
Buttersong/Live And Undrugged (Pt. 1 & 2)/Thin Line Between Law &
Rape/I Ain't Mad At All/Death Of A Carjacka/I Stand Accused/Godd
Complexx/Hitler Day/Harry Allen's Interactive Super Highway Phone
Call To Chuck D/Living In A Zoo (Remix)

He Got Game (1998)
Resurrection/He Got Game/Unstoppable/Shake Your Booty/Is Your
God A Dog/House Of The Rising Son/Revelation 33 1/3 Revolutions/
Game Face/Politics Of The Sneaker Pimps/What You Need Is
Jesus/Super Agent/Go Cat Go/Sudden Death (Interlude)

There's A Poison Goin On (1999)
Dark Side Of The Wall: 2000/Do You Wanna Go Our Way???/LSD/
Here I Go/41:19/Crash/Crayola/First The Sheep Next The Shepherd?/
World Tour Sessions/Last Mass Of The Caballeros/I/What What/
Kevorkian/Swindlers Lust

The Best Of Public Enemy (2001)
Welcome To The Terrordome/911 Is A Joke/Bring The Noise/Don't
Believe The Hype/Give It Up/Shut 'Em Down/Fight The Power/By The
Time I Get To Arizona/Night Of The Living Baseheads/Nighttrain/
Bring Tha Noize

Revolverlution (2002)
Gotta Give The Peeps What They Need/Revolverlution/Miuzi Weighs A
Ton/Put It Up/Can A Woman Make A Man Lose His Mind?/Public

Enemy Service Announcement #1/Fight The Power/By The Time I Get
To Arizona/Post-Concert Arizona Interview/Son Of A
Bush/54321...Boom/Welcome To The Terrordome/B Side Wins
Again/Get Your Shit Together/Public Enemy Service Announcement
#2/Shut 'Em Down/Now A'Daze/Public Enemy No. 1/The Making Of
"Burn Hollywood Burn"/Gotta Give The Peeps What They Need/What
Good Is A Bomb

Power To The People And The Beats: Public Enemy's Greatest Hits (2005)
You're Gonna Get Yours/Public Enemy No. 1/Rebel Without A
Pause/Bring The Noise/Don't Believe The Hype/Prophets Of
Rage/Black Steel In The Hour Of Chaos/Fight The Power/Welcome To
The Terrordome/911 Is A Joke/Brothers Gonna Work It Out/Can't Do
Nuttin' For Ya Man/Can't Truss It/Shut 'Em Down/By The Time I Get
To Arizona/Hazy Shade Of Criminal/Give It Up/He Got Game

New Whirl Odor (2005)
...And No One Broadcasted Louder Than.../New Whirl Odor/Bring That
Beat Back/66.6 Strikes Again/MKLVFKWR/What A Fool Believes/
Makes You Blind/Preachin' To The Quiet/Either We Together Or We
Ain't/Revolution/Check What You're Listening To/As Long As The
People Got Something To Say/Y'all Don't Know/Either You Get It By
Now Or You Don't/Superman's Black In The Building

Rebirth Of A Nation (2006)
Raw Sh★t/Hard Rhymin'/Rise/Can't Hold Us Back/Hard Truth
Soldiers/Hannibal Lecture/Rebirth Of A Nation/Pump The Music, Pump
The Sound/Make It Hardcore/They Call Me Flavor/Plastic Nation/
Coinsequences/Invisible Man/Hell No (We Ain't All Right)/Watch The
Door/Field N★gga Boogie

Fight The Power!: Greatest Hits Live! (2007)
Brothers Gonna Work It Out/Welcome To The Terrordome/Bring The
Noise/Son Of A Bush/Shut 'Em Down/Black Steel In The Hour Of
Chaos/He Got Game/Revolverlution/911 Is A Joke/Public Enemy No.
1/DJ Lord Solo/Give It Up/Don't Believe The Hype/Rebel Without A
Pause/Arizona (Ball Of Confusion)/Fight The Power (Soul Power)

How You Sell Soul To A Soulless People Who Sold Their Soul??? (2007)
How You Sell Soul To A Soulless People Who Sold Their Soul?/Black Is
Back/Harder Than You Think/Between Hard And A Rock Place/Sex,
Drugs & Violence/Amerikan Gangster/Can You Hear Me Now/Head
Wide Shut/Flavor Man/The Enemy Battle Hymn Of The
Public/Escapism/Frankenstar/Col-Leepin/Radiation Of A Radiotvmovie
Nation/See Something, Say Something/Long And Whining Road/Bridge
Of Pain/Eve Of Destruction/How You Sell Soul (Time Is God Refrain)

Most Of My Heroes Still Don't Appear On No Stamp (2012)
Run Till It's Dark/Get Up Stand Up/Most Of My Heroes Still.../I Shall
Not Be Moved/Get It In/Hoovermusic/Catch The Thrown/RLTK/
Truth Decay/Fassfood/WTF?!

The Evil Empire Of Everything (2012)
The Evil Empire Of.../Don't Give Up The Fight/1(Peace)/2 (Respect)/
Beyond Trayvon/...Everything/31 Flavors/Riotstarted!/Notice (Know
This)/Icebreaker/Fame/Broke Diva/Say It Like It Really Is

Chuck D (selected discography)

Autobiography Of Mistachuck (1996)
Mistachuck/No/Generation Wrekkked/Niggativity...Do I Dare Disturb
The Universe?/Free Big Willie/Horizontal Heroin/Talk Show Created
The Fool/Underdog/But Can You Kill The Nigga In
You?/Endonesia/The Pride/Paid

Flavor Flav

Flavor Flav (2006)
Let It Show/Flavor Man/Unga Bunga Bunga/Two Wrongz/I Ain't
Scared/Baby Baby Baby/Wonder Why/Interlude: Latasha Break/No
Loot/The Jookz/The Rest Of My Life/Hot 1/Platinum/Guess Whooz
Bak/Get Up On The Dance Floor/Bridge Of Pain/One And Only
Original Flavor Flav/Col-Leepin/Bonus Track/Hotter Than Ice

Professor Griff (selected discography):

Pawns In The Game (1990)
Pawns In The Game/The Verdict/Suzi Wants To Be A Rock Star/Real
African People Rap Pt. 1/Pass The Ammo/Real African People Rap Pt.
2/Love Thy Enemy/Rap Terrorist/1-900 Ste Oreo Type/Last Asiatic
Disciples/The Word Of God Griff On Duty/The V Amendment/The
Interview/It's A Blax Thanx

Terminator X (selected discography):

Terminator X & the Valley of the Jeep Beats (1991)
Vendetta... The Big Getback/Buck Whylin'/Homey Don't Play Dat/
Juvenile Delinquintz/The Blues/Back To The Scene Of The Bass/Can't
Take My Style/Wanna Be Dancin'/DJ Is The Selector/Run That
Go-Power Thang/No Further/High Priest Of Turbulence/Ain't Got
Nuttin'

BIBLIOGRAPHY

Books:

Battino, David & Richards, Kelli. *The Art Of Digital Music: 56 Visionary Artists And Insiders Reveal Their Creative Secrets*

Charnas, Dan. *The Big Payback: The History Of The Business Of Hip-Hop*

Coleman, Brian. *Check The Technique: Liner Notes For Hip-Hop Junkies*

D, Chuck & Jah, Yusuf (Ed.). *Lyrics Of A Rap Revolutionary*

D, Chuck, with Jah, Yusuf. *Fight The Power: Rap, Race, And Reality*

Dylan, Bob. *Chronicles: Volume One*

Ebert, Roger. *Roger Ebert's Book Of Film*

Ferris, D.X. *Reign In Blood*

Flav, Flavor. *Flavor Flav: The Icon The Memoir*

Fuchs, Cynthia (Ed.). *Spike Lee: Interviews*

Gabbard, Krin. *Black Magic: White Hollywood And African American Culture*

Gueraseva, Stacy. *Def Jam, Inc.: Russell Simmons, Rick Rubin, And The Extraordinary Story Of The World's Most Influential Hip-Hop Label*

Lee, Spike, with Jones, Lisa. *Do The Right Thing*

McLeon, Kembrew & DiCola, Peter. *Creative License: The Law And Culture Of Digital Sampling*

Moskowitz, David. *The Words And Music Of Jimi Hendrix*

Myrie, Russell. *Don't Rhyme For The Sake Of Riddlin': The Authorised Story Of Public Enemy*

Natapoff, Alexandra. *Snitching: Criminal Informants And The Erosion Of American Justice*

Ogg, Alex. *The Men Behind Def Jam: The Radical Rise Of Russell Simmons And Rick Rubin*

Rooksby, Rikki. *Lyrics: Writing Better Words For Your Songs*

Weingarten, Christopher R. *It Takes A Nation Of Millions To Hold Us Back*

Documentaries and concert films:

Downloaded, directed by Alex Winter

Kill the Messenger, directed by Marty Callner

The Million Man March – The Untold Story, directed by Angela Muhammad

Interview discs:

Muse Sick-N-Hour Mess Age

Revolverlution

Periodicals, Newspapers, Podcasts, Radio Shows, Television Programs And Websites:

ABC News, Adweek, Amazon, American Songwriter, Antigravity, AOL, The Arsenio Hall Show, The Associated Press, The Atlantic, The Augusta Chronicle, The A.V. Club, Beats, Billboard, Business Insider, The Charlie Rose Show, Chicago Sun-Times, Chicago Tribune, CNN, Comic Book Resources, Crack, Creative Loafing, The Daily Beast, Davey D's Hip Hop Corner, Deadline, Ego Trip, Electronic Beats, Entertainment Weekly, ESPN, Exberliner, Forbes, The Gainesville Sun, God Is In The TV, TheGrio, The Guardian, Guitar Center, Hard N Heavy, HipHopDX, The Hollywood Reporter, Innerviews , Jet, KPFA 94.1 FM Berkeley, LA Weekly, Los Angeles Times, Melody Maker, Miami New Times, Mixmag, Mother Jones, MTV News, Musician, Myrnb, The Nervous Breakdown, New York, New York Post, The New York Times, Nightline, NME, Option, O'Reilly Digital Media, Origin Magazine, Perfect Sound Forever, Philadelphia Daily News, The Philadelphia Inquirer, Phoenix New Times, Pitchfork, The Pitt News, Playboy, Popeater, The Progressive, Propellerhead Software, Props, The Quietus , Rane, Rapstation, Red Bull Music Academy, Remix, Reuters, Right Wing News, Rolling Stone, Scratch, Self-Titled, SF Weekly, Shutemdown.com, 60 Minutes, Slate, The Source, Spin, The Starting Five, Stay Free!, The Stranger, Synchronicity And Subculture, Tampa Bay Times, Tastes Like Chicken, Tavis Smiley, This Is Not A Test, This Week In Music, Time, The Times-Picayune, TMZ, USA Today, Vibe, The Village Voice, Virginia Living, Vlad TV, Vox, Vulture, The Washington Post, The Washington Times, WHO?MAG TV, Wired, Wondering Sound, XXL, Yahoo!

ABOUT THE AUTHOR

Tim Grierson is a film and music critic whose writing has appeared in numerous publications, including *Rolling Stone, LA Weekly, Playboy, Screen International, The Dissolve, Gawker, Revolver, The Village Voice, Vulture, Wired, Blender* and VH1.com. He is a member of the Los Angeles Film Critics Association. This is his third book for Omnibus Press.